THE LION'S TRIUMPH

"Exhibits the same humor, wit, poignancy and vulnerability that endeared folks to Foley—even those who, in the words of the late Gorilla Monsoon, 'wouldn't know a wristlock from wristwatch.'"
— *Long Island Press*

"I thoroughly enjoyed A LION'S TALE! What I liked best was how Chris Jericho's charm rings through on every page."
— BRET "HITMAN" HART

"Funny, insightful, and compulsively readable . . . His hilarious and detailed descriptions of his many bouts, especially his 1995 'calling card' in Japan . . . will leave readers hoping for a sequel."
— *Publishers Weekly*

"A coming-of-age, follow-your-dreams story that is both fun and inspiring. It's a great read!"
— JANET EVANOVICH, #1 bestselling author

"The best book centered around a wrestler I've read."
— JERRY GREEN, *Orlando Sentinel*

"This may be the first-ever autobiographical, action-adventure, how-to-achieve-success book ever written. Dreams do come true. Happy endings still exist. This book proves it."
— JIM ROSS, "The Voice of the WWE"

more . . .

"An excellent look at a journey to dream come true . . . Jericho provides a much welcomed look at himself without a hint of ego, which is why A LION'S TALE earns my recommendation."

—*PWTorch Newsletter*

"I can honestly say this is one of the best, if not the best, wrestling books I've ever read."

—LANCE STORM,
**WWE Intercontinental Champion
and founder of the Book Marks Book Club**

"A moving story of perseverance and triumph . . . humorous, heart-warming, and a true winner."

—*Graffiti* (WV)

"I was really enjoying this book, empathizing with Chris's plight as an aspiring wrestler, laughing out loud at many of the dead-on depictions of some of the more colorful characters in our business. Suddenly, a wave of momentary panic crashed right into my literary ego. 'Oh no,' I thought. 'What if this book is better than mine?'"

—MICK FOLEY,
**#1 *New York Times* bestselling author
and three-time WWE World Champion**

A LION'S TALE

CHRIS JERICHO

WITH PETER THOMAS FORNATALE

GC

GRAND CENTRAL
PUBLISHING

NEW YORK   BOSTON

If you purchase this book without a cover you should be aware that this book may have been stolen property and reported as "unsold and destroyed" to the publisher. In such case neither the author nor the publisher has received any payment for this "stripped book."

Copyright © 2007 by Chris Jericho
All rights reserved. Except as permitted under the U.S. Copyright Act of 1976, no part of this publication may be reproduced, distributed, or transmitted in any form or by any means, or stored in a database or retrieval system, without the prior written permission of the publisher.

Ted Irvine trading card on insert page 1 and Corazon de Leon card on insert page 5: courtesy of The Topps Company, Inc. Photo of Chris Jericho and Ted Irvine on insert page 1: William Jacobellis/NY POST photo. Owen Hart funeral photos on page 507 and insert page 15: Kirstie McLellan Day, www.pyramidproductions.tv.

Cover design by Flag
Cover photograph by Peter Langone

Grand Central Publishing
Hachette Book Group USA
237 Park Avenue
New York, NY 10017
Visit our Web site at www.HachetteBookGroupUSA.com

Grand Central Publishing is a division of Hachette Book Group USA, Inc. The Grand Central Publishing name and logo is a trademark of Hachette Book Group USA, Inc.

Printed in the United States of America

Originally published in hardcover by Hachette Book Group USA
First Paperback Printing: October 2008

10 9 8 7 6 5 4 3 2 1

ATTENTION CORPORATIONS AND ORGANIZATIONS:
Most HACHETTE BOOK GROUP USA books are available at quantity discounts with bulk purchase for educational, business, or sales promotional use. For information, please call or write:

Special Markets Department, Hachette Book Group USA
237 Park Avenue, New York, NY 10017
Telephone: 1-800-222-6747 Fax: 1-800-477-5925

DEDICATION

For Eddy
Friend, Colleague, Brother, Inspiration

AUTHOR'S NOTE

I started working on this book in August of 2005 and finished it in May of 2007. It was a long process and a labor of love, and when the final manuscript was handed in I was convinced that it was exactly the way I wanted it to be.

The book was typeset and put into galley form (industry talk for pretty much finished, with no more changes allowed), and that was to be it.

But a horrible additional chapter unfolded.

One of the main characters in this book is Chris Benoit. He was a huge influence on my career and on my life, and he is a very important part of this story.

The majority of the events within this book focus on my life from 1990 to 1999. The Chris Benoit in this book is the one I knew within that same time frame. The man that I knew and loved exists within these pages, not the man that existed during the final days of his life.

Due to the tremendous understanding of the people at Grand Central Publishing, I was allowed to break the rules. I was able to make a few changes to the book and to write this message, and I thank them for that.

I just wish to God that I didn't have to, and I pray for the souls of the departed.

CJ

COAUTHOR'S NOTE

First, I want to say that this book is *not* an "as told to" autobiography. My role was to brainstorm ideas and help with organization and structure. The voice is 100 percent Chris Jericho.

Also, we chose to refer to Vince McMahon's wrestling company as the WWF in most places throughout the book, because that's what it was called when the events being described took place. It has since been renamed the WWE.

Peter Thomas Fornatale
Brooklyn, New York

ACKNOWLEDGMENTS

To Jesus Christ for allowing me to live my dream. Thank you sir!

To Jessica my princess and the love of my life, for her belief and tolerance of me. To our children, Ash, Cheyenne, and Sierra, for teaching me how to be a man. Love is too small a word.

To my dad, Ted, for being my biggest supporter and my best friend.

To my mom, Loretta, for being my true hero and for teaching me how to love.

To Chad and Todd Holowatuk for being the brothers I always had.

To Grandma Jesse for getting me into this whole mess.

To Grandpa Jake for granting me amnesty.

To Auntie Joan for encouraging and sparking my creativity.

To Lance Storm, Lenny Olson, Mike Lozanski, and Bret Como for their friendship and for being there from the beginning. We toured the world and elsewhere . . .

To the Palko Family—Jerry, Bev, Brad, and Tyler. Without your love and support this journey never would've taken place.

To Chris Benoit for being a mentor, a big brother, and for always having my back. Love and respect to the man I knew.

To Mick Foley and Andy Summers, whose autobiographies are the templates for what mine aspires to be.

To Pete Fornatale for your advice and assistance as I was writing this masterpiece. I couldn't have chosen a better collaborator.

To Mick Foley for going through the book with me line by line because he cared. His "bestselling author" suggestions and insightful advice were invaluable in making this a better book.

To my editor, Melanie Murray, at Grand Central Publishing, for picking up someone else's vision and crafting it masterfully into her own; and for putting up with my OCD!

To Barry Bloom, Leland LaBarre, and everyone at Diverse, Nicole Nassar, and Kelly Kupper for being the quarterbacks of Team Jericho.

To Rich Ward and Mark Willis for helping to make rock 'n' roll dreams come true.

To Marc Gerald, Seth Rappaport, and Jason Pinter for putting this idea into my head and helping me realize there was something interesting to write about after all.

To all of the promoters who enabled me to turn this fantasy into reality: Vince McMahon, Eric Bischoff, Vince Russo, Paul Heyman, Genichiro Tenryu, Antonio Inoki, Atsushi Onita, Paco Alonso, Carlos Elizondo, Jim Cornette, Rene Lasartesse, Ed Langley, Bob Puppets, Fred Jung, Tony Condello, and Bob Holliday. This is all your fault!

To Owen Hart, Ricky Steamboat, and Shawn Michaels for capturing my imagination and being heroes.

To Jim Ross for writing (as only he can) the perfect Foreword.

To all of those on the long and winding road whose friendship, love, and support helped to make it all possible: Ryan Ahoff, Dave Spivak, Kevin Ahoff, Craig Wallace, Warren Rumpel, Lee Wren, Don Callis, Tonga Fifita, Norman Smiley, Charles Ashenoff, Chavo Guererro Jr., Negro Casas, Yoshihiro Asai, Ajax Olson, Dean Malenko, Shane Helms, Hector Guerrero, Shane McMahon, Ed Aborn, all the past and present members of Fozzy, Sean Delson, Mike Martin, Bob Castillo and all at Grand Central Publishing for their understanding, Flamur Tonuzi, Bonnie Irvine, Paula and Tony Ford, Dave Meltzer for the fact checking, Paul Gargano, Lisa Ortiz, Masa Horie, Stephanie McMahon, Mary Klewchuk, Herb Irvine, Donna, Josh, and Dylan Campanaro, Kevin Dunn, Fred Chase, Zakk Wylde, Michael Braverman, Hal Sparks for the Beaver Birthday Cake line, Dale Thompson for Fistful of Bees, Mike Portnoy, the Irvine family, the Lockhart family, the Wheeldon family, the Malones, the Klewchuk family, the Holowatuk family, Pastor Chris Bonham, Rich McFarlin, and everyone at Grace Family Church, all of the Jerichoholics and Fozzy Fanatics worldwide and, most importantly, YOU!

CJ
www.chrisjericho.com
Phil. 4:13

CONTENTS

CONTENTS

FOREWORD

Are you a dreamer?

Because dreams still do come true and this fascinating book of one young man's dream becoming a reality proves it.

As the son of a former National Hockey League player, when young Chris Jericho was growing up in Winnipeg, Canada, he always wanted to be one of two things when he became an adult. With conventional wisdom tossed aside, Chris dreamed of being either a wrestler or rock star and actively started working toward those goals when he was fourteen years old. Rassler or Rock Star . . . Mom and Dad must have been thrilled!

One distinguishing trait of successful people is that they have the ability to dream and the desire to make those dreams come true no matter the challenges. This book is both a colorful blueprint of how to set one's goals and accomplish them and a story about a young man's adventures on many continents seeking the fame and fortune that had been tugging at his heartstrings his entire life.

I had the privilege of recruiting and signing Chris Jericho to his WWE contract in 1999. I still remember the meeting that Gerald Brisco and I had with Chris at the Bombay Bicycle Club in Clearwater, Florida, one weekday afternoon. For several hours we talked about the biz, told road stories, and worked on convincing Chris to come to the WWE for half the money that WWC was offering him to stay in Atlanta. Luckily we succeeded, as Chris made the decision to continue with his journey, to live his dream, and to run with the opportunity to finally become a superstar in the WWE.

Being active in the wrestling business for over four decades now, I can honestly say that there will never be another professional journey by any wrestler that will remotely compare with Chris Jericho's odyssey to make it to the WWE. Many of today's wrestlers have not been a product of the wrestling territory system like Chris was, because the territorial wrestling promotions have died. Few wrestlers today would even consider traveling abroad so frequently and to literally be challenged to survive in order to learn their craft. Chris Jericho did.

This may be the first-ever autobiographical, action-adventure, how-to-achieve-success book ever written. Chris Jericho is one of the most driven, focused, and talented individuals I have ever known and this unpredictable and offbeat story of one of the most amazing decades of any individual's life will keep you turning the pages from start to finish.

Chris Jericho is the last of a dying breed of unique individuals, the likes of which we will never see again.

Dreams do come true. Happy endings still exist. This book proves it.

Jim "J.R." Ross
www.jrsbarbq.com

A LION'S TALE

THE COUNTDOWN

15…14…13…

The crowd was buzzing like a fistful of bees, each one of them counting down with the clock. The Rock, one of the biggest names in WWF history, stopped his promo mid-sentence as the Countdown to the New Millennium graphic ticked down from 15 seconds toward zero.

Sixteen thousand fans in the Allstate Arena in Chicago knew something huge was about to happen.

The countdown continued . . .

12…11…10…

Standing backstage in the darkness behind the curtain of the massive *Raw* set, I knew that nothing I'd accomplished before this moment meant a dang thing now.

9…8…

Vince McMahon didn't care about any of the successes I'd achieved or about any of the countries I'd traveled to in my quest to make it to the WWF.

He didn't care that I'd been a heartthrob in Mexico or a champion in Japan. All he cared about was what I could do when the clock struck zero and I walked out into the arena to verbally joust with The Rock. If I hit a home run, I'd be on my way to superstardom. But if I struck out, there would be no second chance.

7... 6...

It was hard to concentrate as the roar of the crowd grew to a deafening crescendo, but I tried to forget about the Jericho Curse and focus on what was about to happen. When the clock hit zero, the double pyro display would explode and my new entrance video and ring music would begin to play.

5...4...

Trying to calm the pounding of my heart and the nerves that were running rampant, my mental Rolodex shuffled through all of the experiences that had led me to this moment: Vince McMahon's house, Brian Hildebrand's tribute match in Knoxville, the feud with Goldberg in WCW, Super Liger in Japan, the ECW Arena in Philly, the Super J Cup—Second Stage, the match with Ultimo Dragón in Ryogoku, pickpocketing Christopher Lloyd in Roppongi, wrestling with a broken arm in Tennessee, hanging out with strippers on the Reeperbahn in Germany, getting held up at gunpoint in Mexico City, playing bass with los Leones, my mom's crippling injury, meeting Lance Storm on my first day at the Hart Brothers Pro Wrestling Camp in Okotoks, PummelMania, watching wrestling at my grandma's house in Winnipeg . . .

CHAPTER 1

SHUT UP, KID,
OR I'LL SLAP YOUR FACE

The first time I ever watched pro wrestling was with my grandma in her basement in Winnipeg when I was seven. She was a quiet lady but whenever the AWA was on TV, she would freak out and start yelling and screaming. AWA stood for American Wrestling Association and was one of three major wrestling companies in North America, along with the WWF (World Wrestling Federation) and NWA (National Wrestling Alliance).

My grandma's name was Jesse and the wrestler who most drew her ire was a do-ragged-sporting, Elton John–sunglasses–wearing bad guy named Jesse "The Body" Ventura. Ventura, who sported a fashionable jewel in the dimple of his chin, was part of a tag team with the biker-looking Adrian Adonis. Jesse was a flamboyant loudmouth and I couldn't get enough of him. My grandma couldn't stand the Body or his antics.

My family went to my grandparents' house every

Saturday night to watch the Holy Trinity of Childhood Television™, which began with the *Bugs Bunny/Road-runner Hour* at five, followed by the AWA at six, and ending with *Hockey Night in Canada* at seven. My dad's name was Ted Irvine, and he played hockey in the NHL for ten years with the Los Angeles Kings (where he assisted on the very first power play goal in Kings history), the New York Rangers (where he went all the way to Game 6 of the Stanley Cup final in 1972, only to lose to Bobby Orr and his Boston Bruins), and the St. Louis Blues (where he ended his career in 1977). He was known as the Baby-Faced Assassin and was one of the most feared players in the league. Legendary tough guys like Dave Shultz and Keith Magnuson would challenge him to try and make a name for themselves. But he could also score and ended up with a total of 170 NHL goals and with his combination of skill and strength he was one of the original power forwards. So hockey was a big part of our family, but pro wrestling was beginning to become an even bigger part.

My grandma smoked a lot, which gave her a raspy voice which got raspier when she yelled at the TV, "Come on! Hit him!" I wholeheartedly joined my grandma in cheering our favorites and jeering the guys we hated . . . although I stayed neutral when the Body was on. Whenever my aunts or my dad said anything to her about wrestling being staged, she refused to acknowledge it. She also refused to acknowledge it years earlier when my dad had his first ever close-up on the nationally televised *Hockey Night in Canada* after missing a breakaway and greeting the nation with a resounding "FUCK!" "He never said that," she said. "He would never say that."

The first wrestler to become my hero was Hulk Hogan.

The Hulkster was in the AWA before he became a national star with the World Wrestling Federation, and I loved his huge mustache and long blond hair. He had the biggest muscles I'd ever seen and his charisma was off the charts. To me, the combination of all these qualities made him cooler than the Fonz. He was also the first wrestler that I became emotionally attached to because of a story line, when champion Nick Bockwinkel and his evil goons injured Hulk's arm and put him out of action. I couldn't wait for him to return and exact his revenge.

Eventually, my dad took me to the matches at the Winnipeg Arena. The old barn was big and dark and I was so excited when we got to our seats. All of my eight-year-old dreams and thoughts of what seeing wrestling would be like in person were about to be realized! Only the lights above the ring were illuminated, creating a mystical atmosphere, accentuated by the thick clouds of cigarette smoke that hung in the air underneath the lights. The place was packed. I had never before experienced such a range of emotions from a group of people watching the same event. There was cheering, booing, taunting, happiness, anger, elation, and disappointment.

All of the wrestlers seemed larger than life and I had a list of favorites. The High Flyers: a good-guy tag team made up of Jumpin' Jimmy Brunzell and Greg Gagne, who was AWA promoter Verne Gagne's son. I watched their match with intense concentration, cheering them on, begging for Greg to make the tag to Jimmy after being beaten on for what seemed like an hour and absolutely *exploding* off my seat when he finally did. King Tonga, a 300-pound Islander, who had a huge scar on his arm that was apparently caused by a shark attack on his native island . . . a shark that the King was forced to kill with his bare hands! Jerry Blackwell was a short, disgustingly obese guy the crowd tortured by chanting "Fatwell" during his match. After he threatened to "slap the shit out" of me when I yelled at him timidly as he passed by me on his way to the ring, I joined in the chant with extra vim and vigor (what the hell does vim mean anyway?). Then there was Baron Von Raschke, a bald, strange-looking dude who resembled one of the mutants from *The Hills Have Eyes* and spoke in a thick, hard-to-place Eastern European accent. But he was a Winnipeg favorite and I went nuts for him as he paraded around in his black tights and red cape, threatening to administer his devastating finishing move, the Claw, to his hapless opponent.

There was also Gorgeous Jimmy Garvin, who was accompanied to the ring by his valet, Precious, an attractive blonde in a tight spandex shirt and hot pants. I was *shocked* when the crowd began to chant "Show Your Tits!" I was double-shocked when the crowd began to chant *"Asshole!"* at Garvin when he covered Precious with his jacket. I sat there thinking, "You can't say tits and you sure as heck can't say asshole! When my dad hears that, he is not going to be happy." But he just laughed it off. That's when I figured out that the normal rules of conduct for a hockey or football game didn't apply at the wrestling matches. I liked this rowdy crowd.

At the intermission, the company would sell tickets for the next month's card and my dad and I always bought them. The ring announcer, Mean Gene Okerlund, would say "Get your tickets now . . . doncha dare miss it!" and we didn't. Wrestling became me and my dad's thing. No matter what was going on, we always knew that once a month, we'd be able to spend time together at the matches.

Since my dad had retired from the NHL years before, he had taken a side job as a radio commentator for the Winnipeg Jets. That job helped him make some major connections for his day job as a financial planner. Because of that he was able to get me autographs from some of the top wrestlers like Black Jack Lanza and Nick Bockwinkel. The fringe benefits continued as my dad scored us front-row tickets to one of the biggest cards in Winnipeg history, featuring the main event of new champion Rick Martel against the evil Russian Boris Zukoff in a steel cage match. John Ferguson, the GM of the Jets, was the special referee. Sitting so close to the action opened a whole new world for us as fans and as observers. You could see and hear things that you couldn't see on TV. You could feel the force of the blows . . . or lack thereof. The reactions of the guys in the ring were more pronounced as well. A newcomer named Scott Hall gave a guy a back drop and said to his partner in disbelief, "Hey, did you see how high he went?" My dad and I both heard it and shot each other an astonished look.

A true conflict arose one month when a famous hypnotist known as the Man They Call Raveen came to town. I had to see Raveen . . . I needed to see Raveen . . . I begged my mom to take me to see Raveen! She finally agreed to take me to see damn Raveen but what I didn't know was that Raveen had the audacity to schedule his show the same night as the AWA. At this point after all the begging and the pleading that I had laid onto my mom, I couldn't back out. So my mom and I went to see the amazing mind controller hypnotist, and my dad and my aunts went to see the amazing mind controller wrestlers. As soon as I got to the Raveen show I realized I had made a huge mistake. After a few minutes of watching the Wolfman Jack look-alike in a velvet jacket making people bark like dogs, act like babies, and smell nonexisting farts, all I could think about was how Hogan was getting revenge on Bockwinkel only a few miles away at that very moment . . . and I was *missing* it!

The first thing I did after Raveen had restored everyone back to normal with a simple snap of his amazing fingers was to call my dad to find out what had happened at the Arena. I was pretty pissed off that I'd made the wrong decision and chosen something lame instead of the sure bet of wrestling. It never happened again.

Then one month when I went to the AWA show, I was surprised when the ring announcer welcomed us to the debut of a new wrestling league at the Winnipeg Arena. With no warning, the AWA had been replaced by the World Wrestling Federation. Vince McMahon, the head honcho of this new company, had muscled his way into taking over the Winnipeg wrestling scene, replacing Gagne's show with his own. It didn't take long to realize that the WWF show was all that the AWA was and a whole lot more. These guys had glitzier names—like Jake the Snake, Macho Man Savage, and Ricky "The Dragon" Steamboat—and they were *huge*, massively built muscleheads who were the complete opposites of the skinny or beer-bellied athletes the AWA was offering. But the real kicker came when the WWF's new champion walked through the curtain on his way to the ring: Hulk Hogan was back! If the Hulkster was down with the new boss, then so was I. I instantly turned traitor on the AWA and embraced my new favorite wrestling league.

When I entered my teens, I started to expand my wrestling fanaticism, as just going to the matches and watching them on TV wasn't enough. Someone found out that all the wrestlers stayed at the Polo Park Inn, adjacent to the Winnipeg Arena, when they were in the Peg and worked out at the Gold's Gym across the street. So when the matches came to town, I'd take the bus down to the Arena after school, watch the guys work out at the gym, then go hang out in the lobby of the Polo Park Inn hoping to catch another glimpse. When I got a little bit older, I started sneaking into the Polo Park Inn bar using a fake ID that my friend Warren and I made. Inside the bar, I stared as all the wrestlers hung around talking to girls and drinking Labatt's Blue. I couldn't believe the size of them, especially when I stood next to Andre The Giant. His hand was as big as my head. A few minutes later I saw the Hulkster himself, so I summoned all my courage and asked if I could shake his hand. Not only did he say yes but he asked me my name as well. I flipped out. The Hulkster knew my name! "We're friends!" I thought as I began to skip and dance around like Ed Grimley after he met Pat Sajak.

I always felt more comfortable approaching the smaller guys. Shawn Michaels was a member of the Rockers, my favorite tag team, and wasn't much taller than I was. After seeing him do a back flip off the top rope on TV, I decided I had to do one. When I saw him at the gym I asked him how and he said, "You just have to go up there and do it, brother." While the advice made sense, the fact that he called me brother didn't. To the best of my knowledge we weren't related. I didn't know that I had just been exposed to *the* most frequently used word in pro wrestling vernacular.

It was even easier for me to talk to a lower level guy named Koko B. Ware. Not only was he shorter than me but he also had the goofy gimmick of walking to the ring with his pet bird, Frankie. He barely ever won as it was but after I saw him wrestle in dress pants and dress shoes (his gear bag had been lost by the airline), his intimidation factor was lost to me forever. So anytime I had a question about wrestling, I just asked Koko.

"Hey Koko, I wanna gain weight. What's the best way to do it?"

"You have to drink a lot of beer."

Words to live by for aspiring athletes, street urchins, and chubby, parrot-packing grapplers. The conversation with Koko also started my tradition of asking wrestlers very stupid questions upon meeting them.

"Hey Koko, how do you plan on beating the Warlord? He's so much bigger than you."

"I'll just try to duck and dip around him." Also great advice . . . for dodgeball players.

When he proceeded to lose to the Warlord that night in like three minutes, I thought to myself with pure sincerity, "Damn, I guess dodging and ducking just didn't pan out for him."

The WWF had just released a record album (remember those?) called *Piledriver* which featured wrestlers, including Koko, singing. I brought my copy to the bar for Koko to sign, telling him that not only was he a great wrestler but a great singer as well. He looked at me quizzically as he signed, like even he didn't believe my statement.

I befriended Craig Wallace, aka Wallass, in gym class when we discovered that we both knew how to do a DDT (hands down, the most popular wrestling move for fans from my generation). He was as fanatical about wrestling as I was and we devised a plan to get our pictures with the wrestlers. Since neither one of us had the guts to simply ask them, one of us would stand by a wall in the hotel while the other stood nearby with a camera. When a wrestler walked into the frame of the guy standing next to the wall, the camera guy would say the wrestler's name. "Hey, One Man Gang!" "Hey Outback Jack!" or whatever. When the wrestler turned to look, the cameraman would snap a quick picture and shazam . . . instant personal portrait.

When I took pictures for Wallass, they always came out perfect. But whenever he took pictures for me, the wrestler wouldn't be looking or there'd only be half of me in the shot. It happened so many times that when my picture of Wallass and Bushwhacker Luke was perfect and his picture of me and the Honky Tonk Man was butchered, we got into a fistfight.

The first time I ever got an inkling that wrestling might not be completely legit was when I saw Sika, half of the Wild Samoans, at the hotel. On television, he spoke no English and had a manager who did the talking for the team. I wanted to get his autograph but he was alone, so I approached him gingerly with pen and paper in hand and spoke slowly and simply. "Mr. Sika," I said, pointing at the paper with my pen. "Autograph. Please. You sign. Here," I explained while pantomiming signing motions with my pen.

He looked at the pen and paper in my hand and then looked straight in my eyes and said in perfect English . . .

"Fuck off, kid."

I was shocked! I was agog! And not because he told me to fuck off. Oh no dear readers, I was shocked because I had discovered that Sika *could actually speak English!* "Oh my gosh! He speaks *English!* Did anybody else hear that?" I shouted to no one in particular. But alas, it was like seeing the head of the monster rising from the depths of Loch Ness with nobody else on the boat. I alone had discovered the savage Samoan's secret.

The dissing continued when I saw the Dynamite Kid sitting in the bar, pecs bursting out of an open dress shirt, drinking beer. When he saw me approaching with my pen, he glared at me and said in his thick Cockney accent, "Don't even fookin' try it." I turned on my heels and walked straight out of the bar without missing a beat.

My mission to be assaulted by a wrestler continued when Wallass and I decided to follow the Four Horsemen's limousine in my mom's car after we saw them buying beer at a vendor. After a thirty-minute cat-and-mouse session, they simply put the limo into reverse at a red light and began to chase us backward on and off the curb. We were desperately trying to escape, all the while envisioning the horrible fate that awaited should they catch us. Satisfied that their message had been delivered, they drove away laughing and taunting us all the way down the street. Tully Blanchard stuck his head out of the window and yelled, "You little fuckheads need to get girlfriends." Girlfriends? I had no time for girlfriends . . . I was too busy obsessing about wrestling.

I was a model WWF fan, the perfect sheep that could be manipulated into liking or hating whoever the TV show told me to. I was a huge fan of all the good guys and I hated all the bad guys. Before each match, I made my way down through the crowd to boo them as they came to the ring. I antagonized the Honky Tonk Man so much once, that he said to me in his thick Southern accent, "Shut up, kid, or I'll slap your face!" This time I was no timid amateur like I was when Fatwell threatened me. This time I challenged Honky Tonk to a fight. He just walked away and I'm lucky he didn't stab me with his sideburns.

Even as I got older, I was a firm believer that wrestling was one hundred percent legit. There was no Internet back then giving away the secrets of the matches, no insider newsletters discussing every last detail about the business. Of course some people said it wasn't real and there were moments—like my encounter with Sika—that made me wonder. But no one in my circle knew for sure. It was like Santa Claus. You believed in him because everyone told you to. It was that blind faith that made being a wrestling fan a truly magical experience. Sadly, the magic of those days is long gone and being a true wrestling fan in the year 2007 is an entirely different animal than being a true wrestling fan in the year 1987 . . . and I'm not sure that's a good thing.

CHAPTER 2

GROTTO VALLEY DEATH MATCH

People always asked me, "Are you going to be a hockey player like your dad?" The truth of the matter was even though I'd been playing hockey since I was four, I really wasn't very good. Of course I was a hockey fanatic; there wasn't much to do in Peg in the winter other than play hockey, drink beer, and fight, and at four years old I was too young to fight. I enjoyed playing sports but it was my creativity that really fueled me. I was a huge comic book collector (with Batman and Archie being my favorites) and a voracious reader with the Hardy Boys (the death-defying mystery-solving brothers not the death-defying acrobatic wrestling brothers) and Stephen King leading the way. I loved *Star Wars* (I waited in line for twelve hours to see the first showing of *Return of the Jedi*), James Bond, *Star Trek* (I sent away for a Chekov autograph), and horror movies. My addiction to horror probably started when I awoke one night with my parents searching through my hair, looking for a 666 on my head after they'd just seen *The Omen*. Each week I perused the *TV Guide* and circled the late night horror movies that I wanted to see. My mom allowed me to watch them, but I had to go to bed at my normal time of 10 P.M. and set my alarm to wake up at midnight if I wanted to check out Lon Chaney Jr. as the Wolfman or Boris Karloff in *The Mummy*. Oh the days before TIVO, my children . . . But along with wrestling it was rock 'n' roll that really captured my imagination. I had every Beatles record by the time I was ten and read every book about them I could get my hands on by the time I was twelve. I was fascinated by their music, the details of their lives, how they shaped the entire destiny of pop culture. But in the early 1980s the Beatles' popularity had been usurped (great word) by Martha and the Muffins and Rocky Burnette. "You don't like Loverboy?" my friends would ask. "What's wrong with you? Forget the Beatles; the Little River Band is where it's at." I'm happy to say that when I'm walking in the park and reminiscing, I'm quite proud that I stuck with listening to the legendary Beatles instead of the not so legendary Little River Band.

In addition to my burgeoning interest in the Beatles, the Who, the Beach Boys, and Rick Dees ("Disco Duck," which for some reason was my favorite song for a time), I was also a very creative kid. So much so, that my Auntie Joan, who was the dean of the University of Manitoba, used me as an example of a highly imaginative child when she gave lectures to teachers. I wrote my own songs, tried to teach myself how to play guitar, and made my own tape-recorded radio shows. I acted out battles, adventures, and odysseys for hours with the most impressive collection of Star Wars and *Star Trek* dolls this side of Mos Eisley. I was obsessed with *Dungeons and Dragons* and was convinced that the Loch Ness monster actually existed . . . I still am. I liked to draw my own comic book movies—which were basically just comic books done in movie storyboard fashion, complete with opening and closing credits. A lot of these movies starred the Mr. Rogers Band, a Beatles-influenced rock group that I'd created. I'd storyboard their movies, and draw their album covers and included every detail: the song titles, lyrics, credits, even clocking the song times. I'd cut a circle of black construction paper to represent the actual LP and slide it between the stapled front and back covers.

When I started high school, I had the attitude and look of a rocker, including a sweet mullet that I made worse by using a crimping iron to straighten the back. It fried my hair and earned me the nickname Steel Wool. But I also played hockey and was an all-star water polo goalie, the master of the egg beater (don't ask), so I had a lot of jock friends too. I had the same combination of athleticism and creativity that had originally attracted me to wrestling.

Meanwhile, wrestling was becoming a bigger part of my life. I missed the original WrestleMania, the WWF's version of the Super Bowl, but when it was time for WrestleMania 2 I took the bus down to the Winnipeg Arena and watched the show on closed circuit television, the archaic version of PPV. You paid for a ticket, which gave you the privilege of going to the Arena to watch the damn thing on a giant out-of-focus movie screen.

The glitz and excitement that surrounded WrestleMania took wrestling to a different level for me and I realized that the business was a hell of a lot bigger than what I saw in the Winnipeg Arena every month. I started to dream that maybe someday I could become a wrestler. The problem was that most of the guys in the WWF were huge and I was not. Another friend, Dave Fellowes, was also incredibly into wrestling and we had this crazy idea: Maybe if we hung out together at the Arena in muscle shirts, the British Bulldogs would see our muscularity and decide to take us under their wing and train us to be the Winnipeg Bulldogs. Of course they could just as easily have taken us to the basement, put ball gags in our mouths, and given us to the Gimp, but we'll never know now will we?

In 1986, Winnipeg started getting broadcasts of Stampede Wrestling out of Calgary. This new company looked cheap and was broadcast out of a livestock field house but the wrestling was off the charts. It was fast, hard-hitting, action-packed, and completely ahead of its time. It was a melting pot of styles, exciting to watch, and I realized that the WWF wasn't the only game in town.

There were a couple of other wrestling shows on the tube as well, and I watched them all. We had the local WFWA based out of Winnipeg, the UWF based out of Oklahoma, and the IWA based out of Montreal. The IWA featured all these guys with thick French accents who could hardly speak English and the show was even cheaper-looking than Stampede. But they had some great characters. There was a guy called Floyd Creachman who managed the Man of 1,000 Holds, Leo Burke. Creachman was doing an interview and said that Burke was the Man of 1,002 Holds, to which the interviewer butted in, "But I thought he was the Man of 1,000 Holds?" Creachman deadpanned, "He learned two more." That to me was the greatest line ever—a line so good I ripped it off a decade later.

Then came the day when my life's path became written in stone. I was watching my weekly dose of Stampede Wrestling when a music video of Bryan Adams's "Hearts on Fire" began to air. But instead of featuring clips of a pockmarked, greasy-haired rock star, the video featured clips of a blond-haired, solidly built wrestler performing the most mind-blowing, acrobatic moves I had ever seen . . . and I was completely blown away. The video continued and I watched in total astonishment as this guy who couldn't have been more than five years older than me executed moonsaults, back flips off the top rope, back flips off other wrestlers' backs, and the grand finale where he grabbed a guy's hand, leaped straight to the top rope, sat down on the top rope and flipped onto his feet, only to throw the other wrestler halfway across the ring! I was always more into the high-flying guys in the WWF like the British Bulldogs and Randy Savage, but they didn't have *anybody* there who could do this type of stuff. When the video ended, the name that appeared on the screen was Owen Hart, and he instantly became my new hero. He was the youngest son of the promoter of Stampede, Stu Hart, and the brother of another one of my WWF faves, Bret "The Hitman" Hart. When I saw Owen do his thing, I was struck by a feeling of desire so strong that it might as well have been a bolt of lightning sent straight from the heavens above. I didn't just *want* to be a wrestler . . . I *had* to be a wrestler.

Owen wasn't 6 foot 8 and 300 pounds like most of the wrestlers in the WWF seemed to be. He was my height and had the kind of muscle that I could have if I trained

1987. The picture I drew in math class of me and Owen Hart as Stampede tag team champions. I would attend his funeral less than 12 years later.

hard and ate right. Plus, Calgary was in my universe. It was a city I'd been to and seen with my own eyes. It wasn't like the faraway places where the WWF toured, places I couldn't just get on a bus and visit. I decided that somehow, someway, I was going to go to Calgary and have Owen Hart teach me how to wrestle.

All my friends and I could think about was wrestling, and during class we drew pictures called *Classic Wrestling Moments*. I drew a picture of Owen and me holding the Stampede tag team championships and Wallass drew a picture of King Bundy dropping an elbow on the midget Little Beaver, during WrestleMania 3. Fellowes drew a picture of Roddy Piper destroying Adorable Adrian Adonis's Flower Shop talk show set (Adonis had gone from being a tough

biker to a sissy). I drew another picture of Andre the Giant
pinning Hulk Hogan, while a corrupt referee counted to
three, which was inspired by the craziest wrestling angle
we'd ever seen.

It was one of the most important matches ever in wrestling: Hogan vs. Andre the Giant for the WWF title on
prime-time TV. I had a job at a deli and that night I had
to work so I was going to have to miss the show. I told
Wallass with a tear in my eye, "I have to miss the Hulkster's match, so as soon as it's over, you have to come
straight here, do not pass Go, do not collect $200 (Ca-
nadian), and tell me what happened!" A few hours later,
Wallass staggered breathlessly into the deli. "Oh my God,
man! Oh my God! There were two referees!" He stuttered
and stammered, barely making any sense. "And one got
plastic surgery to look like the other one . . . and he had
money in his pocket . . . and Hogan lost the belt."

I stopped him right there in disbelief and shook my
head. "What did you say?"

"The Million Dollar Man paid off an evil look-alike
referee to cheat," Wallass continued, ". . . and . . . and . . .
and . . . and Hogan lost the belt."

I felt my stomach drop. Hogan had been the champ
since I became a fan of the WWF four years earlier. He had
been the victim of the ultimate double cross, when the official of the match had been kidnapped and replaced by his
evil paid-off twin brother who fast-counted the Hulkster's
shoulders to the mat, causing him to lose the World Wrestling Federation heavyweight championship to Andre the
Giant! Then Andre turned around and, in his words, sold
"the World World Wrestling tag team title" to his boss, the

Million Dollar Man, Ted DiBiase. You couldn't write stuff this good!

Finally it sunk in that Hogan had lost the title. I was devastated and it was just about the worst night of my life. I felt like, "Hogan lost. What are we going to do? Where are we going to go? Who's gonna save the free world from the evil commies now?"

In order to boost our flagging spirits, Wallass and I had an idea. We began going to our high school gym every Wednesday night for what we called Wednesday Night's Main Event. We simply told the gym teacher that we wanted to practice gymnastics and he allowed us to set up the PORTaPIT, which were gym mats that were bigger and thicker than mattresses. We spread them out over the hardwood floors and biggity bam, we had our own personal wrestling ring. After some brainstorming, the best name we could think of was the Big Time Wrestling Federation and biggity-biggety bam, the BTWF was in business baby!

So we had our matches and we had a whole roster of guys who we'd pretend to be. They were either parodies of WWF characters like the Memphis Man or the Wild Warden or original characters like the BFG—the Big Fat Guy—or the Vid Kid. We'd spend hours in class putting together elaborate story lines and spend more hours having the matches themselves, which would always end with a cliff-hanger to lead us to the next week. Due to our fanatical watching and studying of the WWF TV shows we were able to figure out most of the moves . . . DDTs, suplexes, body slams, pile drivers, whatever. We could also both take back drops and land on our feet. Keep in mind that we were beating the crap out of each other on school

property WITH the teacher's permission . . . a highly sue-
able offense in today's world, doncha think?

The matches continued every Wednesday, finally building up to the biggest show in BTWF history . . . Pummel-
Mania. This show was to be the culmination of all the big
feuds we'd been working on for months. One of the main
feuds featured Sheriff Bobby Riggs (the corrupt Southern racist cop) against the Spirit Walker (an Indian mystic
whose name we'd ripped off from a Cult song). They finished off their feud for the Intercity Title at PummelMania
with what we called a Segregation Match. The ring had a
line in the middle and you had to pin the guy on your own
side of the ring for the fall to count. And of course, we did
a big false finish where Sheriff Bobby Riggs pinned the
Spirit Walker on the wrong side of the line, only to get
rolled up by the wily Spirit Walker and lose the match. I
still think that's a hell of an idea for a match that could be
used today . . . are you reading, Vince?

The heavyweight champion of the BTWF was a character I played called the Eastern Crowbar. I have no idea why
we gave him the name, why he was our big star, or why
he spoke with a hybrid Schwarzenegger–Canadian Indian
accent saying things like, "I'm Eastern Crowbar coming
for to get you." His big rival was the Galangoo Man, who
hailed from a small island in the South Pacific and was
rumored to be a cannibal. They feuded over the BTWF
title, which was a very prestigious piece of hardware that
we made out of cardboard. The big main event for PummelMania was a special Grotto Valley Death Match for
the championship. I have no idea what a Grotto Valley
Death Match was or how we thought of it. But it was an
angry match, my friends, and it culminated with the East-

ern Crowbar crawling up a twenty-foot (or six-foot) steel ladder on his way to certain victory. Just as the Crowster reached the top of the ladder and prepared to jump off onto the helpless Galangoo Man for the win, the gym door opened and the janitor walked in. Everyone called him Egypt because nobody could understand the gibberish he spewed out of his mouth, but it was easy to understand his intent as he started screaming at me, "Downnoo . . . Youga downnooa!" I tried to negotiate with Egypt by explaining that I just had to do this one move and then we would split. Egypt's words were still muddled but were becoming more distinct, "No owne zing. Youga doooowwnnnnssss!" He then shambled over and stood over the Galangoo Man, which gave me no choice.

I jumped off the ladder and kicked the son of a bitch in the face.

Actually, I climbed down the ladder with my tail between my legs and the legendary PummelMania main event was declared a no contest.

In the summer, we took the matches to my swimming pool where we organized a massive Intercity Title tournament, using the edge of the pool for . . . ummm . . . dives and splashes. We also published a BTWF magazine that featured articles on all the wrestlers in our company and had ads for such things as BTWF plum and coconut cookies. We created the BTWF Orchestra to record theme songs for the wrestlers and put together *Suplex: The BTWF Wrestling Album,* featuring all our guys singing songs.

We were both pretty much raving schizos at this point.

In the midst of all this imagination, I was hit with a cold shot of reality when my parents decided to get a divorce. My parents had been married twenty years, but over the last few years they had been unraveling at the seams. I used to lie in my bed and listen to them arguing, sometimes flat-out screaming and swearing at each other, just praying that they would stop so I could get to sleep with a clear conscience. About a year earlier, my parents had started sleeping in different rooms. They didn't say anything regarding the reason why and they didn't have to; it was obvious they were having MAJOR problems. It all came to a head one night when I forgot to put the milk back in the fridge and my mom just exploded on me. Things quickly spiraled out of control and my parents got into this monster fight. I jumped into the escape pod of my friend's car and split and when I came back home, my dad was gone. A few days later he came back and my mom and dad sat me down and told me he was moving out. My dad was really upset, almost in tears, but my mom was very calm and matter-of-fact about it. I was furious that they made me sit there and be in the middle of the whole thing. Their contrasting emotions—him so sad, her so businesslike—just confused me even more and made me feel worse. As a result, instead of asking what the problems were about, I just clammed up and waited for it all to be over. My way of dealing with the situation was to just tune out. I just completely ignored the situation and totally committed myself to my friends, my music, and my wrestling. Their divorce also skyrocketed my desire to get out of the house, to escape from Winnipeg and to make something of myself. I still loved both of my parents but just because their lives were messed up didn't mean I was going to mess up mine too. It was now clear what my life's mission was . . . wrestler be thy name!

CHAPTER 3

BODY SLAMS, BISCUITS, AND BIBLES

After my dad moved out, he got an apartment close to where my mom and I lived and made a concerted effort to remain a part of my life. This was really apparent when he started showing up at my church on Sundays. I had been going to church with my mom since I was a little kid but at some point we just stopped. As I got more and more into music, heavy metal in particular, one of the genres I dug the most was Christian metal. A lot of kids in school were into the satanic metal bands like Slayer and Venom and that made me even more curious about what it was like on the other side of the Cross. Bands like Stryper, Bride, and Barren Cross sounded cool, looked cool, and convinced me that you could be into Jesus and still *be* cool. Listening to those bands influenced me to go back to church and I started going by myself on Sundays. I took confirmation classes and I even became a Sunday school teacher at sixteen, with my long steel-wool hair, rumpled dress shirt, and all. The minister at St. Chad's was an ex-hippie named Tony Harwood-Jones who was a very good guy and easy to relate to. He encouraged me to explore my relationship with God. His attitude about being a Christian was "it isn't what you wear as long as you are there." I never missed a Sunday at church after my parents split. When my dad first started showing up, he just came to hang out

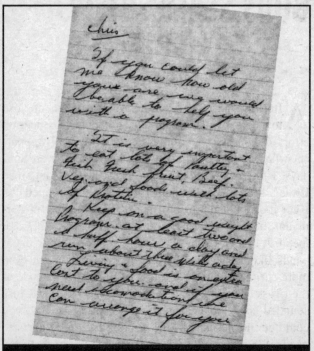

The original reply letter I received from Ed Langley, telling me to work out two and a half hours and run three miles every day.

with me, but after a while he got more into it and came to hang out with Jesus too.

We also made a point of spending time together at his office, which just so happened to be upstairs from a convenience store that rented WWF videotapes. So we rented the latest tape, ate some Kentucky Fried Chicken (well what *did* you think KFC stood for?), and watched wrestling. My relationship with my dad at that time was based on body slams, biscuits, and Bibles and we became closer as a result of the three.

Now that I'd decided the course of my life, I knew I would have to get a whole lot bigger. I joined a gym, stuffed myself with protein (along with a sock), read every muscle magazine I could find, and ordered the Arnold Schwarzenegger EZ Curl Bar to "Get 21 inch arms just like Arnold."

One day while watching Stampede, my heart jumped out of my mouth when I saw an ad for the Hart Brothers Pro Wrestling Camp. This was my chance to be trained by Owen and the entire Hart family, including Stu Hart himself! I wrote to the address on the screen and a couple of weeks later when I opened the reply, I found out two things:

1. I had to be eighteen to go to wrestling camp, and
2. I should be about 225 pounds.

The letter had been written by a guy named Ed Langley, who was the representative for the Hart Brothers Camp. His advice on weight gain was to eat beef, fish, liver, and to drink only milk . . . a direct violation of Koko B. Ware's rule. He also advised me to lift weights for two and a half hours a day and run three miles a day. So I ate raw eggs and liver (trying not to barf) and lots of fish and beef. Every shift at work, I'd weigh myself on the deli scale to check my progress. I started at 175 and my grand plan was to be 235 pounds by the time I left for wrestling school.

I'd decided on 235 as my target weight about a year earlier when I met Ricky the Dragon at an annual car show called the World of Wheels. The show featured fancy funny cars, soap opera stars, Playboy Playmates, and more importantly, a WWF wrestler! Of course I couldn't give a shit about seeing Michael Knight from *All My Children* or meeting Miss March, Mary Jane Rottencrotch, I just wanted to meet my hero himself, Ricky "The Dragon" Steamboat! I met Wallass at the show and tried to decide what I was going to say to him, as we figured we'd have time to ask the Dragon one question. We got our tried-and-true picture system ready and when I reached the front of the line, my big question for Ricky was "How tall are you?" (Hours to think of an inquiry or a witty anecdote and "How tall are you?" was the best I could do. The trend continued.)

Ricky replied that he was 5 foot 11 and when I asked him how much he weighed, just as he answered 235 pounds, Wallass snapped the picture. When I got the picture back we were both actually in the shot, even though Steamboat's eyes were half closed and I looked like a complete tool with bad hair and my mouth wide open like a Muppet. Wallass's photographic ineptitude had struck again.

Steamboat was the same height as me but a whole lot bigger. From that moment on, working out became my second biggest hobby. My biggest hobby was my band.

April 1988. Ricky "The Dragon" Steamboat answers my question of how tall he is just as Wallass takes the picture.

I started playing bass guitar when I was fourteen years old when my cousin lent me his Paul McCartney Hofner bass. I kinda knew my way around a guitar, after taking lessons when I was nine from a guy called Brad Roberts. Coincidentally, Brad would become internationally famous as the leader of the Crash Test Dummies, best known for the song "Mmm Mmm Mmm." I knew they had really made it big when Weird Al Yankovic parodied the track.

When I entered junior high, I made the rock 'n' roll decision to give up the guitar and take up the trombone instead. You could hold a gun to my head and ask me why I felt the need to be a member of the brass section but I still can't come up with an answer. I'd like to tell you that there was a hot French horn player or that I was into

Count Basie, but there wasn't and I wasn't. Trombone? Even being an oboe player was cooler.

My trombone phase not withstanding, I was getting more into heavy metal, especially when I noticed that all the girls I liked were wearing shirts of bands like Ozzy Osbourne, Iron Maiden, Judas Priest. I decided if I ever wanted to actually talk to a girl, I'd better figure out who these guys were, pronto. So I bought *Blizzard of Ozz* by Ozzy and it instantly corrupted me. The Beatles were great, but Ozzy had become the new sheriff in town.

I completely immersed myself into the metal scene and became the Clive Davis of my neighborhood by discovering Metallica, Anthrax, Raven, Saxon, Trouble, Nasty Savage, Megadeth. I'd go to the record store and look through the bins to check out album covers and the band pictures, buying the ones that I thought looked cool.

I was such a metaller that I created major controversy with my metal friends after an appearance I made on the local video program *CitiVision*. "Chris, do you like Bryan Adams?" the host inquired.

"Yeah, he's okay," I said, not caring that I really thought he sucked. I just wanted to be on TV.

But the second I said it, I knew I'd made a horrible mistake. To the Iron Maiden crowd in my school, admitting that Bryan Adams was "okay" was akin to treason . . . the ultimate sin! Any true metalhead should spit on the grave of Bryan Adams and flash his family their nutsacks. As a result of my miscue, I was subjected to the worst buggings I'd endured since I was seen crying after Spock died during Star *Trek II—The Wrath of Khan*. "You cried when Spock died! You like Bryan Adams!" Becoming a Mathlete seemed to be my fate, until I quickly did something to regain my street cred. I formed a band.

My friend since birth, Kevin Ahoff was a really good guitar player and we started jamming together. While most teenagers dabbling in guitar first learn songs like "Smoke on the Water" or "Iron Man," the first song I ever learned on bass was a complex little ditty called "Revelation (Life or Death)" by Trouble. Then we recorded the obvious follow up to a Trouble song . . . the theme from *Peter Gunn*. I don't get the connection either. But it was the first time I'd experienced the magic of playing a piece of music with another musician . . . and I was hooked.

When I started high school, the first band I was in was called Primitive Means (great name), which was like a punk version of Chicago; ten guys in the band with three or four guitarists and anybody who came over could join in. We'd write riffs and make up lyrics on the spot. Since nobody else wanted to sing, I decided to pull double duty. Warren the drummer's nickname was Rocky and after a few weeks of messing around, only he, Kevin, and I were left, so we formed another, heavier band named Scimitar. We jammed for months every day after school in Rocky's garage. When the popular hot chicks who lived down the street were walking home, we impressed and regaled them with our version of "You Really Got Me," Van Halen style. We'd crank it up just as they walked by and play "Da Na Na Nah Na" 100 times in a row. They still wouldn't give us the time of day in school, but for those 2 minutes and 45 seconds of rock stardom they were our groupies.

Scimitar rocked Westwood Collegiate for our entire high school run, mostly doing Iron Maiden and Metallica covers—pretty intense stuff for a bass player in a three-piece. When a citywide Battle of the Bands was announced we entered and were accepted. We played a cover of "Peace Sells . . . But Who's Buying" by Megadeth and a glam/prog rock original called "City Nights." For my stage outfit I made a pair of jeans with mirrors glued on the sides, cut the feet off a pair of socks for wrist bands, and drew a big, black ? on a T-shirt, which was my subtle way of questioning foreign policy against Aborigines . . . or something. When the battle began, our set got off to a rough start when Kevin stepped on his cord and pulled it out of his guitar. We had to restart "Peace Sells" from the beginning and I felt like we were fucked. But we pulled it together, the crowd responded, and we rocked to the second round!

In round two, we totally threw down, inspired by the kids in the crowd who were singing along to "City Nights." I'd like to say that we won the battle and surpassed the Guess Who as the biggest Winnipeg band of all time, but I can't. We ended up losing to a band called the Fourth Floor who did a kick-ass version of "Back in the USSR" by the Beatles. Beaten by my own favorite band! Even though we lost, it was still an amazing night. We were backstage in our own dressing room/closet playing in front of kids from all over the Peg who knew our song. Stepping onto the stage under the glow of the stage lights in front of what felt like 5,000 (50) screaming fans was the ultimate rush. I began to think that I could do that for a living.

The battle was filmed for a local TV show and we got one tape of it that we were supposed to share. We decided we'd take turns with it and when the tape got to my house, I watched it once and it ruled. The next morning, I went downstairs to watch it again, only to be mortified when I saw that my mom had accidentally taped over it with an episode of *The Love Boat*! Scimitar's finest hour had been erased forever, replaced with Isaac serving mai-tais to Charo and Jonathan Winters.

The need to perform continued and I landed the role of lead villain Bill Sykes in our high school musical *Oliver!* I threw myself into the role by spray-painting my hair black, introducing an Indiana Jones–style bullwhip into Sykes's repertoire, and practicing my English accent constantly. The play culminated with my big death scene as I plummeted off the back of the stage (landing on a BTWF regulation-sized PORTaPIT), causing the entire crowd to erupt in glee. I felt like Eugene Levy in *Waiting for Guffman*, when he looks at the camera and says, "I have to perform, I must entertain."

My résumé continued to grow as my group of buds and I became the masters of the Air Band. Air Band was a lip-synching competition where a group would get up on stage and pantomime a song—and we were the best in the city. Instead of doing one song straight through by one band, we took two songs from two different bands and put them together. "Wake Me Up Before You Go Go" by Wham! was combined with the heaviest metal song we could find, "Damage Inc." by Metallica. We called ourselves the Wham Bangers and the crowd yawned as they saw another group of guys dressed in black leather and studs, miming the opening of the Metallica song. But their yawns turned to looks of confusion, as right when it was about to explode, you heard "Jitterbug," and Wham! kicked in. Then balloons and confetti fell on the stage as a pair of hot preppy girls came out and started dancing.

Then—boom—it's back into the super-fast guitar solo from Metallica. It was so original and entertaining that we won the city championship.

Not to be outdone, the next year we took the original country version of "Take This Job and Shove It" by Johnny Paycheck and combined it with the punk version by the Dead Kennedys. Then we had the Johnny Paycheck part sung by a little person named Gary Dyson. At our high school, we had more midgets than black people (two midgets, one African-Canadian) and we took advantage of that. We won again, took our prize money, and blew the entire wad on hookers and blow. Actually we got nothing as the cash was donated to the Student Council. When we won again the next year with a Village People dance extravaganza called the Village Inn Guys, we made sure to have the check written out to Chris Irvine Esquire. Then we blew it on hookers and blow.

CHAPTER

MATH FOR HINDUS

I was only seventeen when I graduated from high school, which meant I had to wait another year before I could go to wrestling school. When Wallass told me he was going to apply to Red River Community College to take a course called Creative Communications, I was intrigued. More importantly, CreeComm would give me something to do until I was old enough to go to wrestling school.

As the college year began, my dad played in a celebrity hockey game at the Arena. I decided to check it out and was killing time downtown before the game when I walked past this big dude, wearing a white-tasseled leather jacket. And I knew only one guy that wore a white-tasseled leather jacket, because he wore it on every episode of Saturday Night's Main Event: Jesse "The Body" Ventura.

I sidled up next to him and began talking. It turned out that he was in town to play in the celebrity hockey game. The Body was the Shits at hockey but after the game, there was an after-party, so with my friends Gouge and

Fellowes, we crashed it. I zeroed in on Jesse and for the next two hours I never left his side, talking about wrestling, movies, and his lack of hockey-playing abilities. He was the coolest, most informative guy and he gave me some great advice about being in the wrestling business:

1. If you want to be a wrestler, you have to be prepared to live every day in pain.
2. If you want to be a wrestler, you need to make sure you have something to fall back on when it ends.
3. If you want to be a wrestler, you have to remember it's not what you earn, it's what you save.

I told him about my plans to attend the Hart Brothers Camp and he laughed and said "Watch out for Stu Hart, he's crazy. I've heard the tapes from the Dungeon where he literally tortures guys. But the toughest wrestlers in the world come from Calgary and if you can make it there, you can make it anywhere."

He told me a story about filming *Predator* with Arnold Schwarzenegger. Jesse would figure out what time Arnold worked out in the morning, get there five minutes earlier, and put water on his face so when Arnold got to the gym he would see Jesse "sweating" and already training. Then he would work out and not leave until after Arnold did. Governor Schwarzenegger never knew when Governor Ventura started or stopped training—and it drove him nuts to think that the Body trained harder than he did.

I wrote an article about my meeting with Jesse for the college paper and got a good response. So when the National Wrestling Alliance came to Winnipeg for the first time, I was able to get an interview with Jim Cornette, who was one of the great heel (bad guy) managers of all time. Jim gave me an awesome interview explaining the angles he was involved in and the business itself. It wasn't the last time Jim Cornette would explain the wrestling business to me.

After my stories got good reviews from the college crowd, I decided to see if I could get a gig at one of the major newspapers in the city. The AWA was launching a comeback, so I contacted the *Winnipeg Free Press* to see who was covering the show. I figured they had a whole team. It was surprising to me when they said nobody was. So I bought my own ticket, submitted the story, got paid fifty beans and the next day I got my first noncollege by-line. I became the wrestling reporter for the *Winnipeg Free Press*.

I'd also landed a job as a cameraman at a public access UHF station that featured such programs as *Math for Hindus*. I literally fell asleep filming this laugh riot and the camera kept dipping toward the floor, which I'm sure frustrated math-loving Hindus across the province.

The *Free Press* promoted me to be its low, low, low-end sports reporter so I got to cover swim meets, CFL fashion shows, and an actual Tiddlywinks tournament. Seriously. That's when I decided that instead of writing about other people, I wanted to be the guy who was being written about.

In the summer of 1989, my dad got invited to Calgary to play in a charity golf tournament. We both thought it would be a good idea to visit the Hart camp, so I went with him.

The camp was in the little town of Okotoks, about

forty minutes outside Calgary. It took a few minutes to find the school, because it was inside a garage behind a Petro Canada gas station. I thought to myself, "This is the Hart Brothers Camp? What happened to Stu Hart's basement? What happened to the Dungeon?"

But I was instantly taken by the dingy place with the dirt floor. Keith Hart (one of Stu's sons who I'd seen on Stampede TV) was in there, the ring was set up, and there were some weights lying around. There were Stampede Wrestling posters on the wall of Brian Pillman, Bruce Hart, Chris Benoit, and Owen Hart and I knew it was only a matter of time before my picture would be beside theirs. I'd worn a tight muscle shirt, jeans, and cowboy boots so I would look as big and as tall as possible. After speaking with Keith for a few minutes, I flipped the fuck out when he asked me to go into the ring. Once inside, he asked me to take a fall onto my back. I did and Keith claimed to be quite impressed. I was stoked but I couldn't believe I had to wait a whole other year before I could train for real.

Later that summer, local promoter Bob Holliday decided to start his own company, the Keystone Wrestling Alliance. He organized a tour of northern Manitoba Indian reservations and he hired me to be part of the ring crew along with Caveman Broda, a short, weird little guy with a crazy beard who coincidentally looked like a caveman. Broda was famous for going into supermarkets while on the road and denting canned foods on the metal shelves, ripping off the labels, and then demanding discounts for the damaged goods. He usually got the discounts, but was left with a duffel bag filled with unlabeled, dented tins of food. He never knew exactly what he was going to eat and constantly talked about "surprising" himself for dinner.

Broda was just one of a motley crew of wrestlers that had been assembled for the tour, including Man Mountain Mike (although since he'd lost about 175 of his 400 pounds, he was more like Man Mountain Stretchmark), a one-handed guy named the Iron Duke, and a big black dude named Catfish Charlie, who ended up being my roommate. But the big star of the tour was my old hero, Baron Von Raschke. Imagine my surprise when I found out that in reality he was really a mild-mannered schoolteacher with a Minnesota accent named Jim Raschke! Once the tour began it was my job not only to set up the ring, but to take ring jackets, sell programs, help with the luggage, and get coffee. I was also in charge of wrangling girls back to the hotel, but I was horrible at it. I didn't have a lot to work with considering that most of the wrestlers looked like orcs.

The tour started in Riverton, Manitoba, and I invited a girl I had a crush on to come to the show. Soon after she arrived, the ring broke. I tried to fix it while the match continued by crawling under the ring and holding it up with my feet. I'd bragged to this girl how I was coming to Riverton with this big wrestling company and here I was on my back attempting to hold up the damn ring with my feet, while Jim Raschke the schoolteacher stomped around above me, threatening to administer the Claw to his fat opponent in front of fifty people. She left early.

As the new kid on the block (Wahlberg represent, yo!), some of the boys targeted me for the age-old wrestling tradition of ribbing. Ribbing is a form of initiation where you are made fun of incessantly and constantly. The guys called me Prettyfer and would say things like, "Why don't you give us a kiss, Prettyfer?" For seasoned veterans it's nothing to get upset about, but for an eighteen-year-old rookie it was the ultimate insult. They kept pushing me until I got so pissed off that I began plotting my revenge.

Fortunately for me, Catfish Charlie was a great guy. He was a journeyman wrestler who never made it to the big time, but he took a liking to me and filled me in on the wrestling business. When I complained to him about the dudes calling me Prettyfer, he sat me down and said, "You know what? If you're going to be in this business, you need to learn a few things."

Charlie sensed that I was dead-serious about becoming a wrestler and he also realized that I had no clue about how it really worked. He explained that in the wrestling business there was a tradition of weeding out the guys who didn't belong and weren't tough enough to make it. If the guy being made fun of got upset, the heat was turned up until he snapped. He continued and explained that wrestlers weren't really fighting each other during a match but were working together to put on a show. I wasn't stupid and at this point he was simply confirming my suspicions. But I was in for a real shock when he answered my next question.

"Yeah, I guess I see what you mean about the lesser guys, but the champions are really the best, right? I mean, they really win their matches."

He looked me dead in the eye and said, "No, the champions are just like everyone else. They win when they're told to win and lose when they're told to lose."

That was a hard one for me to fathom. The idea that when Hulk Hogan won a title it was actually given to him by the promoter didn't compute. I was crestfallen. He explained that there really weren't good guys or bad guys, just guys playing the parts that the promoter decided on. The way that Wallass and I had put together the BTWF was the way the business actually worked. I couldn't believe how smart we'd been, yet how inadvertently stupid we'd been at the same time not to realize it sooner.

Shortly after my talk with Catfish Charlie, I was setting up the ring with Broda. "I hear you want to be a wrestler? Do you want me to show you how it's done?"

This was what I'd been waiting for and I said yes instantly.

Broda picked me up before I knew what was going on and body-slammed me. Surprisingly the slam didn't kill me and as I applauded myself for not crying, I looked up from the mat and saw him climbing to the top rope wearing these ridiculous black rubber boots that he always wore. He must've seen the worried look on my face as he looked down because he said, "The most important thing in wrestling is trust. Either you trust me, or you don't. And if you don't trust me, go home now."

This was the moment of truth. The time to put up or shut up . . . shit or get off the pot . . . a penny saved is a penny earned . . . well you get the idea.

I could get up and leave my dreams on the mat to get crushed by the Caveman or I could stay down and leave my skull on the mat to get crushed by the Caveman. Either way the result would end my wrestling career for good. I thought about closing my eyes but before I could, Broda jumped off the top rope. I saw his crazy hair swaying to and fro. I saw his rubber boots flopping in the air. And I saw his knee start small and slowly grow bigger until it enveloped my whole field of vision like Godzilla's foot. At the last parsec I closed my eyes and awaited Jesus to take me home. Except he didn't. Even though I'd never heard of Caveman Broda and had never seen him wrestle, he had just given me a textbook knee drop from the top rope and I hadn't felt a thing.

Using Broda as an example, I started gaining confidence that I could learn the art of pro wrestling and make a go out of it. My confidence was boosted even further because, Catfish Charlie aside, I looked more like a wrestler than most of the other miscreants on the tour. On top of that, some of the BTWF matches that Wallass and I had in the Westwood Collegiate gym were better executed and more convincing than the ones these guys were having.

Besides the Baron, none of these guys had any kind of unique personalities or interesting gimmicks that would capture the fans' imaginations. I had already begun thinking about the gimmicks that I could use when I started wrestling. My first idea was to be a Christian wrestler named Christian Chris Irvine, who would stand up for what's right and be a role model for all. I would throw Bibles into the crowd on my way to the ring and would wear yellow and black tights just like the biggest Christian metal band Stryper did. Granted it wasn't exactly the Undertaker, but it was a hell of a lot better than Prettyfer.

I also studied the Baron's matches. He was the most popular wrestler on the tour and the only guy that truly understood how to involve the crowd and get them into a match. He couldn't do anything athletic in the ring, but it didn't matter because he was able to manipulate the fans' emotions almost at will. It was the biggest lesson I learned in the Keystone Wrestling Alliance: You have to connect with the audience.

With my apprenticeship complete it was time to learn many more important lessons as a student in the Hart Brothers Pro Wrestling Camp.

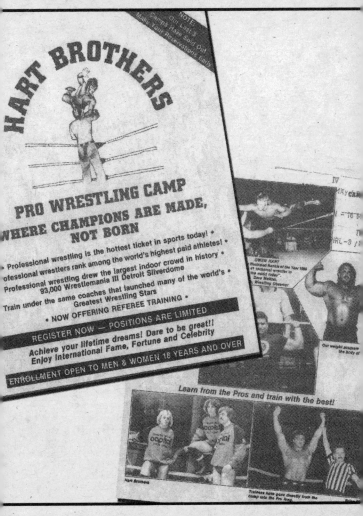

NOTE: Our Last 3 Camps Have Sold Out! Make Your Reservations Early!

HART BROTHERS

PRO WRESTLING CAMP
WHERE CHAMPIONS ARE MADE, NOT BORN

• Professional wrestling is the hottest ticket in sports today! •
• Professional wrestlers rank among the world's highest paid athletes! •
• Professional wrestling drew the largest indoor crowd in history • 93,000 Wrestlemania III Detroit Silverdome •
• Train under the same coaches that launched many of the world's Greatest Wrestling Stars •

• NOW OFFERING REFEREE TRAINING •

REGISTER NOW — POSITIONS ARE LIMITED

Achieve your lifetime dreams! Dare to be great!!
Enjoy international Fame, Fortune and Celebrity

ENROLLMENT OPEN TO MEN & WOMEN 18 YEARS AND OVER

OWEN HART
"Illustrated Rookie of the Year 1988 of technical wrestler in the world today"
Dave Meltzer,
Wrestling Observer

Our weight program the body of

Learn from the Pros and train with the best!

Hart Brothers

Trainers have gone directly from the camp into the Pro Ring.

THE OBVIOUS TRANSITION FROM ARCHERY TO WRESTLING

In January of 1989, six months before I was planning to leave for Calgary, Stampede Wrestling went out of business. It was a huge blow for me and I was terrified that the Hart Brothers Camp was going to close too. My fears were somewhat alleviated when a story appeared announcing that the Canadian National Wrestling Alliance was planning to pick up right where Stampede had left off. I was relieved that there was still going to be a wrestling company in Calgary and that the school was still going to be operating. But the relief was bittersweet because my goal was to be a *Stampede* wrestler, not a CNWA wrestler.

But you can't stop rock 'n' roll and you couldn't stop Christian Chris Irvine either. I steamrolled on and made my arrangements to attend the camp. The price for the eight-week session was a cool 2,000 bucks and I would have to fork out an additional four hundred bucks a month to stay at (according to Ed Langley) "Okotoks' finest hotel," the Willingdon. I planned to cover the costs with a $5,000 bond that my dad had cashed in for me. I made all of my reservations and six days after I graduated with honors from Red River Community College (I'm a freakin' genius), I packed up all my belongings into the trunk of my '76 Volare and left the nest. I was nineteen years old.

After kissing my crying mother goodbye, I pulled out of the driveway fully intending not to come back until I'd made it. As I drove away, I looked in the rearview mirror and waved goodbye to my mom as she began to walk back into the house. I would never see her walk again.

My '76 Volare had a lot of character, which is the automobile equivalent of saying that a girl has a nice personality. The color was a mesh of bottle green and rust red and featured a standard transmission that had been modified so that reverse was where first gear would be, third gear was where reverse would be, etc. Sometimes when I tried to put the car into gear the tranny would jam and I would have to crawl underneath the car to pull the gears back into place. But the Volare was my baby and I'd used the 400 bucks I'd earned as the Keystone Wrestling ring boy to buy the chariot that was going to transport me to the land of the big bucks.

So I popped the new Ratt cassette into the stereo that had only one working channel and began the twelve-hour journey to Cowtown. I drove past Westwood Collegiate on my way out of town and saw the big sign on the front lawn that said HAVE GOOD SUMMER (no joke). I thought to myself, "Someday my name is going to be on that sign." It took fifteen years, but eventually it was.

After almost falling asleep an hour into my drive, I put on some Iron Maiden and began to think about all of the negative feedback I'd received about my decision to follow my dream. One event in particular stuck in my head. When Tony, the minister at my church, announced to the congregation that I was leaving Winnipeg to become a wrestler, there was a ripple of noise in the crowd when they started to laugh. Not all-out belly laughter, but it was enough to really piss me off. Tony didn't make the announcement to make fun of me, he did it because he was proud of me. But to the general public, leaving town to become a pro wrestler was akin to wanting to become a sword swallower or a mime (mimes rule!). I had been dealing with people telling me I was too small to wrestle for years but this was much worse. These people were supposed to be a support group for me and I'll never forget the stabbing embarrassment or the white-hot anger that I felt when I heard their scattered laughter. I vowed to prove them wrong. I never, ever went back to that church again.

I drove all day, stopping eight hours later in Medicine Hat, Alberta, and rented a hotel room for the night—the first of thousands. I checked into the room and ordered a movie from the pay channel called *Great Ballz of Fire*. I didn't realize until it started that it wasn't the Dennis Quaid flick about Jerry Lee Lewis, but actually a porno spoof of it. In retrospect, it was probably the better film.

I found my way to Calgary using a yellow highlighted map that my dad had given me and followed the signs to Okotoks. About forty-five minutes later, I turned off the highway into a storybook Norman Rockwell town of 5,000. I was looking forward to staying in "Okotoks's finest hotel" . . . until I finally saw it. It wasn't a beautiful chalet or a quaint mountain inn, but a run-down, two-story, faded pink dive.

I went inside the bar and checked in with Zig (the oh-so-friendly owner), got my key, and tried to figure out how the hell I was going to lift my trunk up the stairs to the second-floor room. I pulled the trunk out of the . . . um . . . trunk and was dragging it toward the stairs when this guy with a crew cut, skinny legs, and a potbelly walked up to me and said, "Are you here for the Hart Brothers Camp?" Startled that my secret had been exposed, I nodded and asked the guy if he was there for the same reason.

"Yes I am. Let me help you with that trunk."

Like the scene in *Planes, Trains & Automobiles* when Neal Page helps Del Griffith lug his trunk across the field, this guy with stick legs and a spare tire helped me carry my trunk up the steps. It was ironic that the first person I met in Okotoks ended up being one of the best friends I'd ever have in the wrestling business: Lance Storm.

I got all my stuff into the room and noticed that it had no phone, a TV with only three channels, and a bullet hole in the window . . . you know, just the basics. The Willingdon itself was a typical small-town hotel attached to a bar and a smelly old restaurant called the Tray, which I quickly renamed the Ashtray. But Ed Langley wasn't lying, it was the finest hotel in town. It was also the only hotel in town and it was where the class of 1990 was staying. And what a class it was.

On the plus side there was Lance, whose last name at the time was Evers. I have no idea why I thought he had stick legs and a spare tire (maybe it was the muumuu he was wearing), because the guy was muscular and ripped. I had come into camp at a solid 195 pounds (falling forty pounds short of my Steamboat goal) but Lance looked like he had at least ten pounds of muscle on me. I had been worried about being the smallest guy in the camp and my heart sank when I saw how big he was. My heart resurfaced when a short little guy with huge chipmunk cheeks who looked like Andy Kaufman came out of his room and said with a big smile, "I'm Victor DeWilde. I guess we're gonna become famous wrestlers together huh?" I smiled and took stock of this pixie, who looked like he weighed about 160 pounds soaking wet while holding a brick. Victor was a former archery champion who had decided to make the obvious transition from archery to pro wrestling. It only got worse from there as I met Wilf, who had one eye pointing off to the right and one eye pointing off to the left, Dave, a sloppy-looking lumberjack, Edwin Barril, a 400-pound farmer shaped like—what else?—a barrel, and Deb, the only girl in the bunch, who had the IQ of a kumquat and a face to match.

After meeting all of these misfits, I thought to myself, "Thank God Lance is here."

Lance and I were the only ones who even remotely looked like wrestlers. Hell, we were the only ones who looked like we'd ever seen the inside of a gym. Not only was I not the runt of the camp, muscle-wise I was the second biggest one in the group. Judging all these books by their nonathletic covers, Lance and I instantly gravitated toward each other. Later on he told me, "Until you got to the hotel, I was considering just packing up and moving back to Ontario. But when you came in, I was relieved to see that there was at least one other guy who was taking this camp as seriously as I was." I felt the exact same way.

The look of my fellow students wasn't the first indication that the camp wasn't all it was cracked up to be. A few months earlier I had approached Bret Hart at Gold's Gym before a match in Winnipeg and told him I was going to go train in Calgary at his brothers' camp. He replied with great surprise, "I didn't know the camp still existed." I figured that all the Hart brothers talked about everything, so how could Bret not know about the camp?

I decided to do a little name dropping to refresh his memory.

"Oh, well, it starts in a few weeks and I've been talking with Ed Langley about it."

Bret looked at me blankly and said, "I don't know who that is."

Maybe Bret Hart had forgotten who Ed was, but Ed was still the guy who wrote me the letter urging me to run three miles a day, work out in the gym for two and half hours, and eat all the fish, meat, and eggs I could. If that was his personal routine, he must be a badass motherfucker and I was stoked to meet him.

A buzz came over my fellow students when the word spread that Ed had arrived at the hotel. I held my breath, flexed my biceps, and waited for my new mentor to walk in. When a sixty-year-old-looking man wearing his hair parted to the side with thick glasses and a giant beer belly sauntered in, I stared in disbelief at the real Ed. It was like thinking you were having phone sex with Jessica Alba and finding out you've really been beatin' it to Bea Arthur. No wonder Bret had never heard of him—who in the hell was this guy? I found out that when Stampede closed, Keith Hart had bought the rights to the school from his brother Bruce and hired Ed, a former Stampede referee, to run it.

Ed acted like he was the Grand Poobah of pro wrestling and throughout the course of the camp regaled us with stories about his career and his life. Maybe his name should've been Langley Gump, because according to him he'd done it all. He had:

- Wrestled as the masked Dr. X in the WWF . . . which of course couldn't be proven since Dr. X wore a mask.
- Taught ballroom dancing as an Arthur Murray dance instructor.
- Been a Scout leader who'd removed the ruptured appendix of a kid who'd fallen out of a tree while hiking in the desolate Rocky Mountains . . . and then sewed him back together with fishing line.
- Been a pilot who'd landed a plane on a deserted section of highway when the left engine (Ed was very detailed) conked out.
- Been a stock car driver who would crash his car for fifty bucks and would roll it for an additional fifty.
- Been working in a New York meatpacking plant when a slab of meat fell on him leaving him paralyzed. He was despondent and pissed off until he met a surgeon in a bar who operated on him, enabling him to walk again.

- Been a landscaper in Saudi Arabia. (What exactly did he landscape . . . sand?)

Ed would spew out these nuggets at any time with no regard of how ricockulous they sounded or how far from the truth they appeared to be. He was also the only guy I'd ever met above the age of eighteen who lied about his age to be *older*. He claimed he was sixty-two, but one day Lance found his driver's license and found out he was actually only fifty-two.

He lied about his age because when he got in the ring to wrestle, he wanted people to be amazed by the agility and stamina of this sixty-year-old man. He was the first bullshit artist I met in wrestling and he was far from the last. But the problem was, this bullshit artist was now in charge of my career.

I WOULD'VE SIGNED AWAY MY UNIT

After moving from behind the gas station in Okotoks, the camp's new location was inside the Silver Dollar Action Center in Calgary. The name of the place sounded promising, as action and dollars are always good and silver is a fun color. However when we pulled into the parking lot, the place wasn't silver at all. The Silver Dollar Action Center was actually—PINK! What was the deal with all the pink buildings in this area anyway? The Pink Dollar Action Center was a combination bowling alley and bingo hall as well as the new home of the Hart Brothers Pro Wrestling Camp.

Ed had rented a large room in the back of the center and when we walked inside the first thing I noticed was the honest to goodness real wrestling ring set up in the middle. Out of the corner of my eye, I saw Deb (who'd just butchered her hair when she'd attempted to "cut the roots out" of her dyed blond lid) gasp in amazement. It was like seeing the Taj Majal up close . . . an amazing, legendary structure. The room itself was just a big empty space that smelled of stale coffee, like a church gymnasium after a bake sale, with a low roof and a few mats scattered on the floor. There were bathrooms on each side where you could change and that, my friends, was about it. But there was an actual ring and that's all that mattered!

We were absorbing the surroundings when Keith Hart walked through the door. My heart began pounding because this was an actual Hart brother from the actual Hart wrestling dynasty and he was here to teach us how to wrestle! Even though we'd met the year before when I was a mere civilian, since I had officially started my career Keith and I were now on the same level. I wondered if he would remember how impressed he was with my awesome tryout twelve months earlier and invite me out for a beer after class to exchange stories of the road. Or maybe he would take me under his wing and make me into an honorary Hart brother . . .

I was zapped out of dreamland when Keith's first words were, "I'll need to get everybody's money before we go any further."

Then he passed out contracts for us to sign that stated we had to pay 10 percent of all future pro wrestling earnings to Hart Brothers Pro Wtestling. Yeah, it said *Wtestling*. But if we didn't sign them, Keith said we couldn't continue on, so I signed the contract even though it was under duress. There was never another mention of the 10 percent, but it didn't matter anyway because I would've signed away my unit for the chance to wrestle. Quite frankly, some girls I knew might have thought I already had.

I don't remember much of Keith's introductory spiel

because I was so in awe of the whole situation, but it was along the lines of, "There are no guarantees that you're going to make it, but if you work hard and train hard maybe you will," blah, blah, blah, that type of thing. Then he asked us if we had any questions and the Chris tradition of asking stupid questions upon first meeting continued when I blurted out, "How many matches have you had?" Keith got an annoyed look on his face and said he had no idea. How could he not know? And there was no real way to find out. If I wanted to know how many games Wayne Gretzky played in the NHL I could look it up in a record book, but there were no such record books around for wrestling. I decided right then and there that I was going to keep a list of every match I ever had and from my first match on October 2, 1990, against Lance, until my one thousand eight hundred and seventy-seventh match on August 22, 2005, against John Cena, I did.

Then Keith said, "I want everyone to get into the ring and we'll go over a couple things." I couldn't believe Keith's invitation. I'd never been in a wrestling ring as a professional and I wasn't sure I was worthy. I slowly pulled myself onto the ring apron, stepped through the ropes, and stood on the hallowed ground. The ring was solid and sturdy yet it bounced ever so slightly as each one of the students entered. Even though I hadn't had one minute of training, the ring welcomed and embraced me like a new lover. It was where I belonged.

With all of us in the ring, Keith asked a couple of the guys to do a forward roll and showed another how to take a basic back bump to the mat. Then out of nowhere, he grabbed me and said, "Take a back drop, Gear Box." I didn't question him or his lame insult, but I was freakin' out when he backed me to the ropes and pushed me off.

To just throw a novice off the ropes is dangerous; you have to teach one how to do it first. I had zero idea of how to hit the ropes, how to measure the distance of the ring in steps, or how fast to run. If I did, I wouldn't have shelled out two large to come to the Pink Fucking Dollar in the first place! I found out quickly that the twine ropes, which were stretched tight and wrapped in tape, were very unforgiving. If you hit them properly, they sprung you back. If not, you hit them and stopped dead, receiving the equivalent of a baseball bat to the breadbasket and the bruises to match. I also had no idea how to do a proper and safe back bump, which is the most important factor to not getting hurt while wrestling. Learning how to bump is a long process, in which you start by lying on your back and hitting the canvas with your hands hundreds of times in a row. So when Keith threw me off the ropes for a back drop, it was both a dangerous and a bullshit move. I must have pissed him off when I asked him the question that he didn't have the answer to in front of the class. Now he was getting his payback.

After I hit the ropes and felt like I had been kicked in the ribs by Bruce Lee, I ran into Keith, who was bent over ready to launch me up into the air for the back drop. Technically, I was supposed to flip my body in midair and take a back bump on the mat from about six feet off the ground. But when he threw me in the air, I over-rotated and landed on my feet just as Wallass and I had done during countless BTWF matches in the high school gym. I'm proud to say I nailed that bitch with a perfect

10 landing. Carly Patterson couldn't have dismounted that beautifully.

The class was even more amazed than I was with my acrobatic feat and started clapping and cheering. After channeling the abilities of Owen Hart, I figured that my position as the superstar pupil of the class of 1990 had been cemented. I soaked in the adoration of my public, until Keith circled around behind me, wrapped his arm around my neck, and drove his knee into my hamstring, forcing me down to the mat.

He trapped my arms behind my back (in what's known as a grapevine) and applied pressure down on the top of my head and up on the bottom of my chin at the same time. I flashed back to Jesse the Body warning me about the infamous Hart technique of inflicting major amounts of pain and humiliation on the rookies in training.

I kept silent as Keith crushed my jaw together, until it felt like my front teeth were going to snap right in half. He applied so much pressure that I actually felt them bending. I was scared, but I didn't say anything, which I think was my saving grace. I found out later that the classic Hart method was to wait for their victims to scream and then they would administer more torture. A lack of screaming was your ticket out and when I didn't, Keith eventually got bored and released me. I'd like to say that I didn't scream due to my superhuman tolerance for pain, but in reality I didn't scream because I couldn't open my mouth. If I could've, I would've been screaming like a twelve-year-old girl at an Ashlee Simpson gig. (Please don't tell anyone, okay?)

After showing off his dick size by attacking me from behind and beating my ass, Keith collected the rest of the money from everyone and walked out of the building. He never came to the camp again, and Keith's thirty-minute cameo was the only appearance by any of the eight HART BROTHERS for the entire duration of the HART BROTHERS Pro Wrestling Camp.

When the only link to the Hart dynasty left the building, I figured out that the wrestling business wasn't quite what it seemed to be. Fortunately for us, Ed had a training manual that Stu Hart had written in the 1960s, and was following it word for word. Even though Stu wasn't training us himself, in a way he really was. Ed Langley may have been a bullshitter, but he followed Stu's words of training wisdom to a tee and along with an excellent in-ring assistant named Brad Young, Ed was a pretty damn good teacher.

Meanwhile, the Willy wasn't what it was supposed to be either. It was tacky yet unrefined, boasted more ants than a family reunion, and employed a smelly maid who stunk up every room that she cleaned. On the first night of my stay I was sound asleep in my room, when all of a sudden the fire alarm started ringing. I awoke with a start, convinced that I was going to burn to death in Okotoks, the worst-named town ever. I hastily packed up all my stuff (bass guitar and bicycle included) and hauled everything down the stairs in record time. The rest of the Apple Dumpling Gang gathered in the parking lot and waited until Zig wandered outside and said with a smirk, "Don't worry about the fire alarm. It goes off all the time for no reason."

Five nights later it went off again and I figured if the shithole was on fire, I was gonna burn with it. I opened my door in time to see Lumberjack Dave rip the alarm out of the wall. I thought about asking him what would happen if an actual fire started, but I saw the look in his eye and the bullet hole scar on his stomach (matching the one in my window) and decided to catch some sleep instead. After all, I had a big day of getting the shit kicked out of me ahead.

The class trained from 6 to 10 P.M., five days a week for eight weeks. For the first two weeks all we did was stretching (not the Hart kind), running, and calisthenics. We did windsprints and then ran a mile both forward and backward. Ever run a mile backward? Give it a try, junior, it ain't easy. Then we did standing hack squats, starting with twenty-five and increasing every day until we hit 500. Ever done 500 hack squats? I'll personally come to your house, wash your windows, pleasure your dog, and make you a sandwich if you can. Okay, maybe I won't wash your windows.

We'd follow up by doing bridges with only our heads and legs for support, starting with thirty-second increments and increasing them to five minutes. It was brutal and there were countless times I bridged until tears came out of my eyes and my muscles were begging to be released.

We went through a smorgasborg of stretching, including a pleasant exercise where Brad would put his hands on the inner side of one ankle and his feet on the inner side of my other ankle. He would slowly push them apart until my legs were totally straddled out beside me. From behind, Ed would then push my back toward the ground until I kissed the mat. It felt like I was being drawn and quartered and the tears flowed once again.

Every time the stretching mercifully ended I thought, "What does this have to do with wrestling?" The stretches had a lot to do with wrestling because they were designed to test our discipline and tenacity to see if we would be physically and mentally tough enough to make it. It was no surprise that most of my classmates didn't.

After the second day, two of the fourteen students in our class dropped out. As the weeks progressed students continued disappearing like campers in a Jason movie; although being beheaded by a mutant in a goalie mask would've been less painful than the training we were enduring.

Dave the Lumberjack quit after two weeks, proving that even lumberjacks aren't tough enough to be wrestlers. Archers on the other hand apparently were, because as goofy as he was, Victor DeWilde was doing fairly well in camp. Did the rigors of the quill properly prepare him for the rigors of the ring? Only Robin Hood knows for sure.

I wasn't impressed with most of my classmates, but I was starting to respect Wilf. Even though he couldn't see straight, he was working his ass off and never complained once about the shit kicking we were taking. Once when we were practicing sunset flips, he jumped over his opponent and landed straight on his bean, which made a sick, squishy sound when it drove into the mat. Everyone went silent as Wilf stumbled to the change room, complaining of heartburn. He came back a few minutes later and continued doing his drills as if nothing had happened. He was as tough as a three-dollar steak and he was driven by his goal of being a job guy (a guy who always loses) for the WWF. Later on, I heard that he accomplished his dream when he worked a TV taping for the Federation.

I raise my glass to him for that.

CHAPTER 7

ROB BENOIT

The cornerstone to becoming a wrestler is learning how to take bumps, which in laymen's terms is learning how to fall. There were back bumps, side bumps, and front bumps (flopping on your face like Ric Flair). One of the students took a front bump, rolled out of the ring, walked out the door, and was never seen again. We had to take these bumps over and over, dozens of times a night, which led to some very painful mornings. Trying to get out of bed was a science and carefully swinging one leg at a time over the side of the bed just to get out of it made me feel like I was sixty years old instead of nineteen. I invented the fashion trend of stuffing a bag of cotton balls down the back of my shorts to pad and protect my protesting tailbone.

I suffered the common training injury of heeling yourself, which occurred after taking a bump without landing your feet flat on the mat. The heel would hit first, which in turn caused a bolt of pain to shoot up your leg, making it difficult to walk for a few days. But quitting wasn't an option, so I sucked it up like a Third Avenue hooker and continued training the next day.

After a few weeks we finally learned how to properly hit the ropes. The secret was to take four steps in crossing the ring, pivot with your left foot while grabbing the top rope with your right hand, and spring off with your right foot forward. We practiced the timing by hitting the ropes over and over again, until every one of us developed huge bruises and welts from our armpits to our waists. We did forward rolls from one post to another to get the feel of being in the ring. This helped us to develop our timing and to build the basic foundation of how to have a match. But it was amazing how many wrestlers I would meet whose foundations were almost nonexistent.

The Action Center became a refuge for out-of-work wrestlers who thought they were the shit because they'd had a few matches. I wasn't very impressed or excited about most of these guys, because I hadn't heard of them and they were as flabby and out-of-shape as most of the students in my class.

One night a guy showed up in the middle of class who I assumed was the building janitor. He was sporting a sweet mullet, thick Coke-bottle glasses, a porno mustache, and a pretty impressive beer belly. I was mildly surprised when Ed called Lance and me over and said, "This is Bob Puppets. He wrestles and promotes shows and we're gonna be working together."

A promoter? This guy who looked like Mark Borchardt raking leaves at a church picnic was an actual promoter! My mind went haywire thinking of all the places he could potentially book me. I asked him where he promoted his shows and I anxiously awaited his answer of Edmonton or Vancouver or Moscow or . . .

"Innisfail."

Innisfail? Innisfail was a dumpy little farm town two hours outside Calgary. I smelled the beer on his breath as he continued. "I run a lot of shows and I'd like to use you guys." Then he turned his Coke bottles toward me and said, "You look like Chris Benoit. I want to book you as his brother, Rob Benoit."

How exciting was it that a promoter from the bustling metropolis of Innisfail was taking an interest in me? I

August 1990. Giving Lance a gorilla press in class, while Deb looks on and thinks about kumquats.

liked the idea that I reminded him of Chris Benoit because I was a fan of Chris's work in Stampede. So if I
could parlay a passing facial resemblance to him into a
steady gig, I was prepared to milk Rob Benoit for all it
was worth.

The cavalcade of locals continued as other wrestlers
who worked for Puppets showed up. There was Lee
Barachie (say it fast), who worked a gay pianist gimmick
and certainly had the body for it. There was a guy named
Bret Como, who I'd seen wrestling for the WFWA in
Winnipeg. I figured that anyone who wrestled on TV was
a rich superstar, so I instantly respected him. But the one
thing I noticed about all of them from Puppets to Como
to Brad Young was how small they were. It was inspiring to see that many of these working wrestlers were my
size. All of the self-doubt I'd amassed over the years from
people telling me I was too small to be a wrestler was
being erased.

Despite getting tips from the pros, the guy I learned
the most from was Lance. He was a tremendous athlete
and as much of a wrestling fan as I was, and we pushed
each other to the limit on a daily basis. He was also my
personality polar opposite, as I was loud and friendly,
while he was stoic and slightly stand-offish. But we got
along well because we knew that almost everyone else in
the camp sucked and we only had each other to work and
grow with. To this day we both admit if one of us wasn't
in the camp, the other one wouldn't have made it.

Ed knew that we were his star students and began treat-
ing us as such. He showed up at the hotel to talk wrestling,
took us to dinner to tell us about the upcoming shows in the
area, and began letting us train in the ring by ourselves on

our off-days. That's when we really started making giant strides as workers because we could polish our skills at a faster pace without the other students slowing us down.

I held an advantage over everyone at the start because I already knew how to do body slams and suplexes from my years of doing them in the BTWF. But Lance was a quick study and surpassed me quickly. While everybody else was still learning how to give simple arm drags, Lance and I were giving each other intricate moves like head scissors and Frankensteiners.

Lance wasn't only pushing me physically, but mentally as well. He was such a great athlete and it pissed me off when he outperformed me. If he could stand in the ring and jump straight up to the top rope, that meant I had to do it too. I was furious at myself when I tried and failed miserably. He could do a picture-perfect leg drop after the first day of camp and I still can't do one to this day. Every time I tried, Lance would give me this smug little grin that made me want to knock his fucking block off. There was no doubt in anyone's mind who the best student in the camp was and it drove me nuts.

About a month into the camp my dad came to visit. He understood what it was like to leave everything behind to follow your dream because he had done the same thing at nineteen to play pro hockey. No matter how much flak I received for wanting to wrestle, I always knew that my dad stood behind me 100 percent. I don't know what he thought when Ed and Brad stretched the shit out of my groin and hamstrings until I screamed, but he respected my decision all the same.

After observing the session he said, "You sure are lucky that Lance is here." He thought that we were the best two in the class by far, but then again he also loved Vic when he showed up wearing a stethoscope and a smock in his new gimmick of Dr. Love.

I guess there's no accounting for taste in my family.

When we started working short matches with the other students, Lance and I shamelessly showed off. Lance decided that he would be an evil Russian (I guess he was looking to exploit the Cold War of 1990) and wore a black singlet with CCCP written on the straps. I sported a pair of gray gym shorts as we ran through our roster of Moves for the Advanced Student stolen from Shawn Michaels and Owen Hart. Meanwhile the rest of the guys still couldn't take a hip toss.

Ed worked a lot of matches with us too, and if you've ever heard the theory that some people are better teachers than performers, well, that was Ed. He would get in the ring as the Goto Hills Savage, dressed in a costume that included furry checkerboard boots and a matching furry vest that looked like they were made out of toilet seat covers. Whenever he did a move he would yell, "Hyaa!" Once when he hip-tossed Dr. Love, he said "Hyaa!" and his false teeth flew out. Nuff said.

Hyaa!

When we weren't in class, Lance and I spent a lot of time watching videos in his room at the Willy since he'd brought a VCR and his extensive wrestling tape collection with him from Ontario. He was a big NWA fan and I really wasn't, but I soon became quite familiar with the work of Ric Flair, Sting, and Lex Luger. Right away I noticed the major difference between the two companies. The NWA favored wrestling while the WWF favored showmanship. That's also a good analogy of Lance and my respective career paths.

As the camp neared completion, Ed and Brad gave a speech to the remaining survivors similar to the one Catfish Charlie gave me. They'd waited until they'd weeded out the pretenders to fill in the remaining blanks of how wrestling worked. I learned a new rule when Brad explained that in the ring it was up to the more experienced worker to control the flow of the match and to decide what was or wasn't done. Some of the depleted Apple Dumpling Gang reacted to the speech with the same denial that I did when I learned that wrestling wasn't a real contest.

After the speech, Lance and I worked each other to a ten-minute Broadway (draw) and I overheard Deb say with a confused look on her face, "I thought Lance could beat Chris, he's so much better." Even after eight weeks of training she still had the IQ of a kumquat. But kumquat or not, her statement hurt my feelings and increased my jealousy of Lance.

Our graduation from the Hart Camp was nothing special. Those of us left at the end graduated with no ceremony, no diploma, no square hat; just a half-assed congratulations and a guarantee of nothing. While I was proud of myself for making it through the camp, I now had to contend with the more difficult task of finding a job.

CHAPTER 8

IRON WILL

I was feeling uneasy about my future and my only plan was to stay in Calgary to try and get work. Thankfully, Ed erased some of the uncertainty when he allowed Lance, Victor, and me to continue training at the Action Center free of charge.

I was thrilled to have a place to continue training, but that didn't solve my more pressing problem of running out of cash. Luckily, I had some extended family that lived in Okotoks who knew a lady named Bev Palko and her husband, Jerry. She and her family lived outside town and were looking for someone to paint the fence in their backyard. It didn't sound like the most exciting of jobs but I was thankful for the chance to make some money and I accepted the offer.

The next day I drove outside Okotoks until I saw a distant farmhouse surrounded by what seemed to be a five-mile long fence. Not only was this the Palko house, but the Palko FENCE as well. Instead of painting a little old lady's picket fence, I was going to have to whitewash the Great Wall of Alberta.

Bev met me at the door and she was one of the friendliest people I'd ever met. She was in her mid-forties with salt-and-pepper hair and an infectious laugh and I liked her right from the start. She took me out to a garage filled with gallons of whitewash and paint rollers and told me to get cracking.

After I loaded the trunk of the Volare it took me five minutes to drive across the field as my car bumped and lurched like a cheap drunk over the groundhog holes and rocks. Cows were grazing on haystacks while horses neighed in disgust and Lil Chris realized he wasn't in Winnipeg anymore.

I reached the end of the field, popped in the new Anthrax cassette and began to paint . . . and paint . . . and paint. Four hours later I was totally exhausted, with only seven feet of painted fence to show for my efforts. I'd just finished two months of the most intense physical training I'd ever experienced and now I was reduced to this?

But there were benefits to painting the Palkos' fence. Considering that I'd eaten most of my meals that summer at the Petro-Can (paying for them with my dad's gas card), when Mrs. Palko yelled down the field that she'd made lunch, my stomach jumped for joy. The spread was basic but it was one of the best meals of my life. A thick ham sandwich served on homemade bread; fresh out-of-the-oven chocolate chip cookies, and an ice cold glass of milk. It was so heavenly it may as well have been made in the Vatican; or at least it seemed that way after eight weeks of burritos and Twinkies.

The Palkos had two sons: Brad, another friendly Palko

who I met at lunch, and Tyler, who ended up becoming like a brother to me. You wouldn't have guessed it the first time we met though. No one had told him that I was going to be painting the fence, so he was quite surprised when a strange longhair in a bottle green jalopy pulled up at his isolated farmhouse and began rummaging through the garage. I was loading up my trunk on the second day when he came outside and eyed me up.

"You must be Tyler," I said. Then we both stood there staring at each other. After an eternity, he said "Yup" and went inside to ask his dad who in the hell I was.

The Palkos had taken in foster kids for years and when they heard my story and figured out that I was dying to get out of the Willy, they offered me their spare room. They suggested I could stay there in exchange for painting the fence, so I moved in with the intention of staying four months and ended up staying four years. They became my second family and were a blessing because no matter how uncertain my wrestling career was, I always knew I had a stable home to go back to. As broke as I was, rent was never a problem either because I only had to pay a scant $10 a day and pitch in with the chores. Since we were on a farm, those chores included chasing escaped cows off the highway, shooting invading gophers in the field, baling hay into the barn and stuffing chickens into coops to ship to the Colonel. But it was a small price to pay, as their love and kindness helped me to become as successful as I did and for that I'm eternally grateful.

Unfortunately, not everything in my life was going as well as my housing situation. In a botched attempt to make myself look like one of the Nelson twins (whether it was Gunnar or Matthew I'm not sure), I bought a box of cheap dye and ended up with a head of fried canary yellow hair. Then I hit a deer and totaled my precious Volare. But the worst was yet to come.

A friend named Shane Lanoway had moved with his family to Calgary the same time I did. I had spent the night at his house and was mowing their lawn as a thank-you for letting me stay, when Shane's mom came out and told me that my dad was on the phone. I felt my stomach step into a pothole because my dad had no clue where I was. Something very bad had to have happened for him to do the necessary detective work to find me.

I answered the phone and was chilled by the severity of my dad's voice when he said, "You have to come home right now. Your mom has been in an accident." My heart raced and I asked him if she was dead. "No, but you have to come home right now. She's in the hospital. She's in intensive care and she may not make it through the night."

My dad picked me up at the Winnipeg airport and told me what had happened. A few months after my parents had split up three years earlier, my mom had started seeing her new boyfriend. Being a rebellious teenager, I was very cold toward them and whenever they came over to our house to swim or hang out, I split. I still hadn't gotten over the splintering of my own family and wasn't interested in trying to adopt a new one.

I was pissed when they first started dating and after countless fights between my mom and me, she finally said, "I'm not expecting you to accept this right away but I have to go on with my life. I want to be happy and you should want that for me too."

I drove her to her boyfriend Danny's house every Friday and then got her car and our house to myself for the whole weekend. Not a bad consolation prize for a teenager living in a broken home I guess.

My mom was in the ICU because the night before she and Danny had gotten into an argument on the front lawn of our house. During the fight, my mom charged at him and was accidentally back-dropped onto her head when she landed. She instantly became a quadriplegic. She told Danny that she couldn't move, but he didn't realize what had happened and he picked her up, put her on her bed and left the house. *Hours* later when he realized how serious the situation was, he finally called the ambulance.

The last time I had seen my mom, she was walking up the driveway after seeing me off to the Hart camp on a sunny day in late June and all I could smell was the sweet scent of summer flowers. The next time I saw my mom, she was in an intensive care unit two weeks after I'd graduated from the Hart camp on a gloomy day in mid-September and all I could smell was the sickening scent of hospital disinfectant. Since then, whenever I smell that distinct hospital odor I get transported back in time to that exact moment.

When I walked into the room I didn't recognize the frightened person with the swollen face lying there and I thought I was in the wrong room. Then I realized that the face belonged to my mother. She gave me a faint pencil line of a smile and I completely fell apart. All of the hard work that I'd done, my dream of making it into the WWF instantly evaporated when I saw her in that bed. My number one priority was now my mother and I didn't give a damn about anything else. I sincerely hope that none of you sharing this with me right now will ever experience the feeling of seeing one of your dearest loved ones lying motionless in a hospital bed, with a medical halo screwed into their head so tight that you can see the drops of plasma (not blood) creeping down their waxen forehead. I rubbed my hand along her cheek since it was one of the only places that she still had feeling and she looked up at me with another wan smile. But it didn't mask the sheer terror in her eyes.

I left the room after a few minutes, in order to compose myself and to decide how I was going to murder Danny. I wanted to kill him *and* his kids. I'm not exaggerating. A policeman waiting for me in the hallway saw death in my eyes and as I walked by, he stopped me. He was a big man with a thick mustache and I sensed that he wasn't one to mess with. I also sensed that he wanted to help me.

He very deliberately said to me, "I'm sorry about your mother, but if you touch this guy, you're going to jail. If you do what you're thinking about doing, it's going to be the end of three lives: his, yours, and your mom's."

I didn't quite register what he was saying. He was talking like there was a choice. But there was no choice. I had to end him.

"The law will—"

I stopped him and said, "Fuck the law. I'm going to kill him."

What he said next probably saved Danny's life . . . and mine as well.

"If you do, you'll go to jail and then your life will be over. Do you want to go to jail at nineteen? Think about it, it's not worth it. Your life would be over before it even started and that would make your mom's life even harder and unhappier than it is right now."

In the back of my head a little worm of rational thought began to crawl through my brain. What the cop said made sense. As much as I wanted to call some of my Hell's Angel friends and organize a little party, I started comprehending that it wouldn't change a thing. My mom would still be severely injured and my life would end up in shambles. How could I help her if I had to spend the rest of my life in prison? I knew that wasn't what God wanted out of my life either.

Over the next few days the reality of the situation hit me. I was scared that she was going to die but I began to think how hard her life would be if she didn't. I held on to the hope that she would start to move her arms, her legs, a finger, anything. Every night when I went to sleep I prayed that something would improve and every morning when I woke up nothing had.

But every day when I went to see her, she was incredibly strong and never once broke down in front of me. Her attitude began to rub off on me, and I stopped breaking down in front of her. This was the situation; it wasn't going to change and it was time to deal with it. I'd been having a pity party of my own, but that ended pretty quickly when I saw how mentally tough my mom was being.

I was a mental mess though. I'd just gotten confirmation that my first match had been booked in Alberta a few weeks later, yet there was no way I was going to leave my mom.

I had already begun to make plans to move back to Winnipeg. But when she gained enough strength to have a conversation with me, one of the first things she said was, "I don't want you to change anything. I want you to continue doing what you're doing. You have a dream and you're so close to making it happen. I'm not your responsibility."

When I protested, she said, "You've worked too hard and I'm not going to spoil this for you. I'm proud of you and I want you to do this and be the best that you can be!"

As broken-down as her body was, her mental drive and iron will were stronger than ever. If she'd asked me, I would've moved home in a second, but that wasn't the way she wanted it.

Even though my dad was a hard-nosed NHL tough guy, I think I got most of my mental toughness from my mom. She lived as a quadriplegic for fifteen years and during that time she went through enough trials and tribulations for fifteen people, yet she never gave up or stopped fighting. When she gave me her blessing to continue on with wrestling, there was no way on God's green earth I was going to let her down. Her iron will became my iron will and failure was no longer an option.

I had to make it big for her.

CHAPTER

THE PIED PIPER
OF PONOKA

When I got back to Calgary, I knew it was where I was supposed to be. When I'd seen all of my old friends back in the Peg, I realized how much I'd grown and changed as a person. Now that I had something to believe in, there was no turning back.

October 2, 1990 (just over a month before my twentieth birthday), was the day of my first match, and it was rapidly approaching. Lance, Victor, and I had been booked to make our professional wrestling debut with the Canadian Wrestling Connection, which was owned and promoted by none other than the CWC champ himself, Bob "The Judge" Puppets.

Puppets was notorious for being a terrible promoter. He never advertised his shows, and most of them bombed like a Ben Affleck/Jennifer Lopez movie. He once promoted a show at a college in Rimby, Alberta, on the same night as the homecoming free beer bash. Final total: Free

Beer Bash—1000 tickets sold, Puppets Show—seven tickets sold. I guess those seven people were on the wagon . . . or nerds.

But Puppets's promoting track record meant nothing to us because we had a match to prepare for and names to decide on. Since Dr. Love had already solved his name problem, only Lance and I were still struggling.

We all agreed that Puppets's Rob Benoit idea was lame and I decided that Christian Chris Irvine wasn't flashy enough, so I was leaning toward my new choice of JACK ACTION. Jack Action was perfect and I had already worked out the most important part of any name: how to sign my autograph. Paul Stanley from Kiss signed his name with a star at the end of his Y and I ripped him off by signing a star at the end of my N. Hey, it was better than the X that I signed for the Ranger fans who wanted my autograph just for being Ted Irvine's son when I was four years old!

Lance, however, didn't think that Jack Action was the moneymaking merchandising machine that I did and he told me so.

"I saw you autographing your notebook as Jack Action and you can't call yourself that. It's a terrible name. It sucks." Always the diplomat, that Lance.

I denied old Jack quicker than Peter denied Jesus and said, "I know Jack Action is stupid. I was just messing around." Even though I thought the name was amazing, Lance's typical bluntness had killed the Action Man forever.

Then I experimented with different variations of the last name Skywalker. I thought Shawn Skywalker would be cool but I didn't want my name to be too much like

Shawn Michaels. I had already stolen his look, his costume, and his canary yellow hair, so taking his name too would've been a bit much. I tried to think of other decent S names to match Skywalker. Shane Skywalker? Seamus Skywalker? Shakira Skywalker? Nothing fit.

Then I remembered a name that I'd flirted with when I was trying to go the Christian route . . . Jericho. There was a lame comic book character named Jericho and a great record by the German metal band Helloween named *The Walls of Jericho* and I thought it sounded cool. I felt I might have something with Chris Jericho.

I was nervous about my choice because choosing a name is like choosing the side of the bed in a relationship—once you pick one, you're stuck for life. And the situation got more stressful when it came time to pronounce my new moniker to Lance, the great communicator.

So I took a deep breath and announced that my name was going to be Chris Jericho. Surprisingly, Ed and Lance smiled and said it had a nice ring to it. I was proud of my marketing genius and decided to give myself a hero cookie. Lance proclaimed that he would now be known as Lance T. Storm. Ed pointed out that the T. was his idea and stood for THUNDER . . . as if it could've stood for anything else. From the look on Ed's face you would've thought he'd just discovered the cure for fucking cancer, but whatever.

However, Ed also had a name idea for me. He was going to call me Cowboy Chris Jericho from Casper, Wyoming. I kept a poker face as my throat swelled like an erection. I didn't like country music, I didn't like cowboys, and I sure as hell didn't like Casper, Wyoming! (Now that I've been there, I'd like to say that Casper is a nice town filled with nice people.)

"You're going to be Cowboy Chris Jericho. You'll come to the ring with chaps and a cowboy hat." What, no lasso?

I'd gone from Vince Neil to the Village People in the space of two minutes.

I was irate when I spoke to Bret Como, who I'd met at the Hart camp, and told him Ed's idea. But he'd been around a bit and gave me some advice. "Just don't do it," he said.

Just don't do it . . . words of wisdom! I didn't realize that I had a choice.

So I told Ed, "I just don't feel comfortable with it. It's not me and I don't want to do it." His reaction proved that Ed really hadn't been around the wrestling business much. If I was in charge with fifteen years experience under my belt and some punk kid with ZERO matches under his belt said no to one of my suggestions, I would've fired him on the spot. Or I would've turned him into the most ridiculous cowboy of all time; I'm talking *Dumb and Dumber* cowboy hat, assless chaps, the works. Instead, Ed respected my wishes.

Sort of.

Ed and Puppets had decided that for our first match Lance and I would work against each other and Victor wouldn't wrestle, but would serve as Lee Barachie's manager. Vic wanted to save the moneymaking Dr. Love gimmick for his wrestling debut and was stumped in trying to think of a manager's name. I saw his driver's license and noticed that his full given name was Victor Benson Cyril DeWilde. Just like Rick Fliehr and Rick Roode, Vic had been born with the ultimate wrestling name. So he got himself a suit and a neck brace (which he wore for no apparent reason) and became Lee Barachie's stuck-up, snotty manager Benson Cyril.

Now that we had solved the name problem, the next order of business was to get actual wrestling boots, as simple tennis shoes wouldn't suffice any longer. I was looking forward to getting a pair of the shiny, patent leather beauties that all of my favorites wore. Instead Ed took us to a cobbler friend who made us boots out of a flimsy soft leather that flipped and flopped all over the place. I had to put rolled-up magazines inside just to keep them standing straight up. I'd also made the controversial decision to order black boots instead of white, as my idea was to have a yellow and black costume like Stryper, who were famous for their yellow and black threads.

"You can't have black boots," Ed said, horrified. "You're going to be a good guy, a babyface. If you walk to the ring wearing black boots, everyone is going to think you're a bad guy and boo you." It was an old-time tradition that babyfaces wore white, but white didn't fit my gimmick, man! Once again, I held my ground and told Ed that I was going with the black boots. I hadn't even had my first match, but I was already a pain in the ass for my boss. This was a trend that would continue for most of my career.

After a short debate Ed eventually gave in again. "Okay, wear black boots, but don't blame me if people think you're a big heel." I thought if I did my job and played my cards right, the people would cheer for me if I had frozen turkeys on my feet. I was right.

Even though my costume was designed, I was having

a problem finding someone who could actually make it for me. Then Vic told me that he'd met a wrestler named Lenny St. Clair whose mom made wrestling tights. They had started hanging out together when Lenny was working the night shift at the Petro Can. I had seen Lenny St. Clair wrestling on TV, so I was confused as to why he worked at a gas station. He was a television wrestler, so didn't that mean he was too rich and successful for a menial job? The realities of the wrestling biz continued to seep in.

Lenny's mom was very good at her job and he had the rep around Calgary for having great wrestling outfits. While most of the local guys wore the same style of tights with lightning bolts on the legs and stars on the ass, Lenny sported a plethora (great word) of different-colored, intricately designed costumes with matching ring jackets. So I bought a yard of yellow and black spandex and his mom made me a pair of black and yellow tights with black and yellow frills and wristbands to match. Voilà—Colorful Chris Jericho was ready for business.

Our first match was in the town of Ponoka, Alberta, which was famous for its mental institution. The irony that I started my wrestling career only miles away from an insane asylum has not been lost, believe me.

My stomach was a butterfly cage and my heart a floating bobber in my chest as we pulled up to the Moose Hall (which to me might as well have been Madison Square Garden), the venue where Jeric-History would be made. I walked through the banquet hall, past the ring, and up a flight of stairs into the dressing room. I read through the program, which to my chagrin still had me listed as Cowboy Chris Jericho from Casper, Wyoming. I guess being a cowboy in name only was much better than actually having to wear a bandolier and a Stetson.

I suited up in my spandex armor, laced up my EVIL black boots, and taped up my wrists just because everyone else was doing it. Ed had decided that Lance and I would do a ten-minute Broadway, and we'd been working on the match for weeks. Even though I had a good idea of what we were going to do, I started feeling nauseous and nervous as I heard the crowd filing into the hall.

The first match on the show was Como versus Brad Young. They worked together often and had a really good match.

After they were finished, the moment of truth arrived. I said a quick prayer as the strains of Poison's "Unskinny Bop" played through the muffled banquet hall speakers. I took a final deep breath and walked out of the dressing room into the arena/room.

Thousands . . . hundreds . . . dozens of indifferent faces looked up the staircase at the canary-haired, bumblebee-looking wannabe with the maniacal black boots. There were around 100 fans in the place, which was a huge crowd for a Puppets show and for a teenager having his first match. Lance was already in the ring wearing a pink (there's that color again) singlet, and Ed was our referee. The bell rung, we locked up, and suddenly Chris Irvine was possessed by CHRIS JERICHO.

The nervousness was gone, replaced with the confidence to entertain and succeed. I began wrestling the match just as I had been taught for the last three months. Lance and I worked solidly and believably, incorporating unique moves that no one else on the card was doing.

After going through our routine for about five minutes, I noticed that there was actually a crowd watching us!

I had just dropped a knee on Lance's arm when a kid in the crowd said, "Do it again!"

Surprised that someone was paying attention, I searched the crowd for my biggest fan. When I saw a kid smiling at me, I looked at him and said, "All right bud, this one's for you!" and dropped another knee. Someone else yelled for me to do it again so I did. My shameless pandering started paying off as the fans clapped and cheered me on. I responded by clapping my hands in time, which the crowd copied in unison. I'd become the Pied Piper of Ponoka and the crowd ate up my every move.

The match ended after ten minutes and the crowd voiced their disapproval when it was announced as a draw. We shook hands and I walked out of the ring, high fiving all the kids and feeling like the King of the World. Lance was waiting for me in the dressing room and we exchanged hugs and babbled excitedly about our success, until we noticed the other guys staring at us. We'd been taught that one of the unwritten rules of wrestling was never to brag or argue about a match in public. So we went into the bathroom and Lance said excitedly, "You were like Hulk Hogan out there, man!" In retrospect, there were probably like ten people cheering, but it didn't matter. The important thing was that our first match had gone off without a hitch and turned out pretty good. Lance still claims that it was the best match on the show.

Later on that night we also worked in a battle royal, which Lance won. It kind of bothered me that he got to win, but I took solace in the fact that I was the new Hulk Hogan, not him.

After the show, Puppets gave me a white envelope with JERICO written on it. The fact that he'd left out the H in my name was forgiven when I opened the envelope and pulled out a ten and a twenty. Thirty bucks! I used to make forty bucks a week for eight hours' work at the deli and here I'd made almost the same for ten minutes' work. I couldn't believe how much money I'd just made for something that I loved to do.

I was an official working wrestler and it felt amazing.

CHAPTER 10

HOW TO DRINK LIKE A WRESTLER

My next match at the Moose Hall about a month later wasn't quite as amazing. I was in a tag team match and was booked to suffer my first defeat. Nobody likes to lose when they first start out and I was no exception, but if I was told to lose to a turtle I would've done it. Instead I was involved in one of the dumbest finishes of all time. Both my partner and the referee went down and I was attacked by my two opponents, their manager, Benson Cyril, and their bodyguard, Big Titan. But the mighty Chris Jericho could not be beaten by four men, so they pulled out a bottle of ETHER. The idea was they would pour some on a cloth, hold it over my mouth, and pin me when I passed out. The kicker was they filled the bottle with rubbing alcohol. I was huffing and puffing after a brutally bad match, when Titan held the cloth soaked in rubbing alcohol over my face. I could see the little birdies circling around my head as my brain melted. They used the alcohol, they explained, so if the people in the front row smelled it, they would know it was real. Weren't they supposed to be using ether? Does rubbing alcohol even smell like ether? I'm confused . . .

Meanwhile, later in the show Lance beat Bob Puppets to become the CWC champion in his first month of wrestling. Life just isn't fair sometimes.

Our next match was the following week in a Quonset (look it up) in Strathmore, Alberta, another small town near Calgary. The promoter was a young guy named Fred Jung and he had booked Lance and me as a team named Sudden Impact. Fred's show was a little more organized and show business gimmicky than Bob's was, featuring guys with names like Luscious Bubbles, Earthquake Muldoon, and the Black Mamba. Also booked on the show in his debut was Dr. Love! Vic wore a pair of spandex tights with the sides of the legs cut out and replaced with mesh, which accentuated his chicken legs and made him look absolutely flabulous. He faced the Kaos Kid, Fred Jung, and I'll give you two guesses who was booked to win.

Sudden Impact's first match as a team was also our first abortion. In wrestling vernacular the term abortion means a shit match and, believe me, this match was a double helping of steaming shit.

First, the tape deck played my Poison tape backward and we had to walk to the ring to a loopy, psychedelic mishmash of spaceship noises. Then our opponents Steve Gillespie and the Goto Hills Savage himself, Ed Langley, led us through the most nonsensical match of my career, consisting of them beating us up and then beating us up some more. Oh yeah, I forgot to mention that they beat us up. Finally Ed told me to do a big comeback and just as I got started, he nailed me right in the plums. In camp we were taught that if you got hit with a nut shot you were done, so I played dead while he kept trying to stand me up. Then he said, "Get up! That wasn't a nut shot . . . it was an inner thigh shot!"

A nut shot in wrestling IS an inner thigh shot. How was I supposed to tell the difference? Not to mention, how was a shot to the inside of my leg supposed to hurt me? How was I supposed to react? "Oww help me, my inner thigh is broke . . . "

The night of comedy didn't end there. Lance, Victor, and I had volunteered to drive the ring back to Calgary and on our way we blew out a tire and got lost, which turned the ninety-minute journey into an eight-hour marathon. In the course of one week I had experienced the yin and the yang of the wrestling business.

Fred Jung was maybe twenty-two years old and looked like the love child of Jay Mohr and Sandy Duncan. He badly wanted to be a famous promoter and had two of the key skills required to succeed as one. He was a smooth talker and a convincing liar.

But Fred did have legitimate connections with a Japanese company named Frontier Martial Arts Wrestling. FMW was a new company that focused on the table-breaking, barbed-wire-using bloody style that would become known as Garbage Wrestling. Fred used his connection as blackmail by telling all of the local wrestlers that if you wanted to work in Japan, you weren't allowed to work for anyone but him. That was all fine and dandy except for the fact that Fred didn't run any shows. But getting the chance to wrestle in Japan was a big deal due to the prestige and respect shown toward the sport in the

country. All the guys in Calgary wanted to go because
the crowds were bigger, the style was more technical, and
the money was better. Making it in Japan also wasn't as
contingent on size as it was in North America and smaller
guys that could really wrestle had a better chance of becoming huge stars, like I'd heard Eddy Guerrero and
Chris Benoit had done.

When Fred booked Big Titan in Japan his credibility
went through the roof. But he was still hard to trust. He
ran a crappy little wrestling show on Calgary cable access
that he refused to let Sudden Impact wrestle on, because
he claimed that Vince McMahon watched the tapes every
week and would steal us away. In reality, he just didn't want
us to outshine the rest of his rotten roster.

The bullshit continued flowing like wine when
he showed us a signed contract for Big Titan that he'd

November 1991. LTS, Lenny St. Clair, Fred Jung, Big Titan, and me. We're all
thinking how full of shit Fred is, but he's our only link to wrestling in Japan, so
we make happy faces. The Era of Nelson Hair is in full swing.

received from Ted Turner's WCW. The contract was a typewritten piece of paper with a photocopied WCW logo on top, which he had obviously cut out of a magazine. It looked so bush-league but I kept my mouth shut and nodded approvingly because Titan had gone to Japan and I hadn't. After six more months of putting up with Fred's bullshit, I eventually got my chance. But I got tired of waiting for my turn and kept hustling for work in the meantime.

Lance was the first wrestling friend I met, but Bret Como was the first wrestling friend I met that I had a lot in common with. Bret had a laid-back attitude, long hair, and appreciation for heavy metal and we got along well and hung out frequently. Through him, I met Mike Lozanski, who I'd seen wrestling on TV in Winnipeg. Like the Puppetses and the Langleys, Mike was quite a talker but unlike them he was also a doer. To me he might as well have been Marco Polo, as he'd traveled to New Zealand, California, Mexico, and the Maritimes. With his friendly personality and award-winning smile, he'd made a lot of connections and it was through those contacts that I got booked for my first match outside Alberta.

When Mike told me that he could get me on a show in British Columbia, I asked him if he could get Lance booked too. Despite the rivalry between us, he was my partner and I didn't want to leave him out. But Mike laughed and said, "You're not going to be a tag team forever. You have to take the bookings when you can and there's only one slot open on this show. Do you want it or not?"

I felt bad telling Lance but to my surprise he had no problem with it. He understood that you couldn't be picky about bookings and gave me his blessing. So with an extra

100 bucks in my pocket that Jerry Palko insisted on giving me because I was broke, I packed my bag and left on my first wrestling road trip.

Como, Mike, and I began driving the fourteen hours to Vancouver. When I was a kid and we traveled long distances during family vacations, we'd stop for the night at eight and get a hotel room. Much to my chagrin, a wrestling road trip didn't work that way. We left at 8 P.M. and drove all through the night, stopping at dawn when we arrived. I hated traveling at night because I couldn't sleep sitting in the car. Now I can sleep underneath the hood but back then I needed my wittle beddie-weddie.

We drove through the mountains on winding roads with 300-foot drops on either side, watched diligently for deer, and arrived in the early morning. We stayed at the house of a seasoned vet named Tim Flowers, and over the next few days he taught me some very important lessons about the wrestling biz. More specifically, he taught me how to drink like a wrestler. He took us to a bar and bought rounds of drinks for everybody. When it came time for the second round, I still hadn't finished my first one and that didn't fly very well. In his world, you finished your drink as soon as you got it in preparation for the next one. It was also very important to have a drink in your hands at all times even if you weren't drinking it, because if you did nobody bothered you. If you didn't, you became a target.

I learned to keep my thumb on the top of the beer bottle at all times, because there were always guys around who thought it was funny to spike your drink with Halcion pills. After you fell asleep from them, you would be the recipient of a free eyebrow shaving and bonus Lloyd

Christmas haircut. But I was a fast learner and I'm proud to say that after fifteen years of wrestling, I still have the same eyebrows I had when I was soiling my diapers.

Wrestling is a hierarchy and the guys on top dictate what to do to the guys on the bottom. There is no specific rulebook issued to rookies explaining wrestling etiquette, but you'd better figure out the rules quickly and pick them up fast or you'll be weeded out. Rule number one is you have to drink with the boys. If you didn't feel like drinking, you poured some water into a beer bottle and carried it around as if you were. As long as you were smart about it, nobody noticed or cared.

The match itself was in Agassiz, British Columbia, where the movie *First Blood* was filmed and "Sasquatch Crossing" signs were posted on the road. The promoter asked my opponent and me to do a ten-minute Broadway but my opponent was greener than I was and asked, "What do you mean, you want us to act it out?" The promoter sent the guy packing and I worked with Como instead for a cool twenty bucks.

Even though I was rolling in the dough from wrestling, I decided to supplement my income by becoming a stand-up comedian. I went to an open mike night at Yuk-Yuk's comedy club and did a set based on what the golden topping on movie popcorn REALLY was. It turned out I was the only one in the club who thought that comparing golden topping with golden showers was hilarious.

After accepting that the world wasn't ready for my comedic genius, I got a job working at a new family fitness center in Okotoks. I had been training in the Palkos' barn like Stallone in *Rocky IV*, so the arrival of the new gym not only brought in extra cash but allowed me to again build muscle with weights, not haystacks.

The gym was also the perfect place to meet girls. It became the hot place for all the high school kids to hang out and the fact I was the muscular wrestler working the front desk made me the Fonz. Girls like the Fonz. After not meeting anyone all summer, I now had teenage girls flirting and hanging all over me. Being nineteen years old with a badass car (or just a bad one), I had become the proverbial magnet of the chicks. If you've ever seen the *Three's Company* episode where Jack has three different dates at the same restaurant and has to run himself ragged so that none of them finds out about the other ones, you'll get an idea of what I had to deal with. There was a certain hot tub room that was a favorite rendezvous spot of mine, and let me take this opportunity to say, Thank goodness for chlorine.

The girls may have dug me, but the local Popo did not. One John Cleese–looking, Inspector Clouseau–sounding cop in particular named Dan Powers was always looking for ways to mess with me. He pulled me over for going the speed limit ("It's so suspicious") and watched me buy lunch at the Petro Canada just to make sure "I wasn't stealing anything."

One evening, a few older ladies that I didn't recognize came into the gym. I chatted for a few minutes with each of them and then they left. The next day, Powers called me at the Palkos' and told me to come down to the station immediately. When I arrived, Cleese Clouseau proceeded to tell me that there'd been a rash of obscene phone calls in town and guess who he was accusing? He'd told the victims that I was the guilty party and sent them to the gym to speak with me to clarify it. The power of suggestion is a tremendous thing, my friends. If the Pope said you would burst into an order of onion rings if you read this book, would you have placed your filthy hands on this tome so quickly?

When he called Jerry Palko to check our phone bills, Jerry told him to either get a search warrant or leave us both alone. The lack of evidence soured Powers and that was the last time I ever had any problems with him or his mustache. I resumed making calls later that night.

PROPER CRACK-BUYING ETIQUETTE

After the Powers debacle, I welcomed the opportunity to take another road trip. This time to Wichita, Kansas, of all places. Mike had established contact with a promoter named Christopher Love (no relation to the illustrious Dr. Love), who was starting up a promotion in the central states. He'd gotten himself booked and had convinced Love to give Como and me shots as well. So the 1-2-3 Stooges got into Mike's car and began the drive from Calgary to Wichita under standard wrestling driving rules of course.

Being the rookie, it was my job to drive all night and after a few hours I fell asleep at the wheel. I opened my eyes just in time to see the hood of the car nuzzling with the ass end of a four-wheel-drive. I slammed on the brakes and smelled the rubber burning as we skidded to a stop on the side of the highway. Once again I became John Candy in *Planes, Trains & Automobiles,* as the guys woke up and angrily asked if I was going to keep driving.

"Yes I will," I said. "Yes I will."

I'd like to mention that it's very hard to drive when your pants are filled with dookie.

We stopped the next evening when we hit Denver. Instead of checking into a hotel or getting a decent meal, we went straight to Shotgun Willy's.

The strip clubs I'd been to in Winnipeg were just glorified pubs with the occasional bored naked girl wandering around, but Shotgun Willy's had scantily clad gorgeous goddesses everywhere. I promptly fell in love with a lovely lady who told me she was stripping simply to put herself through college. I admired her gumption and after my attempt to fund her entire higher education, she gave me her address (no e-mail in those days, kids). Mike and Bret laughed when I told them that this girl was different from the rest and I planned to keep in touch. They'd been through many towns and many strippers and knew that dancers were con artists just like we were. That's why wrestlers and strippers are so attracted to each other; we're both in the business of selling fantasy. But speaking from experience, it costs a whole lot more to buy what the strippers are selling.

After leaving Shotgun Willy's, Mike and Bret decided that they wanted to indulge in a little of Grandpa's secret stash. We ended up on a street corner in the middle of a downtown Denver ghetto and once again because I was the greenhorn, it was my job to procure the loot. I should've just said no to drugs but I had to prove I was one of the boys; possible felony and extradition be damned!

I got out of the car and a few minutes later a mean-looking dude walked by. I suddenly morphed into Larry David and said these exact words: "Excuse me, sir, do you have any marijuana?"

Instead of assaulting me on the spot for massive nerdery, he pulled a plastic bag out of his pocket. It contained a handful of what looked like small, clear pieces of hard candy.

He said, "I got this and I think you should buy it." I began to protest until he opened his coat and revealed a Crocodile Dundee knife. I was sold so I gave him Mike's money and took the bag. I wasn't sure of the proper crack-buying etiquette, so I thanked him, gave him a thumbs-up, and sprinted back to the car.

I threw the bag of crack in the front seat, told the boys that we were going to be fricasseed if we had any problems with the service at the drive-thru, and Mike floored it.

A serious debate followed as we tried to decide what we were supposed to do with a bag of crack. Do we smoke the crack? Do we eat the crack? Do we put a pin in the crack and wear it as a brooch? It didn't take long for us to decide that we should get rid of the crack as soon as possible. So we stuffed it in the bottom of a Coke bottle and dumped it in the garbage. If there were any garbage-picking vagrants in the area that night, they found a whole lot more in that can than just orange peels and coffee grinds.

We arrived (crack-free) in Wichita and went to Christopher Love's fancy adobe-style house. A guy dressed as a butler answered the door and announced in an overexaggerated serious voice, "Mr. Love will see you now."

Sitting behind an oak desk, book-ended by a fat black

man and a fat white man, was Christopher Love, who was fatter than both of them. He looked like a pissed-off Louie Anderson.

Love surveyed the three of us and from the way he stared at me as if I was a triple cheese with curly fries, it didn't take Dr. Phil to figure out that he was quite gay. He introduced the white guy as the Zebra Kid, even though he looked nothing like a Zebra and less like a kid. He introduced the black guy as Rudy and nodded to the RUBBER CHICKEN Rudy was holding in his hand.

"Say hello to Rudy's manager, Cluck." We smiled at his lame joke, then noticed that nobody else in the room was laughing. Rudy's gimmick was that he asked his manager Cluck for advice, except it didn't seem like a gimmick—everyone took the Cluckster quite seriously.

Zebra broke the silence by complimenting Como on his signature move, the Shooting Star Press, which nobody else in the U.S. was doing. The move was similar to a gainer in diving and it was very difficult to do (I broke my arm attempting it, but that's a story for another chapter). Como had been a trick skier and was agile as a cat. He had mastered the move as a result and had built his reputation on it.

"I've seen you do the Shooting Star Press," Zebra Kid said. "I can do that too."

Looking at the short dumpy guy in front of me, my mind drifted to a Weeble wobbling through the air. Then Love gazed longingly into my eyes and said, "Wow, you look just like Shawn Michaels. I can do a lot with you."

I'm sure he could.

He had a party later that night to celebrate the opening of the company and—surprise, surprise—it was a freaking freak show. The guy dressed as a butler was there, Zebra Kid was there, Rudy was there, Cluck was there. The champion of the company was also there and looked as gay as they come with spiked dyed blond hair and an Errol Flynn mustache. Another wrestler named Rex King was trying to put together a crib for no apparent reason, but was too loaded to figure out how to do it.

The room burst into gales of laughter when one of the referees downed his drink after returning from the bathroom. Apparently this guy had never heard of the "hold on to your drink" rule, because when he was gone someone had used their swizzle stick as a swizzle stick.

"Ha! You just drank a Penis Colada," Rudy said as Cluck guffawed with the rest of the gang. "We got you! We got you with the Penis Colada!" I would have gone postal and kicked the crap out of everyone and their coladas, but this guy just laughed and said with a sheepish grin, "The Penis Colada . . . oh you got me again!"

Again?

AGAIN?

When a commercial aired for the upcoming big show, the whole room hushed up as everyone watched intently. When it ended, the room exploded out of their chairs jumping up and down like the clock had just struck twelve on New Year's Eve. Then they lined up to give Christopher Love a high-five, laughing and screaming to each other while he stood there with a proud knowing look on his face.

I was sitting on the couch trying to make sense of the ridiculosity, when I felt a pair of hands in my hair. I turned around to see that the hands belonged to Christopher Love.

When I asked him what the hell he was doing, he told me, "I'm just playing with your hair."

I bit my tongue and suggested in no uncertain terms that it would probably be better if he stopped. His whole demeanor changed and he waddled (awesome word) off in a huff.

The next day, Zebra called us at our hotel to say that there were too many guys on the show and since Christopher thought I was too green, I was the first one eliminated. Just like Celebrity Duets. We all agreed that I was cut because I balked at Love's hair fondling. But the three of us had come down together with the promise of a booking and that's what the three of us expected to get. We'd arrived as a team and we decided to cut our losses and get the hell out of Dodge (or should I say Wichita) as a team.

We stuck together when the chips were down, which was a unique situation in itself. Wrestling isn't known as a business where you make a lot of trustworthy true friends. But I made two that day.

My dad still points to that experience as a big reason why I always fought for what I believed in during my career.

CHAPTER 12

A HOT DOG AND A GLASS OF ORANGE JUICE

When we returned from Love Land, Mike got me a shot with the CNWA, the company that had formed from the ashes of Stampede Wrestling. They had two major pluses, in nationwide TV on TSN (the ESPN of Canada) and the announcing talents of the famous commentator Ed Whalen. Ed's broadcasts were fairly corny but he was *the* voice of Stampede Wrestling and it was one of my major goals to have him announce one of my matches.

I made my TSN/CNWA debut with another ten-minute draw against Como. We had a decent match despite the white underwear that also made its debut on TSN by continually sticking out of the back of my yellow and black Stryper tights. The best part was watching the tape and hearing Ed Whalen call the match using his ricockulous catchphrases like, "There's a malfunction at the junction" and "It's a ring a ding dong dandy!" I don't know what they mean either, but it was cool to hear Ed say them about me.

It was also a thrill when after the match, Ed looked directly into the camera and said, "I like this Jericho kid." Since the match was shown across Canada, my friends and family got to see me wrestle for the first time and Ed's endorsement not only gave me instant credibility, but also gave people the idea that my name was the Jericho Kid.

Backstage, it was the first time I'd ever dealt with an actual booker and a TV run sheet that listed the down-to-the-minute details. The booker was Bulldog Bob Brown, who'd wrestled for Stampede for years and was the biggest star I'd met so far. He didn't look like much with his crew cut, big gut, chicken legs, and jug handle ears, but I'd watched him for years on Stampede so he was okay in my book—at that point anyway.

I did well enough that I was invited back the next week and a few weeks after that I brought Lance in to work with me as Sudden Impact. In our first week we had to do our first televised interview and it was the best promo of ALL TIME. We were supposed to talk about the big fan appreciation night that was taking place the next week. As I was driving to the Action Center before the show, I heard a radio interview with David Lee Roth. It was vintage Diamond Dave. He was talking all the shit that made him the greatest frontman of all time, and I was digging it huge. When he responded to a question by saying, "There's a fine line between a pat on the back and a kick in the pants, so let's dance!," I thought it was the coolest line ever even though I had absolutely no idea what it meant.

We began our interview and when I was asked about

the upcoming show, I said, "You know, there's a fine line between a pat on the back and a kick in the pants, so let's dance!" The interviewer was like, "Huh?" Lance was like, "Huh?" I was like, "Huh?" I didn't know what to say next and since I didn't have Diamond Dave to help me, I blurted out the only thing I could think of: "Next week we've got midgets coming!"

Bob Brown equated midgets with boffo box office and had told me to "push the shit out of the little bastards."

After discovering that the Roth style of promo wasn't for me, I learned an important lesson—the first of three seminal moments in my promo development. I had done an interview about my first match with Bulldog and I was talking about how old and slow he was, just burying him. I thought it was pretty good, until I walked back to the dressing room and Bulldog stopped me in front of everyone. "What the hell are you doing? Yeah I'm old and everybody knows it. But I want you to think about this. If I beat you, and I WILL be beating you, then you just got beat by an old man. If you beat me, and you WILL NOT be beating me, then you just beat up an old man. If you talk about how much experience I have and then I cheat to beat you, then at least you got beaten by an experienced vet. And if you beat me, well fuck, then you just beat an experienced vet. The way it stands right now, you just pissed all over yourself. You look like a fool either way."

He walked away muttering to himself, and I realized he was right. The first big lesson I learned about promos (get out your pens, kids) was: "Never Totally Bury Your Opponent." You can tell jokes and insult them all you want, but if you don't build them up to some extent, you're just burying yourself.

The CNWA locker room was filled with guys I recognized from the Stampede roster and I was awestruck to be changing and shooting the breeze with all of these wrestlers that I'd watched on the tube. Johnny Smith, the Great Gama, Gerry Morrow, Bad News Allen. Bad News looked like a bigger, meaner Ving Rhames, who demanded respect and got it from every member of the locker room. He had a hot cougar of a wife named Helen who I had the good fortune of meeting when I was leaving the building, after everyone else had cleared out. I was talking to her and turning up the Jeri-Charm, when from out of nowhere, News appeared like an apparition. He was wearing a head-to-toe suit of red leather, with earrings in both ears and one of those Jim Brown brimless hats; and he was staring a wormhole through me.

The Jeri-Charm instantly turned into Jeri-Terror. I was scared to death. Time stood still, and I strained to come up with something clever to say to break the iceberg.

"Hey Bad News, how many earrings do you have?"

The tradition of saying stupid things to wrestlers upon first meeting continued.

Shortly afterward CNWA lost their TV deal and while they kept running shows, the attendance declined. With the TV deal gone there was no reason to stay in Calgary, so Mike called another connection and this time the 1-2-3 Stooges sailed off to California to find our fame and fortune.

We drove for three days to get to our match at a Spanish flea market in Pomona, just outside Los Angeles. The ring announcer couldn't speak English and introduced me to the crowd of dozens as Chris HerraChico. Paul Heyman still calls me that.

Mike and I were working Bret and an old Mexican wrestler named the Great Goliath who must've been sixty, looked like he was seventy, and wrestled like he was eighty. The ring was rock-hard with ropes made of green rubber garden hose and there were hardly any people there, but I still wanted to put on a show in case there were any scouts in attendance. I was still green enough to think that reps from the WWF and WCW scoured every small show looking for talent—not that I had much of it at that point anyway.

Goliath was lazy and I'd been in the ring with him the whole match, so when Como tagged in, I went straight to the top hose and gave him a drop kick. The hoses had no leverage, so when I jumped I slipped and landed right on my hand. I instantly knew I was hurt.

Wrestling is a hard-hitting form of entertainment and you really do live each day in pain just as Jesse the Body had warned me. As a result, you get to know your body to the point of recognizing the difference between an injury that will go away on its own and one that will need medical attention. This one needed medical attention. I finished the match, didn't get paid the 100 bucks I was promised, and drove to the hospital. After a four-hour wait, I was denied care because I didn't have insurance. I called my dad, who gave me his credit card number and the doctor told me I had a hairline fracture in my hand. After all was said and done, I drove 3,000 miles, got ripped off 100 bucks, and ended up with a $1,000 hospital bill just for the privilege of wrestling one match in a flea market. That, young grass-hoppers, is what is known as paying your dues.

At least I got to meet Lars Ulrich a few days later on the Sunset Strip . . . if your definition of "meet" is being brushed off and totally ignored in the middle of the street, that is.

My job didn't get any more lucrative when I returned to Calgary and I hit the bottom of the Jeri-Chasm when Ed booked my next match at a kid's seventh birthday party. You heard me.

Lance and I showed up at a farmhouse outside Okotoks to find six kids and their moms wearing parkas and party hats in the middle of the frozen barn. Ed was friends with the kid's dad and wanted to show off, so he arranged for the kid to get his own private wrestling show. I got Kedzo the Klown for my seventh birthday party, and this kid got two full matches including ring entrances. Afterward the kids were excited and the moms were excited and all of them were having their pictures taken with the half-naked muscleheads with the frozen nipples. Since I'd just entertained a bunch of kids with a match and provided a bunch of ladies in mom jeans with Chippendales On Ice, I was expecting a nice payday. And I got paid all right—with a hot dog and a glass of orange juice. They didn't even give me any ketchup, and at that point my career wasn't cutting the mustard. (Funny author's note: Rumors that Ed later booked me at a bar mitzvah are unfounded.)

With my options drying up in Calgary, I was stoked when I got a call from Winnipeg promoter Tony Condello, who'd decided to bring Chris Jericho back to his hometown for a series of shows—the conquering hero returns! None of my friends had ever seen me wrestle live and I was excited that the first show was a TV taping in a beautiful nightclub called Club Taboo. It was the perfect place to prove to everybody that I was making it big.

Tony was taping a month's worth of TV and when I walked to the ring for the first of four matches that night, the crowd exploded. It was one of the best feelings I've ever experienced, as it seemed that every single person I'd ever known in Winnipeg was there chanting "Jericho! Jericho! Jericho!" It felt even better when I scanned the crowd and saw my mom in attendance.

After a lengthy hospital stay, she'd returned home to her newly renovated house and had started getting acclimated to the huge change in her life. One of her first outings was to Club Taboo to see me wrestle and I'll never forget looking into her face and seeing how proud she was of me. She was living vicariously through me and after urging me to continue following my dreams despite her accident, she'd become my biggest fan.

I made quite an impact with my matches that night and due to my Calgary training I stood head and shoulders over most of the other wrestlers. Throw in the fact that the crowd was going bananas over me and for the first time since I started wrestling, I felt like a star.

A few days later I was cruising down the avenue feeling like a real hotshot and basking in the glow of my newfound celebrity. I was thinking about my next match when I drove past a bar called Georgie's, a local tavern that my friends and I used to go to for beers. The sign on the marquee said FRIDAY NIGHT WRESTLING. It made me smile to think of the low-level sad sacks who would be wrestling at Georgie's. I thought about checking out the show for a laugh, but remembered that I also had a match on Friday night. The slight touch of a moth fluttered in my stomach as I started to put two and two together.

I called Condello to find out where we were wrestling

on Friday and, sure enough, we were booked in the Georgie Dome.

It felt terrible to come back to Winnipeg as the big cheese, wrestle a TV taping in the big venue, and then be reduced to working in my local pub. I was convinced that people would laugh at me for being such a nobody and working in a shithole like Georgie's.

To make matters worse, the pub ring was the size of a king-size bed, which made it impossible to get pinned, because you could break the count by putting your foot on the ropes no matter where you were.

I had to change across the street and walk across the road in my yellow spandex, with cars honking and people laughing all the way. The match was abominable, climaxing when I jumped off the top rope and put my head right through the tile of the low ceiling. Dust and debris floated down onto my back as I pinned my foe, who of course had his foot on the rope. I made the decision right then that I would never wrestle in a bar again.

Due to my refusal to participate in all of the reindeer games, Bob Brown decided that he wanted to work with me for the rest of the tour to teach me a lesson. What he taught me was how not to have a wrestling match.

Working with Bob was brutal because he would always put himself over by beating all the younger guys, which hurt everyone involved. Except for the Bulldog.

Another problem in working with him was that he just wasn't very good. He'd always boast about his ninety-minute matches with Ric Flair or how he tore the house down with Bruiser Brody in Japan. He bragged that he had trained Shawn Michaels, Marty Jannety, and Chris Benoit. I'm sure he worked with them and beat them, but

of doormen to help. He gave all of us nicknames that suited our looks and dispositions. There was Hammer, Creampuff, Guru, Hoop, Turnip, Grizz, Fuji, Chang. I became Biff because I looked like I was from California and Lance became . . . Lance. He was too serious for a nickname.

We slowly eliminated the barroom brawling crowd by using friendly tactics instead of typical bouncer methods. One night at closing time I told a table of bikers that it was time to finish up and they told me in no uncertain terms that they weren't leaving. When I calmly reiterated that they had to leave, one of the boys who probably tipped the scales at three bills said, "If you want me to leave, you're gonna have to beat me in an arm wrestling match."

What Steppenwolf didn't know was that I had worked ring crew for a show that featured Scott "Flash" Norton, a world champion arm wrestler who became a world champion pro wrestler. Like a smartass, I challenged Flash to an arm wrestling match in the dressing room and he beat me in about one googleth of a second, almost tearing my shoulder out of its socket in the process. But he admired my chutzpah and in turn showed me a foolproof technique that guaranteed arm wrestling victory.

So I agreed to the contest and the members of our respective groups surrounded the table like the Sharks and the Jets and began to cheer us on. We gripped hands and began the battle. I used Norton's trick and beat the mutha-trucker, barely. My group cheered, his group groaned, but to their credit they all got up and walked out the door without protest. What's the trick, you may ask? I ain't telling. If you want to learn it, come ask me if you run into me on the street sometime. If I'm feeling froggy, maybe I'll jump.

When things were slow in Malarkey's, I'd get behind the bar and start pouring drinks. I was obsessed with Paul Stanley and Kiss (I dressed as the Starchild for a record-setting seven Halloweens in a row), especially his rap at the beginning of "Cold Gin" on the *Alive* record. He bragged about drinking vodka and orange juice in his thick New York accent and I thought it was the coolest-sounding drink ever. So vodka and orange juice became my drink, except I eliminated the middle man and simply called them Paul Stanleys. It wasn't long before all of the bartenders, managers, doormen, and regular customers called them Paul Stanleys too. I didn't stop there, as rum and cokes became Gene Simmonses, whiskey and Cokes became Ace Frehleys, and gin and tonics became Vinnie Vincents. There was no drink named after Peter Criss because nobody cares about him anyway. If you ever meet someone who worked at Malarkey's, ask them what a Paul Stanley is. They'll know exactly what you're talking about.

Working as a doorman was another great way to meet girls. Everyone wants to be your friend and hang around with you and it's like shooting fish in a barrel—you can basically take your pick. The only drawback is most barflys are crazy. At least the ones that I met were.

When I gave one such fine lass a ride home one night, we parked outside her house and became fast friends. Suddenly, I heard the sound of breaking glass and the passenger window spiderwebbed. I looked through the splintered glass and saw a guy standing there with a hockey stick. "Shit," she said. "It's my fiancé!" Here we were making out, her shirt flung on the dashboard like a used tissue, in front of her own house while her future husband (maybe not after this) was inside. She was either the gutsiest or the stupidest human being on the planet. I kicked her out and sped away, counting my blessings that the guy only had a hockey stick and not a shotgun.

I felt I was better off without a girlfriend anyway because my career mind-set had been influenced by two rules Paul Stanley lived by. His first motto was that the only people who told you that you couldn't do something were the ones who had failed. Words to live by. He also said if you want to make it and be famous you have to get rid of your women. I got his point and since I wanted to wrestle wherever I could, a girlfriend would only deter my plans to travel around the world in spandex.

MY NAME IS CHRIS TOO

My job was a joke, I was broke, and my love life was DOA, so it was time to hit the road again. My dad had begun dating his future second wife, Bonnie, who lived near San Francisco and while watching a small cable channel at her place he saw a wrestling show called Bay Area Wrestling. I needed the exposure and Bonnie said I could stay with her, so for the second time in my career I went to California.

I walked into the tiny TV studio where BAW was filmed and the first thing I noticed was how low the ceiling was. Were there ANY rings in the free world where you could jump off the top rope and not put your head through the roof? The crew was another ragtag bunch of misfits who hadn't been trained properly and once again even with my limited experience, I stood out. Unfortunately, the company couldn't wait to take advantage of that. I worked my first match against promoter Woody Farmer's son and lost quickly. Then I worked the illustrious Spanish Hitman, who was managed by an ancient lady named Johnny Mae Young (yeah, *that* Mae Young and she was already older than Methuselah). She was a lunatic and after she caused me to lose the match, she beat the shit out of me and it hurt.

When I was booked to beat a guy called Luscious Larry, Woody asked me if I was excited that I was "getting a big win." At that point I could've cared less, I just wanted to get it on and get it over with. Winning or losing wasn't as important as having the best match I could in front of the fifty fans in this tiny studio and hopefully be seen on TV by someone who could get me another job. After wrestling three matches for zero money, I got a small victory when I did my first interview with a nationally distributed magazine called *Wrestling World*. The reporter took a few pictures and wrote a total bullshit story about the young gorgeous newcomer that had taken California by storm and was on the brink of superstardom. It was the second time my name had appeared in a wrestling magazine; the first via a letter that had been written by a fan named Clint Bobsky, who said that Chris Jericho was the best new wrestler he'd ever seen. Clint Bobsky was of course the nom de plume of moi.

During my BAW time, I met a guy named Billy Anderson who had the dubious distinction of being the 500th best wrestler in *Pro Wrestling Illustrated*'s annual top 500 wrestlers issue. I struck up a friendship with him and his girlfriend, exchanged contact numbers, and parted ways.

A few weeks after I returned to Calgary, I got a call from Billy's girlfriend, Rebecca, who had gone through his phone book while he was in the shower and stolen my number. She said she was enamored with me and just had to call. The situation got even weirder a few weeks later when she called me at 4 A.M. and told me she was being chased by the Yakuza (the Japanese mafia, more on them later) and was terrified.

"I'm so scared . . . they're after me," she said. "I don't know what to do!"

I sure as hell didn't know what to do either, as I envisioned the Yakuza finding my number and coming after me too.

"Help me, please Chris help—" she said and then the line went dead.

Either she had hung up the phone and had a laugh at my expense OR the Yakuza had actually gotten her. I never found out because I never spoke with her again.

I did however, speak to the Great Gama, who was putting together a one-night-only Stampede Wrestling revival show at the Victoria Pavilion, the home of the promotion for forty years. When he told me I was booked against the 350-pound female Monster Ripper Rhonda Singh, I still did a Jeri-jig because I was finally going to get to wrestle for Stampede Freakin' Wrestling!

I was in the dressing room getting ready for my match, when Mike Lozanski walked in with my long-lost brother Chris Benoit. I'd been a fan of Benoit's from Stampede and had followed his career ever since. From Canada to Japan to Germany to Mexico, he'd built his reputation as one of the best wrestlers in the world. He was also an inspiration to me because he'd started in Calgary, wasn't a giant, and had established himself as an internationally respected superstar. I wanted my career path to emulate his. I racked my brain to think of something to say that would show him how much I respected him. I walked up to him, stuck out my hand and said, "My name is Chris too."

Benoit looked at me sideways and muttered hello. As he walked away, Lenny, who was sitting beside me, mimicked my voice and said, "My name's Chris too . . . my name's Chris too . . . " He broke into a gale of laughter and I told him to fuck off.

Lenny and I had grown quite close and we spent a lot of time together. We were both obsessed with *This Is Spinal Tap* and called ourselves the Lovely Lads, after David and Nigel's first band. He played guitar and to kill time between gigs, we formed a band named Blackstone Menace. We used a drum machine in lieu of a drummer so for the band photos we had Lenny's brother Ajax stand in as the skinsman. We sounded like a cross between the Ramones and Mötley Crüe and we spent weeks in Lenny's basement recording our first demo, "My Brain Hurts." When it was ready, we drew the cover, handwrote the lyrics, and produced 100 hand-laminated copies. We took them to a record store in Okotoks and sold them on consignment. The final sales at Big Rock Records had Blackstone Menace outselling Nirvana, Kiss, and Elton John, five copies to three copies.

We were huge rock stars.

We kept releasing different demos under the band names Mr. Filthy, Great Caesar's Ghost, Love Weasel, or Jesus A Go-Go and sent them out all over Canada. If you were a fan of unsigned Canadian bands in the 1990s, look through those old boxes of cassette demos and maybe you'll find one of ours.

Our musical peak arrived when a national music magazine named *MEAT* reviewed the Blackstone demo and said, quote, "This demo has very catchy songs and the band has an original sound to them; either that or the tape I got is fucked up." What more could you ask for in a review?

While chasing our rock 'n' roll dreams, Lenny and I were still wrestling in Calgary. The quality of workers was deteriorating because there wasn't much work in town, so once again with the tremendous training we'd both had our skills were better than the majority of the guys around, and that pissed some people off.

The booker of the weekly Calgary show was Karl Moffat, who had wrestled in Stampede as the original Jason the Terrible. He was an arrogant prick and he didn't like the fact that Lenny's booking ideas were better than his. So he decided to put a bounty out on Lenny, which would be collected by the first guy who kicked the shit out of him in the ring for real. The stupid thing was that Moffat bragged about his plan to anyone who would listen and the word trickled back to us.

We knew that the ambush was going to happen that week courtesy of a big fat farm boy named Shane Croft, so we devised a plan of our own. Moffat had booked us in a tag match, and when it was over, I was supposed to fight to the back with our opponents, leaving Lenny in the ring. Croft was then going to hit the ring and give Lenny a brutal beatdown. But instead of fighting to the back, I was going to remain at ringside and if Croft was too much for Lenny to handle, I was going to perform an ambush of my own.

So we had the match and when it was over, I hustled back to the ring just as Croft arrived. He got in the ring and started lacing into Lenny and it was obvious that the shit was on. Lenny gave me the sign and I hit the ring ready to rock.

While I was envisioning a Three Ninjas attack, it ended up a Three Stooges bit. I got in the ring and started pulling Croft's hair to get him off of Lenny. The more I pulled the less he moved, so I kept pulling and pulling until I heard Lenny yell, "Stop it man!" I looked at my hand and saw that I was pulling Lenny's hair instead.

The comedy routine continued when Lenny aimed a punch a Croft's moving head, but popped me in the jaw instead. At that point I'd had enough, so I reached down and grabbed his ballbag—Croft's this time, not Lenny's—and squeezed it as hard as I could. To my dismay, the guy didn't flinch. Not even a little. That's when I knew we were in trouble. He was still pummeling us with his massive hamhock farmer fists, so I rolled out of the ring and grabbed a chair. When I came back inside, I hit that bitch in the head from behind harder than I've ever hit anyone in my entire life. There was a sick crack and he grabbed the back of his head and said in the saddest voice, sounding just like Mongo from *Blazing Saddles*, "What did you do that for?"

Croft had had enough but Lenny sure hadn't. He walked over to the gimmick (souvenir) table and picked up the stack of Shane Croft 8x10s. Since Croft hadn't sold a damn one of them, I'm sure they were lonely and enjoyed the attention that Lenny gave them when he ripped each and every one of them in half. He threw the pile at Croft's wife and yelled, "What are you going to do about it, you CUNT!" Them thar's fighting words, cowpoke.

We went downstairs to the dressing room and grabbed the weapons we'd brought with us: my tire iron and Lenny's hockey stick with nails driven through it that he had made just for the occasion.

We stormed into the booking office where Moffat was cowering and chewed him out like a beaver's birthday cake. Then Croft walked in the room and Lenny said, "I just called your wife a cunt. What are you gonna do about it?" Both Croft and Moffat had apparently noticed something interesting on the tips of their shoes because they both refused to look up. "You guys got anything to say?" Lenny continued. When neither of them did, I said, "Well then get the fuck out of here." And they did. We'd kicked them out of their own office. Lenny sat in Moffat's chair, put his foot up on the desk, and said, "My scalp is killing me."

Later that night an old Japanese wrestler named Mr. Hito was impressed enough with my wrestling skills . . . or my ballbag-grabbing skills . . . to ask me if I wanted to train with him the next week. He was looking for guys to work with his Japanese students and since I was constantly looking for ways to get a shot in Japan, it was a no-brainer. I could hardly contain my excitement when he said, "I see you on Monday at Stu's house." Stu's house? That meant I was finally going to get to train in the infamous Hart Dungeon!

The next Monday, I pulled up to a house that resembled the Addams Family mansion, only the family that lived inside this house was much stranger. I knocked a few times and there was no answer, so I walked inside the unlocked front door and introduced myself to Stu and his wife, Helen, who were sitting right inside the foyer. I guess they didn't feel like answering the door. Hito was there with a few Japanese kids and he grunted in my direction and led me down the steps into the Dungeon. I saw right away why it had that name. It looked like the basement of the house in *The Texas Chainsaw Massacre*, dark and damp with pipes hanging from the low ceiling and a mat slightly raised off the floor that served as the training ring. There were some weights lying around with HART branded onto the plates (years later before the house was sold, Bret gave me one of them as a gift). Overall, the world-famous Dungeon was just a big unfinished rumpus room. But it was a rumpus room haunted by the screams of a thousand wrestlers.

The first thing Hito made me do was take 500 back bumps in a row. I was numb after the first fifty, but I kept going. This was true Japanese wrestling training and I wanted a taste. After about 300 bumps I started slowing down from the fatigue and when Hito told me to speed up, I said, "No problem."

Hito threw his hat at me and yelled, "Yes, there is problem! You are problem! Just do what I tell you and no speak!"

I shut up and continued training with Hito and his students for the rest of the week and taking around 3,000 bumps in the process. I learned different wrestling holds and techniques that I'd never seen before and I had highly intense practice matches with the Japanese guys. The highlight of the week arrived when Stu shuffled down the stairs and hung around the ring watching like a predator. I sensed the danger and with Jesse's words of warning echoing in the back of my head, I tried to stay inconspicuous. Stu was in his mid-seventies, but he still got off on stretching guys the same way that his son Keith got off on stretching me. Thankfully Stu never put his hands on me but he did stretch the shit out of the one Japanese kid who made the mistake of shaking Stu-San's hand. After the greeting, Stu held on to the guy's hand and said, "Let me show you something." He pulled the kid closer and stuck one arm on the kid's head and the other under his chin. As Stu applied the pressure, I realized where Keith learned the hold that he'd locked on me during my first day of camp. But this kid didn't contain his screams like I had and his cries of pain joined the legions of others that already haunted the Dungeon.

CHAPTER 14

THE WORST BALL-HUGGERS EVER

After finally experiencing the legend of the Dungeon, I felt that I'd gone as far as I could go working in Calgary. My career had been in a constant state of one step forward, two steps back and I'd grown stagnant working in the same places against the same guys. If I was going to get better, I needed a change of scenery and a change of style. I put together a promo tape filled with nonsensical high spots and flashy moves performed in front of twenty-five fans in high school gyms, and sent it to promoters around the world. I'd received bupkus in response and it was getting discouraging.

That's why it was such a blessing to get a call from Mike Lozanski asking me if I wanted to go wrestle in Mexico. Mike had gotten the opportunity to work for a company based out of Monterrey and since Mexican wrestling was based around tag team matches, the promoter wanted Mike to have a permanent partner.

I jumped at Mike's offer, and a few days later we bought our own tickets and flew via Mexico City to Monterrey, in the northern part of Mexico.

The promoter, Carlos Elizondo, didn't have work visas arranged for us, so when we went through customs in Mexico City, we were to claim that we were on vacation. Of course, if anybody pushed the issue and checked our duffel bags filled with wrestling gear, it would've made things a little hard to explain. I guess I was supposed to use the Jedi mind trick to deter any official questions if asked. When I got to the front of the customs line I had to press a big black button that was attached to a traffic light. If the light blinked green, I was free to go. If it blinked red, it was plastic glove time. My finger shook slightly and a bead of moisture formed on my upper lip as I pressed the button. It flashed green and I breathed a sigh of relief that I wouldn't have to claim that my fancy spandex tights were for a cabaret. The Jedi mind trick was saved for another day.

Monterrey was a fairly modern city with cool, dry weather, nestled in a scenic mountain range. The wrestling business was booming there and Elizondo's company ran four shows a week, the biggest of which took place in a 10,000-seat bull fighting arena called Plaza Monumental every Sunday. I couldn't imagine what it would be like to work in front of that many people and I wondered how I would handle it when the day arrived.

We decided to stay in an American-style Holiday Inn and Elizondo agreed to pay half of the bill. He also agreed to reimburse us for our plane tickets (he never did) and to pay each of us 2,000 pesos a week, about 700 bucks, with a minimum of two matches a week. We could also eat for free at Cuatro Milpas, the restaurant he owned. Throw in the fact that it was my first steady job in the wrestling biz and you'll see why I was a twenty-two-year-old happy campero.

I didn't speak any Spanish at all, nothing, zilch, nada . . . okay, bad example. Mike however had spent a lot of time in Mexico and thought his Spanish was fairly good. But the more he spoke, the more I realized that he didn't know any more than I did. He always ordered a *jueves* for lunch, thinking that it was a "type of sandwich." What he was really ordering was a Thursday, the actual definition of *jueves*. It didn't take long to realize that it was imperative to learn Spanish. Without it, I couldn't eat, buy, sell, talk to girls, or put together a wrestling match.

Mexican wrestling is known as lucha libre, which loosely translated means free fight. Lucha is a high-flying style of wrestling with different rules and traditions that made it hard for me to understand. Lucha is to American wrestling as the Canadian Football League is to the National Football League. The same sport but with different rules. Most of the matches were six-man tags and were decided by the best two out of three falls. The majority of the performers—especially the natives—wore masks and had elaborately made colorful costumes with capes to match.

When I heard that Elizondo had an idea for my ring costume, I was intrigued. I was hoping for something cool, like a rainbow-colored mask with a silver cape and streamers shooting out of my hands. I almost had a heart attack when he gave me a little handful of spandex instead. He didn't speak any English but I could see he was quite excited about the tiny yellow Speedos he wanted me to wear. Did I mention that he was openly gay? Seriously, was there something in the water that these promoters drank? I smiled back and when I motioned that I wouldn't feel comfortable wearing the flashy handkerchief, his face darkened.

He pondered my reaction for a few minutes and then mumbled something to the costume maker, who reached into his bag and pulled out plan B. These tights were a little longer than Speedos but were much tighter. As a matter of fact, they were probably the worst ball-huggers ever worn. You doubt me? Check out any of the pictures of me wearing them and you'll know what religion I am.

Once I was issued the banana hammock, it was time to give me a new name. It was obvious from the Pomona HerriChico experience that the Chris Jericho nombre wouldn't play in Pechuca, so I had to think of something else. Since Mike was known as Tigre Canadiense (Canadian Tiger) and we were partners, I had the idea to call myself Lion Heart.

But Elizondo hated it because he'd already come up with a name for me.

He-Man.

I'll write it again . . . HE-MAN.

And not only did he want to call me He-Man, he wanted me to dress like the fucking guy as well. I'm talking the whole deal . . . furry boots, short tights with an H on the crotch, broadsword. Just what was I supposed to do with a broadsword? Behead the referee after a controversial call? He-Man made Cowboy Chris Jericho look like Stone Cold Steve Austin in comparison. I didn't want to complain too loudly, as I still wanted the job, but as much as I tried to come to grips with the concept, I knew I could never make He-Man work.

I had the costume maker translate my words as I reasoned with the boss.

"If you think about it, Lion Heart is perfect. You brought me in to be Tigre Canadiense's partner and if you use my name, we can be Lion and Tiger, the Canadian Wildcats!"

My pitch completed, I flashed Elizondo a Brad Pitt smile (although in retrospect I should've flashed him my ball bag). He liked the Gatos Salvaje (Wildcats) idea but didn't feel that the fans would understand what a Lion Heart was. He toyed with the idea of calling me León d'Oro (Golden Lion) but after a few minutes decided he still liked He-Man best.

Elizondo was being such a name stickler because he had big plans for me in his company—he wanted to make me a star. He'd already started building up my debut by placing full-page ads of me in my crotch holder in the local papers, offering free tickets to the first fan who could correctly answer three questions about me:

1. What was my real name?
2. Where was I from?
3. When was my debut match?

It was straight out of *Tiger Beat* and he wanted me to be a teen heartthrob like I was the Canadian member of Menudo.

He had also booked me on the local TV show *Lucha Esta Noche!* (Wrestling Tonight) to introduce me to the fans of Monterrey. So far, I was feeling pretty especial.

After two days, I was already the subject of a contest in the paper AND the special guest on *Lucha Esta* frickin' *Noche!* Finally after years of hardship, my ship was coming in.

But the damn ship sank seconds later when it was brought to my attention that my name was going to be decided by the viewers of the show. Elizondo's idea was to have the fans watching *Lucha Tonight* vote on what my name should be. I figured that he would use León d'Oro no matter what the actual vote tally was, but Elizondo assured me that the voting process would be totally legit. The viewers would make their choice from three available names . . . He-Man, León d'Oro, or Chris Power. Chris Power? Granted He-Man was horrible, but it was better than that shit sandwich of a name.

The show began with the two masked hosts and me sitting around a desk looking serious. Sure luchadores are the superheroes of Mexican culture who hide their identities behind a mask, but why might I ask were the HOSTS hiding their faces? Did they have to conceal their identities from the evil TV hosts who were out to destroy them?

Even though I was a sexy beast, the episode of *Lucha Esta Noche!* was probably the worst show in Mexican television history. This was the result of an interviewer who spoke no English having an in-depth conversation with a guest who spoke no Spanish.

I fumbled through the disaster of a show, knowing that I had zero control over the upcoming decision that would forever change the course of my career.

Finally, a mariachi band began to play and the mysterious host hyped the big moment. The time had come!

He was handed an envelope as if I was about to win a shitty Emmy. The winner of the Worst Name in Wrestling is . . .

After some babble about nombres and votas, the hostador finally opened the envelope. My heart pounded and a chorus line of Skeletors danced around inside my head like satanic Rockettes as the host revealed my new name of . . .

León d'Oro!!!

I morphed into Meg Ryan in *When Harry Met Sally* as I jumped up and down screaming, "Yes! Yes, yes, yes, yes!"

The show ended with confetti falling and the mariachis throwing the fuck down. After the hosts shook my hand and walked off the stage, I noticed that they'd left the paper with the vote tallies written on it. I read it and the results were:

León d'Oro—412 votes
He-Man—410 votes
Chris Power—52 votes

I had three thoughts:

1. I was spared He-Man by two measly votes.
2. I was shocked that there were fifty-two people in TV Land who actually liked the name Chris Power.
3. Only 874 people had watched the show.

CHAPTER 15

TOILET WATER IS TOILET WATER

Shortly afterward, I made my lucha libre debut with my new name, León d'Oro. The show took place in a parking lot, lit with a string of Christmas lights and a pair of headlights from an '82 Chevy parked in front of the ring.

Mike had warned me to watch out for the Mexican wrestlers who were unhappy about the foreigners invading their territory. So it was no surprise when the first guy I got in the ring with, el Ranger, punched me in the face as hard as he could right off the lockup. I understood what was happening and after the second swing connected harder than the first one, I punched the bastard back. Just to make sure there was no confusion, I tattooed him a second time and after that he was very easy to work with. When the match was over he was quite friendly and never mentioned the stiff shots. Go figure.

After working exclusively in North America, I found

the strange lucha style to be like wrestling trigonometry. There was a lot of rolling and tumbling in the ring, a direct contrast to the impactful bumps I'd been trained to do. The luchadores were throwing each other off the ropes with one hand and barely touching each other on tackles and clotheslines. They were working so light with each other that everything they did looked—dare I say—fake.

The stories told during the matches were strange as well. Falls would end only when every member of a team was pinned. We would work a fall for five minutes or so until all the members of the losing team got pinned or submitted one after another, only seconds apart. Then the second fall would start and the same thing would happen. You could also win by diving outside the ring onto another guy, but only if he wasn't the captain. The captain could only lose if he was pinned or submitted. Confused? I am and I wrestled there for three years.

Another major difference was, when you worked a match in Canada or the States, you worked on the left side of your opponent's body. You focused on his left leg or his left arm; you locked up at the beginning of the match with your left leg forward. But in Mexico, everyone worked on the right side. During my first match, I had no prior knowledge of this and it was like I was driving a car in England. I was bumping and crashing into things like Mel Gibson in Malibu, until I figured it out.

I was glad that I had the parking lot match to work out the kinks because my next match was in the Plaza Monumental, the massive bull fighting arena. The ring was set up in the middle of a large dirt floor and the mat was covered in a coat of dust that mushroomed into the air with every bump. When the show started, the Plaza was jam-packed with 10,000 screaming fans, the majority of them girls and kids. When I looked into the crowd during my previous matches, I could see each face, each person. But with a crowd this large all I noticed was a living, breathing monster, moving and shifting just outside the glow of the ring lights. It was the first time that I felt like I was in the big leagues. This was no community center or bar; this was a legitimate arena with tiers of padded seats, wandering popcorn vendors, and a full PA system. After working here, I knew I could never go back to the minor leagues of Canada again.

While the situation was memorable, the match was not. We'd been booked with the legendary Mil Mascaras. Earlier, he'd been bragging in the dressing room (while standing on his toes and wearing his mask) that he'd:

a) Trained Arnold Schwarzenegger on Venice Beach in 1968,
b) Was the best technical wrestler in Mexican history, and
c) Was a superstar in every country in the world . . . even Luxembourg.

After all his talk I was expecting something special, but in reality Mil was rotten. He didn't want Mike and me to do any offensive moves, as he said the thousands of fans in attendance wouldn't believe in us. Yet he did nothing in the ring, besides flexing his saggy pectorals and dancing around like he had antalones in his pantalones. But the massive crowd went nuts for him anyway. After the match was finished he kept his mask on the entire time he was in the building, even while standing in the shower.

I was buzzing over working in such a big venue when I opened the backstage door to leave. I walked into the parking lot and couldn't believe what I saw. Hundreds of fans were swarming around, all of them screaming and yelling. Chicks and guys, kids and old ladies, farmers and teenage girls, all of them pushing and hustling toward me. People were grabbing me and shouting, "León, León! *Una foto* (a picture)! *Un beso* (a kiss)!" Girls were clutching and pulling my hair and planting kisses on me with lips covered in cheap red lipstick. They were pinching my ass, grabbing my plums, and trying to steal my gear bag (I'm glad it wasn't the other way around). It was like being in the middle of a scene in *A Hard Day's Night* and I was the fifth Beatle. I felt fine.

I'd quickly become a bona fide celebrity in Monterrey and I was in demand. People wanted more than just the luchador and Elizondo booked me for a personal appearance at a factory Christmas party for a cool 600 pesos (200 bucks). It was easy money and all I had to do, according to him, was show up, shake some hands, kiss some babies, and I'd be on my merry way. It was a much better deal than wrestling in front of seven people in Bimby, Alberta.

I got to the factory and went to the party area. Streamers and balloons were taped to a bunch of tables, all of them facing the stage at the end of the room. I asked where the signing area was and was surprised when I was told there wouldn't be one. This was going to be easier than I thought!

But when a lady introduced herself and said she was my translator for the speech, the night got a whole lot harder. "Speech?"

"Yes. You'll need to have your speech on ecology translated for the kids, won't you?"

That's when I found out that Elizondo had booked me at the party to give a speech to the kids on the importance of ECOLOGY. I didn't know anything about Mexico or anything about Spanish and I sure as hell didn't know anything about ecology! I walked on stage and faced a bunch of kids wearing Santa hats staring at me with expectant looks on their faces. They had no clue who I was and were wondering what the hell I was going to say.

So was I.

I walked up to the podium and said "Hola," the only Spanish word I knew. I followed up in English with "We are gathered here today," and it just went downhill from there, as the translator repeated my every word in Spanish. Considering that I had no idea what I was saying I can only imagine what *she* was translating my words into.

"We all know that ecology is very important to the world today. It's very important to love the trees because trees are our friends," I pontificated wisely.

"His mother likes bananas," the translator translated.

The kids stared at me with faces as blank as the Vote For Pedro guy. The parents whispered to each other in the back of the room, probably asking one another, "What is this jack-off talking about?"

I continued: "Make sure that you don't chop the trees down. Don't use a lot of paper, and don't use gas-guzzling cars when you're old enough to drive."

"He worked a match in exchange for a hot dog and an orange juice," the translator continued.

I finished off with a Feliz Navidad, and smiled broadly. A cricket chirped. A tumbleweed blew by. A child picked his nose. I walked off the stage and signed autographs for a mob of six kids. When I got my 600 pesos, I smiled and said thanks to the people in charge. They said the Spanish equivalent of "Whatever" and walked away in silence. I counted the cash and decided if even one of those kids became a future car-pooler, my speech was not in vain.

Our next match was in a small town outside Monterrey called Matamoros. The arena in Matamoros was straight out of the movie *Bloodsport*: dark and dingy and surrounded by a fence of chicken wire that separated the fans from the ring. During the matches, the fans held on to the chicken wire and pushed it in and out like rabid wolverines. It was a real-life Scorpions video.

The ring was a boxing ring that had absolutely no give and was not made for bumping. My opponent, an American named Fabuloso Blondy, warned me that we wouldn't be able to do much of anything during the match. I figured he was just being lazy and called a hip toss. He ran off the ropes saying "Fuck that," and hip-tossed me instead. When I landed on what felt like concrete, I nearly pooped my pants. No shit. We did nothing but exchange holds after that. It wasn't worth the money we were making to blow out our O rings in this dumpy town. Not to mention that we got ripped off by the promoter anyway.

After the match I was covered in dust and grime from the filthy ring and I wanted to clean up. I changed my mind when I saw that the shower was a garden hose stuck in the back of a toilet tank. A guy had sucked on the end until a lonely flow of water trickled out. I threw up in my mouth a little because even though the water wasn't out of the actual bowl, where I come from toilet water is toilet water.

The biggest star in the country at the time was

another Canadian named Vampiro Canadiense. Everywhere you looked you saw the image of the vampire wrestler with the Alice Cooper makeup and the long red and blue braided hair. At his peak he was the Mexican equivalent of Hulk Hogan or Steve Austin. He'd arrived in Mexico just as lucha libre had exploded with increased TV exposure and he had ridden the boom to superstardom. There were Vampiro dolls, T-shirts, comic books, chocolate bars, soap bars, singles bars, everything.

So when it was announced that he was coming to Monterrey to challenge the heavyweight champion, Black Magic, for the title, the city went wild with anticipation.

The Monumental sold out quickly, but on the day of the show Vampiro showed up at the airport on crutches. He had suffered some sort of injury and couldn't work that night. Elizondo needed a suitable replacement and he picked me. It was ironic because when I first arrived in Monterrey, Elizondo had toyed with the idea of calling me Vampiro Americano to try to cash in on Vamp's popularity. A few years later, he gave the name to a Dallas-based wrestler named John Layfield, who went on to become WWE champion JBL.

Black Magic was an American from Florida named Norman Smiley, who was thrilled to be working with another foreigner and was quite responsive to my ideas. I called most of the match even though he was more experienced than me. He ended up holding my tights to win the third fall, but even though he had beaten me, Magic gave me my first great match in Mexico. The fans went loco when I beat him in the first fall and as the match progressed they started to believe that this hot young upstart could win the title. The champ took me to a different level by allowing me to hang with him and I'm still grateful for that. He could've telephoned in his performance against the nobody and sandbagged me but Magic worked his ass off to make me look like a superstar.

When I walked back to the dressing room, Elizondo congratulated me by giving me my pay envelope containing $1,000. It was a Mexican tradition to receive a double payoff for a title match and I was shocked to have made that much money for one match. The next person to congratulate me was Vampiro, but he didn't seem very sincere. Later on at the Cuatro Milpas, he took me aside to give me advice on how to survive in Mexico. He said that all of the Mexican wrestlers were jealous of me and that I couldn't trust anyone.

"But you can trust me. I really want to help you make it here." Then he told me if I wanted to make it big, I needed to start wearing a different outfit.

"I know this country and I know what the people want. If you wore a loincloth, you'd be huge." Aside from the fact that if I wore a loincloth people would know I wasn't that huge, his advice didn't make any sense. If a loincloth was what was needed to make it big in Mexico, than why the fuck wasn't he wearing one? A loincloth would destroy my credibility and make a fool out of me. Maybe that's what he wanted. It seemed that he didn't like the fact that I had rocked the Plaza that night with a great match. As big a star as he was, he was jealous that there was a new kid in town.

I walked over to Mike, who was getting the cold shoulder from Konnan and Love Machine, two other massively popular foreigners who'd worked that night for a rival company. Konnan had long braided cornrows and Love

Machine (whose real name was Art Barr) held a cup of chewing tobacco spit in his hand that he—Phbbt—kept adding to constantly. They both grunted a cursory greeting and moved on, ignoring me.

Besides Mike and Magic, was every foreigner in this country a jerk?

At least the natives treated us well, especially the girls. Mike and I were experiencing different female representatives of the fine city on a nightly basis. One night we ended up at a Señor Frog's on the night of the Monterrey Arm Wrestling Championship and, as local celebrities, we got front-row seats. After a grueling tournament a winner was crowned. He turned his attention to the two of us and started babbling in an aggressive manner.

One of the girls informed us that he was issuing an arm wrestling challenge. In the same way that every war in history has started, the girls batted their boobs and my machismo took over. I stepped forward and the patrons of the bar began chanting my name.

As the sounds of "León!" washed over me, I sat across from the champ and locked grips. This guy didn't know about Scott Norton's secret trick . . . but I did. I beat that bad boy in about thirty seconds and became the new Arm Wrestling Champion of Monterrey. I was doused in beer by the elated patrons like I'd just won the Stanley Cup. I was given a little tin trophy that said CAMPEÓN, which I gave to one of the girls the next morning.

Despite the available women that were seemingly on twenty-four-hour call, I was still a virgin. I guess I took Paul Stanley's advice about leaving the women behind a little too literally. Don't get me wrong: I'd had my dalliances, but because of my Christian beliefs I hadn't done any full-fledged shagging. But when I met Raquel the temptation was just too much to resist. She was a Modelo girl, which was like a Budweiser girl, and her picture was on posters all over Mexico. She had the classic Latina body, built like J-Lo, with long black hair and a gorgeous face.

I met her at a party after the matches and you could cut the attraction with a knife. It was one of those times when you know it's on from the very first glance. In one of the most awkward situations ever, I invited her back to my hotel where Mike was sleeping in the other bed. Maybe it was the alcohol, maybe it was the nervousness, maybe it was the fact that the lights were on and Mike was pretending to sleep only a few feet away, but my first sexual performance lasted all of twenty seconds. It was quite frankly THE worst sexual performance of all time and a real waste because, like I said, Raquel was smoking hot. Here's a few words of wisdom from Uncle J: If the girl you just had sex with for the first time is giggling and patting your shoulder, it's not a good thing. Sorry Raquel—I gave it my best shot.

CHAPTER 18

THE GOAT BUS

Shortly after my short (in more ways than one) performance, Mike and I headed back to Calgary for Christmas break and I received a call at the Palkos' from a toymaker I'd met in Monterrey. His company made all of the luchador action figures and he told me that Paco Alonso, the Vince McMahon of Mexico, was interested in hiring me. Mexico City was the big time and wrestling there was a major step up the food chain. I'd hoped to work there from the moment I arrived in Monterrey.

I flew to Mexico City to meet with Paco in his office in Arena México, the oldest wrestling arena in the world. He made me a great offer and told me I could work for him as long as I wanted.

He didn't want to call me León d'Oro, as he already had a wrestler named Oro. So when he asked me if I had any other name ideas I pulled out the old standard Lion Heart. He liked it and liked the Spanish translation of Corazón de León even more. Why an English-speaking guy would have a Spanish name like Corazón de León, while a Spanish-speaking guy like Silver King had an English name made no sense, but who was I to judge?

Paco said he was going to book me on shows with veteran wrestler Hector Guerrero, so Hector could help me learn the ropes of surviving and getting by in Mexico. Hector was a member of Mexico's most famous wrestling family, sired by Gory Guerrero, one of the greatest luchadores ever. I'd also heard a lot about Hector's younger brother Eddy, who was making a worldwide name for himself, and along with Chris Benoit was one of the guys I hoped to pattern my career after. I looked forward to meeting and wrestling him.

Paco put me up at the Plaza Madrid, a high-end hotel in the middle of the city, and Hector made a point of introducing me to all of the other guys who were staying there, including my old chewing tobacco buddy Art Barr.

Art was much friendlier now that we were neighbors. He also almost got me fired on my first night, when he took me leather jacket shopping and caused me to be ninety minutes late for my Empressa Mexicana de Lucha Libre debut. I finally arrived at the Arena Coliseo and entered into the new world of the EMLL locker room.

The Coliseo had been owned by the Alonso family for decades and it looked it. The dirty, humid dressing room was on the second floor, lined with ceramic tiles that were as smudged and greasy as some of the guys walking on them. Some of the other luchadores were sitting around in the nude, smoking and drinking whiskey straight from the bottle. Two others were going over their match, while one of them sat naked on the toilet taking a dumpski.

The toilets had no toilet seats (you had to sit directly on the porcelain bowl) and the stalls that housed them had no doors. Instead of flushing the used toilet paper down the toilet, the tissue was dropped beside the bowl building a mountain of poopy paper. I walked around looking for a place to change while all of the guys had a "who the hell is this guy" expression on their face. Right then, I figured out another reason why Paco had placed me in Hector's care: Being associated with him gave me credibility in the locker room. Hector was adamant about introducing me to every member of the roster from top to bottom. I shook the hand of every person in the locker room and to not do so would have been a cardinal wrestling sin. It's a tradition that must be followed in every wrestling locker room at every level in every country.

As we discussed our match with our opponents Hector changed into his Lasser-Tron outfit, which made him look like a red and blue piñata. But his costume was nothing compared to the guy who was wearing what appeared to be a Tony the Tiger costume. He was sporting a complete head-to-toe furry bodysuit of orange and black tiger stripes and looked completely ricockulous. His name was Felino and, to his credit, he was very agreeable to all of my suggestions once Hector translated them. As a matter of fact, he was Grrrrrrrrreat.

We were in the semi-main event and for some reason my entrance music was "Everybody Dance Now" by C&C Music Factory. There were about 5,000 seats in the Coliseo arranged in tiers that went straight up like an upside-down wedding cake. The fans sat in sections according to their affiliations holding homemade signs that said, "Sección de Rudos" (Bad Guys Section) and "Sección de Técnicos" (Good Guys Section). The fans dueled each other with chants of "Arriba los rudos!" countered by "Arriba los técnicos!"

I worked mostly with Felino, who seemed to understand my style and worked hard for me during the match. He was a member of the Casas family, who were famous for being great luchadores, and I had the feeling that Paco had asked Felino to make me look good—which he did.

The match culminated with my huge swan dive over the top rope onto Felino. The crowd responded with a huge cheer and I think they were surprised that a pretty-boy gringo with long blond hair could actually wrestle the way I did.

The next day, a big picture of me doing the dive appeared in *Afición* and *Ovaciones*, newspapers in Mexico City that boasted millions of readers. Fans all over the country read the reporters' opinions that my debut had been a success. When the lucha magazines filled with my pictures arrived on the stands later that week, I officially became a national star.

My schedule filled up instantly and a typical week saw me working in Guadalajara on Sunday, Naucalpan on Monday, Puebla on Tuesday, Acapulco on Wednesday, Cuernavaca on Thursday, and Mexico City on Friday and Saturday. There were so many shows across the country that I was working as many as ten matches a week, including four matches on Saturdays.

I was twenty-two years old and making three or four grand a week with no expenses. But I was working hard for my money. I had to travel to the shows by bus and while some of the lines offered first-class service, most of them didn't. So I had to make the four-to six-hour trips on glorified school buses.

Even when all of the seats were filled it didn't stop the bus driver from picking up other passengers. We'd be driving down the highway in the dark in the middle of nowhere and the driver would pull over on the dirt shoulder whenever any Tom, Dick, or Javier waved him down for a ride. People would get on the bus with dogs, cats, goats, chickens, and once even a parrot that wouldn't stop squawking in Spanish. The seats and the aisles of the goat bus would be full of people chattering, animals barking, baying, clucking and I would be wondering what the hell I was doing.

"Vaya con Dios . . . SQUAWK . . . "

While I had learned decent Spanish from watching Spanish language TV shows (*Sábado Gigante* rules) and having various girls teach me, I still couldn't pronounce Irvine in a way that people could understand. So the name on my bus ticket went from Chris Irbo to Chris Irbin to Chris Ririn, until I gave up and started calling myself José Sánchez. It saved a lot of hassle for both me and the ticket sellers.

In the meantime, I was learning the art of lucha libre and the man I learned the most from was Negro Casas. Negro was known as the Ric Flair of Mexico and one of the best wrestlers in Mexican history. He was from the same famous lucha family as Felino and was one of the smartest performers I've ever worked with. He was the perfect example of a guy who got over (wrestling vernacular for being popular with the fans) because he knew exactly what his audience wanted to see. He knew his people. He was so good that all the fans respected him and knew he was the best no matter what role he was playing. When he was a rudo (and he was the best rudo in the country) I had the feeling that people booed him just because they were supposed to and not because they really hated him. But he was the master of working a crowd and always had them in the palm of his hand. With a simple gesture or facial expression he could make them cheer or boo at the drop of a peso.

Negro taught me when to do a certain move and when not to. He taught me timing, how to use the crowd's reactions as a blueprint for the match, and how not to get frazzled when things went wrong. "Nobody knows it's a mistake unless you let them know," he said in his broken English.

He also taught me not to obsess about a match if it didn't work out the way I wanted it to. "Don't worry when you have a bad match, tomorrow there will be another one. Are you going to worry about the match that's in the past or are you going to do better tomorrow? Tomorrow, this match doesn't mean anything." His point was that you can't change the past, you can only learn from your mistakes and make the future better. I still live my life (both in and out of the ring) by that philosophy.

CHAPTER 17

AN EMBARRASSING WAY TO DIE

A lot of American wrestling experts feel that luchadores aren't actual wrestlers because of their unorthodox style. Nothing could be further from the truth. Some of the wrestlers in the EMLL were the best in the world. Aside from Negro, performers such as Dr. Wagner Jr., Emilio Charles Jr., and el Dandy were tremendous. The tag team of Los Cowboys, Texano and Silver King (aka Ramses from *Nacho Libre*), were two more of my favorites. They worked a stiff fast-moving, Japanese-Mexican hybrid style, which was different from what most of the other luchadores were doing.

The first time I worked with them they nailed me with every kick and punch and I thought they were fucking with me. After a few more matches against them, I realized that that's just how they worked and they expected to be hit the same way in return. That made them different from the other luchadores, who worked pretty light, which is one of the criticisms that people within the business have of lucha libre. But the marquee names in the EMLL were top-level major-league performers and the more I worked with them the better I got.

I also got better at living in Mexico City. The hardest part was getting acclimated to the altitude and the pollution. The city was high above sea level and engulfed in smog for most of the year, which made breathing difficult. It sat in a valley and during certain times of year when there was no rain or wind, the smog would settle in like a fog, which caused me countless nosebleeds and irritation.

But natural disasters like poisonous air and earthquakes weren't the worst dangers I'd face in Mexico. The biggest danger came courtesy of another human being.

One of my favorite restaurants in the country was VIP's, a diner similar to Denny's that served tremendous American-style food. I was eating my favorite dinner of a steak sandwich with a fruit plate, when I noticed a really cute girl staring at me from across the crowded room. I waved at her and she beckoned me to come over to the table she was sitting at with another guy. She spoke decent English and admitted that she and her brother (bonus!) were fans of mine. We spoke for a few minutes and she asked me if I wanted to go to a party with them. Did I? She was a knockout and I wanted to rock with her big time, so I accepted immediately. I played big shot and paid for their meals, then got into their car and left.

Her brother was driving and I was in the back seat with Ingrid and we were getting to know each other's tonsils. The scenery began to get darker and more desolate the farther we went, so I asked Ingrid's brother where the party was. He simply replied, "Está bien," (it's okay) as Ingrid poked her tongue into my mouth again. Even though she was a great kisser, I started to get the bad feeling that maybe there was no party. My suspicions were confirmed when we pulled over on the side of the barren road. When Ingrid's brother got out of the car, came around to my window, and calmly pulled a gun on me, I literally almost pissed my pants.

Ever had a gun pulled on you? Trust me when I say that it's the coldest, most helpless feeling you could ever have. Your life lies completely in another person's hands and there's not a damn thing you can do about it.

"Get out of the car," he said in perfectly clear English.

I slowly got out, cursing my stupidity for putting myself in that position. He switched back to Spanish and said, "Take your money and put it on the roof of the car."

I never carried around much money in case I got robbed, but I gave him what I had. He put the few hundred pesos into his pocket and pointed the gun directly into my face. It was going to end for me on a darkened road in a foreign country. It was an embarrassing way to die and the worst part of it was that nobody even knew where I was. All I could think of was my poor mom.

He stared directly into my eyes and I stared directly into the barrel of his gun. It was so close that I could see the grooves inside, like at the beginning of a James Bond movie. The seconds seemed like hours, his stare never wavering, until he lowered the gun with a smirk, got back into the car, and drove away. I saw Ingrid laughing at me as they sped past on the dirt road and my only thought was, "That bitch robbed me and I just bought her dinner."

With the taste of her lipstick still in my mouth, I breathed a sigh of relief that my brains weren't spattered all over the countryside. But I was still on the darkened outskirts of one of the most dangerous cities in the world; a gringo who had no money and couldn't speak Spanish. I also had no clue where I was. It might've been easier if the guy had shot me.

A pair of scrawny dogs joined me as I walked toward the faint glow in the sky that I assumed came from the lights of the city. After about an hour of hoofing it, I waved down a passing taxi. When the driver slowed down enough to see me, he sped up and left me hanging. A gringo walking down a deserted road in the dead of night? I wouldn't have picked me up either.

I walked for another hour until finally another taxi driver risked his life to pick me up. When we finally got to the Plaza, I had to borrow money from the doorman to pay for my ride.

The moral of the story is twofold:

1. Don't pick up strange women at restaurants.
2. Don't pay for their dinners if you do.

I learned another lesson the hard way when I drank Mexican tap water. I was constantly careful to only drink sealed bottled water, but I made the mistake of drinking a bottle of unsealed water in the dressing room in Guadalajara. It was common for the vendors to refill empty bottles with tap water and resell them unsealed. A few minutes after I drank it, there was a knock on the door.

"Mr. Jericho, meet Monty Zuma."

It was the shits.

I began to feel the effects as soon as I boarded the plane back to Mexico City: The moment I sat down, I felt some gurgling. We got stuck behind another plane waiting to take off so I wasn't allowed to get up to go to the bathroom. Then as we sped up for the takeoff, the pilot slammed on the brakes at about 100 miles an hour. I flew forward, snapped back into the seat, and promptly filled my pants.

I looked out the window, whilst squirming in my soiled chair and noticed that the cargo door had snapped open and a bunch of bags had fallen out of the hold onto the runway. Of course mine was one of them. My bag had bounced across the runway and settled into a puddle of mud . . . similar to the one that currently resided in the pants of the mighty Chris Jericho.

At least Hector Guerrero didn't have a problem hanging out with Poopypants Jericho and wanted to introduce me to his brother Eddy, who had just returned from a tour of Japan. Eddy's reputation as a great wrestler and a great person preceded him. If he was anything like his brother, I had a feeling we would get along great right off the bat.

We didn't.

When I walked into Hector's room, I found Eddy sprawled upon the bed wearing only his underwear. He looked like I thought he would: little mustache, big arms, big shoulders, big back, and big mullet. But he didn't act like I thought he would. The first words out of his mouth to me were, "Who the fuck do you think you are?"

I wasn't sure how to answer that.

Then with a sneer, he asked me what my name was. I was confused, as Hector had just introduced me as Chris

Jericho, so I thought he was asking me what my wrestling name was.

"I wrestle as Corazón de León. It's Spanish for Lion Heart."

He said disgustedly, "I'm Mexican . . . I know what Corazón de León means." He followed with, "What are you, some kind of mark? I don't mean your wrestling name. I mean your real name."

A mark is a term for a fan or for a wrestler who believes in his own hype and isn't exactly a term of endearment.

I reiterated to him that my name was Chris (too) and assured him that I was not a mark. He grunted a few more choice words for me under his breath, rolled over, and went to sleep. Eddy Guerrero, supposed sweetheart, had turned out to be a complete ass.

When I saw him at breakfast the next day, he instantly apologized to me. When I asked him what for, he said, "For whatever I said or did last night. I'm not sure exactly what it was, but I figured I should apologize." I laughed at his honesty and his complete change of character. I accepted his apology and it was the start of a friendship that would last until his death twelve years later.

My link to the Guerrero family continued when Paco informed me I was going to be winning the NWA middle-weight title. Eddy and Hector's father, Gory, had been one of the first men to wear the belt some fifty years earlier. Subsequently, the title had been held by some of the biggest names in Mexican wrestling history. Now it was my turn and I wanted to take the title with a brand-new move I'd been working on. My idea was to do a splash from the top rope with a full 360 degree spin in midair. It was both acrobatic and unique and I was ready to debut it that night.

I was warming up in the dressing room before the match with the champion, Mano Negra. I wanted to do the spin a few more times to prepare, so I went into the bathroom for some privacy. I jumped up and spun around on the spot a few times and decided I needed more rotation. But as I jumped again, I slipped on some water on the floor and landed ribs first on the side of a sharp corner of the sink. I fell to the ground with the wind knocked out of me and gasping for air, while my ring music pounded throughout the building. I dragged myself out of the bathroom and down the backstage hallway. I felt like barfing as I lurched to the ring as a knitting needle stabbed me in the side every time I took a breath. However, once the match started, I managed to get through to the finish.

I executed my brand-new maneuver—which looked like shit—and won the title. But even though I was a babyface, the people began to boo. The patriotic Mexican fans didn't like the idea of a gringo winning a championship from one of their own, no matter how much they hated Mano Negra. As popular as I was, some fans were never going to fully accept me because I was a foreigner.

Some of the office employees didn't want to accept me either. The first time I wrestled in Guadalajara, I received an amazing reaction from the fans who'd never seen me before. But the referee, of all people, had an attitude toward me and didn't seem to want me there. This was proved correct when I got in the ref's face during the course of the match and instead of backing down as a ref should, he slapped me in the face. I was furious but I finished the match like a professional.

Afterward, I stormed into the dressing room and confronted the son of a bitch. To my surprise, he slapped me again. I had alls I could takes and I couldn't takes no more, so I tackled him and paintbrushed him from the mount. He was a small, wiry guy in his mid-fifties and it was like trying to hold down a greased pig. Finally the boys pulled me off him. I was completely embarrassed, but all of my frustrations of being a stranger in a strange land boiled over when this dick had taken advantage of me.

In Canada, I learned how to wrestle. In Mexico, I learned how to be a star. But as big of a star as I was, I was still an outsider.

CHAPTER 18

CORAZÓN DE POLLO

After my grueling fight with a fifty-year-old man, I needed some R & R. Hector had driven his car to Mexico from Texas, so he, Eddy, and I decided to check out the ancient Mayan Sun and Moon pyramids, a mere three hours' drive from Mexico City.

It was surreal to stand beside the massive structures (built by aliens I'm sure), and feeling the life-force of countless beings that had stood where I was standing thousands of years earlier. There were still bloodstains on the altar of sacrifice on the Sun Pyramid. But as eerie as it was, there was only so much you could do at the pyramids before you got bored. So when we walked the steps of the Moon Pyramid, we decided that it was only apropos to drop our pants and hang a moon. It's a wonder why the rest of the world thinks that Americans are idiots, isn't it?

It was always a relief to return to the Plaza where I could blow off steam with the other outsiders who dwelled there. Our gang had been joined by another gringo that I knew from watching the AWA years before, King Haku.

After the AWA, he'd gone on to become a star in the WWE and had even been a tag team champion with Andre the Giant. Haku was huge, standing 6 foot 3 and weighing over 300 pounds, but he was one of the kindest men I've ever met, with a heart of pure gold. We both worked for Paco, so we saw each other almost on a daily basis and bonded quickly.

Haku's real name was Tonga UliUli Fifita and he was from the isle of Tonga in the South Pacific. When people asked him questions about his background it usually turned into an Abbott and Costello routine.

"What's your name?"

"Tonga."

"Where are you from?"

"Tonga."

"So, what's your name?"

"Tonga."

"But where are you from?"

"TONGA! My name is Tonga and I'm from Tonga! Get it?"

Tonga started his career as a sumo wrestler in Japan before making a name for himself in the States. He was the first major WWF star I'd met and I deluged him with countless questions about working for Vince McMahon.

"When you were in the WWF, who made your costumes for you?"

"Do you have to come up with your name or does Vince McMahon?"

"Do you have to pay for your own plane tickets?"

"Do you wear boxers or briefs?"

Tonga finally snapped. "Why do you ask me so many questions? Stop asking so many questions. You're like a child!"

I started to weep.

The first show we were booked on together was in Acapulco and since we were in the main event, we convinced the promoter to fly us in. That saved us from another of Marlin Perkinez' *Wild Kingdom* bus rides.

I arrived at the airport late for my flight, so I checked in quickly and ran through the concourse to security. When the guard asked to see the contents of my bag, I explained that I only had minutes to make my flight. He flashed a gold-toothed grin and slowly unzipped the case. He pulled out a tube of toothpaste and asked me what it was. When I told him it was a tube of toothpaste, he said he didn't believe me. I looked at my watch and saw my flight was leaving in ten minutes. He examined my deodorant and my gonch (sicko). Then he found my title belt and mockingly placed it around his waist, doing a little jig for his fellow guards. He was obviously fucking with me and I lost my cool.

Maybe it was because I was a luchador, maybe it was because I was a gringo, but it pissed me off that he was going to make me miss my flight, so I grabbed my Right Guard and threw it at the Wrong Guard. I started swearing and throwing a temper tantrum, which was the worst thing to do and I knew it but I couldn't help it. I was digging my own grave and I'd gone too far to turn back. In mid-tirade I felt a hand on my back, so I turned around and gave its owner a solid push to the chest, causing her to fall down.

That's right . . . HER.

I'd shoved a female guard and she'd fallen hard to the floor. "Oh shit . . . here we go," I thought.

The guards surrounded me, shouting in Spanish. It was like something out of a bad Van Damme movie (was there ever a good Van Damme movie?) as the platoon advanced toward me. I had no idea what I was going to do, when suddenly in the distance I heard a deep voice yelling, "HEY! WHAT'S GOING ON DERE?"

I turned to look and I've never in my life been so happy to see a 300-pound Tongan. Tonga entered the fray and immediately pawed two of the cops out of his way. When another guard got in his face, he lifted the guy off the ground by his jacket. Pancho's feet were kicking in midair just like Darth Vader's first victim in the beginning of *Star Wars*. Moments later Tonga and I were back to back like gunfighters in the O.K. Corral. Then for the second time in my life I had a gun pulled on me, this time by an airport policeman.

The guards marched us through the concourse while travelers stared at us like we were a pair of criminals, which at that point we were. They left us in a little room with no chairs or windows so we sat on the floor and discussed how things got out of control so quickly. After about an hour, an official-looking guy in a suit came in and spoke to us in perfect English.

"I want you to tell me what happened."

I told him step by step what went down and how sorry I was. I also told him that Tonga was only trying to help and was not at fault. I explained that we were stressed out but loved living and working in Mexico and felt blessed that we were able to support our families from the money we made in his beautiful country. It was a desperate ass kissing, but I was a desperate (yet still sexy) man.

He told us that he was the manager of the airport and noted that besides my overreacting and a little pushing and shoving, nothing that terrible had happened.

"I could have you charged with assault, but that won't be necessary as long as you tip the security guards," he explained very seriously.

Tonga and I looked at each other and read between the lines. When you're facing the threat of being charged with a felony, the difference between a tip and a bribe blurs considerably. We pooled our resources and gave the guy about 1,000 pesos (350 bucks). He pocketed the cash and assured us that the guards would be quite happy, although I'll bet you a Gerardo record that those guards never saw one peso of our tip. Then he opened the door but before we could leave he asked us for autographs for his kids.

The comedy never ends.

Tonga and I hung out a lot afterward and I found it frustrating that whenever we went anywhere, he always paid the bill. Tonga had trained to wrestle in Japan, and it was a tradition that the veteran paid for the rookie. When Tonga was a young boy (*kohai*), his mentor (*sempai*) paid for him and now he was carrying on the tradition. I respected Tonga for his accomplishments, his demeanor, and his treatment of others and I would have taken a bullet for him. I learned from him to respect those who came into the business before me and to teach that same respect to those who came into the business after me.

Tonga also taught me that a Canadian could never outdrink a Tongan, no matter how hard I tried. One night after drinking mescal (which tastes like a dirty ashtray) until five in the morning, I stumbled into my room and passed out on the floor. I was awakened two hours later by

Tonga hammering on my door, wanting to go do aerobics. I ignored him for as long as I could but when he didn't go away I was forced to get physical. When we arrived at the gym, Tonga stopped aerobicising after five minutes but encouraged/threatened me to continue for the rest of the session. He was too loaded to argue with . . . come to think of it, so was I. When the class ended we were the only two people left in the studio. We stank so bad as the stench of day-old booze emanated out of our pores that everyone else had left, including the teacher.

May 1993. My first piece of merchandise. The guy who made and sold the bootleg shirts outside of Arena México wouldn't give me a free one, so I had to buy the damn thing myself.

While I needed work on my jazzercising, my in-ring persona was developing nicely. It was fun being a técnico but I enjoyed it when crowds turned on me from time to time. I found it easier being a rudo because it's a lot harder to make people like you than it is to make them hate you. A simple scowl or a cocky walk to the ring was all you needed to be rewarded with a chorus of boos and a pelting of garbage.

I learned this from watching Negro Casas, the best heel in Mexico. He taught me that a heel should always cheat and take the easy way out of a situation. His theory was that a rudo was a coward at heart.

The theory worked too well when I had a championship match against a small but technically skilled wrestler named el Dandy in Acapulco. The arena was stiflingly humid and I was drenched in sweat before I even left the dressing room. I worked the match as grimy and dirty as I felt. The crowd was in a frenzy after I won the first fall by hoofing Dandy in the frijoles behind the referee's back and pinning him with one foot on his chest. While the fans barraged me with garbage, I saw a commotion in the front row as a bunch of security guards dragged a guy out of the arena.

"Chinga Tu Madre," I yelled after him in defiance, happy to know that I'd done such a great job of being an asshole that this guy had tried to jump over the rail. The crowd responded by chanting "Corazón de Pollo!" (Heart of a Chicken), which earned points for originality.

Despite my evil tactics, Dandy won the next two falls and retained his title. I scuttled back toward the dressing room in shame while threatening a little kid in the front row (the same way that Fatwell had done to me a decade earlier), when I was hit in the side of the head and mouth by a plastic cup filled with beer. Then a rancid smell hit me and I realized that the fluid in the cup wasn't beer—it was urine. And it was warm.

I was sitting in the dressing room covered in piss, when Dandy returned from the ring with one of the security guards.

"You remember that big commotion in the crowd after the first fall?" he asked. "The reason the guards took the guy out of the arena was because he was heading toward you with a gun."

For those keeping track at home, that was the third time a gun had been pulled on me during my sojourn in scenic Mexico.

How much did someone have to hate me to want to shoot me because of a wrestling match? For that matter, how much did someone have to hate me to pull out their wiener in a public place and throw a cup of fresh piss at me?

By the way, did you know that pee tastes salty?

Thankfully I was tasting success along with pee pee. As a result a plethora of Corazón de León merchandise had hit the market, including trading cards, balloons, clocks, official T-shirts, bootleg T-shirts (I had to buy one from the bootlegger when he refused to give me a freebie), and a comic book that saw me having adventures with the assistance of a magical talking frog. I was on the cover of every wrestling magazine (there were over a dozen at the time) and receiving critical acclaim. I was honored when *Arena* magazine, the most prestigious lucha magazine in Mexico, voted Corazón de León and Ultimo Dragón vs. Negro Casas and el

Dandy the match of the year for 1993. I was awestruck, as there were thousands of matches in Mexico every year. The match had been almost an hour long and was a breeze since all four of us had similar styles and attitudes. Our only goal was to make the other guy look good and we did.

There was a Mexican tradition that when the crowd felt they had seen something special, they would throw money into the ring. After our match Negro began to encourage the crowd and a domino effect occurred. Soon the entire ring was littered with bills and change. We split it among the four of us along with the two referees who were assigned to the match. It was a nice pat on the back and getting hit with a handful of cash was much more pleasant than getting hit with a cupful of piss.

Another lucha tradition was settling major feuds with a mask vs. mask match, where the loser would have to unmask for good. For wrestlers who didn't wear a mask, hair vs. hair matches, where the loser shaved his head, were just as popular. When I was booked in my first hair match, the possibility of me losing my trademark blond mane became a big draw.

The angle started when a trio of wrestlers called the Cavernícolas (the Cavemen) attacked me, leading to me beating two of them and challenging the third to a hair vs. hair match.

A loud crowd of 8,000 fans filed into Arena México on a Sunday afternoon three weeks later to see me shave the fat bastard bald.

It was the first time I was ever involved in a multi-week story line and it was rewarding watching the crowd grow week after week as the story built. The Cavernícolas weren't a big act on their own, but the cliff-hanger angle made them into an attraction, teaching me that with the right push even an average performer could be made into a star and draw a crowd.

CHAPTER 19

HALCION BOWLING

I was working a crazy schedule and when I had a rare day off I liked to chill out by listening to music and reading a book on the roof of the Plaza. It was a solitary, peaceful place to collect my thoughts and get some alone time. So I was disappointed when I went to the roof one afternoon and found Art Barr, the Chewing Tobacco Kid, already there. I was jealous that another person knew about my private sanctuary.

We knew each other a little but weren't exactly best friends, so the meeting was a little awkward at the start. Our conversation was stilted until we spotted a guy nailing a chick from behind in the window of the building directly across from us. The girl had massive guns (and probably weighed about 250 pounds) that were squishing up against the glass with each thrust. The guy finally noticed us mid-coitus, gave us the finger, and closed the drapes. We started howling with laughter and if there was ever a better icebreaker in history, I'd like to hear it.

Art and I started hanging out on our days off and

one day he called me to ask if I wanted to check out a movie set. WWF Hall of Famer Rowdy Roddy Piper was in Mexico shooting the movie *Immortal Combat* (Oscar winner for the best picture of 1994) and was good friends with Art from his days wrestling for Art's dad in Oregon. Piper invited him to come hang out on the set and Art invited me.

We both ended up getting cast in the greatest movie ever. Art landed a role as a waiter and I landed a role as a punching bag. Martial arts legend Sonny Chiba played Piper's nemesis and was filming a scene where he got into a brawl with a group of toughs, one of whom was me. As we shot the fight scene over and over, Chiba's endurance started to poop out. He was really good at pulling his punches and kicks during the first few takes but by the tenth take, he was kicking the shit out of me.

When the movie was finally released directly on video I wasn't listed in the credits. As a matter of fact, unless you paused the flick at the exact right spot you wouldn't even see my face. If you did, you'd see my nose and a bunch of hair flying around for two frames. But I looked sexy and it was a screen debut on par with Haley Joel Osment in *The Sixth Sense*.

A few days later when Art came up to my room to tell me how awesome Piper thought he (not both of us) had done in the movie, I couldn't figure why he'd brought a little kid with him.

Art made me uncomfortable as he swore and talked his typical shit in front of this child, who couldn't have been more than ten years old. The kid looked like Chicken Little, about five feet tall and weighing no more than 130 pounds, standing silent with a big perma-smile on his face. I almost had a heart attack when Art pulled out a joint and asked me for a light.

"What are you doing, man? Not in front of the kid! Why are you hanging out with him in the first place?"

Art laughed and explained that the kid was actually eighteen years old and was a wrestler. I looked at his scrawny build and thought, "Bless his tiny heart . . . he doesn't stand a chance."

I asked to see some ID and when he showed it to me, he said in perfect English, "I'm a fan of your work and I'm looking forward to wrestling you someday."

I nodded and thought that the kid would be lucky to carry my ring jacket, let alone work with me. But I ended up working with him dozens of times when he became Rey Mysterio Jr., the greatest high-flyer of all time.

Art and I invented the stupidest sport of all time when we created Halcion Bowling. Halcions are sleeping pills that work very well if you take them with the intention of sleeping. But if you took one and stayed awake, you ended up stumbling and mumbling around like you were drunk. We rounded up Eddy, Tonga, Black Magic, Mike Lozanski, Miguel Pérez, José Estrada, and a pair of twins known as the Headhunters who were distinguished by the master marketing names of Headhunter A and Headhunter B. We downed our Halcions and had the worst bowling game in recorded history. It featured such highlights as Eddy getting a strike by walking down the lane and rolling the ball six inches away from the pins, Tonga getting a strike by rifling the ball into a different lane, and me getting a strike when I fell down the stairs and knocked over two rows of stacked chairs.

When I wasn't falling on my face like Kramer at a

comedy club I was inventing signature moves. In 1993, using a moonsault (a top rope back flip into a splash) was not a common move like it is today. I'd seen it done on a Japanese wrestling tape by the Great Muta and stole it to use in Mexico. When other guys began using it, I wanted to come up with a different variation.

I called Lenny to ask him for ideas and he said, "Have you ever thought about doing the moonsault from the middle rope?"

The idea had come to him in a dream and I asked him to elaborate. He explained that if I used the middle rope to do the moonsault across the ring, it could be done quicker with less setup and would be totally unique. It was just what I was looking for.

So I went to Arena México during the day and practiced my new creation in front of 17,000 empty seats. I filled a duffel bag with dirty clothes and used it as my target. After a dozen practice runs, I figured out how far the guy had to be from the ropes so I wouldn't land with my knees in his face.

The next night I slammed Negro Casas exactly four paces from the ropes and performed the Lionsault for the very first time. I used it almost every night afterward for the next twelve years.

It's an acrobatic move and because the ropes in the Mexican rings were always either too loose or too tight, doing the Lionsault every night was a risk. So in addition to my nightly pre-match prayer, I decided to try and stay on God's good side by doing good deeds. Whenever I pulled up in the taxi to the Arena México stage door, there were always a lot of kids hanging around asking to carry my bag, so they could get inside the arena and see the show for free. I admired their ingenuity and let a different kid carry the bag each night.

It was a tough life for the poor kids in Mexico and it used to break my heart to see them begging with their dirty faces and sad eyes on every street corner in the Zona Rosa. Zona Rosa was a hip section of the downtown area filled with restaurants, record stores, and movie theaters. It was also filled with the smell of sewage and boasted rats the size of small cats that I saw out of the corner of my eye. I wasn't sure just how big, until one of them ran across Magic's sandal-covered foot one day.

I had a soft spot for the kids and frequently gave them decent amounts of money. That changed one day when I saw all of them gathered around an older man, giving him the money they'd collected. The kids belonged to a begging syndicate and this guy sent them out all over the city (like in *Oliver!*), collected the cash, and gave the kids a percentage. They were probably making more money than I was.

As soon as kids in Mexico were old enough, they were expected to contribute to the income of their household. Everywhere you looked you saw kids working: washing windows and selling gum at traffic lights, peddling fruit from carts on the street, performing dance routines or playing music for change.

I was strolling through a park in the center of the downtown area when I came across a band of kids playing rock music. I'm not talking about a few acoustic guitars and a plastic bucket. I'm talking about a full-on professional setup. Two guitars, keyboards, bass, drums, all surrounded by stacks of monitors and amps. They were playing Black Sabbath, Deep Purple, Kiss, Rush, pure 1970s heavy metal . . . and they were amazing. When they finished the set, I went and introduced myself and found out the band was called los Leones. They were made up of four brothers and a sister ranging in age from fifteen to twenty-two. The Heredia family's sole income was made up of the change collected by los Leones after each set.

Each sibling was a virtuoso, especially Jair the lead guitarist. He was only fifteen and his guitar was almost bigger than he was, but he played like Eddie Van Halen on peyote. He broke into a huge grin when I told him that he was my new favorite Mexican guitar player. They all spoke English from listening to American music and we talked for a long time about rock 'n' roll and Mexico. When they found out that I played bass, Corazón los Leones was born.

The next day, I showed up and we jammed on "Paranoid," "Roadhouse Blues," "Domino," "Love Gun," classic songs we all knew and loved. Even though we came from different worlds and had never played together before, we threw down like seasoned vets. They announced that I was Corazón de León from Arena México and the crowd got larger as people came to check out the wrestler ruling the bass. At the end of the set the whole promenade was packed and we had to pass the hat around about a dozen times because it filled up so fast. My share of the earnings was a solid forty pesos and I've never been prouder of a payoff.

They gave me a videotape of our jam and if you watch it, you'll never see a guy with a bigger smile on his face than the one I had when we were playing. The power of music transcends everything: language, country, race.

CHAPTER
20

WHEN YOU LOSE
A BROTHER

I was walking back to the hotel after experiencing
maximum rockicity when I ran into Magic. He had
moved into a downtown apartment and invited me over
to his place to check out a new show that the WWF had
on the USA Network called *Raw*. Watching the show
while trapped in Mexico made me remember how much
I wanted to wrestle there. Mexico was a great living and
a great experience, but to me the brass ring was still
the WWF. With the stardom I'd achieved in Mexico, I
felt like I was on the path toward my ultimate goal of
working there, but I didn't have the contacts to get in
and I still didn't think I was ready yet. Yeah, my in-ring
work was improving and I had learned how to work as
both a heel and a babyface, but I hadn't developed my
own character and I hadn't done any promo work since
I left Canada. Even though my Spanish was good by
this point, lucha wasn't based around interviews like in

American wrestling. But seeing the *Raw* broadcast from the Manhattan Center in New York City reminded me what my final goal was.

As for *Raw* itself, it was edgier, slicker, and better than anything I'd seen from the WWF before. The company was putting more emphasis on smaller guys like Bret Hart and Shawn Michaels. When I saw the 1-2-3 Kid (a scrawny dude who didn't even look like he worked out) beat Razor Ramon, one of the top stars in the company, I was psyched. At that moment, I knew that the size hurdle was less of an obstacle to making it to the WWF than ever before.

It was fun going to Magic's to watch the show, except for the fact that Vampiro (the guy who suggested I wear a loincloth) was also there. The more time I spent in Mexico, the less I wanted to be around Vamp. Ever since I'd arrived in CMLL, I'd gotten a big push from the company and he didn't like it. The two of us were the main foreign babyfaces in the company, but I was no threat to him. His position as the company's biggest star hadn't changed. Even though we were both from Canada and into music, Vamp's actions showed me that he had no interest in being my bud.

- When I first got to Mexico City, he gave me his phone number and told me to call him if I ever wanted to hang out or if I needed any help. When I called, the number he'd given me belonged to an old lady named Rosa who'd never heard of any Vampiro.
- EMLL referee Roberto Rangel told me that Paco wanted to create a Canadian trio consisting of Vamp, Wild Pegasus (Benoit), and me. When Vamp heard

about the idea, he threatened to quit if Paco paired him with me.
- Marcos, the head of payroll, informed me that Vamp quizzed him weekly about how much money I was making.
- Paco called me into his office for a meeting one day and was very concerned. He asked if everything was okay and when I assured him that I loved working in Mexico, Paco confessed that Vamp had told him that I hated Mexico. He said I didn't like Mexican people, I didn't like the food, I wanted more money and a bigger push, and I was planning to walk out of the company. I informed Paco that it wasn't the case and he said, "Well that's just Vamp being Vamp."

When Vampiro wasn't trying to bury me, he was burying himself by coming up with new bullshit stories on a daily basis. Vampiro had taken a page out of Ed Langley's book by claiming:

- He'd been a bodyguard for Milli Vanilli.
- He played minor league pro hockey for the Winnipeg Warriors. When I told him I grew up in the Peg and was a huge fan of the Warriors, he suddenly remembered that it was the Moosejaw Warriors he had played for.
- He was a kung fu master.
- He was a master chef.
- He'd never watched or liked wrestling as a kid but when he went to a lucha show while on vacation in Mexico, a scout saw him and recruited him.

I've met a dozen wrestlers since who confirmed that they worked with him on shows in Canada years before he came to Mexico.

I figured out the best way to deal with him was to just ignore him like a mouthy little kid. He was a brat and I treated him as such. Whenever he started talking his Vampshit, I'd make like a tree and get out.

On the opposite side of the coin, I had become really close with Art Barr. As we spent time together, I learned more about his background. He grew up in Oregon where his father, Sandy, was a wrestler and promoter. He'd grown up in the wrestling business and had gotten a break when Roddy Piper became his mentor and got him a job in WCW. He was given the gimmick of the Juicer, based on the movie *Beetle Juice*. Sporting white makeup and crazy hair, he became very popular with kids due to his undeniable charisma.

When he left WCW, he was considered too small to work in the WWF and was floundering, until Konnan brought him into Mexico to work for Paco. When the two of them jumped to the rival AAA promotion, Art met Eddy Guerrero and formed los Gringos Locos, one of the greatest heel tag teams in Mexican history.

With his newfound success Art was forced to spend weeks, sometimes months, away from his wife and two kids. That my friend, is the worst part of the wrestling business: the constant travel that separates you from your loved ones. As great as the fame and the money are, sometimes I wonder if working at a Taco Bell and being able to tuck your kids in at night isn't a better gig.

Fortunately, all of us at the Plaza Madrid had developed into a second family for each other (or in my case a third family if you included the Palkos). We talked about our problems or our feelings and just hung out and had a great time with each other. I was close with guys like Lance, Lenny, and Como, but it was a different situation with those guys because we were in our own country. But in Mexico because we were fish out of water, there was more of a family-type bond between me, Eddy, Tonga, Black Magic, Mike, and Art.

On the outside, Art was egotistical, sarcastic, and obnoxious, but once you got to know him he was a blast to be around and impossible to dislike. Art and Eddy were still working for AAA and after losing one of the classic matches of all time to Octagon and el Hijo del Santo, Eddy got Art booked on a tour with New Japan. Art's ridiculous amount of charisma combined with his solid wrestling skills made him an instant success in Japan. He was at the top of his game, making big money worldwide, and was finally able to take some well-deserved time off to spend with his family. Life was good.

The day before he left to go back to Oregon, we met up to hang out in Zona Rosa for the day. We went to a Carl's Jr. burger joint for a bite and got into a big debate over whether or not Loverboy was a cool band. We'd seen one of their videos at the Plaza and were discussing how lead singer Mike Reno's headband and lame leg warmers completely contradicted their kickass songs. Art decided to buy a headband to wear all day as a tribute to Loverboy. Years later on WCW *Nitro* I accused wrestler Lenny Lane of stealing my Loverboy tape as a tribute to Art.

After lunch, instead of taking a bus back to the Plaza we saw one of those rickshaw guys and Art suggested we get a ride back. Imagine the ridiculosity of two hetero males, one with long blond hair, one with a Loverboy headband, sitting side by side and being pulled down the street in a rickshaw.

Back at the hotel before we parted ways, Art reached into his pocket and gave me his room key. Because Art and Eddy were exploding as big-time draws for AAA, they had top-floor suites in the Plaza complete with a VCR, fridge, and stove. I was in a normal room, so this was like giving me the gold key to Disneyland. It was also strange because, to my knowledge, Art had never given his key to anyone and he certainly had never given it to me. He told me I was welcome to watch movies, cook dinner, or just hang out in his huge room. Then he gave me a hug and said, "I love you man."

Saying "I love you" is not something that guys feel comfortable about, but it takes a real man to be able to tell another man that you love him as a brother. I reiterated the statement and we parted ways. Forever.

A couple of nights later after watching a few movies in Art's room, the phone rang. I answered it and was surprised to hear Magic's voice. I asked him what was up and a chill enveloped my body when he spoke two simple words: "Art's dead."

Time went into half speed. I looked at the push buttons on the phone and tried to figure out what they were for. I was infatuated with the numbers on the squares embedded into the base of the phone: 1, 2, 3 . . . I hit the floor before I got to 4.

My knees turned into water balloons and wouldn't support my body. I collapsed like a house of cards. Some would say I fainted except I didn't black out. I could still smell the dust on the brown carpet and the polish on the oak night table.

A zombie spoke into the phone: "What are you talking about?"

"Art is dead. He died at home."

I felt as paralyzed as my mom. My limbs weren't responding to my commands and I couldn't pick myself off the floor.

Magic explained that Art had died during the night while his young son Dexter slept beside him.

"Magic, what are we going to do? What are we gonna do?" I kept asking over and over. "What are we gonna do?"

I couldn't grasp what I'd just been told. I didn't understand how a guy who had eaten a hamburger and discussed Loverboy only days earlier could now be dead.

I hung up the phone, grabbed a pen and paper, and just started writing. In some way, writing a letter to Art helped me to comprehend what I'd just heard. I poured my feelings onto the page, covering it with the ink of my emotions, and the next day I faxed it to the inside trade paper *The Wrestling Observer.* It was printed on the front page of the following week's issue. I felt weird reading it because I didn't remember a word of what I'd written until I read it back.

When You Lose a Brother

Trying to forget the news
That you're gone so soon
It leaves me crushed and broken
I don't know what to do

A brother is more than blood
More than just a name

Even though we have different families
We were brothers just the same

We weren't brothers in flesh and blood
We were brothers of circumstance and means
Sharing stories and good times
Sharing the same visions and dreams

I remember so many times
When each other was all we had
Helping to conquer the difficulties
Of being two strangers in a strange land

Yet I'm very thankful
At the end of that one day
When we exchanged the words "I love you"
As only true brothers can say

Because even though you have gone
To a place we all shall see
We shared respect, love, admiration, and fun
And you will always be with me

Lionheart Chris Jericho
Mexico City
Thanksgiving, 1994

Art's death is still a mystery. There are lots of conflicting theories and reports as to what happened but I have a theory of my own. Art took a lot of pills during his everyday life. I believe that as a result of taking so many his body became confused about when to wake up and when to go to sleep and as a result it simply stopped working.

November 1994. I took this picture of Art Barr from his hotel room the night I found out he'd died. Every time I see it, it takes me right back to the moment I received the devastating news from Black Magic.

When I finished writing Art's requiem, I went back into his room to do a cleanup operation. I didn't know what I'd find, but I knew that his death would be a huge story and I didn't want the police to discover anything that would cause his family any further pain. There wasn't all that much to hide but I cleaned up what I thought should be cleaned up, out of respect for my friend and his family. I took one more look around the room and was about to turn the lights out and leave when I saw a photo hanging on the wall. It was a picture of Art dressed in a nice suit with a classic Love Machine devil-may-care look on his face, taken at a Christmas party the year before. I had no right to take it off the wall and keep it, but I did. It was something of his that I could hold on to and remember my brother by.

A few short weeks after Art's death, the Mexican peso crashed hard. Suddenly I was making a third of what I'd been making as the exchange on 1,000 pesos went from $340 to about $125 in one day. The peso crash was the icing on the cake anyway, because after Art died the fun of wrestling in Mexico was gone. The whole vibe had changed and it was too painful to stay at the Plaza with all of the Art memories surrounding me. God was telling me that it was time to move on and it was no coincidence when a few days later I received an offer from the perfect place to continue my quest.

CHAPTER 21

THE TRIANGLE OF DECADENCE

Even though I was a main-event performer all across Mexico, a heartthrob, a match-of-the-year participant, a champion, and a fairly well off twenty-four-year-old, I still felt like I was at square one when it came to breaking into the big time in North America. I didn't think that I had enough experience or was good enough to go to New York (wrestling slang for the WWF), but as I said I didn't want to stay in Mexico.

Once again I felt complacent as a performer and I was getting tired of living in what was basically a Third World country. I'd gotten everything I could out of lucha libre, so I set my sights on getting booked elsewhere. Since Japan wasn't knocking on my door, I started thinking about Europe. The style there was based more on techni-cal wrestling (something I wanted to get better at) and less on masks and fancy ball-boasting costumes. Lance had built a name for himself working in Germany and

Austria, with the same company Chris Benoit had worked for a few years before. I respected both guys, so I started to investigate.

I'd met another American wrestler staying at the Plaza named Solomon Grundy who'd spent the previous fall working in Hamburg. I asked him for the address of the promoter so I could try and get myself booked. I figured that the Beatles got their big break in Hamburg, so why not me? Solomon gave me the address, and the next day I wrote promoter Rene Lasartesse a letter . . . how archaic!

A few weeks later I received his reply. He explained that the promotion ran a tournament out of the same building six nights a week for six weeks. I'd sent him a beefcake picture of myself wearing only a pair of ripped jeans and he said that his daughter was in love with that picture and she had insisted he invite me.

I was surprised at how easily I'd been accepted, but I guess I shouldn't have underestimated my sexocity. I wrote him back to find out how much my guarantee would be, where I would get my work visa from, where I would stay, and how I would get my plane ticket. He responded that I wouldn't be getting a visa or a plane ticket but I would get 150 deutsche marks a night. He also agreed to pick me up from the airport and make a reservation for me at the hotel where all the boys stayed. It wasn't the best of deals but I was stoked to go to Europe so I didn't mind the pay cut. I was intrigued by the idea of working in the same venue in front of the same fans every night. In that scenario, there would be no complacency or shortcuts allowed. I would have to challenge myself to do something different every night. It would be a great way to sharpen my skills and keep me mentally and physically in shape . . . like Pilates.

January 1993. This is the picture that Lasartesse's daughter fell in love with, which got me the gig in Germany. The jeans were again influenced by Nelson, and I used to wear them in -20° weather in Calgary. Freezing my nis was a small price to pay to look cool.

In Germany, wrestling is known as Catch. The name referred to the catch-as-catch-can style of wrestling, which doesn't make much sense. Then again neither does gesundheit and that's a German word too.

So I paid for my own plane ticket to Hamburg, thrilled to add another country to the expanding list of destinations my career was taking me to. When I got off the plane, I looked for the customs area and was surprised not to find one. I could've walked off the plane with two hockey equipment bags full of pure Denver crack and nobody would've known.

I did have two hockey bags, but regretfully they were filled with clothes not crack. The tour was six weeks long so I'd packed accordingly. I brought exactly three weeks of clothes . . . twenty-one pairs of socks, twenty-one pairs of gonch, etc., so I'd only have to do the washing once. Genius, huh? I also brought a slew of cassettes (remember those?) and a four-speaker ghetto blaster. There was no way I was going to let anything stop me from rocking for six whole weeks.

I lugged my bags into the bright sunshine looking for the friendly face of Lasartesse. I had no idea what he looked like, which wasn't a problem because nobody was there.

Nobody.

I was by myself in Germany, didn't speak the language, and didn't have any contact numbers or for that matter any contacts. All I had was the address to the Hotel Domschanke, the place where Rene had booked me.

I found what appeared to be the only taxi driver in Hamburg lounging in the coffee shop and gave him the address. We drove for twenty minutes until he dropped me off at what looked like a large house, not the fancy joint with picture windows and revolving doors that I was expecting. I lugged my overstuffed bags up a flight of stairs and walked into what I thought was the lobby.

It was actually a pub and it was just like the bar scene in *Animal House*: Everyone stopped talking and turned to stare at me. The smile crawled off my face as the beer steins clinked down on the tables and everyone took a good look. I put my bags down with a double thud and asked the big-boned woman behind the bar, "Excuse me, where's the front desk?"

She said nothing and a few of the patrons snickered at my question.

Awkward . . .

"Dis EES de front desk," she said with a scowl in a thick German accent.

I told her that I had a reservation at the hotel.

"No you don't, ve're full."

"I'm sure I do. Renee Lasartesse made it for me."

"I'm sure you DON'T, ve're full," she insisted.

So Rene hadn't picked me up from the airport or made me a reservation, but I wasn't surprised. This was wrestling, after all.

I decided to let it go and I asked her if she knew where the Catch tournament was. She pointed out the window, to a thumbnail of a tent in the middle of a huge park.

"Right over dere," she said and gave me my Welcome to Germany present of a basket of puppies. Actually, she stared at me as if I'd murdered David Hasselhoff, and motioned toward the door.

I headed through the park toward the tent as if I was Dorothy walking to the Emerald City. I cursed Lasartesse as each step seemed to add another brick to my hockey bags. Hot, wet, and dripping with sweat, I finally reached the venue, which seemed better suited for Oktoberfest than for wrestling. It was a big circus tent with a wooden floor and various flags hanging from the ceiling. Parked on the outside was a line of motor home trailers. When I knocked on the first trailer hoping to find Lasartesse, I was astonished when Davey Boy Smith opened the door.

It took me two seconds to realize that the guy wasn't as big or as handsome as Davey, but he was damn close. He didn't look happy to be disturbed and growled in a strong English accent, "What the fuck do you want?"

When I told him I was looking for Rene, he lightened up and invited me inside.

His name was Boston Blackie and the trailer, or caravan, was his. Most of the wrestlers from the U.K. lived in caravans for the six weeks of the tournament and were able to save a lot of money as a result.

We shot the breeze for a bit until he asked me, "Are you a villain or a blue-eye?"

It took me a minute to figure out that blue-eye meant babyface. Blackie was a blue-eye, which was exemplified by the stack of Davey Boy Smith (one of the most popular English wrestlers ever) pictures on his table that were signed "Boston Blackie."

Blackie wasn't the only Englishman that was copying a famous WWF gimmick, as soon afterward a droopy dog of a man named Johnny South came into the caravan. Johnny looked vaguely like Hawk from the Road Warriors but instead of being known as the Legion of Doom, he was the Legend of Doom (they have the Big Mac, we have the Big Mic). He sported the same makeup, mohawk, and spiked shoulder pads as Hawk, but there was one major discrepancy. Johnny was about a foot shorter and fifty pounds lighter. He also had a nasty divot across his bald head.

My curiosity got the best of me and I asked, "Where did that dent come from?"

"I got chopped in the head with an ax," he said matter-of-factly. "It was stuck in me fookin' scalp."

Fair enough.

Blackie told me that Lasartesse was inside so I walked into the tent and encountered a huge, white-haired man, sitting at a desk counting money.

"Are you Rene?"

"Yes. Who are you?" He was from Switzerland and spoke in a hybrid French/English accent that made him sound like Andre the Giant.

"I'm Chris Jericho."

He gave me the once over. "Wow, you looked better in the picture."

He continued to bolster my ego when he explained that he simply forgot to pick me up and hadn't got around to booking me at the Domschanke.

He offered to make up for his forgetfulness by giving me a ride to the nearby Reeperbahn where I could find a place to stay. We got into his two-seater Trans Am that was so small I had to sit with one of the clunky hockey bags on my lap. We drove to a street bathed in the neon light of signs, advertising all things porno from strip clubs to S/M shops to XXX theaters to live sex shows. The Reeperbahn is one of the most famous red-light districts in the world. And for the next six weeks I would be living there.

I price-checked a few hotels but they were all too

expensive for my limited budget. I was only making 150 DM a night (about 175 bucks) and these places were 100 to 120 DM a night. Throw in the two grand I'd forked over for the plane ticket and it was paramount for me to be as frugal as possible. The further we traveled up the Reeperbahn the cheaper the hotels got, both in price and quality.

I finally settled on the illustrious Hotel Rheinland for a cool 75 DM a night. Anything cheaper and I'd be sleeping on the back of a cockroach. At the Rheinland, I just roomed with them.

The good thing about the Hotel Rheinland was its proximity to what I called the Triangle of Decadence™. To the right was a strip club called the Cat Meow, to the left a McDonald's, and across the street a heavy metal club called the Docks. I believe that covers all three of the major-party food groups and I knew I was in for an adventurous six weeks.

CHAPTER 22

THE JERICHO CURSE

The tournament took place during the cold and clammy months of September and October. Because of all the moisture in the air, the damp got through your clothes and chilled you to the bone. My room was always cold because the radiator didn't work very well. Things got worse when I first opened the door to the bathroom and found only a closet.

I went downstairs to the front pub desk to inquire where my biffy was. The fat guy behind the bar snickered and explained in Europe there was only one bathroom on every floor of the hotel and that was it.

"Where are you from ... America?" he scoffed in a patronizing way.

"Uhhh, I'm from Canada, pal," I fired back with great aplomb and stormed out of the pub. My dramatic exit would've worked much better if I hadn't returned a few moments later because I'd locked myself out of my room.

So I dealt with the community potty by putting toilet paper on the seat before every dumpski and using the sink in my room as a urinal. Then washed my face immediately afterward . . .

I keed.

I waited a few minutes before washing my face.

The key to my room was an old-fashioned skinny skeleton key. But nobody told me that you had to put the key into the lock and turn it clockwise in order to lock the door. I just assumed that as soon as the door shut, it locked automatically.

On the first night in my room I was lying on my bed reading *The Stand* by Stephen King, when the door flew open and a skinny guy dressed in black walked in and started screaming at me in German. I have no idea why he was screaming at me, but before he could pee on my rug I shouted, "Go away . . . get the hell out of here!"

He didn't budge and his tone grew angrier. When he first busted in he'd scared the shit out of me, but now I was pissed off. I started yelling, "Fuck off, Fuck off, Fuck off," while pointing to the door with authority, figuring that he had to smell what I was cooking. When he didn't budge, I whipped the 1,100-page novel at him. It smacked him on the noggin and he stormed out the door, screaming all the way down the stairs.

I have no idea what his deal was, I was just thankful that he hadn't pulled a gun. I learned my lesson and made sure to always turn the key in the lock every time I walked into my room. After all, I didn't want anyone interrupting me while I was peeing in the sink.

The next day I when I showed up for the first night of the tournament, I was introduced to the strange traditions of Catch. At the beginning of the show all the wrestlers in the tournament had to parade out of the dressing room in single file and march around the inside of the ring. Then we all had to stand in a circle staring at each other, units in our hands, while the announcer introduced us individually.

When I heard "From Canada, Chris 'Lion Heart' Jericho," I would have to walk into the center of the circle and wave like I was on *Catch Soul Train*. Even if you were involved in a fight-to-the-death blood feud, you still had to stand side by side with your hated rival every night.

I made my Catch debut against Indio Guajardo, a sixty-year-old wrestler from South America who lived in Germany and spoke no English whatsoever. We were able to string together a match by speaking Spanish, but there wasn't much to talk about as he really didn't want to do anything. He was a Hamburg wrestling institution—he'd been working there for decades—but when we got into the ring it was horrible.

Instead of trusting Indio's judgment and doing the type of match that he wanted to do, I tried to do a bunch of moves that totally clashed with his style. I tried to give him a monkey flip but when I jumped on his thighs to flip him back he just stood there and I threw myself onto my back for no apparent reason. I tried to give him a leapfrog but when I leaped into the air he just stood there and I did the splits in midair for no apparent reason.

Instead of working for the match I worked to showcase myself, which made us both look like shit. I finally suplexed him—a big deal because he never left his feet—and got the win, but it was too late.

The match was one of the first occurrences of what I came to refer to as the Jericho Curse. Every time I debuted in a new company my debut match sucked. Most of the fans and the guys in the back thought I was the shits. That night I learned the very important lesson that while having a good match takes two people, having a bad match only takes one.

I was feeling like an ass afterward when I was approached by two of the other guys in the tourney. "Don't worry about it, mate," one of them said. "Indio has been here a long time and he doesn't really have good matches anymore."

I still felt like the worst wrestler ever but I appreciated their attempt to make me feel better. They introduced themselves as Robbie Brookside and Doc Dean from Liverpool. I was instantly impressed because they hailed from the same city as the Beatles! They were also my age, and had long hair to boot. They'd been coming to Hamburg for a few years and knew a girl who gave them a cheap rate at the hotel she ran—they just had to make up the difference in other ways. Aside from the giant bloodstain splattered across their hotel room wall, it seemed like a good deal.

It was a constant learning experience hanging out with my new friends because they spoke in their own language. Traditionally, wrestlers spoke a secret code called carny, which was one of the first things I was taught when I finished wrestling school. The basic premise was you would add an E-Z sound in the middle of a word to disguise it. If you wanted to comment on a girl's boobs when she was within earshot, you would say, "Look at that gezzurl's teezits." It didn't take a mental giant to figure out what teezits meant when you were staring directly at the girl's chest, but that was the idea. However, the English wrestlers had a much more clever code to disguise what they were saying.

We'd be standing around talking when one of them would say something like, "Look at those Scotch eggs," as a girl walked by. I smiled and pretended I had a clue as to what was being said, but in reality I was completely in the dark.

After a few more of those types of statements, I had to know what the funk was going on.

"What are you guys talking about? What is a Scotch egg?"

Robbie laughed and explained that they were speaking Cockney rhyming slang. They would take a word that rhymed with the word they wanted to say and replace it. Therefore, Scotch egg would be used instead of leg. When they said, "Look at those Scotch eggs," they really meant, "Look at that girl's legs."

Not just any rhyming word would do either. The term "boat race" was used for "face," but you could only use "boat race." You couldn't say, "Look at that girl's mace" . . . it didn't work that way. There were specific words and you had to use them properly.

A Donald Duck, or a Donald, was a fuck.

A syrup and fig, or a syrup, was a wig.

Red reels of cotton, or red reels, meant rotten. And so on.

As cool as it was, this new code was much trickier to figure out than stinky old carny. It was simple to discern the meaning of, "I'd like to beezang this cheezick with the nice leezegs."

But try to figure out: "Even though that bird with the syrup has a red reels boat race, she does have great Scotch eggs and I'd like to take her for a Donald."

Huh?

But once I figured out the Cockney slang, I moved

into the inner circle of the English boys. It didn't hurt that I'd grown up singing "God Save the Queen" in elementary school and watching *Fawlty Towers, Benny Hill,* and *Monty Python* on the CBC, since Canada was a member of the Commonwealth and was very English-influenced.

Robbie and Doc also knew the best places to eat in the city. My favorite was a little hole in the wall called Freddie's Imbiss. Freddie had the meal of a half roast chicken, noodles, and a liter of milk waiting for us every day. The meal was right up there with Mrs. Palko's ham sandwich and chocolate chip cookies as one of the best meals I've ever had.

After the matches most of the crew went to a place called Ante's, a Yugoslavian bar and grill run by a guy named—wait for it—Ante. He was always happy, his smile hidden by an enormous walrus mustache. His gorgeous daughters made us the Ante's special, which was a plate of sausage, steak, and lamb. There was a jukebox filled with old blues tunes and all the boys and fans who knew about the place danced and drank until dawn every night. Then we'd all sleep till noon, hit the gym, go to Freddie's for lunch, catch a nap, and go to work. We never had to travel to a different town, so the routine never changed. Tough life huh?

Everything in Hamburg was perfect—except for my matches. Because of my shit debut, I'd been booked into a series of opening matches with the rookie German guys. I just couldn't get it going and I became the victim of another Hamburg tradition: If you had a red reels match, you would have to bring a case of beer into the dressing room as a peace offering. But you wouldn't have to buy too many cases in a row because if you stunk it up too much Rene would simply give you the night off. You would still get paid, but it was like being benched by the coach. It was not a good sign. After I'd bought a case of beer two nights in a row, I decided that I'd bought my tournament limit.

The next night, I brought a case of beer and put it in the dressing room before the match had even started, which got a laugh. I wanted to show that I had a sense of humor about the whole thing, but I was also on a mission to whip ass and show everyone in the place what I could do.

I explained to the guy I was working that night that I was going to take control of the match and call the entire thing. The pressure of being in the new territory had worn off and I became myself again. I relaxed and let the crowd tell me what they wanted to see. They really got into watching the exchanging of holds known as chain wrestling, so we did a succession of unique reversals and the crowd responded. We ended up having a decent match and my reputation was redeemed. When I left the arena that night, I took my case of beer with me.

CHAPTER 23

THERE'S SOMETHING ABOUT JERICHO

One of the guys who'd been riding me about my initial performances was a Scotsman named Drew McDonald. He'd been working for a decades and was always one of the top workers in the tournament and had made a bunch of snide remarks about my work after the first few nights. I was drinking a few pints at Ante's after my acquittal, when I saw him staring at me.

"Mr. Canada, do you want to be a big dog?" he yelled over at me. "If you want to be a big dog, you've got to sit in the big dog corner."

We started bullshitting and he told me that I'd earned his respect with my work that night. So we clinked our steins and proceeded to act like the big dogs that we were—until seven the next morning.

The more time I spent with Drew, the more I learned about his extremely disgusting side. He'd worked for Stu in Stampede as one half of the tag team Ben Doon and

Phil McCraken (say the two names together quickly, junior) and he had the reputation for getting his rocks off by licking women's toilet seats. He was also known for having no problem drinking a cup of pee, even if it wasn't his . . . he would've loved being a rudo in Mexico. So it wasn't a shock when he asked me if I wanted to go to one of the peep shows on the Reeperbahn.

We went inside and were ushered into separate darkened rooms the size of closets. I put a deutsche mark coin into the slot and a little TV came on with forty-four choices of movies . . . like cable.

On channel 12, I was introduced to the screen gem known as Caviar, which featured people eating each other's feces. It had crappy reception, so I switched to channel 32, which featured a guy having sex with his foot. You know what they say about guys with big feet.

I flipped around for a few more minutes until I switched to Blumpkin, which saw a guy getting head while on the toilet. Are there enough people doing this that we need a name to describe it?

I was disgusted by Blumpkin and after watching for five minutes I left the booth.

Drew was waiting outside and asked me excitedly, "What did you think!"

"What did **I** think? What did **you** think?"

"I love this place," he said. "I came here this morning, had a wank and wiped it on the door handle for the next guy."

I recoiled in disgust.

"Couldn't you have told me that before I went in there? How do I know that you weren't in the booth I was just in?"

"You don't," he said and smiled.

As we walked out of the peep show, "Hold the Line" by Toto was blasting out of the speakers continuously on a tape loop.

I used to like "Hold the Line." Now whenever I hear it all I can think of is Drew McDonald whacking off and wiping the product from his Scot knob onto the door knob. Does anybody have any hand sanitizer? There's Something About Jericho . . .

As disgusting as Drew was, he was also very talented and taught me that the less you have to do in the ring the better it is for everyone.

The fans in Germany were very easily entertained. But I'd say that 65 percent of them were there every night, so it became a challenge to keep them on their feet without constantly relying on the same old tricks. When Drew and I worked the crowd into a frenzy without even locking up one night, I was impressed. Drew kept getting in and out of the ring until the fans became rabid. They wanted him IN the ring and wouldn't settle for anything less. The next thing we knew, the clock on the wall had moved forward ten minutes and we hadn't done a damn thing.

"That's what it's all about," he said after the match. "To not do anything for ten minutes and still have the people going crazy is a wet dream! I wish we could have that every night!"

I wasn't sure if he meant good matches or wet dreams.

Another Catch routine the heels followed was the instigating of fines. If a referee spotted someone breaking the rules, they would fine the offender for bad behavior. A good villain would do something dastardly during the match that everyone but the ref would see. When the blue-eye had no choice but to retaliate, he would get busted and fined by the ref. If the gimmick was done properly, the fans would be furious and volunteer to pay the fine for the innocent man. After the match, the paid fines were split up three ways with your opponent and the ref.

Because we were wrestling in front of a lot of the same fans every night, working the fine wasn't something you could pull off regularly. It also wasn't something that just anyone on the card could sell to the customers; you had to be good at it and have a certain level of heat with the crowd.

The best fine producer in our tournament was a guy from Tennessee named Moondog Randy Colley. He'd spent a few years in the WWF as part of the Moondogs tag team and claimed to have invented the leather-clad face-painted gimmick of the tag team Demolition, which Vince then stole from him. I liked Demolition better when they were called the Road Warriors anyway.

Randy was great at getting the crowd to hate him, which made it easy to get them to pay the fines that he caused. He also used solid ring psychology and everything he did made perfect sense.

He carried a giant dinosaur bone to the ring that he would use as a foreign object during his matches. Whenever he won it was because of the bone and whenever he lost it was because of the bone. It was a simple rule that I'd learned in camp . . . if you have a gimmick, make sure to use it. Moondog used his gimmick every match and the bone became his trademark.

Another of my opponents was a New Zealander named

Rip Morgan. Rip's gimmick was performing a Maori haka prior to every match. The haka was a combination dance and chant that became one of the highlights of the night—the fans loved seeing it.

Rip asked me one night, "Have you ever thought about going to New York?"

"I don't feel like I'm ready for the WWF yet."

"Really," he replied. "I think you should send them a tape. You'd be perfect for Vince."

I was honored that he felt that way, but I told him I wanted to get more experience first. What I didn't tell him was I would've gone to New York in a New York minute, except for the fact that nobody had ever asked me.

There were some very good workers in our tournament but there were also a lot of bad ones too, the worst being our boss. Rene Lasartesse had been one of the most hated and feared heels in Europe in the 1960s and 1970s but now he was just plain red reels. He was in his late sixties and insisted on wearing this ricockulous Dracula cape to the ring, because it "scared children."

He wrestled every night, his version of wrestling consisting of standing in the corner throwing the worst kicks and punches imaginable. Worst of all, since he was the booker he won all his matches and won them with the worst finishing move of all time . . . a cartwheel.

With his victim lying prone on the mat, he'd put his hand on his throat and do the worst old-man cartwheel ever with the idea being that he crushed his opponent's larynx. It reality, he only crushed their pride.

One night as Rene was feebly kicking me, one of my contact lenses popped out and crumpled up on the mat like a dying spider. I deftly rolled over, grabbed my little buddy and put it in my mouth. Storing the lens without swallowing it while trying to carry Rene to a good match was like trying to pat my stomach and rub my head at the same time.

But it wasn't just the wrestlers that made it hard to have a good match. The tournament's referee was an Englishman named Mal Mason who was a true mark for himself. He was the only ref I've ever worked with who insisted on having his own ring music.

Yeah that's right, referee ring music.

As soon as the first verse of Right Said Fred's "I'm Too Sexy" hit, this skinny fifty-year-old man with a horse face jogged to the ring, as serious as a heart attack. I laughed my ass off the first time I saw him do it. I stopped laughing when he dropped down to his stomach during the match as I ran off the ropes, forcing me to jump over him to avoid tripping and crashing to the floor.

I confronted him afterward and asked, "Why the hell did you do that?"

"Well, I felt it added to the realism of the match, mate."

"Interesting. Well here's an idea . . . why don't you add to the realism of the match by staying out of the way?"

Quick Rule: A good ref is one that you never notice is there. A bad ref is one that drops down in front of you when you're running the ropes.

As enamored as Mal was with himself, he didn't hold a peace pipe to Suni War Cloud. Suni was a French-Canadian Indian who spoke little English. When he got the night off, which was two or three times a week, Suni waltzed around bragging, "You guy workings again tonight. I not working but make same money!"

The truth was that he wasn't working because he wasn't very good. He was really bragging, "I'm getting paid so I don't stink out the joint tonight."

One night we went to the red-light district on the Reeperbahn. At the end of a dark alley there was a big gate and when you walked through it you entered what was basically a pornographic zoo. Behind full-length walls of glass stood some of the most beautiful (and ugliest) girls I'd ever seen. If a fine lad was so inclined, for the right price he could enter the goddess's glass house and throw some sexual stones.

We walked by a spectacular blonde and Suni decided, "The blond one, she like me I can tell. How could she no like sexy Suni? I take off my shirt and show her what real mans is!"

He stripped off a shirt that was too small for a twelve-year-old and unleashed a pair of man boobs that would've made Fatwell jealous. He continued with a posing routine so red reels that it could've embarrassed Schwarzenegger into making a movie about male pregnancy.

Suni was like one of those guys at Lambeau Field in December with a painted stomach and no shirt. The pretty young thing watched his flabby pectorals bob to and fro, lit up a smoke, and pulled down the window shade.

Hamburg was a European Las Vegas that never shut down and offered anything and everything that a decadent heart could desire. And since it was also the city where the Beatles got their start over three decades earlier, I made it my mission to try to find the clubs where they played. Happily, I found that a few of them were still around. Sitting in the Kaiserkeller drinking cheap draft beer and watching a crappy German rock band play "Bad to the Bone" or smelling forty years of cigarette smoke ground into the walls of the Star Club was like being on hallowed ground. Hanging around in the same bars that John, Paul, and George had rocked decades ago was one of the high points of my trip. This was what life was all about—being paid to do something you loved while traveling the world to places that you heard about your whole life.

Since there were so many things to do and holes to crawl into on the Reeperbahn, being a Catcher didn't have the same allure to the Hamburg locals that it did to the Mexicans. Most of the people in the city didn't even realize that there was wrestling in the big tent downtown, since Rene refused to advertise. He figured the word of mouth from forty years of running shows would be enough. It wasn't. Within a few years the tournament would shut down. But the one group of people that knew about the matches in Hamburg were the strippers. I single-handedly generated a lot of the advertising by hanging out regularly in the Cat Meow. As I learned in Denver, wrestlers and strippers easily connect with each other and I proved it by connecting with a few of the frauleins. My new supporters also had a lot of cash, which they were very generous in sharing with me. I made sure to use the starving wrestler poverty card whenever one of my friends stayed the night enjoying tea and strumpets, so I could get said friend to pay for my room.

One morning when I went to pay the rent—again—I was surprised when the guy behind the desk said, "Last night you had a guest in your room, you have to pay me 125 deutsche marks."

That was a fifty DM increase and I was perplexed.

How did he know I'd had a guest? I scanned the bar for a secret mirror or a video screen, anything that would've helped him to find out, but there was nothing.

A couple of days later another of Hamburg's finest impressed me with her hospitality and the next morning I was charged 125 deutsche marks again. I still had no idea how he'd found out, until I heard a couple of beeps coming from behind the desk. Upon closer inspection, I saw what appeared to be a telephone switchboard. This was strange because there were no telephones in the rooms.

When I went back up to my room to investigate, sure enough there was an electric eye embedded in the wood at the bottom of the staircase. Whenever someone walked up to their room it would set the eye off. If it beeped twice, they would know that two people had walked up the stairs and if that didn't match your registration, they would know you had someone in for a shag or a piss in the sink or whatever.

Now that I'd figured out the secret, the next time I had a visitor I hoisted her over my shoulder as I walked up the steps. I don't know why I wasn't charged extra when the drunken dude barged into my room during my first night. I guess the first accosting from an inebriated German was on the house.

I did quite well on the German meat market despite the fact that I was sporting a Michael Bolton hairstyle. Because of the heavy humidity in Hamburg I had some serious Shirley Temple sausage curls. The problem was that the hair dryer I used to blow out the curls blew its circuits the first day I arrived. Once I realized that Europe was on a different power system, I couldn't afford a

European-powered dryer and was forced to rock the poodle lid for six weeks.

Fortunately, I noticed from hanging out at the Docks that most of the rockers in Hamburg had hair just like me.

CHAPTER 24

MY FIRST FELONY!

Every Monday there was a metal concert at the Docks and since I just so happened to be off on Mondays, I was able to check out some of my favorite groups. I got to see such mega-bands as Gamma Ray, Saxon, Accept, Manowar, Green Jelly, and Morbid Angel, who were all very popular in Europe, yet practically unheard of in the U.S. The highlight for me was getting to check out Helloween, whose *Walls of Jericho* album helped inspire my name. An extra bonus occurred when I got to meet their singer, Michael Kiske, one of my top three favorite vocalists of all time. I was starstruck and even though I'd tasted some degree of worldwide stardom and success, meeting him transformed me right back into a fifteen-year-old fan. If I met James Hetfield from Metallica tomorrow, I would act the same way.

I thought I did meet James during one of my first nights wrestling in Hamburg, when I looked into the crowd and saw him sitting there. I kept looking over at him during my match, trying to figure why in the hell the mighty Hetfield would be sitting in a tent on the Reeperbahn.

After the match, I asked Robbie Brookside, "Am I crazy or was that James Hetfield out there tonight?"

Robbie laughed and said, "That was my friend Jorn. Everyone thinks he's Hetfield when they first see him. You have to meet him, he owns a record store and he plays bass in a band." He sounded like my kind of dude.

When I met Jorn Ruter after the show, he was sooo easygoing and impossible not to like. He played bass and sang in Torment, a Motörhead-influenced band, whose biggest hit was the pretty little ditty "Bestial Sex." He also owned and operated both a record label and a record shop named Remedy Records. Jorn knew his stuff and we spent hours debating and discussing all things metal.

You have to understand that in Germany heavy metal isn't just music, it's a way of life. The people of Hamburg seemed to me to be strict, cold, and tough with a pissed-off edge. Heavy metal was the perfect soundtrack for their lives.

Jorn showed that toughness by cruising the streets of Hamburg with his friends, one of them being Kai Karczewski, whose father, Uwe, painted the cover of the *Walls of Jericho* album . . . see how it all ties together?

They roamed the city looking for fights . . . with skinheads. While the Nazi-influenced punks patrolled the Reeperbahn looking for drunken partiers or homosexuals to beat the hell out of, Jorn's gang patrolled the Reeperbahn looking for skinheads to beat the hell out of.

There was still a big Nazi influence in Hamburg existing even in its architecture. In the middle of the city, there was a black fortress of a building perched like a bloated spider casting a dark shadow across the streets. It gave me a bad vibe, so I asked Jorn what it was. I found out it was called the Hafenbunker, a Nazi stronghold where Hitler himself stayed when he was in Hamburg. If there was ever such a thing as a haunted house, the Hafenbunker was it.

One night Jorn and I went to Ante's for a few beers. But the beers he ordered were a lot different from the Labatt's I was used to drinking. He'd got me a Guinness and I couldn't believe how dark and syrupy it was. It was like drinking a stein of Aunt Jemima's and I was still forcing down my first one when the next round came. Apparently German drinking rules are similar to wrestling drinking rules. Jorn got angry and sternly told me, "You are in Germany. You must drink like a German!"

So I did.

I ended up totally loaded and spent the rest of the night going absolutely crazy. The highlights of which included a foot race between Jorn and me over the roofs of cars parked on the street and a schnitzel-eating contest, which was not a good decision. Holy heartburn, Batman!

I woke up the next morning next to a naked hermaphrodite—whose picture was in the stack of porno magazines scattered across my room. I had spent all of my deutsche marks on such classics as *He's a Woman, She's a Man, Midget Titties,* and *Caviar Deluxe* (normal Caviar wasn't enough for this mag) and didn't remember a damn thing.

Later that night in the dressing room I told my *Caviar Deluxe* story after taking a post-match shower, while Doc messed around with a movie camera he'd brought with him from Liverpool.

"Hey Lion Heart, what would you do if I was filming right now?" he inquired.

I checked and saw that there was no blinking red light on the camera, so I decided to put on a show.

"I'd take off my towel and shake my shit like this!" I whipped off the towel and started flapping my horn back and forth like a paddleball.

Then I performed a sweet electric slide and a swank Pee-wee Herman tequila dance while my Arthur Digby Sellers whipped to and fro.

"And what if I told you I really was filming?"

"Well, you're not. The red light's not blinking." I started to pogo.

"Actually, it is," he said and ripped off the piece of black electrical tape that had been hiding the blinking red light.

I scrambled to cover up my Uncle Albert/Admiral Halsey with the bunched-up towel at my feet. "Promise you won't show that to anyone," I begged. "It's freezing in here!"

Later on, all the boys and a ton of fans congregated at Ante's for the nightly after-show party. I was making some headway with one of Ante's gorgeous daughters when the whole place suddenly burst out laughing. I turned to the big-screen TV behind the bar and saw my Tico Torres staring back at me with a one-eyed grin.

I felt like George Costanza as I explained how cold the dressing room was. And that shower . . . there was NEVER hot water in that damn shower. The laughter got louder when my Pee-wee (poor choice of words) Herman dance began.

I was furious and I didn't speak to Doc for a week.

He finally cornered me in the dressing room and said, "Listen man if you want to get even, get even, but the fact you're not talking to me is killing me. Please . . . rib me back already."

I racked my brain and decided to exact my revenge by stuffing raw eggs into his wrestling boots and cutting the laces minutes before his match. I put my plan in motion and stifled a giggle when Doc stuck his foot into his boot, cracking the eggs. I waited for him to freak out, alerting everyone to my master plan. Instead he diabolically diffused my rib by silently cleaning out his boots and tying knots in his laces and nobody was ever the wiser.

I learned two important lessons that day:

1. Never sell a rib, and
2. Never whip out your Dustin Diamond in front of a camera.

Did I mention how cold the dressing room was?

Now reunited, Robbie, Doc, and I had a couple of strippers take us on the two-hour drive to Hanover to visit the boys in the CWA. The Catch Wrestling Association was the WWF of Germany and I wanted to check out the difference between Rene's promotion and the big leagues. Their tent was fancier than ours and the crowd was a little bigger, but other than that it was pretty much the same scenario as Hamburg, with one notable exception.

The quality of the workers in Hanover was head and shoulders above our group. The best of the lot was Fit Finlay, an Irishman who was the king of the heels in the company. That night I watched his match and he commanded five fines against a young guy I'd never seen before or since. Fit was a friend of Robbie and Doc and when they introduced me he said, "What are you doing here?"

"I'm wrestling in Hamburg right now."

Finlay smiled his gap-toothed grin. "Give those guys in Hamburg a message for me," he said cheerily.

"Sure," I replied just as cheerily.

"Tell those cunts to fuck off."

I returned to Hamburg and told everyone that Finlay had wished them well in their future endeavors.

Toward the end of the tourney, a sign was posted in the dressing room announcing that Kinder Catch would be held the following Sunday. Kinder Catch was probably the worst idea I'd ever heard. The basic premise was that you would baby-sit a bunch of kids under the age of ten and tell them wrestling's secrets. We should have told them that Santa Claus was bullshit too while we were at it. Now playing the role of Catfish Charlie . . . Chris Jericho.

I arrived that morning straight from the Kaiserkeller sporting a horrible hangover. Rene had all the kids line up in the ring and showed them our tricks, like a turncoat magician at a child's birthday party. The kids ran around the ring doing drop kicks and taking bumps while we tried to make sure they didn't break their Kinder necks.

When the last day of the tournament arrived, nobody seemed to know who was in the final. When the tournament started there'd been a chart in the front lobby listing all the standings, but it had been taken down a few days later because I don't think Rene knew how he wanted the tournament to end.

I was *in* the tourney and I was confused, so I can just imagine how the fans felt. It wouldn't have been hard to figure out a point system or a round-robin bracketing, but Rene was just too lazy. He didn't think people would care about such details, even though it was a TOURNAMENT.

But I found out that I'd advanced to the semifinals (who knew?) and would be facing Drew McDonald to decide the third-place winner. There'd been zero buildup for the match but the crowd was still buzzing when we stood across from each other in the parade. It was hard to keep a straight face during the staredown as he was flexing his thigh and the tits of naked girl tattooed on his leg's were bouncing up and down. It was actually a lot cooler than it sounds.

We had great chemistry and the match went perfectly. During the entire tournament, Drew had been trying to convince me to try a move he'd thought of where I would do a Frankensteiner with the both of us standing on the top rope. I thought it was impossible but he kept bringing it up and I finally agreed to do it for the last match. We both climbed to the top and I jumped up on his shoulders, back-flipping him into the ring while the fans went nuts. I liked the move so much that it became one of my signature moves (and almost led to my death four years later).

Drew ended up pinning me but we were both winners, as Rene told me it was the best match he'd ever seen during his time in Hamburg. Considering my less than auspicious start, it was nice to end the tournament with a bang.

The final match was Blackie Boy Smith winning the tournament by beating Rene (Rene was in the final? What a surprise.) and they had no chance of following Drew and me. I took great pride in that.

Even though I'd been wrestling for years, I'd never experimented with steroids. I didn't have the guts to try them. Plus I didn't know where I could get them and after my crack-buying experience in Denver, I'd proven that I didn't have much flair for purchasing illegal drugs.

But when I found out that they were easy to obtain in Germany, I decided to pop my sterry and bought 150 tablets of Dianabol. The Dianabol looked exactly like these little sugar tablets that Germans use to sweeten their coffee. They came in this Tic-Tac container type thingy, so I bought one and replaced the sugar pills with Dianabol pills. I'd discovered the perfect way to smuggle contraband over international borders, but I got paranoid and became convinced I was going to get caught. I wrapped the dispenser in a pair of dirty undies, but that still wasn't enough. So I stuffed the gonch into a stinky sock and then stuck the stinky sock into a pair of sweaty tights. But I needed more protection, so I put the whole rolled-up wrinkly mess into the bottom of my laundry bag. I figured if the customs guys found my stuff after all that, I deserved to get busted.

I was freaking out when I took my bags through German customs, even though there still wasn't a customs area. When I approached Canadian customs I felt like I was packing a shoe bomb, but thankfully my bags weren't searched.

So it was official. I had transported illegal substances across international borders.

My first felony!

(Apologetic Author's Note: If any customs officials are reading this book, please don't search me as I promise to never smuggle illegal contraband again. I don't know why I even bothered because the Dianabol didn't do shit for me. As a matter of fact, I think they actually were sugar pills in the first place.)

CHAPTER 25

AIN'T NO PARTY LIKE A WAL-MART PARTY

After returning from Germany I decided it was time to get serious about working in the States. I'd thought a lot about Rip Morgan's comment that I was ready to break into the WWF and wondered if he was right. But even though I'd achieved some worldwide notoriety, the WWF still hadn't acknowledged my existence or sent out any kind of feelers toward me. Since they were essentially compana non grata, it was time to look elsewhere for mainland exposure.

I called Lance to touch base and share stories about working in Germany and I asked him what he had coming up next. He mentioned that he'd been talking with Jim Cornette (who I had interviewed years earlier for my college newspaper), now the promoter for Smoky Mountain Wrestling, one of the top independent companies in the States.

SMW was based out of Knoxville, Tennessee, and it

had been getting a lot of recognition because of Cornette's involvement. He'd been a successful manager and assistant booker in both the WCW and WWF, before getting tired of the grind and walking away to form his own company.

SMW offered more of a slower-paced, old-time style of wrestling than what the glitzy WWF was selling. To a certain extent the fans in the Southern states preferred Smoky's style to the WWF's, with a lot of them still believing that they were watching a legitimate sport and behaving accordingly. This included automatically cheering or booing a wrestler based solely on whether he came to the ring from the heel or babyface locker room.

The company also relied more on wrestler interviews to build up the big matches. This was the opposite of wrestling in Germany or Mexico, where there was less emphasis on cutting promos. If I was ever going to get to the WWF, I would have to learn how to deliver a better promo, and working for Jim Cornette, one of the greatest promo men of all time, would help me to do that. I got his number from Lance and gave him a call.

I was surprised when Jim called me back excitedly the next day. He'd already seen some of my work via an audition tape Lance had sent him chock-full of highlights of the two of us wrestling each other. One of the clips featured me taking a crazy bump over the top post straight to the floor and Cornette wouldn't stop raving about it. When I brought up that I'd interviewed him for my college newspaper five years earlier, he laughed and then cut to the chase. "I would love to bring you and Lance in to work as a tag team."

There was more emphasis on tag teams in SMW and the

top stars in the company were the Rock 'n' Roll Express. Ricky Morton and Robert Gibson were former NWA and WCW tag team champions and one of the biggest drawing acts of the 1980s. I thought Lance and I would be a perfect fit for the company. I didn't want to spoil any of Lance's plans though, so I called to ask his opinion. He liked the idea and we were Tennessee-bound.

Cornette's plan was to put us together as a young and fearless team called the Thrillseekers. Our gimmick was that we were more extreme than the rest of the performers in SMW. This extreme didn't mean that we broke tables or shot staple guns into our heads; it referred rather to our devil-may-care attitude as we walked the earth seeking thrills . . . or something like that.

The idea was that we'd explode into the territory performing flashy moves and working diverse styles that had never been seen by these fans before.

Cornette made the arrangements to fly us down to Knoxville to sell us on his company. He also had an idea of what he wanted us to wear in the ring and sent us a few rough designs. They featured a pair of stickmen wearing singlets, resembling a Southern Spirit Squad. Cornette's notes stated that our first names were to be written on the front in "gold lamé or similar material."

It was lame all right. We would've been better off wearing loincloths.

We were both excited about the prospect of working full-time in the States and we had no idea what kind of money we could expect to make. I had left Mexico on good terms and even though the peso had crashed, I knew I could go back and make a good living. But I felt at this stage of my career it meant more to get the gig with SMW even if it meant a huge pay cut, although Cornette didn't need to know that. So it was time to do some hardball negotiating.

From the moment Lance and I stepped off the plane in Knoxville it was as much of a culture shock as being in Mexico City the first time. For starters, even though we were still in North America I had a real problem understanding a damn word the people were saying. Trying to figure out the Southern accents was harder than trying to decode carny and Cockney combined.

Cornette met us at the gate wearing a tight SMW T-shirt that barely covered his ample belly and a pair of Zubaz workout pants that were in style a decade earlier. He had a haircut like a first-grader, short and parted with an ax to the side, and was sporting a pair of Coke-bottle glasses.

"Hey y'all."

"Pardon?"

"Jeet yet?"

"Excuse me?"

"Jeet yet?"

I just nodded politely until I decoded that he was asking, "Did you eat yet?"

When I finally jate, the food was just as alien as the accent. Blooming onions, grits, okra, BBQ that wasn't actually BBQ at all, but some kind of mystery meat covered with a cold, slimy sauce. And what the hell was a Waffle House?

The culture shock continued when I saw a huge billboard on the side of the highway featuring a familiar face.

"Why is there a picture of Burt Reynolds from *Smokey and the Bandit* on that billboard?"

"Burt Reynolds?" he asked in amazement. "That's not Burt Reynolds, that's Richard Petty . . . one of the most famous NASCAR drivers ever!"

I'm from Canada. What the hell did I know about NASCAR?

He took us to a fancy riverside restaurant and began the hard sell about how good it would be for our careers to work with SMW. Jimmy unveiled his plan to build us up by introducing the Thrillseekers to his fans with television vignettes.

We filmed the first one in the Smoky Mountains at Pigeon Forge, the home of Dollywood (me likey Dolly). We wandered around the tourist attractions while Jim filmed us performing such death-defying thrill-seeking activities as ice skating, horseback riding, go-cart driving, video game playing, and the extreme coup de grâce of jumping onto a Velcro wall whilst wearing a Velcro suit. Another wacky scene showed Lance throwing treats into a bear pit only to pan down and reveal that it was really me jeeting the treats. HILARIOUS!

The whole concept of the vignette was goofy to begin with (now I know why Jim's nickname was Corny) but I made it worse with my horribly cheesy overacting. I was bopping along to Danger Danger's "Rock America" (Corny couldn't have picked a worse hair metal entrance song for us if he tried) once again trying to be David Lee Roth and once again ending up as Screech. If you didn't know me you might've thought, "This guy's an idiot." (Then again, you might think that even if you do.)

Then he wanted to end the clip with the two of us banging our fists together, which would cause a lightning bolt (to be added in post) to shoot out of our hands.

"Wonder twin powers activate! Form of Dweeb."

The next (and worst) one was set to "I'll Sleep When I'm Dead" by Bon Jovi, and began with me rousing Lance out of bed at 8 P.M. to go party. Apparently, one half of this hot young tag team had to be in bed before sundown. This was to show that Lance was the straitlaced guy and I was the rock 'n' roll animal.

The video continued with me and my reluctant party partner in the bar drinking mugs of milk and winking to each other about it like we were too smart to be seen drinking beer on camera. Later when I propositioned a pretty Southern belle, she promptly slapped me in the face. I guess this was to show that the Thrillseekers were so cool, girls would rather slap us in the face than speak to us. At the end of the video, Lance knocked on the door of my room at eight in the morning and I'm passed out drunk with the goofiest generic drunk face. You might as well have drawn X X over my eyes.

Beer bottles were lying all over the room and I was wearing the same clothes that I wore the night before. Then again so was Lance, who apparently went home, got a good night's sleep, and put on the same clothes to come wake me up. This folks, is your new babyface tag team.

The last vignette showed us working out in the gym wearing the shortest of short-shorts and string tank tops, close-ups of our butts in slow motion, the works. It was almost as if the territory was based in San Francisco not Knoxville. Then we return to our hotel room and find two girls waiting for us. When I saw them I begged Jimmy to give me two minutes to go to a strip club, a Hooters, a mall, a nunnery, anywhere, so I could find two different girls. Hell, I could've thrown a dart into a crowded street and hit a hotter chick. But he insisted upon using *these* girls and we were forced to act excited that we were going to get lucky; high-fives and all.

The hot young babyface tag team had just picked up a couple of skeezers and had it captured on tape, killing our sex appeal and our cool factor in one fell swoop.

With the vignettes in the can (in the toilet would have been more appropriate) we attended SMW's "Sunday, Bloody Sunday" at the Knoxville Coliseum.

Three or four times a year Jimmy would blow off (wrestling speak for the end of a feud) the hot angles of the company with a big show at the Coliseum. He had a lot of credibility and a good name throughout the business and was able to book some legendary names for his big shows. Earlier in the night I got to meet Terry and Dory Funk, two of the biggest stars in wrestling history. I was agog when Terry busted out a moonsault during his match with Bullet Bob Armstrong. He worked his ass off and so did the entire crew as the show brought out the best in the company, its wrestlers, and its fans. Seeing 4,000 fans going crazy for the matches in this big arena made it seem like SMW was the place to be.

The Thrillseekers were ready to come aboard. We just had to agree upon the finances, so after the show we met with Cornette to talk numbers.

There was no way Corny could afford to pay me what I'd been making in Mexico and I didn't expect him to. After what I'd just seen, I wanted to work in SMW more than ever but I still wanted to make the best deal I could. Lance had given me his blessing to work out the deal for both of us, so I decided to swing for the fences. I told

Jimmy I couldn't come in for anything less than $850 a week and of course Lance would have to make the same.

Without a word, Jimmy grabbed a pen and after a few minutes of number crunching, he said he might be able to do it.

A major revenue stream for the workers in SMW was the sale of merchandise, or gimmicks. Guys would peddle T-shirts, pictures, mugs, buttons, anything. They would have sold turds if there was a Sharpie that could write on them. Cornette told us he could guarantee the $3,400 to each of us monthly by keeping the proceeds from our gimmick sales.

I think he figured he could pay us 100 bucks a match for four matches a week and make up the remaining $1,800 with Thrillseeker gimmicks. It might have been possible except I think Corny forgot that Lance and I would have to generate $1,800 a month in gimmicks EACH to cover the guarantee. Therefore the Thrillseekers would have to sell $3,600 a month in merch for him to break even. So the deal put him in as much of a hole money-wise as our crappy vignettes put the Thrillseekers in image-wise.

What made his offer stranger was that even with the biggest push in history, nothing was going to make us more popular than the Rock 'n' Roll Express in SMW. He'd just made a deal to pay an unproven tag team twice as much as he was paying his top-drawing main event tag team.

The bottom line: great deal for us, bad deal for Cornette.

With Cornette in charge of producing our gimmicks, it wasn't a priority for us to put any thought into what we were selling. It didn't matter if we sold 1 or 100 dollars' worth because we got our monthly guarantee either way. So we refused to take the beefcake pictures of us soaking in a hot tub in Speedos that were standard for babyfaces in the Southern territories. We wanted to be known as serious wrestlers and the only pictures we agreed to take were of us on horseback, wearing jackets and jeans. We didn't even show off our physiques, which was what a lot of the female fans wanted to see. It was a piss-poor attitude to have because Jimmy was paying us a lot of money to play the pretty boy role. It was almost embarrassing to compare our inventory with the rest of the guys who made the lion's share of their income from the sales of merchandise.

The Rock 'n' Roll Express were the kings of the gimmicks. They made hundreds, sometimes thousands of dollars a night by selling anything and everything, including shirts, buttons, dog collars, key chains, can openers, and ball caps. They'd buy a white bedsheet, rip it into strips, write R+R on them in black marker, and sell them as official headbands. Once I saw a fan give Ricky Morton a rebel flag license plate as a gift. As soon as she turned her back, he signed his name on it and sold it ten minutes later for twenty bucks. They'd shamelessly shill their stuff to any fan in the place who had more than a dime to their name. If a dime was all you had, they'd take that too.

The more you schmoozed the fans the more you sold, but the whole concept of whoring yourself out bothered me. Here we were, so-called big-time superstars sitting at a table during intermission, hawking a button for a dollar as if our lives depended on it. You never saw Hulk Hogan at the merch stand at intermission selling red and yellow headbands and I didn't think I should have to do it either. I felt that it really destroyed the larger-than-life status wrestlers were supposed to have. My wrestling motto was No Mystique, Big Mistake.

In retrospect, that mind-set hindered the Thrillseekers from reaching our full potential and from getting over as much as we could have in SMW. I didn't understand it at the time, but selling gimmicks and interacting with the fans was a huge factor in gaining popularity in the territory. But whether I understood it or not, I should have just done it, as it was part of my job and my deal with Corny.

But with the deal done and the contract signed, the next step was to pack up my stuff from the Palkos' house (my North American base for the whole time I was in Mexico and Germany) and move to Tennessee. SMW's referee Brian Hildebrand had found an apartment I could share with a couple of the other wrestlers in Morristown, about forty-five minutes outside Knoxville, so I was good to go.

Brian was a short slightly built man who was one of the easiest guys to talk to that I'd ever met. He was obsessed with 1970s music and had a good wrestling mind and worked the independent scene as manager Hymie P. Schwartz (the best name ever). He had immense respect for the business, as he'd learned to wrestle in Pittsburgh at the same school as Mick Foley and Shane Douglas. But he'd never fulfilled his dream of becoming a wrestler because he was too small for his time so he'd become a referee instead and was now Corny's right-hand man in SMW.

Brian worked at a shoestore by day and became the SMW man Friday by night. He helped book the matches, run the shows, and produce the TV program, a little bit of everything. He had a massive wrestling tape collection from all over the world and knew my entire history from my first match on. He was even familiar with Bret Como (or as he called him Bret Cuomo, like the governor), and wanted to convince Corny to bring him in. We really hit it off and he assured me that my apartment was ready to move into, so I flew back to Calgary to pack up my stuff and make the three-day drive to Tennessee.

Leaving the Palkos' house was quite emotional for me as their home had been my home base for the past four years. No matter where I went or how long I was gone whenever I returned, I went back to live at their house. I was always welcomed with open arms, my mail piled on the freshly washed sheets of my bed. I'd become part of their family and Jerry and Bev treated me like one of their own. I could probably still be living there as the wacky sitcom roommate guy.

I was able to hold back my tears as I pulled out of their driveway for the last time, but when I saw Mrs. Palko waving at me in the rearview mirror the same way my mom had when I'd moved from Winnipeg, the tears dashed down my cheeks. My supposed six-week stay had turned into three and a half years and now I was leaving home for the second time. Once again, if it wasn't for the Palkos, I never would have made it as far as I have in wrestling or in life.

I drove for three days across two countries and finally pulled up to my new digs in Morristown. It was a two-story duplex that I'd be sharing with Anthony Michaels, a rookie from New York who'd moved to Tennessee to find his fame and fortune. I don't know how much fortune he found, but he did have a quick taste of fame when he wrestled as the original Dudley Brother Snot years later in Extreme Championship Wrestling (ECW).

Unfortunately, Anthony was out of town and hadn't informed anybody else in the place that I was moving in. I walked into my room to find Goldilocks in my bed and I recognized him instantly as the guy who'd been too wasted to assemble a crib in Christopher Love's house in Wichita. His name was Rex King and he begrudgingly vacated my bed when I explained that it was my room now.

I found out that my new home had been given the nickname SMF, the Smoky Mountain Flophouse. Wrestler Chris Candido had coined the phrase because anytime a new performer came into the company and needed a place to stay, he would move in there.

No wonder Brian was able to hook it up for me so easily.

Candido was right. There were people drifting in and out of the SMF on a nightly basis. There was no air-conditioning so it was ceaselessly hot and damp inside and I'd never experienced that kind of brutal humidity or the horrible amounts of pollen in the air. After a week of being red-eyed and bushy-haired, I was ready to stick my head in the microwave . . . if only the SMF had one.

Our groovy pad also boasted fake wood paneling right out of the '70s and smelled like a mouse had crawled behind the fridge and died. Coincidentally, when I pulled it back, I found out that a mouse *had* crawled behind the fridge and died.

At least I got along well with my new roommate Anthony. He was into the metal scene and, like me, he'd been born in Long Island. He played guitar and I'd brought my bass, so we formed a glam band called Slippery Nipple. We were the first metal band in history without a drummer or any songs but we rocked all the same.

Living in Tennessee was a big lifestyle adjustment, as I'd gone from living on the Reeperbahn going out every night and meeting all the girls I could handle, to living with a bunch of stinky dudes in a cheap apartment in the middle of a dry county. A dry county meant that there were no bars in all of Morristown, which really limited the places we could go to hang out and meet girls. There was nothing to do, except watch *The Real World* on MTV (that Puck . . . what a rogue) and hang out at the brand-new twenty-four-hour Wal-Mart. Ain't no party like a Wal-Mart party!

In old-school Southern territories one of the responsibilities of a babyface was to, shall we say, service the female gender. This was done to ensure continued attendance and the continued buying of gimmicks by enraptured female fans.

But Lance was married and I had standards, so we drove Cornette absolutely nuts.

"You're not sleeping with any of the girls! What kind of a babyface are you?"

If Cornette had introduced me to ONE female SMW fanatic that caught my fancy, I would've been happy to play hide the blooming onion. But he didn't, so I kissed no grits.

CHAPTER 26

TRUE TO THE CREW

The only pretty girls I met during my whole time in Tennessee were in a strip club in Knoxville called the Mouse's Ear. I had to have a membership card to get inside, but it was worth it when I met a buxom lass with long jet black hair. I was so desperate to rock that it didn't bother me when she said she was a vampire. However, it did bother me when she said she wanted me to unleash my life-force inside of her so she could absorb me into her spiritual being and live with me always. I unleashed my life-force out of her apartment and absorbed myself back to Morristown instead.

My sad-sack existence finally gained purpose when the Thrillseekers vignettes began running on television. As cheesy and overacted as they were, they still created a buzz and when we made our SMW debut at a TV taping in Dungannen, Virginia, the fans went nuts for us right off the bat. A lot of the reaction was garnered simply because we entered the gym from the babyface dressing room. To build us up instantly in the ring, Jimmy had brought in

Well Dunn (Steve Doll and my short-term roommate Rex King), a former WWF team that had ended up in SMW.

They'd been around for years and cut a really good promo airing their grievances about the Thrillseekers. Even though I'd learned a little about promos from Bulldog Bob Brown, I was still so green that I thought that doing a good interview consisted of having the fans cheer every word I said. The fans didn't really know me and I overcompensated for the lack of reaction by shamelessly mugging to them in hopes they would cheer. It was like seeing a bad stand-up comic (golden topping) laughing at his own lame jokes.

I mentioned that my dad had played in the NHL and I said in an overexaggerated babyface voice, "Since you guys are cheaters, we want to help even the odds. We want to face you in the very first penalty box match [crickets chirped]. In hockey if you do something wrong, you have to go to the penalty box for two minutes. In this match if one of you guys breaks the rules, then that guy has to go sit in the penalty box for two minutes as well."

"So what you're telling us," Steve confirmed, "is if you guys break the rules—and you will—there will be two of Well Dunn versus one Thrillseeker."

"Yeah, but if you guys break the rules," Lance fired back, "it'll be two Thrillseekers versus one Well Done!"

You put your chocolate in my peanut butter.

I decided I needed a big finishing line to drive my point home.

"We're going to show you how we do things, the Canadian way," I proudly proclaimed. Problem was we weren't in Canada and we weren't heels. We were babyfaces in

Tennessee, flaunting our foreign roots in the middle of one of the most xenophobic regions in the country.

Cornette was convinced that the penalty box match was a great idea and pushed the concept hard on the TV shows leading up to the first one in Marietta, Georgia. Georgia was the heart of WCW country and Corny was convinced that SMW had arrived. "We're going to stick it to WCW boys!" he bellowed before the show.

He'd arranged for Chris LiPuma, a goon from the Atlanta Knights minor league hockey team, to be the special guest ringside enforcer for the box matches. The pattern of the match was similar to how the fining system worked in Germany; one of the Well Dunns would cheat and the ref wouldn't see it. One of the Seekers would retaliate, get caught, and be forced to sit behind the desk that was playing the part of the penalty box. There were times during the match that I wanted to get up and help Lance when he was being beaten two on one, but the power of the desk compelled me not to.

While the match was an interesting concept on paper, it was a stinker in execution. The idea was too unbelievable and the rules were too complicated to follow. The fans shit all over the match and it was a terrible way to debut a new, supposedly hot team. It was another nail in the Thrillseekers' coffin.

The only thing that got a reaction from the fans was our finishing move, a double drop kick from the top rope. Both of us climbed up to the same top corner post and with perfect timing hit a high double drop kick. It was a spectacular and original move that I've never seen anybody do since.

Politically it wasn't the smartest choice for a finish, as

the Rock 'n' Roll Express also used a double drop kick for their finishing move. The difference was they delivered theirs from the mat and connected about waist-high, if they even connected at all. But they were the top dogs in the company and as the number two pretenders to their throne, we had basically stolen their finish.

It was a breach of wrestling etiquette and a big rookie mistake. Nobody told us not to do it again, but rumors circulated that the Rock 'n' Roll were furious and had buried us to the boss.

They were all smiles to our faces though. It was another of wrestling's unwritten rules that when someone makes a mistake, nobody ever tells him about it. They just tell everybody else instead. It's a confusing concept. I compare it to someone on a hockey team needing to work on their slapshot but never being told about it. Instead, the rest of the team is told and everyone gossips and laughs about the guy's shitty slapshot behind his back. As a result he never gets better, gets cut from the team, and ends up selling fruit on the side of the road.

The Rock 'n' Roll Express were an institution in the South and had earned a lot of money over the years. They were still earning a lot with their lucrative SMW gimmick sales.

Ricky Morton was one of the most underrated wrestlers of all time and one of the top three babyface sellers ever. He would get the shit kicked out of him every night and he made the girls and guys cry out in sympathy for him with his movements and facial expressions. He made them believe that he was in terrible pain and on his last legs. They would be on the edge of their seats begging for him to tag Robert, much the same way I begged for Greg Gagne to tag

Jimmy Brunzell in the Winnipeg Arena. Ricky was small and kind of pudgy and he had a cigarette in his hand at all times before the match, but he never got tired or blew up in the ring. Robert didn't have the work rate or the charisma that Ricky did, but the two of them had chemistry and the IT factor. Because of it, the Rock 'n' Roll always had one of the best matches on the show.

Ricky and Robert were the epitome of tag team, both in the ring and out. They followed each other around everywhere finishing each other's sentences and making jokes like a modern-day Abbott and Costello.

"Ricky, I didn't get much sleep last night."

"I haven't slept for sixteen years, Robert."

"I figure we'll start the match slow, Robert."

"And taper off from there, Ricky."

They continued their wacky duo act by pulling ribs on anyone they could reel in. They'd goad an unsuspecting victim to point at a spot on the wall and then challenge them to try to walk up to the wall and touch that exact spot with their eyes closed. When the guy began to walk toward the wall, Robert would pull down his pants and the guy would end up sticking his finger up Gibson's ass.

I couldn't believe how moist and warm it was.

Another howler saw Ricky take a quarter and stick it onto the middle of his forehead. Then he'd hit the back of his head causing the coin to fall off his forehead into his hand. I thought it would be an easy task, so they stuck the quarter onto my forehead. I whacked the back of my head progressively harder and harder, until I was belting it full force and wondering why the hell the coin wasn't coming off. They broke out laughing when they held up the coin that they'd pressed into my head and then pulled off. The coin still felt stuck to my head and I never realized it was gone.

I'm from Canada. What the hell do I know about NASCAR?

They were also notorious for bragging about all of their wrestling accomplishments. Whenever someone mentioned an old promotion or a Podunk town, Ricky would pipe up, "When we came into (insert name of town here) there were only 200 people in the building. We worked an angle with (insert name of opponents here) and sold the place out. We popped that territory and there were motherfuckers hanging from the rafters trying to get in. We made (insert name of opponents here) look like a million bucks, isn't that right, Hoot?"

"That's right, Punky."

Hoot was Robert's nickname and Punky was Ricky's nickname.

Three days later they'd be talking about another Podunk town. "When we came into (insert name of town here) there were only 200 people in the building. We worked an angle with (insert name of opponents here) and sold the place out. We popped that territory and there were motherfuckers hanging from the rafters trying to get in. We made (insert name of opponents here) look like a million bucks, isn't that right, Hoot?"

"That's right, Punky."

No matter what town or territory came up in a conversation, Rock 'n' Roll told the same story verbatim. It became a game when they started talking, "Ricky's going to tell the story. Let's see if he says the same stuff!"

He always did.

The SMW roster included quite a few other seasoned

veterans and I learned the ways of the road from all of them. When I first met Dirty Dick Murdoch, one of wrestling's true legends, I thought he was a literal dick. He was a potbellied, skinny-legged old-timer with a fat face and a W. C. Fields nose. His nickname was Captain Redneck although at first I thought it was Obnoxious Racist.

So when Cornette asked me to drive Dick around I was pissed. In retrospect, it ended up being one of the highlights of my career. As I got to know him I realized he wasn't a racist, he was just honest and fair. He hated everyone equally.

On the long trips from town to town, he told hilarious stories and taught me how to hit speed limit signs with a beer bottle while driving eighty miles an hour. If you think it's easy, give it a try. It takes a lot of timing, a lot of miles, and a lot of beers to get it right. Murdoch had all three and I never saw him miss a speed sign when he threw a bottle . . . never.

Murdoch was too big a star to lodge at SMF, but Corny's next hire wasn't. Jimmy had seen a guy called Johnny K-9 working in Detroit and recruited him to be a powerhouse heel named Bruiser Bedlam. To save on hotel fees, he invited Bruiser to stay with us at SMF, unbeknownst to Anthony and me. Bruiser was built like a cigarette machine with a head on it and that head was shaved bald with a sole shock of hair sprouting out of the side of his skull. He had gold hoops hanging off each ear, a huge handlebar mustache, and a cache of prison tattoos that he'd received, coincidentally, in prison. The biggest one was an entire sentence written across his stomach saying TRUE TO THE CREW (which was his catchphrase). I saw this tat-

May 1994. The Thrillseekers with Bruiser Bedlam. Note Bruiser's "True to the Crew" tattoo on his stomach and the brand new pair of flipflops that he stole from Wal-Mart earlier that day. The fact that I'm wearing an Iron Maiden shirt and Lance a D.A.R.E. shirt says it all.

too because he never wore a shirt—ever—only flip-flops and gym shorts.

He was really friendly and called everybody "buddy," but the man truly did not give a shit. He'd walk into Wendy's (sans shirt), grab a dirty tray and use it for a buffet plate—no charge of course. When he needed new flip-flops he'd walk into Wal-Mart (party central), put on new ones, and walk out.

He'd bench-press six plates on each side of the bar and, after a few reps, pretend that he couldn't lift the weight off his chest. When people panicked and came to assist, he'd laugh maniacally, yell "Fuck you!" and do an additional three or four reps. He constantly talked about sex and bragged about all the girls who'd enjoyed "Honking on Bobo."

After Bruiser had crashed uninvited with us for a few days, he decided to repay our hospitality by doing the dishes. The next day, I went to get a plate and noticed that it had a bunch of crusty shit all over it. On closer inspection, I found that all of the dishes had crusty shit on them. Fearing the worst, I watched Bruiser the next time he washed the dishes and saw that for him "washing" consisted of holding the dirty dish under the faucet for a few seconds before putting it back into the cupboard. No soap, no scrubbing, no hassle.

He had been getting on my nerves from the first day he stayed with us, and when I told him that I would take care of the dishes from then on, he got really pissed and insisted HE would do them. The debate escalated until I finally boiled over: "You know what, man? You're obnoxious and you're getting on my nerves with this TRUE TO THE CREW bullshit. What does that even mean?"

"Buddy, I'm going to show you what happens when you disrespect THE CREW! I'm gonna whip your ass right now." He put up his dukes and got into a fighting stance. "I'm gonna throw hands, prison-style."

As I said, this guy was a convict and twice my size but I didn't give a shit. It was one of the stupidest decisions of my life, but if I was going down, I was taking him with me. I'd already decided that I was going to rip the pirate hoop out of his ear if he got close enough.

Since I didn't have a CREW to be TRUE to and I'd never been to prison, I wanted to let him know that I was no slouch.

"I'm gonna throw hands Winnipeg-style!"

I wasn't sure what that meant but I was hoping it would scare him.

Instead, a smile broke out on his face. Then he burst out laughing and dropped his dukes.

"You know what, Winnipeg? I've got a lot of respect for you. I'm not going to fight you. You're TRUE TO THE CREW, buddy."

I was a huge fan of the *Shout at the Devil* record, but that wasn't important—Winnipeg had saved the day.

With that, I established myself as the king of the SMF castle. That is until Boo Bradley came a-calling.

Cornette brought Boo (who became Balls Mahoney in ECW) in to be Candido's partner and gave him the gimmick of a strange simpleton. The best gimmicks are extensions of real-life qualities and while I'm not sure if Boo was simple, he sure was strange. He was obsessed with Satanic death metal and constantly sang songs in a high-pitched, King Diamond soprano. He never seemed to have any clean clothes and had a stench cloud surrounding him. Cornette should've given him a Pigpen gimmick.

Even though he reeked, I could've dealt with him, as he was no worse than Bruiser. But the straw that broke the moose's back was when Anthony and I decided to clean his room. It was a mess, so we put on rubber gloves and collected all the garbage strewn about, picked up his filthy clothes, and went to change the sheets on his bed. When we lifted his mattress off the box spring, I almost had an aneurism when I saw the nest of roaches living there. They looked up at me, I looked down at them, and all ninety of us screamed. It was exactly like the movie *Creepshow*: They scuttled off the bed and quickly disappeared.

This stupid bastard would sit in bed and eat sandwiches, but instead of throwing the crusts away he put them between the mattress and the box spring. Apparently the roaches had heard about the fine buffet offered at SMF and decided to set a spell.

Do I even need to tell you that at that moment I was finished with SMF?

CHAPTER 27

STRANGE KENTUCKY PEOPLE

Things were even stranger on the road than they were at SMF.

We'd arrive in a town like Hyden, Kentucky, where the census population was 200 and 400 people would turn up for the matches. People would literally come down from the hills to see the show. I hate to stereotype, but this was pure *Deliverance*–type shit and the evidence of inbreeding was impossible to ignore. I saw one kid with purple skin and another with hands like lobster claws. I know it's a cliché to say that rednecks have no teeth, but it's just plain creepy to see so many people in one place that literally have no chiclets. But they loved to watch their rasslin'.

I don't know where they got the cash, but the people in these towns bought more gimmicks than fans any-where else did. I was signing pictures at the table in Vir-gie, Kentucky, when a guy came up and asked me for an autograph.

"Sure thing, bud," I said with a smile. "I'd be happy to."

He looked at me with sleepy-eyed wonder, his gut peeking out of his greasy wifebeater, and asked with complete seriousness, "How did you know my name was Bud?"

You can't write stuff like this.

I was hanging around between matches at another of our regular towns, Paintsville, Kentucky, when a girl came up to me and gave me a videotape. She stared at the ground while she stuttered and spit out, "Chris Jericho, I love you. I made a tape of your matches just for you. It's got all your matches that you ever had in SMW." Then she turned tail and split. I was honored that she'd put them all on one tape as a present but when I watched the tape, it didn't contain any matches. What it did contain, however, was much more entertaining.

The tape featured the girl and her hillbilly mountain family performing for me . . . and what a show it was. It began with her looking into the camera like a deer in headlights. She resembled Chris Farley dressed up as Meatloaf circa 1977 and was wearing a shirt with a rebel flag on it that said, "You wear your colors, I'll wear mine."

She began her dissertation and said, "I made this tape for you, Chris Jericho [she always called me by my full name]. We love you, Chris Jericho. You're my favorite rassler, Chris Jericho, and I really love you, Chris Jericho." She wiped the snot out of her nose.

Then she became Annie Wilkes from *Misery* and started speaking gibberish like, "Well look. Here's a white googleberry. Fleezin fibble foo!" She began dancing as the rest of her family came into frame like Oompa Loompas. They were all smacking each other's butts and doing the most bizarre version of the Electric Slide, while chanting in unison "Electric Slide, Electric Slide, Electric Slide," like some kind of disco cult.

Then a kid who I'm guessing was her brother or her husband—or both—explained how much he liked watching rasslin', then farted twice. Then his mother or his wife—or both—who literally had NO teeth, patted him on the butt and commented on its fragrance. There was a bed in the middle of the living room and on the wall behind it were two pictures: one of Jesus and one of Ricky and Robert. Both photos were at the exact same level, which I'm sure was a huge honor for the Savior.

Farleyloaf wandered back in and gave a shout-out to Lance. "I like you too, Lance! Here's a wheelbarra," and she started to push around a child's toy wheelbarrow while performing a massive booty shake. The camera panned to her left, only to find the fartster walking like a crab for no apparent reason. Then the camera panned into the yard where there was a battalion of rusted old vehicles, each housing a sad-eyed dog. In the background trying his hardest to stay out of camera range but failing miserably was an old *American Gothic*–looking farmer who I'm assuming was responsible for the whole mess.

The camera spun back around, passing the Amazing Crab Boy™ and settling on a lady with a worse Lloyd Christmas *Dumb and Dumber* haircut than Jim Carrey. She stayed in the shot long enough to say, "I love the Thrillseekers. I want to have two kids named Chris and Lance and a dog named Storm." It was much creepier than it sounds, believe me.

These people were either the greatest actors of our generation or complete lunatics and I don't think they were thespians. Nor do I think they knew what thespian means.

I still don't know why she gave me the tape. Did she think that I'd watch it and become so enamored of her and her family that I'd come over for farts and crabwalks? If I wanted to impress Jessica Simpson, I sure as hell wouldn't give her a tape of me picking my nose and doing the Electric Slide. But then again maybe it's crazy enough to work . . .

Somehow the video got around and became a cult classic on the tape-trading circuit under the name "Strange Kentucky People." Look for it wherever fine hillbilly videos are sold and if you act now, you receive a free Rock 'n' Roll Express/Son of God portrait package!

I was also semiresponsible for another tape-trading classic known as "Jim Cornette vs. the Drive-Thru."

Me, Corny, Lance, and a few other guys were driving back from a show and stopped at a Dairy Queen drive-thru. Everyone was starving and we ended up ordering around twenty burgers. But there was a long line and it took us half an hour to get to the window, which put Corny in an even fouler mood than usual.

"Can I help you?" the girl at the window inquired.

Cornette answered with irritation, "Of course you can help me. I'm picking up my order."

I grabbed my video camera and started filming for the heck of it.

"What order is that?"

"What order is that? The order I placed half an hour ago for twenty burgers."

"Oh, I thought you were joking."

Cornette's face turned beet red as he stuttered in disbelief, "Why the fuck would I be joking? Do you think I have nothing better to do than order twenty fucking burgers and wait in line thirty minutes as a joke? I thought you were fixing my order, you stupid bitch!" I learned in the South, you don't make food, you fix it.

"Sir, if you continue to use that type of language, I'm not going to get you your order at all," she threatened.

I was in the back of the van with the camera zoomed in on Corny's tomato face and I needed more emotion for my epic, so I stirred the pot a little.

"She's fucking with you, Jimmy. She thinks it's a joke."

I would've let it go at that point, but Jimmy was just getting started. His lower jaw jutted forward (giving him a massive underbite) and he continued, "You're worried about my language? I'll give you some language: You cunts better get me my fucking food right now!"

Then he sprang out of the van and stuck his whole upper torso through the drive-thru window screaming that he was going to kill everybody inside and make them all pay.

We eventually got our food, although I'll bet after that whole ordeal our burgers had been garnished with some special snot sauce.

Cornette had a horrible temper and was a hotheaded jerk sometimes but he was able to channel those qualities into his interviews. He was one of the best promo men of all time and he was the most hated heel in SMW by far.

He took great responsibility in trying to train everybody else to do the same type of promos that he could do. Cornette was a master of incorporating the energy, charisma, delivery, and originality that it took to give a memorable promo. I was on the other end of the spectrum because I'd never really had the chance to work on them.

Cornette stressed that interviews were the most important aspect of wrestling. If I wanted to make it to the big leagues, I'd have to learn how to do them properly.

Other guys like the Dirty White Boy and Chris Candido could also do good promos but my favorite guy to watch was Bullet Bob Armstrong, the patriarch of the famous Armstrong wrestling family.

Bullet was in his sixties and rarely wrestled but he was the commissioner of SMW and was responsible for multiple promos on every TV show. He didn't need anyone to tell him what to say or when to say it, he just needed to know the details of what he was supposed to get across before getting the job done in minimal takes.

I popped huge when he was asked to do a detailed promo to explain one of the complicated angles on the show. He listened to what Jim wanted to accomplish with the segment, thought about it for a few minutes, and went in front of the camera. After delivering a classic, Bullet looked at Cornette and said, "It don't get any better than that," then walked out the door without saying another word. Nobody disagreed. That, young Jedi, is known as true confidence.

Even though I was learning from some of the best, my promos were still stanky. I had fire and energy, but my delivery was forced and cheesy. Instead of being cool and likable, I was coming across as insincere and annoying.

Cornette worked with me for hours to help me to improve and when I started using some of his tricks, I got 1,004 times better. Jimmy taught me to stop speaking with the same volume and the same tone and alter my delivery. I started varying my voice, almost speaking with a whisper at times, forcing the fans to really pay attention to what I was saying. That made my point more memorable.

That was the second big lesson I learned about promos. They're like singing. If you scream the whole song it becomes monotonous. But when you sing with emotion and dynamics, it draws people into the vibe of the song. Then when you blow their heads off with a powerful scream, the performance becomes much more effective and memorable. The whole idea of doing a promo is not to just make jokes and repeat catchphrases, it's also to make the people watching at home want to buy a ticket to see you. If the promos are good, fans will be familiar with the angles and the personalities and develop an emotional investment in each bout as a result.

CHAPTER 28

AIN'T YOU SUPPOSED TO BE A FAMOUS WRESTLER?

Unfortunately, Jimmy's business skills didn't match his promo skills, and he tried to offset our huge guarantees by booking us on personal appearances.

When we showed up for our first appearance at a furniture store, I had to look in the mirror to make sure I hadn't transformed into David St. Hubbins because there was nobody there.

I'm not saying there were only four or five people. I'm saying there was Nobody there. NOOOOOBODY!

Only Artie Fufkin begging us to "kick this ass for a man" was missing.

It was embarrassing but the owner of the store wouldn't let us leave.

"You gotta stay for two hours. I'm paying you seventy-five bucks each." I would have paid him the seventy-five myself for the right to split. But we had to sit at a table in the middle of the store on a Saturday afternoon with the customers milling around wondering who the hell the two idiots with the stack of photos in front of them were. A couple of kids finally showed up to hang around the table and one of them said, "Ain't you supposed to be a famous wrestler? How come nobody is here? Where is everybody?"

There's no way to answer that question with any kind of dignity.

I just smiled and shooed them away. When another kid asked Lance, "Are you a famous pro wrestler?" he dead-panned, "Apparently not." The kid wilted under Lance's fuck-off stare and wandered away. The next 112 minutes were long ones indeed.

The silver lining was that the owner of the furniture store had connections in the music business and offered to get me free Metallica tickets. After seeing the huge crowd we'd drawn to his store, it was the least he could do.

So I drove the three hours to Cincinnati and saw Metallica, Danzig, and Suicidal Tendencies. It was a great show and because of my tight connection with Krazy Kelly's Kooky Furniture, I got to hang around backstage like a real rock 'n' roller. I was speechless when I got to meet Metallica's guitar player Kirk Hammett. I was even more speechless when I asked him for his autograph and he replied, "Only if I can use my boner as a speed bump."

Master of Meat Puppets?

After I drove over Kirk's kock with my Kamaro, I struck up a conversation with Rob Dibble, a pitcher for the Cincinnati Reds, who'd helped his team win the World

Series that year. The power of music once again reared its rockin' head and after discussing the finer points of thrash metal, he invited me to come hang out. Let me say that hanging out in the VIP section of the hottest clubs in Cincy with a World Series winning pitcher definitely didn't suck. Rob even lent me his championship ring to wear for the night and I used it to prove to the girls that I was a pitcher for the Reds also.

Back in SMW, Cornette introduced his new attraction: a pair of angry ghetto dudes called the Gangstas. They came out for their first TV appearance with an entire posse dressed either like Louis Farrakhan with the bow ties around their necks or street thugs with the bandannas hiding their faces. They made gang signs, spoke Ebonics, and mockingly ate watermelons and fried chicken to protest the stereotypical "where all the white women at" portrayal of African Americans by certain segments of society.

Jimmy was hoping to tap in to the racism of the South by making the Gangstas top heels. But instead of the controversy creating cash, it did the opposite. The sponsors, the television executives, and the fans were all offended. Corny's act of desperation didn't work, business suffered, and Smoky Mountain Wrestling was losing ground.

Cornette didn't help the situation by returning to the WWF. He'd struck up a working agreement with Vince and in return for Jimmy's managing skills, Smoky became like a feeder system for the WWF. SMW suffered because Jim was spending less time with his own company. Still, I figured his return would lead to a big break for me and Lance. Certainly some scout from the WWF would discover us now! Except nobody did. The closest we got was an offer to do a weekend of house shows losing to the Bushwhackers, until even that fell through.

Since it was clear that the WWF had no interest in me, I decided to flaunt my goods to the other show in town when I saw that WCW was coming to Knoxville. It wasn't a problem getting tickets for the show because I'd received a complimentary pair with my power bill. WCW wasn't doing very good business and they had to give out free tickets to entice people to show up. But I was a poor independent wrestler so I had no problem using the free ducats in order to suck up for a job.

I walked the backstage area of the Coliseum in complete awe of the whole setup. Even though I'd wrestled in the same building with Smoky, this was like catching a glimpse of the promised land. Everywhere I looked I saw legendary figures milling around: Sting, Lex Luger, Arn Anderson, the Steiner Brothers, Terra Ryzing. All of them were eating plates of steak and chicken from an overstocked catering table that made the licorice and cupcakes that made up the SMW catering look embarrassing.

Other guys like Kevin Sullivan and my former AWA idol Greg Gagne seemed to be running the show, holding clipboards and wearing headsets. Tonga was also now with WCW and he introduced me to everyone.

"This is my friend Chris, I worked with him in Mexico. He's a great wrestler."

It was actually quite embarrassing, but I appreciated the props especially when he brought me to meet the booker of WCW, Ric Flair. If you're a wrestling fan you appreciate Ric Flair; if you're a wrestler you idolize him. He's on the short list of the greatest performers of all time.

When Flair shook my hand, I noticed two things:

1. He was immaculately dressed in an expensive suit and tie.
2. He had a huge schnozz that looked like a plantain stuck in the middle of his face.

"Nice to meet you, sir." Why he was calling me sir, I had no idea.

I was happy just to be talking to him, but when he said, "Let me give you my phone number. Give me a call, and maybe we can arrange a tryout for you," I was gobsmacked! An invitation to the big time! Even though it wasn't the WWF, I wasn't going to take it lightly.

I carried Flair's number in my pocket for days, asking myself the same question I'd ask if I'd gotten a phone number from a pretty girl.

How long do I wait before I make the call? One day? One week?

Getting a job was more important than getting laid and I had to weigh the factors much more diligently. I finally decided to call two days later.

That gave Ric a day to recuperate from his travels and another day to settle into his office. I didn't want to wait too much longer because I was pretty sure he was waiting for my call. I dialed the number on the paper and when a female voice answered, I turned on the Jeri-Charm (taken verbatim from the actual call):

"Hello, can I speak to Mr. Flair, please?"

"Who's speaking?"

"This is Lion Heart Chris Jericho. The Nature Boy is expecting my call."

"Okay."

"He's expecting my call."

"Yes, you said that Mr. . . . umm . . . Heart. Hold on, please."

I waited on the line for a while. She came back and said, "Ric is in Aruba right now."

"Oh. Well, when should I call back?"

"He should be back in about a week or so. He's on vacation. So just leave your number and I'll have him call you back."

I wanted to stall a bit longer and really win over Ric's secretary with my charisma.

"Aruba huh? Where is that? Maybe I should fly the both of us over there and we can meet up with Ric? Ha ha."

While it was obvious that she was enamored with my suggestion, she covered it up by stoically saying, "Ric will call you."

I thought it was a little strange that Flair's personal secretary had to put me on hold to find out that her boss was in Aruba. It was almost as if she'd lied to me, but I knew THAT would never happen. Nevertheless I didn't let it discourage me and I called her back one week later to the day.

"Hi, this is Chris Jericho. Can I speak to Ric please? I spoke with you last week and you told me to call you back."

For some reason she acted like she didn't remember my rapier wit and said, "No, I said he'd call you when he came back from vacation. He's still in Aruba."

On it went.

"He's extended his stay for another week."

"He's back from Aruba, but he's in Charlotte now."

"He's washing his hair."

"A dog ate his homework."

I finally got the hint, but I couldn't figure out why he'd given me his number in the first place. It was another fine lesson about the world of wrestling.

So I was 0-for-2 in landing a spot with one of the big companies in the States and I felt like shit because I'd come to Tennessee with the hopes of springboarding into the big leagues. Instead, I'd springboarded into the same high school gyms that I'd already worked in Canada.

The situation was complicated further when I got a call from the Japanese company WAR, asking me to come work for them full-time. I'd already done a few tours with them and had impressed them enough that they wanted me to work for them on a monthly basis.

But if I took the gig it would cause a huge problem. Smoky recorded four weeks of TV in one shot, so if I missed one TV taping I wouldn't be able to be involved in any of the angles or shows for an entire month.

The next WAR tour took place during the next SMW taping so I knew there was no way I could work in both companies. I agonized over the decision for days but in the end there was no way I could turn down a regular gig in Japan. I'd based my career path on Chris Benoit's and after he made a huge name for himself in Japan, he'd gotten a job with WCW. If working in SMW wasn't going to get me to the big leagues, then maybe working in the respected environment of Japan would.

I knew my absence was going to spoil a lot of Jim's plans, so I dialed his number immediately.

Jim didn't understand or appreciate the Japanese style of wrestling and I thought the best way to make him understand my choice was to compare it to a similar situation that he'd been through: "You had a dream to start your own wrestling company and you left WCW and the WWF in order to make it happen. You took a chance and fulfilled your dream. Well, I want to do the same thing. Working in Japan is one of my dreams."

To my surprise, he understood and gave me his blessing. I think he was probably relieved that he wouldn't have to worry about my guarantee anymore. We agreed that he would explain to the fans that I was missing the tapings because I was touring Japan, but it was no secret to either of us that, in the long run, I'd basically given my notice and he'd basically accepted it. However, I still wanted to wrestle for Smoky for as long as I could, and Jimmy still had plans for the Thrillseekers.

He was planning to run a show at the Knoxville Coliseum that would climax all of the major angles of the year and was so sure of its success, he claimed if it didn't sell out he would "strip naked and sing 'Back in Black' in the center of the ring."

Please God, let it sell out.

One of Cornette's big plans for the show was to build a feud between the Thrillseekers and the team he managed, the Heavenly Bodies. The Bodies were made up of Tom Pritchard and Jimmy Del Ray and had been the top heel team until they'd lost a loser-leaves-SMW match, which was an excuse for them to start full-time with the WWF. Cornette received permission from Vince to bring them back for his big show. It was to be our biggest win and the beginning of a serious push for the Seekers.

The build for the angle had started at the previous taping in Warrensville, North Carolina, (I don't know where the heck it is either), when the fine fans in the Ville presented us with a cake to welcome us into the company. In the middle of our ceremony Cornette came out to spoil the party and to put us in our place.

"Well, well, Thrillseekers. You're doing all your fancy moves and you've got your fancy videos and all those fancy costumes. But all that doesn't mean a thing because when it all boils down, in the ring you just ain't that fancy."

The crowd booed but we took the insult in stride, as if he'd meant it as constructive criticism. "You know what, Jim? You're right and as a result, we're just going to step back and give you this cake. We want you to have it."

He went to take a bite and I shoved his face into it.

(Wrestling Rule #24: Whenever a cake appears in the ring, someone will end up wearing it.)

Cornette got his revenge when he orchestrated an attack by two masked man who beat the hell out of us in a parking lot later in the week. The ambush was of course accidentally recorded by an ardent fan and the tape exposed the masked men as the Heavenly Bodies. The shit was on.

TED IRVINE   L. WING
N.Y. RANGERS

TOP
April 1974. My dad and I in the dressing
room of Madison Square Garden after
the Rangers beat the Canadiens in the
first round of the playoffs. The Baby-
Faced Assassin scored 2 goals that
night, while I chipped in with 3 assists.

LEFT
Ted Irvine hockey card from 1970, his
first year with the Rangers. My dad
scored 20 goals that season.

CALGARY

TOP
July 1990. Outside of "Okotok's Finest Hotel," better known as the Willy, my palatial estate for the next 3 months.

RIGHT
July 1990. Inside the pink bowling alley known as the Hart Brothers Pro Wrestling Camp. Wilf Weird Eye, Cowboy Chris Jericho (Rockers T-shirt and all), Lance T. Storm, and our illustrious trainer, Ed "The Goto Hills Savage" Langley.

TOP LEFT
January 1993. Lenny, Como, and
I backstage after a huge show in
Calgary in front of 34 rabid fans.

TOP RIGHT
March 1992. Sudden Impact wearing
the finest in Shawn Michaels tights
and Sgt. Pepper jackets.

BOTTOM
July 1992. Ladies and gentlemen . . .
The Phoenix! I spent a month building
the wings and making the mask, and it
still looked absolutely red reels.

December 1993. I had just won one of the world's oldest titles, the NWA Middleweight Championship, from Mano Negra. These fans were happy, but the majority were miffed that a gringo had beaten a native Mexican, even though I was the good guy.

CORAZON DE LEON

TOP LEFT
April 1993. With Lassar Tron, aka Hector Guerrero, in Mexico City. The Sgt. Pepper jacket travels to its third country.

TOP RIGHT
December 1994. I was so excited about my new outfit for a Super Luchas magazine photo shoot. I was wearing this ensemble because I thought it was very, very cool. I was very, very wrong.

LEFT
May 1993. My second-ever piece of merchandise, from the Topps Ballbag Collector's Series.

November 1993. The crew of the Hamburg Catch Tournament, including Boston Blackie, Suni War Cloud, Indio Guajardo, Drew McDonald, Rip Morgan, the Legend of Doom, the Moondog, the Liverpool Lads, and, in the front row in the red pants, Mal Mason, the only ref I ever worked with who insisted on having his own ring music.

August 1994. My audition in Knoxville for the remake of Carrie did not go well. The redneck who stuck his finger in a pool of my blood, tasted it and was convinced it wasn't real made the moment even more disgusting.

JAPAN

TOP LEFT
February 1996. The evil Fuyuki-Gun, aka Team No Respect and the top heels in WAR: Fuyuki, Jado, Gedo, and Lion Do.

TOP RIGHT
March 1995. Against Ultimo Dragón in the tournament to crown the first WAR IJ Champion in Ryogoku.

BOTTOM
April 1995. The world-famous Lionsault, a move I invented in an empty Arena México with a bag of dirty laundry for a target.

TOP
March 1995. At the Tokyo Hard Rock with Psicosis, Big Titan, and a 14-year-old-looking dude named Oscar. The four of us are striking the famous A-OK/devilhorn /beer can /thumbs-up pose.

TOP
December 1995. The Super J Cup Second Stage lineup. Yes, that is a grown man in a crab mask.

LEFT
January 1997. The mysterious Super Liger at the Tokyo Dome. The match was such a shipwreck that Super Liger's debut and retirement were on the same night.

OPPOSITE PAGE, BOTTOM LEFT
December 1995. After wining the Fighting Spirit Award at the J Cup, I flash the Nixon Victory sign for some reason. The fact that I was completely wasted might have had something to do with it.

OPPOSITE PAGE, BOTTOM RIGHT
December 1995. The Calgary Kids at the Super J Cup Second Stage.

TOP
July 1997. One of the best things about working in WCW was that my mom could see me every week on TV.

BOTTOM
April 1997. Eddy and I adhere to the Benoit dress code while Chavo rebels. However, all three of us adhere to the wrestler fanny pack code.

& ATLANTA

TOP
November 1998. Me and my crew enjoy the moment after the Brian Hildebrand Tribute show. Later on that night, the five of us got annihilated on Brian's prescription marijuana.

LEFT
February 1998. The Good, the Bad Teeth and the Ugly. The legendary head of Jericho Personal Security and my personal hype man, Ralphus.

July 1999. Fozzy backstage in Spartanburg, South Carolina, before our second show ever. A record company bidding war for The Fozz began the following week.

& ATLANTA

TOP
May 1999. At the Hart House after Owen's funeral. How many world champions and hall of famers can you count in this picture? A few moments later, Stu put a chokehold on Brian Blair and wouldn't let go.

BOTTOM
August 1999. The taming of the savage beast: the love of my life, Jessica.

PERO... ¿QUÉ PUEDO HACER YO PARA ALCANZAR MI SUEÑO? NO TENGO MÁS QUE ESTE CUERPO ENDEBLE Y... ESTOY SOLO.

INMENSAMENTE SOLO.

MUNDIAL... EL HIJO DE LAS FIERAS... EL ÚNICO... ¡CORAZÓN DE LEÓN!

June 1993. This is from a comic book that was released in Mexico, which featured me working as a zookeeper too afraid to follow my dreams of becoming a wrestler. Then I meet a magical talking frog who convinces me that I need to follow my dreams the same way that the men who first went to the moon did. I'm completely serious by the way.

MY WHITE WHALE

The angle was a huge success and our match with the Bodies for the big show called Night of the Legends was one of the most anticipated matches on the card. It was going to be a huge night for us and I wanted to debut a new move that would be as monumental as the occasion . . . the Shooting Star Press.

The Shooting Star Press was the move that had been originated in Japan by pioneering high-flyer Jushin Liger and had later been the trademark of my old friend Bret Como (and the Zebra Kid). I'd never done it before but I'd been conned into thinking I could do it by Ultimo Dragón, one of my future greatest rivals. He'd seen me do the Lionsault in Mexico and thought that the Shooting Star wasn't too far off. He was wrong.

When I practiced off the diving board of a swimming pool near SMF, I nailed it every time. Even when I didn't nail it, the worst thing that happened was I took a refreshing plunge into the pool. I wasn't stupid enough to think it would be as easy from the top rope, but I was stupid enough to try it without a practice mat in the ring a few weeks before the Night of the Legends.

I stood on the top rope, repeating "I think I can" like I was the Little Wrestler That Could. Summoning all my courage, I jumped out into the wild blue yonder. But once I did, I had no idea where I was in the air and ended up coming straight down on my head. Even though I was amazingly unharmed, it completely freaked me out. Since I'd started my career, I had a horrible phobia of breaking my neck and ending up paralyzed like my mom. Even though she never came out and said it, I could see in her eyes whenever we talked about wrestling that she harbored the same fear. God was with me that day and I should've learned my lesson. But I didn't.

I couldn't let it go and convinced myself that I'd be less of a wrestler if I didn't do the Shooting Star. It had become my white whale and I was obsessed with mastering it.

On the day of the big show, I arrived at the Coliseum early to practice the Shooting Star as many times as it took to get it ready. I ran into Cornette backstage and when he asked why I was there early, I told him I wanted to practice a few things.

"Well for God's sake, just don't hurt yourself."

I walked into the ring in the middle of the empty Coliseum and climbed to the top rope. Once again I brainwashed myself into believing that I had to perfect the move or else my career would mean nothing. All rational thought had gone out the window and with no spotter or practice mat, I leaped out into the air again.

To my surprise, this time I landed it almost perfectly. Almost. But I rotated too far to one side and landed with all my weight on the right side. I looked at my arm and something wasn't quite right. There was a divot in the middle of my forearm, like a dip in a roller coaster, but strangely it didn't hurt. I rolled out of the ring and walked to the back of the arena where Lance had turned up.

"I saw you land," Lance said with concern. "Are you okay?"

"Look at my arm. Does this look right to you?"

When I moved my arm up and down it was bending like a rubber pencil. It still didn't hurt but I thought it would be best to get it checked out before the match. Before I left the arena for the hospital, I asked Lance, "Did I at least nail the move?"

With a classic Lance response he said, "Not even close."

At the hospital, the doctor messed with my arm a bit. When he was done, he assured me that if it was broken I'd be screaming in pain. However he still wanted to X-ray it. We were both astonished when he got the results and discovered that I had indeed fractured my radius bone.

"We have to get you into surgery tonight."

"Can we do it tomorrow morning instead? I have to sit at ringside at a very important wrestling match tonight."

I knew there was no way in hell he would let me out of his care if I told him I had to actually wrestle a match. He pondered a little and said as long as I was only going to watch, it was okay with him. Sucker . . .

He scheduled my surgery for the next morning, put my arm in a soft cast, and told me that under NO circumstances could I do anything physical. I had zero intention of listening to him and when I saw Cornette back at the arena, he went ballistic when I told him I'd broken my arm.

"I told you to be careful! You stupid idiot! You dumb—"

I cut him off and told him I still planned on wrestling that night. Broken arm or not, I wasn't missing the match.

The redness fell out of his face like a thermometer as he asked me, "Are you sure? Well just be careful."

That was it. It was *the* stupidest decision I ever made in my career. I had no business being in the ring that night and one false move could've ended my career forever. Jimmy knew how dangerous it was for me to be wrestling but he didn't care at that point. Going through with the planned match was the most important thing to him and if my career ended as a result, it was my own damn fault.

Besides Corny, everyone else backstage thought that I was insane to wrestle with a broken arm. Road Warrior Hawk (the real one, not the Johnny South facsimile) told me that I was the bravest and the stupidest guy he'd ever met. Terry Funk told me that I was a bigger dumbass than he was. Strangely, I still felt no pain and I decided that I wasn't going to take one painkiller during the whole healing process. I don't know if it was toughness or stupidity, but I never did.

I even gave my prescription for them to a wrestler named Brian Lee, who was quite concerned. "Hey man, doesn't your arm hurt?"

"Strangely it doesn't," I said. "I don't think I'm gonna need these painkillers."

"Thank God, I was so worried," Brian cooed. Then

his concern melted away and he said, "Can I have your prescription then?"

I spoke to Tom and Jimmy, my Heavenly Body opponents, before the match and told them even with a fractured radius I refused to change a damn thing about the match. We would do it just the way we'd planned it a few days earlier. The iron will that I'd inherited from my mom was in full force that day.

During the match I was a machine, throwing left-handed punches, drop kicks, executing flips, and taking hard bumps. I even slammed Jimmy Del Ray with one arm—not that I had that much to do with it mind you. The Bodies were consummate pros and took such good care of me, you never would have known that I only had one functional arm.

Cornette had worked a deal to have Jim Ross, the greatest wrestling announcer of all time, announce the matches for the TV show. His work in calling the bout gave it a major league feel as he sold both the match and the story line behind it to the fans at home as something special. He also covered for me and said that I'd broken my arm in a motorcycle accident earlier in the day, rather than saying that one of the top babyfaces had broken his arm by screwing up a move that he had no business trying in the first place.

Cornette's plan for the finish was for me to get the living shit kicked out of me, until I ended up covered in blood from the same crazy bump that Cornette had raved about seeing me do on Lance's original audition tape. Referee Brian would make the decision to stop the match but before he could award it the Heavenly Bodies, I would beg him to let it continue. The Thrillseekers would then beat the odds with our courage and win the match putting us at a different level in the fan's eyes. It would've worked too, if it wasn't for those meddling kids and that darned broken arm.

Everything about the match was picture-perfect. Lance called it one of the most incredible experiences of his entire career. The fans were behind us, every move was crisp, and I ended up covered in more blood than Sissy Spacek in *Carrie*. It was as if I had a bucket of it poured over my head. Even Lance was worried and on the tape of the match you can even see him ask me, "Are you okay?"

After Lance super-kicked Jimmy Del Ray, allowing me to roll him up for the 3-count, I rolled onto the floor, my hair soaking wet with gore. Brian came to check on me and both of us were *covered* in plasma, when a stereotypical redneck fan with overalls and a cowboy hat said, "That ain't real blood!"

How could it not be? Did I have an invisible tube running up my back to the top of my head? Did I dump a bag of Karo syrup on myself when no one was looking? Give me a break, assclown! Then he dipped his finger in the pool of my DNA and put it in his mouth.

"Yeah, that's not real," he said knowingly to his friend. Bad call, Foghorn. How did I taste?

My tights were soaked with blood and after I took a shower in the dressing room, the stall looked like an abattoir. I had a three-inch cut on my forehead to match the broken bone in my arm. At least I already had hospital time booked the next day. Maybe I could get a two-for-one.

The night got even worse when I had to hawk Thrillseekers gimmicks during intermission and a plethora of girls wanted me to paint the town red (poor choice of words) with them after the show. I'd love to go, ladies, but I have to get a three-inch plate and seven screws inserted into my arm tomorrow. How 'bout a rain check?

Twelve hours later I was in an operating room with a gas mask over my face. The surgeon told me if I started counting down from 100, I'd be asleep by 85. That son of a bitch double-crossed me because I was out before I got to 97. I woke up after the surgery screaming, "I'm alive! Thank Jesus I'm alive!" I was serious too, because I was terrified before the operation. Fracturing my arm had shown me that I wasn't as invincible as I thought. I was an actual human being that could break.

The doctor told me that I wouldn't be able to wrestle for sixteen weeks. I was an independent wrestler with no insurance and since I'd broken my arm during practice Corny refused to pay for my surgery (that still doesn't explain why he didn't pay for the eight stitches I'd incurred during the match). But I had bills to cover and with a tour of Japan coming up, I used the power of positive thinking, hit the gym, and ate an entire bottle of calcium pills a day. I was miraculously cleared to wrestle after seven weeks. The mental powers of the Man They Call Raveen ain't got shit on the mental powers of the Man They Call Jericho.

About a year later, SMW closed its doors and Cornette returned to the WWF full-time. When he called me in Calgary one day to ask me if I'd like to come work for Vince, my heart soared. I figured that he'd finally put in a good word for me and the WWF brass was going to bring the Lion Heart in with a big push. My heart crashed to the ground like Icarus when he said, "We're going to introduce a group of wrestlers on the show who aren't necessarily job guys (term for losers), but not pushed guys either. They're going to be enhancement guys (fancy term for losers), and they're going to have gimmicks."

I'd been waiting for a chance to work in the WWF for six years, but not under those circumstances. It was an idea that was bound to fail and I had a hunch that it would end up hurting the careers of the guys who agreed to do it. I was right. Don't believe me? Here's a list of the future Hall of Famers who were involved with this plan. Do you remember the Pug or the Goon? How about Freddy Joe Floyd, TL Hopper, Rad Radford, or Salvatore Sincerely . . . (what the fruit does that one even mean anyway)?

I coulda been a contendah . . .

So I politely said, "Jimmy, you know, I'm not really interested. When the time comes for me to go to the WWF, I want it to be the right way. I'm only twenty-four and I don't want to rush to get there, especially if it means that I'd be brought in and not given a proper chance."

"I'll put you down as not interested with an asterisk," Jimmy said optimistically.

Things didn't work out with Jim Cornette the way I wanted them to in the short term, but in the big picture, SMW was the catalyst in helping me learn how to cut a good promo . . . which ended up becoming one of my trademarks. I also learned that acrobatic moves weren't as important as personality or storytelling, and I'm thankful for the time I spent working for Jim Cornette.

Plus I got to meet Strange Kentucky People.

PART SEVEN JAPAN

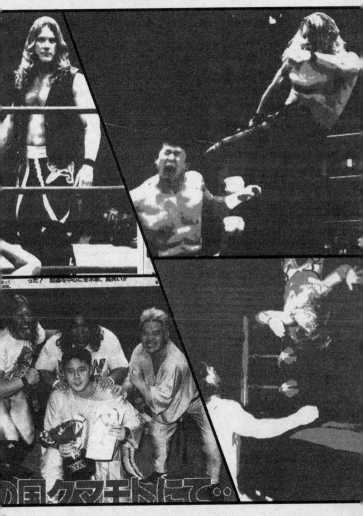

CHAPTER 30

DONALDO MAKUDONALDO

With SMW behind me, I was ready to devote all of my energies into making my mark in Japan. Even though WAR seemed to be impressed with my work, I was nervous because I'd already experienced a few false starts.

Years earlier in Calgary after putting up with all of Fred Jung's bullshit, he'd finally come through and booked Lance Storm and me for a three-week tour of Japan with FMW. The tour was scheduled for October of 1991, only one year after I'd made my debut at the Ponoka Moose Hall. During that year I'd wrestled a grand total of thirty-nine matches, which meant that I was as green as the Grinch and was nowhere near ready for such an international platform. But FMW was a small company and I worked cheap, so the deal was made.

Fred considered himself to be a mastermind and came up with the idea for us to go to Japan as Sudden Impact.

He insisted that the team name was as important as the team itself and was convinced that his name was money in the bank. Lance and I disagreed and thought as a Canadian team the name Northern Lights was a better fit. Fred wouldn't hear of it, as he was convinced that Sudden Impact was the handle that was gonna make us all rich!

I guess it was better than the Dirty Harrys . . .

Fred's other genius idea was to have Sudden Impact wear tights made of fabric that would change colors as we wrestled. I'd never heard of such a magical textile; perhaps Fred was planning on purchasing this mystical fabric from Willy Wonka. But even if an Oompa Loompa was growing the fabric from a Shazbot tree wouldn't the concept of color-changing tights fit the Northern Lights gimmick much better?

The amazing material never materialized, but our Japanese tour did. Fred had us sign contracts supposedly sent from Japan which were pockmarked with white-out and printing errors. In hindsight, it's obvious he'd doctored an old contract and passed it off to us as a new one, the same way he fabricated the WCW contract for Big Titan.

He also promised us work visas and then changed his mind and said we didn't need them. Instead he gave us his friend Ricky Fuji's address in Tokyo and told us if we were hassled at immigration to say we were on vacation and staying at Ricky's place. (Sounds like the name of a sitcom.)

The actual flight concerned me too. I didn't understand how an airplane could stay up in the sky for that long and I was afraid I was going to freak out en route. Unfortunately, since I couldn't take a steamship to the Orient I had no other choice.

When I picked Lance up on my way to the airport, he was wearing a collared shirt and tie for no apparent reason. When I asked him why, he replied, "Well, we're going to Japan, so I thought I should wear a tie." Naturally.

He was already annoyed at me because I was late in picking him up. But that pretty much defined our relationship . . . I was late and he wore a tie.

FMW was still a fledgling company and didn't have a lot of money so they bought us the cheapest plane tickets possible. Therefore we had to fly three hours south to Los Angeles in order to connect and fly the three hours back north on our way to Narita, Tokyo's airport.

When we boarded the plane to L.A., I saw that the Edmonton Oilers were also on our flight—sitting in coach with the rest of us peasants. Mark Messier, Jari Kurri, Bill Ranford, most of the guys who'd eliminated my beloved Winnipeg Jets from the Stanley Cup Playoffs only a year earlier were all there.

I knew that the guy who sat beside me used to play for the Oilers but I couldn't remember his name. It was driving me nuts, so when he got up to go to the bathroom I bent over to examine his carry-on bag stuffed under the seat. I fumbled around until I found the name tag and a cold chill ran up my spine when I saw whose bag it was. Then a warm squirt ran down my undies when a pissed-off deep voice from over my shoulder said, "Get your fucking hands off my bag."

I slowly looked up and faced Dave Semenko, one of the toughest goons in NHL history. Cementhead's sole reason for employment with the Oilers was to annihilate anybody who came even the slightest bit close to Wayne Gretzky.

And now he wanted to annihilate me.

I sat in silence, speechless and quivering in the face of death.

Semenko leaned into my face with the power of 1,000 knockouts behind him . . . and his coffee breath almost made me knockout 1,001.

"Don't touch my stuff, asshole."

When I began to retort he cut me off and said, "Don't even think of talking to me for the rest of the flight either."

I stared at my suddenly quite interesting shoelaces for the rest of the trip and survived the flight to L.A. unscathed. I passed the time by reading my Japanese-English dictionary and making note of all the phrases and words I was going to use when we landed.

So Lance and I arrived in Narita with no work visa, no idea who we were supposed to be meeting, no address for the company that had brought us over, and less than $200 (Canadian) between us. After making it through customs trouble-free (once again without having to utilize the Force), we were met by Ito, the FMW referee. He spoke English, but it didn't matter to me, as I was practically fluent in Japanese after my in-flight crash course.

The dictionary said that *Konnichi-Wa* meant "Good Afternoon." I'd had problems trying to discern the correct pronunciation on the plane, but I figured it out and when Ito introduced himself, I practically shouted into his face, "Kone-Ikki-way!"

He looked at me with a confused smile, so I said it again. "Kone-Ikki-way!"

He explained that the proper pronunciation was *Ko-Ni-Chi-Wah*, so after five minutes in the country I'd already established myself as a patronizing, stereotypical, sanctimonious tourist, who said Good Afternoon at six o'clock at night and mispronounced it to boot. I was the bizarro Long Duck Dong.

The drive from Narita to Tokyo was supposed to take two hours but took nearly four because of the bumper-to-bumper traffic. The rain pouring out of the sky made the Tokyo cityscape seem futuristic and straight out of *Blade Runner*: sleek modern skyscrapers with giant flashing neon signs illuminating highways stacked on top of other highways.

We checked into the tiny Tokyo GREEN Hotel, which strangely had a BLUE logo. My room was the size of a walk-in closet, but it was my first free hotel room and it was amazing. I put on the kimono and slippers that were provided by the hotel and sashayed across the room like I was the Last Samurai.

I didn't want to waste a minute of sightseeing time, so I met Lance and Ito in the lobby and we hit the streets looking for sake and ninjas. We found neither, as all of the restaurants and shops were closed even though it was only nine at night. Finally we found a convenience store named Lawson's Station. I was starving and some 7-Eleven style food, maybe a bean burrito and a Slurpee, sounded appetizing.

Lawson's Station offered neither. What Lawson's did have were such delicacies as corn sandwiches, kumquats, packs of peas in a pod, boxes of chocolate on a stick called Pocky, and shrink-wrapped squid. They had everything . . . except for something I could eat.

I settled on a can of Pocari Sweat (the all-time worst name for a sports drink) and a box of fried chicken pieces.

I bit into the fatty piece of chicken and it was so spicy it burned the shit out of my mouth. The Pocari Sweat tasted like lime-flavored water and was no help in getting the fire out of mouth, so I bought a little plastic bottle of milk, downed it in one gulp, and barfed. It was soy milk or goat's milk or mother's milk, something other than cow's milk and it tasted like piss.

I thought I was going to come to Japan and experience screaming fans and ancient temples. Instead I stood in front of a convenience store puking my guts out in the pouring rain. I could have just spent the night drinking in Calgary and achieved the same results without having to take a sixteen-hour flight.

We finally found a KFC and I was overjoyed. But when I bit into my chicken breast, I discovered a tiny brain behind the wing. I'm talking an actual gray matter brain with lines and ridges. I showed it to the manager and he and his employees huddled in a serious meeting before offering me a new piece.

I'd had enough and asked Ito where McDonald's was. He stared at me in confusion until he finally figured out what I wanted.

"Ohhh you mean MAKUDONALDO!"

That was the name of the famous burger restaurant that featured the red-haired clown mascot Donaldo Maku-Donaldo. I ordered a potato bacon pie and a Teriyaki McRib and shut my mouth.

The next morning, with the remains of the soy milk and Pocky still gurgling in my innards, the whole crew met in the lobby of the hotel and boarded the official FMW bus. That's when I met Ricky Fuji, Fred's illustrious connection to Japan. Unlike Fred he was friendly and down-to-earth. He also had waist-length hair and a strong desire to be Canadian.

"I love Canada man. It's my favorite place, eh. I wish I could live in Canada."

From then on we called him by his new Canadian name, Ricky McKenzie.

He constantly bombarded me with a bunch of oh-so-Japanese-style questions, in that they made sense but really didn't.

"You like rock 'n' roll sex music?"

"You like Richie Sambora's hat?"

"Do you know any hockey players' wives?"

"Do you like jeans?"

"How many pairs of sunglasses do you have?"

Ricky also sported one of the biggest fanny packs I'd ever seen. The fanny pack was a wrestler's fashion staple in the '90s, and my neon green pack was no slouch, but Ricky's pack covered half his torso. He'd look through it for a pack of cigarettes, a pair of chopsticks, a monkey wrench. I'm not kidding about the monkey wrench, by the way.

Once again the power of music was universal and because he liked heavy metal as much as I did, we became instant friends. One night he took me to see a band called the Privates play at a small club. I was amused at how polite the Japanese rock fans were. They didn't make much noise and just watched, clapping politely when the song ended. I soon learned it was the same way with Japanese wrestling crowds.

When we arrived at the arena in Kanagawa for the first night of the tour, Lance took a look at the list of the evening's matches taped to the wall and his face dropped.

"This is terrible."

"What's wrong?"

"We're not on. It's our first night in and we're not even on the show."

I looked at the card and sure enough the names Chris Jericho and Lance Storm weren't on the list. But the names Clise and Runce were—and that was us.

Like Cher, no last names were necessary. It was just CLISE and RUNCE. Clise was a bad phonetic translation of my name with the R sound not being pronounced the same way in Japanese, but I'd been called worse. I was once listed on an ad in the *Calgary Sun* as Chris Cherrykoo.

I also noticed that Clise and Runce were written across from Onita's name, which meant that we were in the main event of the show. Excited by the huge opportunity we suited up in our fancy new multicolored Sgt. Pepper ring jackets with green and black Rockers rip-off tights, both made by Lenny St. Clair's mom.

I threw a few warm-up kicks and said the same prayer that I said before every match. I was almost ready to rock.

I had one more task before the match, and when I went to drop the kids off at the pool I was agog (great word) when I saw the toilets in the bathroom.

They were nothing more than porcelain-covered holes in the ground, and the idea was to squat a few inches above the "toilet" and let it rip. To me, the bathroom is supposed to be a sanctuary, but there's nothing relaxing about straining your legs in a crouch while trying to get the job done.

After a while I became smart enough to look for a

handicap stall, or a Western Toilet. The Western Toilet didn't feature cowboy hats or lassos, just a good old North American dumper. So did the handicap stall and they both featured a diagram on the wall of a stick man sitting on a stick toilet, showing people how to use it.

If you don't know how to use a toilet . . .

I got the job done and hit the ring for the main event of Sudden Impact and Mark Starr vs. Onita, Sambo Asako, and Ueda, a kickboxer who wore boxing gloves during the whole match.

Lance and I made our big entrance by vaulting up to the top rope and back-flipping into the center of the ring. I remembered asking Shawn Michaels back in Winnipeg how to do a back flip and him telling me to get up there and just do it. I'd practiced back-flipping a few times in Calgary but this was the first official voyage. So I got up there and just did it, flipping backward with so much force that I over-rotated and landed on my ass. It was a complete embarrassment, made even worse by the platoon of magazine photographers who captured me falling on my posterior for posterity and the sour look on Lance T.'s face.

I got over my embarrassment when Onita got into the ring. It was a sobering experience to be standing across the ring from the boss of the company and one of the biggest stars in all of Japan.

Atsushi Onita had started FMW after becoming unhappy wrestling for All Japan, when he rallied a few sponsors and formed his own company. FMW was the first company to promote such delicate displays as electrified barbed-wire matches and exploding-ring death matches.

Onita's build was fairly dumpy and he wasn't much of

a wrestler, but he had unbelievable charisma and personality. After his matches the fans would storm the ringside area as he doused himself in water while grabbing the microphone. He would then cut a long promo, bursting into tears every time. He became famous for his crying and the fans cried along with him, because he proclaimed himself to be a warrior for the people, with his tears signifying his fighting spirit.

People bought his shtick hook, line, and sinker and chanted O-NI-TA! while Joan Jett's version of "Wild Thing" blared throughout the arena. He ended up becoming a cultural phenomenon and a senator in the Japanese Diet. Not bad for a marginal wrestler with only one move.

Once the match started, I got stuck working mostly with Ueda the kickboxer. He didn't seem like he had any interest in being there and didn't seem to have any interest in pulling his punches and kicks either. He was basically kicking the shit out of me. But one of the rules of FMW was that there were no rules, so I thought, "Fuck this guy," rolled to the floor, and got a chair. It was Shane Croft in Calgary Part 2—The Return.

When I brought the chair back in the ring, he made the mistake of turning his back on the pretty boy. When he turned around, I hit that sumbitch in the head as hard as I could. He dropped like a sack filled with more potatoes (stiff shots) than he'd hit me with earlier. He could've killed me in a real fight, but just like in my encounter with Bruiser Bedlam, my attitude was if I'm going down I'm taking someone with me.

Much like in Mexico, the Japanese were notorious for taking liberties with the foreigners. If you fired back by taking a few liberties of your own, you earned their respect and it was pure business after that. The rest of the match went fine and Onita ended up pinning Mark Starr. He hadn't pinned one of Sudden Impact because he wanted to see what we had to offer. It must not have been enough because we didn't work with him again for the rest of the tour.

I knew that pro wrestling (or Puro-Resu as they call it) was big in Japan, but I didn't realize just how big until I got there. There were over a dozen different companies operating on an island the size of Montana. Clips of the matches ran nightly on TV, while results from the previous night's matches were listed in the national newspapers next to the baseball scores.

There were two wrestling-heavy newspapers, *Tokyo Sports* and *The Weekly Fight*, as well as two glossy first-class magazines that featured some of the best sports photography I'd ever seen. They were called *Weekly Gong* and *Weekly Pro Wrestling*, which everyone called *Baseball Magazine* because it was published by a baseball magazine company. Got that?

There was something that made perfect sense about calling a wrestling magazine *Baseball Magazine* in Japan. After all, this was the home of television shows named *Heavy Metal L-Game* and *Space Runaway Ideon* and baseball teams called the Nippon Ham Fighters and the Hiroshima Carp. The majority of the Japanese media and high-school-educated people could speak just enough English to where it made just enough sense to not make sense. I call it Japanglish.

It was a thrill to see a full-page color spread in the magazines of Sudden Impact's debut in Japan. The pictures were amazing action shots of the unique moves that we were doing and the text called us Canada's Steiner Brothers. That was high praise, as the Steiners were two of the biggest gaijin (foreign) stars in Japan and a great team.

After an unimpressive debut in FMW (the Curse lives on), Sudden Impact worked mostly in the first half of the future shows. But that really wasn't a surprise, as our technical style didn't fit in with the barbed-wire, bombs, and bloodbaths mind-set of Onita. We stood out in FMW, but not necessarily in the best of ways.

Most of the shows had between 1,000 and 3,000 fans in attendance and even though they were the largest crowds I'd worked in front of, I was surprised at the fans' lack of reaction. It was just like the Privates' concert that Ricky had taken me to—the fans watched politely and didn't say a word for most of the match.

I'd be dismantling my opponent's arm with an impressive array of holds and submissions while crickets chirped in the audience.

"Do I suck? Why is nobody saying anything?"

Then I'd do an acrobatic move or a simple amateur wrestling takedown and the fans would explode with an OOOOOOHHHHH! Then they would go quiet again.

I realized that the fans weren't bored, but were merely watching intently. They understood the moves and the reversals of moves and appreciated the craft of the business. They respected the art of wrestling, and since there wasn't much of it in FMW, they appreciated our work.

A majority of the fans wore nice clothes or suits and it seemed like going to the matches was a prestigious event, like going to the opera. They really paid attention to the story and intensity of the performances. When the match built to the end, the secret was to incorporate a bunch of false finishes ("2 counts" as Wallass and I had called them), to which the fans would count along, "One, Tuuuu, OOOOOOOOOOHHHH!" Then they would give a round of quick applause and silence themselves again. When a match really got cooking, the buzz would pick up until the crowd was screaming and clapping along with every move. It took a while to get used to it but once I did, I got addicted to the unique reactions and began to custom-build my matches in order to get the maximum reactions out of the fans.

THE DOM DELUISE
OF WRESTLING

It seemed to me that Japan as a country had American-ized itself as much as possible. But walking around Tokyo was like traveling through a funhouse where everything inside was slightly warped.

There were MakuDonaldo's and Domino's everywhere but the Japanese versions had a weird taste. People walked the crowded streets in sixty degree weather wearing expensive downhill skiing suits as a status symbol. Guys would dye their hair blond to stand out but would end up with a creepy burnt orange hue instead.

I wanted to ingratiate myself to the Japanese people as much as possible so I informed anybody that would listen that I was a huge fan of the Japanese metal band Loudness. But while Loudness was cool to me, they'd seen better days in their home country. Proclaiming my loyalty to Loudness was like going to the States and saying I was a huge Dokken fan.

But I figured everyone would be impressed by the fact that I had all of their records and knew the singer's name was Minoru Niihara. Finally I was told to step out of the 1980s and get into the 1990s scene and was turned on to Japan's biggest rock band, X.

They had sold out the Tokyo Dome for a reason—they were amazing. My Clive Davis of Winnipeg tendencies resurfaced and I made it my mission to spread the X gospel to all of my metal friends back home.

It was a pleasant surprise to find out how big the metal scene was in Japan. Grunge was taking over America and slowly killing hard rock, but in the Orient I could spend hours at Shinjuku Tower Records checking out all of the new metal releases.

I also discovered that the Japanese versions of CDs from all of the biggest bands included bonus tracks, stickers, and other special treats that you couldn't get anywhere else. The CD booklets contained exclusive pictures, lyrics, and liner notes written by the bands and translated into Japanese. Fourteen years later, it was a thrill for me to handwrite the liner notes for the Japanese pressing of Fozzy's *All That Remains*.

While I spent hundreds of dollars on CDs, I also spent hundreds of dollars when Ricky took Lance and I to a place known as a lobby bar. It was basically a fancy lounge with the gimmick of being waited on head to toe by beautiful Filipinas. No gaijin were allowed in without a Japanese chaperon but once we got inside, the girls showered me with back massages, poured my drinks, and fed me like I was Jerichus Caesar. Then we danced the night away (I wore my neon green fanny pack the entire time) to the most annoying Japanese pop music I'd ever heard. But the girls could move and they even taught me the Lambada (that's the Forbidden Dance!). They treated me like I was King Stud, but just when I thought I was about to have my Pocky played with, the girls escorted us to the door and bid us konbawa. Instead of receiving a happy ending, I received a bill for $500.

Turns out it was the girls' job to hang out and flirt with the customers, while pouring as much whiskey as possible. They got a commission on each $250 bottle that we drank. For that type of cash, they could've at least given us Caviar.

In the BTWF days, Wallass and I had read a list of Japanese wrestlers in a magazine and had seen the name Tarzan Goto. How could you be Japanese and have the name Tarzan? From then on the mere mention of the mighty Tarzan elicited gales of laughter. Lo and behold when I arrived in FMW, who was the number two man behind Onita? Tarzan Muthafuckin Goto!

He was a short, fat, stocky beast with no front teeth and a face only your mum could love. He also had no problem beating up fans if the opportunity presented itself—like when someone clapped him on the back as he walked to the ring.

When a foolhardy fan did just that, Tarzan promptly punched the sorry bastard in the face. Then Goto chased the guy through the stands, grabbed him, and threw him out of the building. In the States if you even look in a fan's general direction, you can be sued. In Japan to be attacked and beaten by your favorite wrestler was a badge of honor, something to brag about to your friends.

But I'm sure to be decked by a guy named Tarzan Goto was a lot more credible than getting the crap kicked out of you by el Pandita. That's right, I said el Pandita. That's Spanish for Little Panda and English for Worst Gimmick Ever.

Asian people are fascinated with pandas and the Pandita gimmick was intended to exploit that obsession to the fullest. This clown's ring costume was a full-body Panda suit; lovable cotton ball tail included. He would skip to the ring, handing out candy to the fans before jumping into the ring and holding his arms out as if to say, "I'm cute and lovable!" During the match, you would have to sell Pandita's terrible-looking offense unless you could grab his tail. That would cause the lovable creature to run around in circles chasing it.

It got worse and his crowd-pleasing big move belongs in the Shit Hall of Fame. Pandita would knock his opponent out of the ring and hit the opposite ropes like he was going to do a dive through the ropes onto the floor. Instead of flying through the ropes, he would jump up and land horizontally in a Playgirl pose with his legs spread open and his chin on his fist like a cute little panda bear. The crowd would go "OOOOOOHHHHH!" and I would wonder what the hell was going on. Guys would butcher each other with barbed-wire baseball bats and in the next match out came the Dom DeLuise of wrestling.

FMW was a smaller company with a will-work-for-food mentality and a lot of the shows were held in outdoor parking lots with makeshift fences erected around them. There were no dressing rooms for us, which meant we had to change on the bus. It also meant that there were no bathrooms or showers and after the matches we'd have to endure a three-hour bus ride covered in dirt, sweat, and blood. It looked like the Spirit of '76 when the crew checked into the hotel and more than once I saw the desk clerk run into the back room to hide from us.

Even though we had separate hotel rooms, Lance and I spent so much time together that we started to get on each other's nerves over the smallest of things.

"You smack your lips when you eat."

"You walk funny."

"Your white boots are pissing me off."

The tension culminated in a dressing room scuffle in Aichi that led to us rolling around on the floor like a couple of eight-year-olds. But when it was time to make the donuts and get the job done, we always worked hard together in the ring. We'd been through so much since training in the bowling alley that we had become like brothers. Sometimes brothers gotta hug, sometimes brothers gotta fight.

But everything came full circle for us when we arrived at the Hakata Star Lanes in Fukuoka . . . another bowling alley. We'd traveled thousands of miles around the world just to end up in the same combination bowling alley/ wrestling venue that we'd started in, in Calgary.

The main event at the Star Lane was a street fight battle royal. I must've missed the memo and I didn't have anything that you could actually wear in a street fight. So while everybody else was wearing jeans, sleeveless T-shirts, weightlifting belts, and cowboy boots, I ended up wearing zebra-striped Zubaz gym shorts tied up with a shoelace and my floppy black wrestling boots from the Calgary cobbler, the most unintimidating street fight outfit in wrestling history. Throw in my canary blond fried hair and you know I was the epitome of TOUGH. It was no surprise that I was the first one thrown out of the ring.

But it had been a good night and I was feeling cocky.

So I decided to go and speak to Onita—something we were specifically told not to do.

"How's it going eh?"

"Okay."

"I really wanted to say thanks for having us on the tour."

"Okay."

"Are you having a good tour?"

"Okay."

"You've got cool ring music."

"Okay."

He was looking at me like I was nuts for breaking the no-talking-to-the-almighty rule. I thought I might have pissed him off with my faux pas, because Ito later told me never to speak to Onita directly again. Yet on the last show of the tour, he told us we were beating the top FMW tag team of Horace Boulder and the Gladiator (or as the Japanese called him, the Grajiator).

I took it as a sign that they had enjoyed our work and were excited about Sudden Impact's future. But when we went to get our payoffs for the tour, instead of receiving the princely sum of $800 a week that Fred's homemade contract had promised, we were only paid $600 a week.

It was bullshit and I was pissed. Granted we were rookies with no name value but we'd still worked our asses off and earned every penny we were promised. We'd impressed the other wrestlers in the company enough that the rookies were stealing our high-flying moves and claiming them as their own. We'd introduced top rope dives to the floor and Frankensteiners to the company and the different dimension we brought to FMW made it a more well-rounded company. Sudden Impact brought to the hardcore FMW what Eddy Guerrero and Chris Benoit brought to the hardcore ECW years later.

When we asked Ito why we'd been shorted $200 a week, he told us the company would wire us the difference. I was still naive enough to think we would get it too. We never did; however, Onita was happy enough with my work to give me a bonus. An official FMW keychain.

On the plane back to Canada I tried to comprehend the strangeness I'd encountered. I'd gone to Japan expecting rice paddies and ninjas, but instead I found corn pizza and porno magazines featuring schoolgirls peeing on the beach. The sexual decadence prevalent in the country was a direct contrast to the bowing and honorable behavior that was expected. The dichotomy summed up the whole country. Nothing really made sense.

CHAPTER 32

PRAY FOR BLOOD

Even though I'd apparently pissed off Onita and we'd been stiffed on our pay, Ito informed us that the boss had really liked our work and was planning on bringing us back "five or six times" over the course of the next year. But it should've raised a red flag when the very next tour featured a tag team tournament and we weren't invited. I still thought it was only a matter of time before we were brought back, but we waited month after month with no offer to return, while a conveyor belt of Fred's Calgary wrestlers went over instead of us.

I was bitter at the whole situation but when my friend Lenny St. Claire got his chance to go, I was happy for him. FMW told him to think up a gimmick a few days before he left for his tour, so he took the mask off a football helmet and screwed a strap onto the back of it. Then he had his costume-making mom construct a straitjacket that he wore over a pair of gas station coveralls and Dr. Luther, a raving lunatic based on Hannibal Lecter, was ready to terrorize.

With his eerie look and total commitment to insanity,

he was an instant sensation. He would burst out of the dressing room door throwing chairs and running directly into the crowd, who would in turn flee in widespread panic as if Godzilla himself had broken loose.

The magazines picked up on him instantly and, after his first week, he was the subject of a six-page color spread in *Baseball Magazine* that proclaimed "Pray for Blood . . . Luther Is Here!" Dr. Luther became one of the most popular gimmicks in FMW history.

Every time Lenny returned from a tour, I'd ask him how it had gone and then, inevitably, "Did anybody mention my name or when I'm coming back?" The answer was always the same: "Nobody mentioned anything."

I'd pretty much accepted that Sudden Impact had been a one-hit wonder, a wrestling version of Chumbawamba, until I finally got a call from Ricky Fuji almost one year later. He wanted to know if we could return for the FMW third anniversary show at the Yokohama baseball stadium.

We were going to have the important task of kicking off the show. It's a general rule in wrestling, if you're not wrestling in the main event then the opener is the most important match of the evening. It's your responsibility to get things started with a great match and set the tone for the rest of the night.

But my excitement was shot down in flames when Lance refused to go. He was still pissed that Onita had stiffed us out of our money and lied to our faces about bringing us back. But neither of us had any steady work outside of the odd match in Alberta or Manitoba and I was itching to go back to Japan. Since New Japan wasn't breaking down my door with offers, FMW was my only option.

Lance had decided earlier in the year that we should break up Sudden Impact and go our separate ways, but I was certain that I'd be able to talk him into a one-time reunion for such a big show. When he said no without hesitation, I was furious.

I wasn't going to let Lance or anyone else spoil my big return to Japan. So after a few days of holding off the calls from FMW, I called Ricky and told him that Lance had decided to retire from the business. Ricky was surprised, but I told him that I'd gotten a new partner and Sudden Impact would be honored to work the big show. Ricky gave me the details and everything was all set.

Now I just had to find a partner.

None of the local Calgary wrestlers could hold a candle to Lance's work rate and since our team was based around flashy moves, replacing him wasn't going to be easy. I finally found a guy I thought would do a decent job in Eric Freeze from Edmonton. He was taller and not as muscular as Lance but he was quite athletic. Even though he wasn't as advanced in the ring as Lance, I thought he was solid enough to get by.

He had a similar haircut to Lance and I thought from a distance people would be fooled and think it was him. It worked, as there are still tapes of that match floating around with Eric Freeze being listed as Lance Storm . . . a fact that does not please good ol' LTS.

I spent the next few weeks teaching Freeze the greatest hits of Sudden Impact. I explained to him that our patented double-team flying elbows and double leapfrogs were so original and unique that after waiting for over a year to see them, the fans were going to lose their minds. It was going to be bigger than the Police reunion.

I kept strictly emphasizing to Freeze how important this match would be and how I was expecting full-page articles in the magazines, mobs of screaming Sudden Impact fans, and lineups of chicks just waiting for us. I taught myself how to say "I'm back!" in Japanese (Kaette-Kita-Zo!), so I could yell it when I entered the ring. I would be the biggest babyface gaijin of all time.

Chris Jericho was going to be *the* shit!

I had a problem tracking down Lance's Sgt. Pepper jacket, because he'd sold it to a fan. But after locating it and paying the guy to rent the jacket that I'd created and designed, I got Lenny's mom to make a matching pair of black tights with full silver sequins on the front. I completed the costume with a silver sequin choker, black-painted nails (nicked from Paul Stanley), and black eyeliner. I was dressed to kill and ready to make my mark in the Land of the Rising Jericho.

But I had one more trick up my choker before the master plan was complete. My coup de grâce was to use an X song for Sudden Impact's ring music. I knew that the fans would go wild when they realized that a couple of gaijins were down enough to enter the ring to a song by Japan's biggest band!

The only thing that stood in the way of my return was the complete indifference to it. The FMW office employees were cordial, but hardly ecstatic, and both the Japanese and foreign wrestlers seemed like they couldn't have cared less. The true indication that nobody gave a damn about us came when we had to walk through the concourse of the stadium to go over the match with our opponents. During the five-minute walk through the crowded corridors, not *one* person gave us more than a cursory glance even though we were wearing full wrestling regalia—and these were wrestling fans that bought tickets to see the show!

When we went over the match, the most important thing we were asked to do was break up the pin when their top young star Eiji Ezaki (who became the masked Hayabusa and ironically ended up paralyzed years later after landing on his head attempting a Lionsault) did a moonsault. The extended back flip from the top rope into a pin is one of the most overused moves in the business today, but in 1992 it was rare to see one performed. Freeze and I agreed to protect Ezaki's big move and the four of us put together what I was convinced was going to be a classic match. There was no question that the fans and the media would have no choice but to take notice of me.

X's "Silent Jealousy" blasted out of the stadium speakers as Sudden Impact ran down the long stadium ramp to the ring. I climbed to the second rope and screamed, *"KAETTE-KITA-ZO!"* I might as well have said, "I'M A WANNABE AND TRYING WAY TOO HARD!"

The match itself should've been canceled due to lack of interest. There was deathly silence as we robotically ran through a preplanned match that was devoid of any meaning or storytelling whatsoever.

Finally, Ezaki set himself up and gave me the big moonsault. He hit it perfectly and the fans finally showed some life, reacting with amazement. Unfortunately, so did Freeze.

He seemed so mesmerized by the image of himself on the stadium JumboTron, he didn't make the save. He was so into watching the match that he forgot he was actually a part of it. At least somebody was enjoying it.

We won the match, but the five-star classic I'd been hoping for was as nonexistent as Freeze's moonsault save.

Afterward when I was changing out of my gear in the dressing room, an old-timer named John Tolos asked if he could borrow my boots for his match. "I don't have boots anymore. Why do I need boots? I'll just borrow yours." I guess that's the difference between a greenhorn and a seasoned veteran. I'd had an entire new outfit made for the show and he didn't even have fuckin' wrestling boots. I'm sure he also made ten times more for his match than the $800 I made for mine.

Onita was infatuated with having boxers and martial artists on his shows (remember, FMW stood for Frontier Martial Arts Wrestling). He'd paid big money to bring Leon Spinks, the former heavyweight boxing champion of the world, over for the show that night. The idea was for Leon to use his boxing skills against the wrestlers but when they told him to pull his punches so he wouldn't kill anyone, Leon couldn't grasp the concept.

"You mean when I give a punch, it's not a hard punch but the guy falls down anyway? That's so funny," he said in his slurred punch-drunk speech.

Leon didn't last long, as he was constantly smiling and laughing during his matches. If boxing is fixed, Spinks sure as hell didn't know because he definitely didn't understand the difference between real and show in the wrestling ring.

After the match, Ricky Fuji took me to the most famous wrestling restaurant in the world, Ribera Steakhouse. It was discovered in the 1970s by Stan Hansen and had been a favorite wrestler hangout ever since.

But the steak was only part of Ribera's sizzle. After the meal, all the wrestlers were presented with official Ribera jackets. They were tacky satin and rayon striped numbers with "Ribera" stenciled across the front and back. They were brutally ugly, but any wrestler given one wore it loudly and proudly like a badge of honor. Ricky joked that Ribera was Japanese for "I'm a wrestler and I've been to Japan."

On the walls of the restaurant hung dozens of signed pictures from all the wrestlers who'd been there. Amazingly, whenever you went you'd find your picture on the wall. Ribera himself would check the tour lineups in the magazines to find out which gaijins would be in the country and for how long. He'd put up those wrestlers' pictures and when the tours were finished, he'd put up photos of the next batch of foreigners. He was more of a worker than the wrestlers.

WRESTLE AND ROMANCE

I left Japan this time with no invitation to come back. It bothered me because I didn't see many guys in FMW who could wrestle better than me. What I did see was a plethora of outlandish gimmicks: the Ninja Turtle, Pandita, Battle Ranger, Ultraman, his giant lobster nemesis Bartak, all of these larger-than-life characters. It was obvious that to be a big star in Japan I needed a gimmick that could match those.

The first idea I had was the dastardly Master Sebastian (named after Sebastian Bach), who would be Dr. Luther's manager. The Master would wear a long black leather trench coat and sport one of those Madonna ponytail hairpieces on the top of his head for no apparent reason.

Then I thought I could be Dr. Luther's brother Mr. Hannibal, a character FMW wanted to create to cash in on Luther's immense popularity. Lenny tried to talk me out of it saying I didn't need to be a copy of him, but I was desperate. FMW turned me down flat for the gimmick anyway. Since I'd already wrestled in the company, the fans knew I wasn't a homicidal maniac.

Then I came up with the Parasite. I painted my face with Alice Cooper style makeup and carried around a can of WD-40. When the time was right, I'd hold a match up to the spray and create a blowtorch. What I was going to do with the torch, I have no idea. I never got that far.

October 1992. When the Phoenix didn't...ahem...take off, I came up with the money-making gimmick of the Parasite. Surprisingly, this genius idea didn't...errr...heat things up for me either.

When Parasite baby bombed like the *Enola Gay*, I got my next gimmick idea from watching an Iron Maiden *Powerslave* concert video. When I saw singer Bruce Dickinson don an Egyptian bird mask, I decided to become the Phoenix.

I designed the whole costume and started assembling it by first buying a bird mask at a costume store. I gave it full plumage by attaching a bouquet of multicolored feathers with a glue gun I found in the Palkos' garage. The costume also called for a pair of Hawkman wings, so I bought some thin aluminum poles from a hardware store and soldered them together into a frame of bird wings. I sewed some black spandex over the frame and glued strips of sequins, fake costume jewelry, and rhinestones onto the material. I ran out of money before I could buy the leather straps necessary to attach the wings, so I tied thin strips of spandex to the frame instead. When I put the costume on, I was quite impressed. The wings were a little lopsided and the mask was a touch too small, but the ensemble looked pretty darn cool and there was no way I wouldn't get a gig this time.

But my carefully constructed wings were brutally flimsy and the wind bent them askew during an outdoor photo shoot. They eventually blew right off my back, forcing me to chase them down like Rocky Balboa chasing the chicken in *Rocky 2*. When the wind died down momentarily, I hastily tied them back on and screamed, "Take the picture now!"

The comedy continued after the shoot, when I tried to practice my big ring entrance. After a few attempts, I found that it was impossible to get into the ring with the wings on. I couldn't climb in between the ropes because they were too rickety and cumbersome. When I tried to jump straight over the top rope into the ring, the damn contraption just fell off my back.

My dreams of going back to Japan were falling apart along with my wings. I was ready to give up, when Ricky finally called me and said FMW wanted to bring me in as the Phoenix and give me a Porsche.

I was a little surprised with the offer and wondered how I was going to drive a Porsche from Japan to Canada. Unfortunately he was saying "push," not "Porsche." Even though a push was almost as good as a Porsche, it was a moot point because FMW was a day late and a keychain short.

The day prior I'd been offered a tour for the bigger and more prestigious Japanese company WAR. I'd started working in Mexico City at this point and had met Ultimo Dragón, a Japanese wrestler who'd made a huge name for himself in Mexico and with WAR in Japan. I hoped to get booked with the company for months, since Dragón was always looking for new opponents and with my Calgary/Mexico/European hybrid style, I knew we'd have great chemistry. Since we both worked for Paco Alonso, we'd teamed together frequently and Dragón was familiar with what I could do and thought I would fit the bill perfectly. Now I had my chance.

Dragón's real name was Yoshihiro Asai and like me his dream as a kid was to be a wrestler, but he'd been turned down by New Japan because of his small stature. He refused to take no for an answer and moved to Mexico, where he became a star under the masked gimmick of Ultimo Dragón. The name translated in English was the Last Dragon, the idea being that he was the last student of Bruce Lee. I guess that would've made him about eight years old when he trained with Bruce. After making his mark in Mexico, he'd returned to Japan and found a home with WAR.

WAR wasn't pronounced in the "What Is It Good For" kind of way, but rather "W . . . A . . . R," an acronym for Wrestle and Romance. It was classic Japanglish in that it was just English enough to make no sense. I was confused as to whether I was supposed to bring the Wrestle or the Romance.

Wrestle and Romance was operated by Genichiro Tenryu, one of the top ten biggest names in Japanese wrestling history. Much like Tonga, he'd started as a sumo wrestler and then achieved huge success when he switched to wrestling. He had the best chops to the chest this side of Ric Flair and worked very stiff, which the fans loved and I learned to hate. One of the ways he was building his company was by focusing on his junior heavyweight division, which was second in quality only to New Japan's crop of high-flyers.

The difference between working in FMW and WAR was similar to the difference between working in Monterrey and Mexico City. You could see the increase in professionalism instantly. The fine people at the newly christened Wrestle Association R (makes even less sense than Wrestle and Romance, don't it?) provided me with a work visa and sent me a notarized contract for the king's ransom of $1,400 a week. I was upgraded accommodation-wise from the Tokyo Green Hotel to the Hyatt Regency and upgraded opponent-wise from kickboxers and Pandas to real wrestlers.

Two of them were Jado and Gedo, who I'd met while they were making pennies working in Mexico. They'd followed Dragón's path and gone to Mexico after being told they were too small for New Japan. They were also tremendous performers and were major contributors to the strengthening WAR junior division.

I got along well with them, because I could speak the legitimate language of Broken English. I learned Broken English by proxy because Jado and Gedo could speak decent English, but only understood certain words. For example, they didn't know what a store was, but they knew what a shop was.

So if I said, "Would you guys like to spend the afternoon looking through the record store?" they wouldn't get it. However, if I said "Maybe you me go CD shop?" they would nod in agreement. Once I figured out what words they understood, I could speak to them for hours.

When touring Japan, the whole crew rode together on the team bus and all the hotels and travel was taken care of. This was the opposite of wrestling in the States, where everyone was responsible for their own arrangements.

Everyone from Tenryu to the ring crew traveled together and there was no tolerance for lateness. I learned that rule very quickly when I showed up at ten one morning for a 10 A.M. departure. Dragón took me aside and sternly told me that my tardiness (I don't feel tardy) had to stop. A 10 A.M. departure meant I was supposed to be there at 9:45. Japanese time was different from Mexican time, where a 10 A.M. departure meant 10:45 or 11. Call me kooky but where I come from a 10 A.M. departure means 10 A.M.

But when in Tokyo . . .

My first match for WAR was in Korakuen Hall, one of the most famous wrestling venues in the world. Korakuen was a 2,200-seat theater on the grounds of the Big Egg

Tokyo Dome (classic Japanglish) but it was *the* place for wrestling in Tokyo. A match at Korakuen could make or break you because it was the media epicenter of the Japanese wrestling business. All the photographers and writers showed up in full force and their magazine reviews of the matches and performers carried serious weight throughout the country much like they did in Mexico.

I heard so much about Korakuen from Lenny. He'd even left me a message written in black marker on the wall of the backstage area saying, "Congratulations, you finally made it, Clise!" It was like finding an Easter egg, so I got a black marker of my own and left a reply. He replied to that and so on and so on until messages on the backstage wall became a tradition before every Korakuen match. It was old-school texting.

Sadly, another Jericho tradition continued when I had another stinker of a debut match. I worked against Rio Lord of the Jungle, a male stripper turned wrestler who later worked in WCW as the Ultimate Warrior rip-off, the Renegade. He was massive and green, which was a tough combination to overcome. We opened the show and when I beat him clean with the Japanese debut of the Lionsault, it was the only good part of the match.

You never get a second chance to make a first impression . . .

I did an interview with *Gong Magazine* afterward where I was asked how it felt to beat the Load of the Jungle. Because of the difference in the Japanese pronunciation of the R sound, Lord became Load. I think if I was a Lord, when in Japan I'd change my name to Boss or Supervisor. I'm sure the Warload and Load Steven Regal would agree.

Despite my load-of-shit match, I liked the WAR style. It was the hard-hitting, no-nonsense, technical type of match that I'd become a fan of from watching Stampede and New Japan. The matches were athletic competitions between two warriors, with a winner, a loser, and no bullshit.

My first tour for WAR was only four shows, but I had a great second match with a junior heavyweight named Masao Orihara, which cemented my spot in the company. The match after that was another stinker with a Korean wrestler named Kim Duk, who had worked in the WWF as Tiger Chung Lee. Tiger walked down the aisle with a confused look on his face while holding a spear for no apparent reason. Was he planning on skewering river trout on his way to the ring?

After meeting him I wanted to skewer myself because he was quite annoying. He'd had bit parts in a few movies, but talking to him you'd think he was Johnny Depp. Our bus had a TV and VCR and he made sure to bring his movies with him so we could watch *Red Heat*, *The Golden Child*, and *Blind Fury* over and over again.

"Why don't you put on *Red Heat*? Arnold Schwarzenegger told me he really liked working with me."

"Let's watch *The Golden Child*. Eddie Murphy thought I was very funny."

"Let's check out *Blind Fury*. Rutger Hauer thought I was a talented actor and wants to work with me again."

Despite having to put up with Inside the Actors Studio Featuring Kim Duk, working for Tenryu was a tremendous experience. He'd worked in the States for a few years, so he understood what we needed as foreigners to be comfortable in a strange land. He spoke good English and had a great sense of humor. While I got in trouble for speaking to Onita, I would've gotten in trouble if I *didn't* speak to Tenryu. Whether we were singing "Summer Lovin'" on a karaoke machine on the bus or smashing plates over drunken fans' heads at parties, Tenryu was as cool as a boss could be.

On my first day of work, he introduced himself and thanked me for coming. Later on in the tour when I sneezed, he asked with concern, "Are you sick?" When I said no, he replied deadpan, "Oh, I thought for sure you were sick. Sick of watching Kim Duk's movies . . ."

(Curious Author's Note: I heard rumors that Tenryu had pearls implanted in his wiener, which was a Yakuza technique used to increase sexual pleasure. I never had the balls to ask him if it was true.)

The last match of the tour was a big show at Ryogoku, an 11,000-seat arena known as the Sumo Hall. Ryogoku was where all of the important sumo matches had been held for hundreds of years.

The Hall was a unique traditional Japanese venue; besides the chairs set up on the floor section there were no actual seats in the arena. There were only sections cordoned off by steel rails that held four people per section. The fans would sit cross-legged on the floor of their area and watch the show.

All of Tenryu's big shows were held at Ryogoku and the draw to this one was a battle between WAR and New Japan. I was pitted against Super Strong Machine, a New Japan wrestler who'd worked for Stampede Wrestling as Sonny Two Rivers. I was nervous and Super Strong Machine kicked the shit out of me, but you know my mantra by now . . . I was taking him with me. I kicked him square in the face and set him up for my new patented move of jumping straight up onto the top rope and drop-kicking him off the apron. Just as I took off running, the referee wandered right in front of me and I totally blew the spot.

I'd been Mal Mason-ed!

But the match still got a couple pages of coverage in the magazines, which was always a watermark of whether something was good or not. There was a great shot of Machine dumping me on my head and another of me caving in the side of his face with a spin kick. When all else fails, just beat the shit out of each other I always say.

CHAPTER 34

YASKY

A few tours later, right after I was asked to be a regular for WAR, I broke my arm in SMW. After using my amazing mental powers to heal myself, I was booked to return to Japan. Even though I wasn't completely healed, I'd already been forced to miss one tour because of my arm and there was no way I was going to miss another one.

While I had to endure the long flight from L.A. to Tokyo in a middle seat of the smoking section, I was happy to get the upgrade for the Calgary–L.A. leg of the trip. I was even happier when I boarded the plane and sat down next to Owen Hart.

Owen was the guy that had made me want to be a wrestler in the first place and I'd drawn pictures of the two of us as tag team champions. Our paths had crossed a few times and while he was always friendly, I'd never had the chance to have a true one-on-one conversation with him. He told me that he was on his way to a WWF pay-per-view that day in L.A. and his brother Bret had given him shit for not leaving the night before.

"An extra night with my family at home is worth the possibility of missing the PPV," he explained. It turned out that we had a lot in common and we started sharing stories about working in Mexico and Germany.

Three and a half hours later we were suddenly in L.A. I apologized for talking his ear off, but he said, "No man, it was great getting to know you a little bit." I walked off the plane grinning ear to ear because he was even nicer than I'd expected him to be. Now I just had to figure out a way to become Owen's tag team partner.

My first match back from my broken arm was in Tokyo against my old buddy Vampiro, who was so saccharine friendly to my face that I felt like I was choking on cotton candy. I was past the point in my career where I worried about wins and losses, but I have to admit that I was ticked off when Tenryu asked me to put him over. It was a matter of principle I guess.

I was wearing a soft cast on my still healing arm since I'd rushed the recovery but the doctor told me I'd be okay to wrestle as long as I avoided taking a blow directly on the break. So I asked Vamp to do me a favor and stay away from my metal plate.

He agreed and did this annoying bow that he'd starting doing, thinking he was ingratiating himself with the Japanese. Instead he just looked like he had a nervous twitch. He should've just played X for his ring music, since it had worked so well for me in FMW.

Vamp considered himself something of a martial arts expert at this point and wore Muay Thai shorts in the ring to prove it. He based the majority of his offense around a variety of kicks that he had no idea how to do properly. He made that apparent when his first move of the match was to kick me directly in my bad arm. The pain spread like panic and he said, "Whoops, I was aiming for your ribs."

The rib was on me for trusting him.

Out of the ring, it wasn't long before Vamp was resorting to the same bullshit he'd tried to pull on me in Mexico.

A few days into the tour, I got a call to meet up with Tenryu after the matches. When I arrived at the Lobby bar, Tenryu wasted no time in asking me, "I'm very happy with your work and I just want to make sure that you're happy working for my company."

I was a little taken aback and assured him that I was indeed very happy. "Of course I am. Why would you even ask?"

"Well, I went out for drinks with Vampiro a couple of nights ago and he told me that you didn't like coming to Japan. He said you weren't happy here and were planning on walking out. Is that true?"

Meet the new ass, same as the old ass.

I assured Tenryu that nothing could be further from the truth and I was planning to work on as many WAR tours as he wanted me to. Then I spared no detail in telling him about my experiences with Vampiro and I made sure to let him know exactly what I thought of him. When the dust settled, the final score was Jericho—twenty-four tours with Tenryu's company, Vampiro—four tours. I guess lil old Lion Heart won that WAR.

Later in our conversation Tenryu brought up an interesting proposition. Since I was going to be working for him on a monthly basis, I'd have to fly back and forth to

Japan every few weeks. He wanted to remedy that and asked me if I would consider moving to Japan for six months to live in the WAR dojo.

A dojo is a combination school and training center, where all the young boys (rookies) lived and trained to become wrestlers. Not every Western wrestler would have wanted to live in Japan—most guys either loved it or hated it. It wouldn't be easy to adapt to the ways of life in a completely different culture but I was intrigued and honored by the proposition.

A major reason I was especially interested in the idea was that Benoit had lived and trained at the New Japan dojo for six months. I had a lot of questions, so I decided to call Chris and ask for his advice.

When he answered after a few rings, I almost hung up the phone like a high school kid calling a girl for a date. But cooler heads prevailed and I introduced myself, "Hi, this is Chris Jericho (My name's Chris too!) and I'm calling you from Calgary. I met you at the Stampede reunion show a few years ago."

His response was curt and cold. I'm sure he got calls from wrestling wannabes all the time. So I got right to the point and told him that I'd been offered a chance to live in Japan for six months.

His tone immediately changed. Not too many wrestling wannabes got the chance to live and train in Japan so that gave me instant credibility. Without hesitation, Benoit highly recommended that I do it and the conversation was a turning point in my life. It not only fired me up about wanting to work in Japan full-time, but it also was the beginning of one of the best friendships I've ever had in the wrestling business.

I had so much respect for Benoit that I developed almost a George Costanza heterosexual crush on him. Whenever he called the Palkos' house, I'd run down the stairs to pick up the phone like an excited schoolgirl. Benoit intimidated me, and it took me years to feel like an equal around him. I learned a lot from Chris, and he became one of the few people I truly trusted during my career.

Unfortunately, a few weeks later Tenryu changed his mind and decided it would be easier on me and cheaper for the company to continue flying me in every month. But a mutual commitment to each other had been confirmed with his offer.

I felt that I not only had a commitment to WAR, but to the Japanese fans as well. They'd accepted me and treated me with respect and I wanted to reciprocate that loyalty. So I bought a set of tapes that told me I could LEARN TO SPEAK JAPANESE IN 8 EASY LESSONS, but it was just as impossible to learn from them as it was to learn from the PLAY BASS LIKE BILLY SHEEHAN tape I'd bought ten years earlier.

The problem was that Tokyo Japanese is slightly different from Osaka Japanese, which is slightly different from Sapporo Japanese, which made it hard to learn any of them. Whenever I tried to speak any Japanese, the people would stare at me in stone-faced confusion. Nothing kills your confidence worse than trying to speak another language and not being understood.

I decided it would be easier and almost as valuable to learn how to read Japanese instead. So I went to a library in Vancouver where I was living with Lenny and grabbed a book of Japanese characters. There are three major different types of Japanese writing: Kanji, Hiragana, and Katakana. Katakana symbols are used for foreign words and resemble our alphabet in that they are made up of minimal strokes and slashes rather than the small works of art that make up the other types. I photocopied a chart with all forty-six Katakana characters and the sounds that each one represented and took them with me on my next tour.

I carried the pages in my back pocket and sounded out the syllables while reading the wrestling magazines and newspapers. I practiced by translating the descriptions and reviews of my own matches.

Instead of sleeping on the bus or watching *Red Heat* for the fifteenth time, I read billboards on the side of the road, names stenciled on the sides of trucks, music magazines, whatever I could to improve my reading. After a while, I was able to read menus and street signs and became the tour guide for the rest of the gaijin. Eventually I was able to ditch the photocopied sheets all together and read things unassisted, which impressed the company, the wrestlers, and the fans. Not bad for a twenty-four-year-old Canadian kid, huh?

My newfound skills made me the liaison between the office and the other gaijin. Whenever a message needed to be passed along, I'd be responsible for explaining it to everyone in English or Spanish (Dragón helped book a few luchadores from Mexico on every tour). I got a nice raise as a result of my new communication officer duties.

I'd become Lt. Uhura without the stockings and beehive.

Now that I could read the language, it showed the

Japanese that I had respect for their country and its people and I don't have to tell you what respect and honor means there.

When I really wanted to impress somebody, I'd sign my autograph in Japanese. When I drew the slashes and lines that spelled out Lion Heart, you would've guessed from the cries of amazement and moans of pleasure that I'd just penetrated them with a Steely Dan. Even though I'd barely displayed the skills of a ten-year-old, the Japanese people were very impressed.

While wrestling fans in general are some of the most loyal and dedicated fans in the world, I think the fans in Japan may be the best. They treated wrestlers with respect and a little fear; the way you might treat a friendly animal in the forest. You want to touch it, but you know it may bite you at any time.

Fans cautiously approached me to sign autographs on these special 8x10 whiteboards they all had. They gave me a plethora of intricately crafted presents, such as clocks with my face on them, kewpie dolls made to look like me (my son plays with them now), banners, hand-drawn and hand-painted pictures, sculptures, CDs of my favorite bands, and Japanese candy. A girl even gave me her baby once.

Actually a guy did bring his baby up to my room during my first tour of FMW. I don't know how he found out my exact room, but he knocked on the door and asked to buy my pants for ten bucks.

When I passed, he asked to take a picture of me with his infant son. I did and when I returned the next year he showed up again. He made a point of getting a picture of me with his son every time I came to Japan.

In 2005, I was in Japan and I got a knock at the door of my hotel in Tokyo. It was the guy and his now teenage son. They'd brought a photo album that included pictures of me and his kid from almost every year of his life. It was both cool and creepy. I have no idea why he decided to document his child's life with pictures of me. If I would've known I could've at least put on a growth chart costume.

I also have no idea why beer was sold out of vending machines on the street or why all the taxi drivers wore white gloves. Japan is a strange country. When it came to making sense of things in Japan, Lenny and I coined the term yasky.

Y ask Y.

A fan named Masa introduced himself to me one day and offered to clear up as much of the confusion as possible. Masa was the most dedicated wrestling fan I've ever met, so much so that he learned English SO HE COULD SPEAK TO WRESTLERS.

That's commitment. I love Jet Li, but I wouldn't learn Chinese just to be able to speak to the dude.

There were a lot of Japanese fans who considered hanging out with wrestlers to be a status symbol. They were known as sponsors and would pay for dinner, bestow lavish gifts, and give away hundreds of dollars in cash to the boys.

Right from the start, Masa made it very clear that he was a fan, nothing more. He said that he sponsored us by buying tickets to the hundreds of wrestling shows that he attended each year. He also made it very clear that he was there to help us with anything we might need. I took him up on his offer and we became good friends—he even attended my wedding. He had a giant photo album with pictures of almost every gaijin who ever toured Japan. If you're a wrestler who's been to Japan and your picture isn't in Masa's book, then you don't mean shit.

CHAPTER 35

THE WHITE URKEL

WAR's roster was a mixture of younger guys on their way up, like me, and legendary veterans at the tail end of their careers, like Bob Backlund.

Backlund had been the WWF champion in the late 1970s and early 1980s, but was now a nutcase. He wore a three-piece suit and a bow tie at all times even though we were in the middle of a horribly humid Japanese summer. One morning with the bus thermometer at 105 degrees, Backlund came on and beelined over to Tenryu, who was in shorts and a T-shirt.

"Mr. Tenryu, I'm sorry that I'm a little bit disheveled today but it's a little warm this morning. I apologize for my appearance." He had the top button of his dress shirt undone and his jacket over his shoulder. He was still wearing the vest.

During the long bus rides Bob never slept or relaxed because he was always reading or talking to somebody . . . or to himself.

He was in the midst of reading a thick book, when

John Kronus of the Eliminators tag team asked him what he was doing.

"Just reading a book about Winston Churchill, one of the paramount orators of our time," he replied to the simpleminded Kronus. "But then again, John, you probably don't know what a 'paramount orator' is."

"I don't even know what a 'Winston Churchill' is," John replied as Backlund looked away in disgust.

Bob looked like a maniacal Richie Cunningham and sounded like the white Urkel. I was sitting on the bus when I heard a mechanical voice behind me say, "Lugubrious: a melancholy state of mind."

I turned around to see Demon Opie shoving a hand-sized computer into my face.

"Look what I've got, Christopher," he said with a voice that resembled SpongeBob on Quaaludes.

"It's a talking dictionary. It gives you the definition of almost every word in the English language," he explained proudly.

This is what years of taking bumps does to you, kids.

"Exacerbate: to increase the severity of something," the computer voice continued.

"Despondent: to feel bad."

"Nomenclature: a name."

At this point Bob looked like he was about to ejaculate: to eject bodily fluids.

Bob also had a rule that a fan could have his autograph only if they could name all the presidents in United States history—in chronological order. I guess he wanted to educate the youth of Japan, one autograph at a time. When one teenage fan finally rattled them off, Bob was so impressed he signed *two* autographs.

The only time I ever saw Bob loosen up was when Dick Murdoch joined the tour. Despite my initial opinion of Murdoch in SMW, I was really happy to see him again. When Dickie was around you didn't need to find a party, because Captain Redneck WAS the party. That evening he peer-pressured Backlund into drinking a ridiculous amount of beer, turning him into a raving drunk.

I was veritably aghast at the magnitude of bock he imbibed.

The tour led us back to the Hakata Star Lane and that night Murdoch was facing one of the WAR young boys.

"Mr. Murdoch, would you mind if maybe we did this high spot?" the young boy asked. Then he described an intricate well thought out series of moves that was guaranteed to get a reaction. Dirty Dick just kept nodding, "Uh-huh. Yeah. Okay. Yeah. I got it. Okay. Okay. Sounds great kid."

As the rookie walked away pleased with his gumption, Murdoch looked at me straight-faced and said, "Ain't no way in hell I'm doing any of that bullshit out there."

Dick couldn't speak much Japanese but he didn't have to. He was in his late fifties but the crowd loved him and ate out of the palm of his hand. Like Negro Casas in Mexico, Dick knew what they liked and how to get them to react the way he wanted. I watched in awe and learned yet another lesson.

In wrestling, instinct means more than being able to speak the same language.

Now the antithesis to Dick Murdoch was Mil Mascaras. He arrived in WAR with the same giant ego and piss-poor attitude that he'd shown me in Mexico.

But the loyal Japanese fans loved him because of his

success as a pioneering high-flyer in the 1970s. Now that he was in *his* seventies, he was a nightmare to work with. I drew the short straw when Tenryu told me he was bringing Mil in and wanted me to work with him every night.

"It's not going to be fun for you I know, but you're a good worker and maybe you can get a decent match out of him."

I couldn't.

But I worked my ass off every night trying to make chicken salad out of chicken shit. I was especially ticked off after our match on the second to last night of the tour when Mil cornered me. "Nobody cares about you. They just care about me. Nobody paid to see you, they paid to see me. So no more of your moves tomorrow night because nobody wants to see them." Then he arrogantly walked away.

Too many blows to the head had left me with a memory problem and the next night I couldn't remember if he'd told me to give him none of my moves or ALL of my moves. Just to be on the safe side, I gave him every damn move I could think of.

He didn't say a thing to me after the match and I've never spoken to him since.

During my career, I developed a reputation for being able to make guys look better than they really were. That skill came from working with guys like Mil Mascaras. I learned if you make your opponent look better, it makes you look better. If you can become a ring general, you will *always* have a job within the wrestling business. Unfortunately it's likely you will always *do* the job as well.

Being a ring general is no easy task and a lot of guys get offended when a younger guy with less experience is better at piecing together a match than they are. Thankfully that wasn't the case when I had my first match against my old friend Tonga (aka King Haku) in WAR.

Tonga had been working for Tenryu for years and was the top gaijin in WAR. He had no problem listening to my ideas, which was a good thing as he outweighed me by 100 pounds and was one of the most feared men in the business. It's a strange feeling to be in the ring with someone you know could kill and eat you in a heartbeat. Wrestling him was like trying hold down an angry Doberman with a blanket. But Tonga went above and beyond to make me look great, not because we were friends, but because he was a professional. He understood that the better I looked, the better he looked and the better the match would be. He did such a good job of making his smaller, little known opponent look good that the fans started to believe that I could beat him.

Getting that reaction wasn't easy because in Japan, Size Matters. The fans equate girth and mass with power and fighting spirit, which is why sumo wrestlers are regarded as true warriors even with their Michelin Man physiques. Tonga looked like he could pick his teeth with me and he made sure to tell me before the match, "You have to hit me hard or no one will believe it."

He didn't have to say it twice.

I worked stiff and made sure to lay it in when I kicked him in the head and punched him in the face. I'd just invented a move where I would jump on the second rope inside the ring and moonsault out over the top rope to the floor and Tonga was the perfect target. He caught me like I was a good-lookin' softball.

We built the match until the fans were ooohhhing every

false finish, stomping their feet on the floor, and cheering everything we did. When he finally gave me his power bomb finish, he told me to kick out at 2. I waited until 2.9 and then lifted my shoulder to the crowd's amazement.

They began to excitedly chant, "Harto-Harto-Harto," due to the fighting spirit I'd shown by spitting in the face of the monster. Fighting spirit, the courage and fire you show in any fight, is the number one quality you need to have for the Japanese fans to respect you as a warrior. When the fans believe that you have that fighting spirit, they'll respect you forever.

So by kicking out of Haku's big move, the fans respected me.

Tonga beat me soon after, but instead of being disappointed they cheered me even harder. It didn't matter that I'd lost. I'd attained more honor and respect by losing and putting up a tremendous fight than if I'd pulled off a fluke win.

The influential *Gong Magazine* recognized our effort and voted the match the Best Bout of the night. I was able to read about it with my own eyes. That match was an important one for me because it was rare for two foreigners to get a Best Bout mention in one of the magazines. It was also the catalyst for my biggest push to date.

THE LOVELY LADS

Tenryu decided to create a heel faction within his company that would threaten to tear WAR apart from within. When Tenryu thought of this idea, the nWo was still a stain in Eric Bischoff's undies. Hiromichi Fuyuki was the second biggest name in WAR and was ready to become the top heel in the company. He recruited Jado and Gedo and the evil Fuyuki-Gun (Foo-You-Kee-Goon) was born.

I was in the locker room one night when I heard ambulance sirens pulling up to the arena, which is never a good thing. I found out that Jado had injured his shoulder and would be out for two months. Suddenly Fuyuki-Gun needed a new member and that's when Lion Do was born.

I don't know if the name was a spin-off of Jado and Gedo or if it meant something else—Fuyuki never told me even though he laughed out loud every time he said it. But becoming Lion Do helped me to become a star in Japan.

We became pure heels in a society that truly got mad

at us for our actions. The fans nicknamed us Team No Respect, which was the worst thing to be accused of in Japan. We didn't give a shit about anything in or out of the ring. This was exemplified by the T-shirts that Jado and Gedo sold at the merch stand that said, FUCK YOU . . . WE ARE JADO AND GEDO!! Definitely the best Japanglish T-shirt to ever hit the market.

Fuyuki was a genius at putting matches together and taught me a lot about developing my heel personality, I stole my patented "Cocky Pin" (putting one foot on my opponent while posing) from Fuyuki. He thought outside the box and came up with ideas like spraying our opponents with fire extinguishers, dousing them from behind with buckets of ice water, or unhooking the top rope to choke our enemies with.

My confidence level soared through the roof from working with some of the top names in Japan in the main events every night. So much of being successful in wrestling is having the confidence in knowing that your company believes in you. It gives you the inspiration to take chances during the matches and transcend into a superstar.

It was a great feeling when Tenryu shook my hand after the match one night and pressed 50,000 yen in my hand at the same time saying, "Thanks you" (not a typo). I would've jumped through fire for the guy because I knew he believed in me.

I became an honorary Japanese as a result of my membership in Fuyuki-Gun. Sometimes I traveled on the Japanese bus and I was the only gaijin to receive one of the black and yellow (Stryper colors!) WAR uniforms that all of the Japanese wrestlers wore. I also had to sit in silence while a half dozen guys put together a match in Japanese before stopping to ask me in English, "What you want do right here?" I had no idea what part of the match they were talking about or what would fit in that spot, so I had to guess and hope that my hip toss idea was a good one. Sometimes, they would all stop talking, look at me and burst out laughing. It's never funny being the butt of the joke, but it's even worse when you're the butt that can't understand a damn thing.

On the nights I wasn't working with Fuyuki-Gun, I was usually booked to work with Ultimo Dragón, the man responsible for my job with WAR. I think that my rivalry with Dragón was one of the best of my career.

Our styles complemented each other perfectly and it got to the point where we could read each other's minds during a match. One of us would say, "Spot number 2," and we'd go through an intricate set of moves without thinking. I can honestly say that we never had a bad match. This was evident when WAR positioned us some nights in the main event, an almost unthinkable deed since the heavyweights usually worked on top.

Like in any other form of entertainment, the bigger a name you became, the better quality of girls were attained. In Japan the groupies (sometimes known as rats) would find out where the crew was staying and simply call the room. If one was in the mood to indulge, one could just invite a girl to his room like sexual room service. The only drag was that you never knew what they were going to look like until they showed up at the door. But that's why peepholes were invented, young grasshoppers.

I got a call one evening and a female voice asked, "This is Fumi. Can I come see you?"

Curiosity killed the JeriCat and I concurred. When I looked through the peephole, I thought, "Ooh, I don't think so."

I didn't answer the door, but Fumi was very persistent and kept on knocking. I still didn't answer and a battle of wills ensued. I wasn't gonna open the door and she wasn't leaving until I did. So I put on my Walkman (old-school), took a Halcion, and went to sleep.

I woke up the next morning to find a letter slipped under my door.

Lion Do,
I am not a rat!! [Then why was she pounding on my door?] I never want to see you again [I'd never seen her before]. I no like you anyway. You are Mr. Bighead. You could never win in Japan again. [Was she cursing me?] I never sex with you. You are gay boy!
Fumi
PS—Call me please!

The comedy never ends . . .

I got another raise in pay and in responsibility, when I was asked to be the foreign liaison for WAR. My duties included helping to book other foreigners that I felt could contribute to the company's growing success.

The first guys I thought of were my friends in Calgary. Lance was an awesome worker at this point and a no-brainer. Bret Como was brought over to be Ultimo Dragón's evil doppelganger, Ultimate Dragon. Big Titan was a big name from FMW and I was able to convince him to jump to WAR. Then there was Dr. Luther himself.

Lenny had been looking to work for a more prominent company and his solid style was a good fit for WAR.

All of these guys were good for the company, but I'd be lying if I said their talent was the only reason I'd suggested them. There's something to be said about traveling around the world with your best friends and living your dreams together. I'd spent enough time alone in Mexico and Germany so getting to hang with my bros in Japan made it almost like a paid vacation.

We always had a blast hanging in the small-town karaoke bars where you could rent a private room for just your party. We stocked up on a sweet Korean drink called Chu-Hi (think a wine cooler crossed with straight vodka) and rocked the hizz by singing whatever English songs were offered in the songbook. Sometimes there were only four or five of them and they'd be the most eclectic mix of songs like "What a Wonderful World," "The Kid Is Hot Tonight," "Heartbreak Hotel," "Auld Lang Syne," and "The Humpty Dance."

So we sang the songs ten times each, then switched it up and did Louis Armstrong singing, "The Kid Is Hot Tonight" or Jackie Mason singing "The Humpty Dance." The more Chu-Hi we drank, the funnier (and better) the songs got.

Of all the guys I helped bring over, Lenny and I had the best time because we lived in our own little world of private jokes and bullshit. Our favorite movie was *This Is Spinal Tap* and we called ourselves the Lovely Lads, which was the name of the Tap before they were famous. We always thought it would be a blast if the Lovely Lads got work in Japan and our dream came to fruition when we were booked as a tag team in Korakuen Hall. I've never been so proud as when I stood in the center of the ring and heard our ring introduction echo throughout the sold out venue, "Dr. Russer and Lion Ha-Toe, the Rovery Rads!"

That night we celebrated the debut and the subsequent breakup of the Lovely Lads (after we lost the match) in an area of Tokyo called Roppongi. Roppongi was jam-packed with bars and restaurants and was popular with all the foreigners in the city. Wrestlers, servicemen, actors, models, strippers, rock stars, botanists; you name it, they went there. When Lenny and I went to the Hard Rock Café for a cocktail, we saw Bono having a drink at the bar and I ain't talking about Sonny. I'm talking about THE Bono himself.

We had long debated the selling out of U2 and were determined to tell Bono exactly how we felt. We discussed what form of venom we would spit and when we were ready I marched straight over to him and said, "My name's Bono too."

Actually, we chickened out and stood there like asses until Lenny spit out "Bono, you're awesome." Then we stared at him with goofy grins until his bodyguard shooed us away.

We got another chance to redeem ourselves when we went into the Gas Panic Club (best bar name ever) and saw Christopher Lloyd. We stared at him from afar until Lenny said, "He's a movie star, so you know he's rich. I'm going to go pickpocket him and see what I can get."

Pickpocket him? Was he going to pull a caper next?

He came back moments later, all excited.

"I got something, I got something!"

He unfolded his hand and we stared at the hotel dry

cleaning receipt he'd stolen. Then Lenny decided, "I'm going to go over to talk to him." He wandered over and they struck up a conversation. I couldn't hear what exactly they were saying, but if Lenny was getting along so well with Christopher Lloyd, then I could too. I sidled up and did my best Dr. Emmett Brown impersonation.

"88.8 jigowatts! What are we going to do, Marty?"

Instead of the raucous laughter I expected, he ignored me and continued talking to Lenny. Len didn't introduce me either and I was dying a slow death.

"88.8 jigowatts! Marty get some plutonium!"

This time Christopher looked at me and said disgustedly, "First off, do you know how many people do that imitation for me every night? Second of all, its not 88.8 jigowatts, it's 1.21. 88.8 miles an hour was the speed the DeLorean needed to get to in order to time-travel."

Embarrassed by my lack of knowledge regarding *Back to the Future* minutiae, I tried to patch things up with some idle chat.

"How long have you been in Japan?"

"Too long," he responded and turned away for the last time. I shuffled away with my bottom lip dragging behind me and sulked in the corner while Lenny and Lloyd had a grand old time talking about acting or spelunking or whatever. They even called Lenny's brother in Vancouver to chat and I thought all the while, "Hello, I'm right here Ignatowski! No long-distance charges required, ya jackass."

While Chris Lloyd wasn't a fan of mine, some of my other fans had a lot more in their pockets than dry cleaning receipts. While a few of my sponsors were highly annoying and obnoxious, others had no ulterior motives and honestly wanted to show respect. They appreciated the hard work that was required to entertain them and wanted to repay us in some small way for the sacrifices we'd made.

My biggest sponsor was Rakutaru, a well-known Japanese television personality, motivational speaker, and comedian. He sat in the front row of every show we had in Tokyo and afterward he always took the whole crew out for Yakuniku. Yakuniku was Korean BBQ and was by far my favorite Japanese food, along with Yakitori (skewers of chicken) and Shabu Shabu, a thinly sliced roast beef that you boiled at your table like a fondue.

After each feast, Rocky gave me cab fare home, but where a cab cost only 1,000 yen, he'd give me 20,000. "Paying for the taxi" was his way of giving me a present (presento) without being obvious about it.

One night I had to take one for the team when he took us out for sushi instead. He ordered one special piece that tasted like the mushy poop it resembled. It was rubbery and gelatinous, but I didn't want to be rude so I took a small bite and swallowed it whole with a gulp of beer. I was pushing the rest of it away, when Dragón informed that it would be better to finish it, as it cost $750 for the single piece. I'd bought my first car for 400 bucks.

Rocky was an awesome sponsor and even took the entire Fuyuki-Gun to Hawaii for the Christmas of '95, all expenses paid. I felt bad telling my mom that I wouldn't be home for Christmas for the first time in my life, but she agreed that I couldn't pass up a free trip to Hawaii.

I was quite the James Bond world traveler as I went skiing in Banff in the Rocky Mountains and less than twenty-four hours later I was surfing in the Pacific Ocean off Waikiki Beach.

The most difficult thing about surfing is paddling far enough out to be able to surf in. What a waste of time! Why can't somebody invent a towrope made of foam to pull lazy Howlies like myself out into the surf? And once you've blown yourself up paddling, you have to actually stand up on the damn thing. I tried and fell down and tried and fell down until I finally got up on the stupid board. The theme from *Hawaii Five-0* started playing in my head and I imagined myself a speck of humanity in the middle of an eighty-foot pipeline.

In reality, I was gliding on two inches of wave until I panicked and fell back into the water five seconds later. As my head popped up out of the drink, I narrowly avoided being surfed over by a pair of giggling eight-year-old girls who pointed at me with laughter as they zipped by.

Bitches, man. Bitches.

CHAPTER 37

YOU'LL NEVER WORK IN JAPAN AGAIN

When I returned to WAR, business was declining. There'd been a huge influx of wrestling companies in Japan (over twenty) and it was getting harder to draw the fans.

I started to see members of the Yakuza sitting in the front row, always wearing their loud Bill Cosby style sweaters. I suspect that Tenryu made a deal with the Japanese mafia to help sell (extort) tickets to the shows in the smaller towns. It was a common practice in Japan for the mafia to launder money through wrestling.

Part of what endeared Tenryu to the fans was his stiff work in the ring. But whenever the Yakuza were in attendance, he worked *extra*-stiff. He wanted to impress them and prove that "his company was real," to ensure their future involvement with WAR.

That meant if you saw Cosby sweaters in the crowd and were booked against Tenryu, you were in for a tough night.

I speak from experience as I woke up many mornings with the pattern of Tenryu's bootlaces imbedded into my forehead. Beat that, Tito Ortiz.

A hardcore Yakuza was covered with head-to-toe tattoos and, accordingly, many public places forbade uncovered tattoos. The rule applied to everyone, Yakuza or not, so guys with heavy ink like Lenny or Perry Saturn from the Eliminators would have to wear long-sleeve shirts to use the gym or the swimming pool.

The mafia weren't to be taken lightly either, as they were a bunch of mean muthatruckas. Len and I found this out one night after we'd been rocking the Chu-Hi. We were playing catch with a flower pot (sounded like a good idea at the time) and I fumbled the pass. The pot shattered on the street, dirt and daffodils exploding all over the place. Seconds later, a black sedan pulled up beside us and two members of the Osaka chapter of the Cosby kids got out of the car speaking angrily in Japanese.

One of them said in broken English, "Why you make mess of this street? That is our flower pot. Pay us for the flower pot."

We were drunk, not stupid, and these guys weren't fucking around. So we gave them all our yen and cleaned the shattered pieces of pottery off the street. Besides, I was happy to do it because I wasn't into the idea of having a gun pulled on me in another foreign country.

Cleaning up for the Yakuza made us feel like the Japanese young boys who were expected to do all of the menial tasks in the dojo. They had to carry the bags, shine the boots, and wash the backs of their superiors as well as train brutally hard in the ring.

There was a vicious hazing process and tactics of

humiliation were used to weed out the pretenders. They were given crewcuts, demeaned and berated constantly, and were the victims of cruel beatings, both physical and mental. The young boys in the FMW dojo rumored to have to jack off into a jar, place it in the fridge, and drink it, *Fear Factor* style. I'd rather eat a worm myself.

They were also expected to set up the ring, work the opening match with little fanfare, and kneel at ringside for the rest of the show, watching and learning from the more experienced members of the crew. When the time was right, they'd be sent away to another country to get more experience. When they returned to Japan, they would be young boys no longer and would begin moving up the ladder. More fun would ensue, as they would get the shit kicked out of them by the veterans. It was Japanese tradition and when Tenryu told me to be extra-stiff with his young boys, I did what my boss told me to do.

It was a powerful feeling to able to smack guys in the head or kick them in the back as hard as I could. It was like having a Get Out of Jail Free card to be as mean and as stiff as I wanted with no fear of reprisal. It was the only time in my career that I won a match with a punch to the face.

But what comes around goes around and after I'd taken advantage of the young boys, I became the one who was taken advantage of.

Koji Kitao was an ex-Yokozuna (sumo's highest honor) who had gotten into wrestling after being thrown out of sumo. Kitao was 6 foot 6, 400 pounds, with a black belt and a bad attitude. He was a nightmare to work with because he just wanted to kick the shit out of everybody.

Guess who had to work with him the most? If you guessed William Hung, guess again.

So I had to suck it up and accept getting the shit kicked out of me night after night. Working with Kitao reminded me of a Tae Kwon Do tournament when I was eight years old. My opponent was a foot taller than me and was beating me up so bad that the ref said, "Fight back already!"

"I'm trying," I replied before eating another toe.

This was the same story.

Kitao helped WAR's business pick up enough that a Ryoguku show was booked for a six-man tag team tournament that featured the first-time pairing of Tenryu and my old FMW boss, Atsushi Onita. Interpromotional matches were rare in Japan and it was a huge deal to see the faces of two big companies tagging together. I was the odd man out of the Fuyuki-Gun that night, so I was paired with Vampiro and a huge bodybuilder named the Warlord for the first-round match against Tenryu's team, which also included Bam Bam Bigelow.

It was weird working with Onita. I still felt screwed over because he owed me money and he'd never treated me with any respect when I worked for him. I talked to him briefly before the match and he claimed to remember me but I got the vibe that he was lying . . . again.

The finish of the match was booked to have me do the Lionsault onto Onita. But before I could get the win, Tenryu would make the save and Onita would pin me with his shitty Thunder Fire Power Bomb finish.

I went for the Lionsault, which I usually hit 9.9 times out of ten. But this time, I nailed Onita square in the face with my knees. Maybe he was out of position, maybe the ring lights hit me in the eye, or maybe it was a Freudian slip, but the bottom line was I knocked the bastard out cold.

I looked into his glazed eyes and I knew he was in Ra Ra Rand. I was in front of 10,000 fans and I'd just knocked out my former boss with my finishing move. Time stood still and a lil devil Jericho appeared on my shoulder saying, "Pin him! Pin him! If you get the clean win over Atsushi Onita, it will catapult you to superstardom! Plus the son of a bitch still owes you $200."

A lil angel Jericho appeared on my other shoulder saying, "Christopher! Don't you even dare. It's so unprofessional and you'll get fired. You'll never work in Japan again!"

In the end I sided with the angel and as the ref counted to 2 I discreetly popped Onita's shoulder up, making it seem like he'd kicked out of my pin. He was still dazed man walking, so I basically power-bombed myself and told him to pin me. That's got to be the first time that someone has been owed money and beaten *himself* up.

After the match, I was admiring my pumped-up postmatch physique in the mirror when the Warlord walked behind me. He was so huge that he made me look like Nicole Richie in comparison.

I said to myself, "Why bother," and grabbed a donut.

The Warload was obsessed with eating an exact amount of carbs, calories, and proteins per day. The more he came to Japan, the harder it was for him to adapt to the schedule and the available cuisine. Most of WAR's shows ended by 9 P.M. and in the smaller towns everything closed at eight. We'd have to eat Bento boxes (boxed lunches) or stop at convenience stores. It was an acquired skill, but I'd learned how to get a decent meal at Lawson's Station.

Each night I enjoyed a hearty dinner of boiled eggs, giant pear apples, bottled water, and cookies.

But the Warload would have none of it and demanded steak every night. Unfortunately it was almost impossible to get a steak at that time. As the bus drove down the darkened roads in the middle of the night, he never stopped grumbling, "I want a fucking steak. I need a steak. I'm a big guy, I'm supposed to eat a steak. This is inhumane treatment." It didn't take long for the humor of watching such a big man acting like a such a baby to get old. We turned up the volume of the Kim Duk movie and ignored him.

The next morning he'd get on the bus bragging, "Well, I had a taxi drive me all over the city until five A.M. and even though I had to spend 100 bucks, I got my steak." He'd look around proudly like we were going to be jealous of his lucky break.

The Load was always bragging about how much he could eat. When they let us into the Shabu-Shabu buffets (most buffet restaurants in Japan had signs saying "No Sumo or Wrestlers") the Loadster would lose control and eat for an hour. One night I mentioned that I could eat more plates of food than he could, which to him was akin to calling his mother a whore.

I could sense he was outraged, so I made it official and challenged him. We started dipping the Shabu-Shabu meat into the boiling water and chowed down. About an hour later, we were both left with twenty-two plates stacked unevenly in front of each of us.

"You must be pretty embarrassed. I'm only 220 pounds. You weigh over 300 pounds and I just ate as much as you did."

"Hold on a second here. This is bullshit. I ate the rice. I ate three bowls of rice. For you to say that proves that you don't even know what you're talking about. I ate more than you. Ha Ha!"

Ha Ha? He'd gone stir-crazy. I expected him to start wagging his finger and chant "Nya, Nya, Nya Nya Nya."

CHAPTER 38

CALGARY KIDS

The junior heavyweight style of wrestling was more popular in Japan than anywhere else in the world and in 1994 the division gained even more prominence when Jushin Liger created the Super J Cup.

The J Cup was a one-night all-star tournament featuring the best junior heavyweight wrestlers from most of the major companies all over the world. Liger had major political pull and put together one of the best pro wrestling shows of all time. Liger, Dean Malenko, Eddy Guerrero, Ultimo Dragón, and Hayabusa were among those competing until Chris Benoit as Wild Pegasus beat the Great Sasuke to win the tournament.

The Super J Cup was technically a New Japan show with Liger as the producer and it was created to be a one-time event. But Dragón scored a major victory when he announced a little over a year later that he would be producing the Super J Cup—Second Stage for WAR.

I was on pins and needles waiting to see if I was going to be involved. After a few days of not hearing anything,

I called Dragón and cut to the chase. "Am I going to be in the J Cup?"

I breathed a sigh of relief when he said, "Of course."

Dragón did a great job orchestrating the tournament and spent months putting together the details. The Super J Cup—Second Stage once again featured the top junior heavyweights from almost all the top companies in the world. Liger, Benoit, el Samurai, Dos Caras, Shinjiro Otani were some of the best on the planet and Lion Heart was now included with them.

This was also the biggest show I'd ever been involved with. Tickets for the tournament at Ryogoku sold out within hours, I was on the cover of my first Japanese magazine with the rest of the participants, I did interviews with newspapers and radio, and was part of a huge press conference for NHK, one of the biggest TV stations in Tokyo.

But even though this was going to be the biggest show of my career, I had to make a major sacrifice to be a part of it. My grandfather had been very sick with cancer for months and passed away the week before the show. When I found out that he'd died, I had two choices. I could go to his funeral or I could stay in Japan and wrestle in the J Cup. My decision was made even harder, as my mother couldn't go to her own father's service because she couldn't travel long distances in her condition.

I decided to stay in Japan and do the show. Career-wise I really had no choice and I might not have gotten to where I am if I hadn't wrestled the J Cup. But I have to live with missing my grandpa's funeral and it's one of the two major regrets of my life. It still bothers me to this day.

December 13, 1995, was the day of the second Super J Cup and the packed house was abuzz as only a sold-out Japanese crowd can be. The fans were known for being on the silent side, but when something special was happening all those stereotypes flew out the window.

My first match was against Hanzo Nakijima and I beat him with the Lionsault. Hanzo was the appetizer and the main course was my second-round match against Wild Pegasus himself, Chris Benoit. Dragón had told me of his plan to book the two of us against each other and it was a dream match for me and the magazines.

The journalists called Benoit and Jericho the Calgary Kids, referring to the similar styles that all wrestlers from Calgary seem to have. The fans were excited at the prospect of seeing the two of us square off for the first time ever.

I was still intimidated by Chris, but I was looking forward to impressing him with all of my great ideas. I'd thought of a plethora of reversals and false finishes, but when I told Benoit my plans, he seemed noncommittal. He explained that he liked to have a few basic ideas for a match, but other than that just preferred to "go out there and do it." So we went over a few things, put together a finishing sequence, and that was it.

My music played and I was a ticking time bomb ready to explode, wearing my yellow and black Stryper tights and a black sequined disco jacket that was given to me by a sponsor. Not exactly the epitome of tough, but at least I looked sassy.

When Benoit's music, "Jump" by Van Halen, blared through the speakers, the New Japan partisan crowd went nuts for the defending champion as he walked to the ring, nary a facial expression to be found. When he entered the ring we immediately stood face-to-face, our noses pressed uncomfortably together.

Wild Pegasus vs. Lion Hart. Benoit vs. Jericho.

This was the man I'd patterned my career after. This was the man I'd depended on for advice. This was the man whose brother I'd almost been. This was the man I was going to beat the shit out of.

The match began and I gave Benoit one of my trademark hard slaps to the face.

"Come on motherfucker!" I yelled, causing the silent crowd to react with a massive OOOOOOOHHHHHHHH!

Saying the word fuck always caused the fans to react in amazement, as if it was the most unheard of and rebellious statement you could ever make. It was a trick that I used nightly.

When I cockily smirked at Benoit, he slapped me in the face right back. If you've ever heard the expression "he slapped the taste out of my mouth," you understand what happened. Except that he slapped the sight, hearing, touch and smell out of me as well. I was momentarily as knocked out as Onita was in the same ring and the same arena, a year and a half earlier.

After the match I said to Benoit, "That slap was pretty crazy."

"Well, I don't really throw a lot of slaps, so I'm not really good at it."

My stinging jaw thought he was *very* good at it.

But I was only dazed for a few seconds and the slap was like getting doused with a bucket of water. The Shit Was On!

We took each other to the max, maneuvering in and

out of European-style holds, exhibiting high-flying lucha libre moves, and beating the hell out of each other Dungeon style. After a brilliant string of false finishes that included an awesome power bomb attempt by Benoit reversed into a Frankensteiner, Chris pinned me with a piledriver off the second rope.

But we'd lived up to the expectation and put on the match of the night. *Gong* gave us Best Bout honors and me a trophy for Best Fighting Sprit.

Dragón booked the rest of the tournament perfectly. Gedo beat Benoit and then Liger beat Gedo in the final. New Japan won, which I'm sure was a political concession for allowing WAR to use Liger's idea of the J Cup in the first place. But having Gedo in the final cemented him as a top junior heavyweight and gave Dragón a new top-level opponent.

Dragón also made another smart move by booking an exhibition match featuring the Japanese debut of Rey Misterio Jr., the guy Art Barr had introduced me to in Mexico a few years earlier. Since then, Rey had developed a reputation as the best high-flyer in the world.

Benoit had never seen him wrestle in person either, so we sat down in front of a backstage monitor to check him out. His match that night against Psicosis was one of the most amazing displays of athleticism that I've ever seen in my life. I think there were probably fifteen or twenty instances where Benoit and I looked at each other and incredulously remarked, "Holy shit. Did you see that?" or "That's impossible!"

Rey was a real-life superhero like Jackie Chan. When Dragón first brought him into the locker room, the president of WAR complained about his size, thinking that having such a small man in the WAR ring would be an embarrassment to the company. As soon as the match was over, the same guy asked Dragón when Rey could be booked again.

All of the participants in the J Cup were required to watch the final match from the ringside area, symbolizing how important the last match was. A few minutes before we went to the ring, I decided to try some of the GHB that I had acquired a few days earlier. GHB was a bodybuilding supplement that was created to help you get cut while you slept. But if you took it and stayed awake, it would help you get cut period.

It had the flavor of salty paint thinner and was pretty much the worst thing I'd ever tasted in my life. But it did its job quickly and I was buzzed by the time I walked through the curtain of the sold-out Sumo Hall toward the ring. I anchored myself to the turnbuckle post across from Benoit and the arena started to spin. Chris was laughing his ass off across from me.

After Liger won, we got into the ring for the final ceremony. I had a befuddled grin on my face; half from appreciating the experience, half from appreciating the GHB. The next week I finally made the cover of *Gong Magazine* with my hair askew and sporting a drug-induced Cheshire Cat grin. Another goal accomplished!

The celebration continued in the dressing room. It was a Japanese tradition for all the members to hold a beer into the air and yell "Kanpai!" After repeating the gesture a dozen times for all the photographers, I was starting to feel sick so I sat in the corner. I bent over to put my head between my legs and watched as the sweat dripped off my head onto the floor.

Drip, drip, drip.

A pool of sweat gathered and I opened my mouth to puke all over the floor of the sacred arena. With my stomach settling, I took a lurching breath and threw up a second time. I felt a little better, so I lifted my head and stared right into the face of Benoit. He was laughing uncontrollably (come to think of it, Chris always seemed to find it hilarious to watch me throw up) while standing next to a New Japan official he'd brought over to show off my vomiting skills.

"Look at this, Kawana," Benoit said, pointing at me with tears streaming down his face. "This guy's got no class."

I was sure that any chance I had of ever working for New Japan had just been barfed out the window.

KENNY AND DOLLY

I flew back to Calgary the next day with the four-foot-tall Gong trophy stuffed into the overhead bin. A few days later, Chris called to tell me he was coming to Calgary to wrestle a show in honor of Stu Hart's eightieth birthday. I hadn't been invited to work the show, as I was strangely never booked on any of the Hart Brothers' sporadic local events.

I picked Chris up in a car that had no heater in the minus-thirty-degree weather and offered him lodging on the floor of my apartment. I was a hell of a host. So the mighty Chris Benoit spent the night shivering on my carpet, covered by an afghan that my grandma had knit for me.

We went to the show and I met Bret Hart for the first time. He was as friendly to me as his brother Owen was on the plane to LAX and it was nice to know that at least two of the Hart brothers knew who I was. Bret asked me where I had worked and when I mentioned Mexico, a light flashed in his eye.

"I'm looking for a fancy pin to use as a finish on a PPV in a few days and I can't think of anything original. I know in Mexico they do a lot of interesting roll-ups. You have any ideas?"

Bret was facing Davey Boy Smith at the *In Your House* PPV a few days later. He didn't want to beat Davey with his finish, as that was too decisive an ending and they were in the middle of their angle. The WWF world champion was looking for a cool pinning move and he'd asked lil old Lion Heart for ideas!

Immediately I thought of Negro Casas's finishing move, the Magistral. Negro would hook his opponent's arm, roll over his back, and trap him in a pin. I told Bret I might have one for him and asked the 1-2-3 Kid if he would play guinea pig. Bret watched in silence as I did it a few times on the dressing room floor and finally nodded in agreement.

I gave a little cheer a few days later when I watched the PPV and saw Bret actually use my (Negro's) move. I'd still never been contacted by anyone to work for the WWF but at least I could say that I'd taught the world champion his new finishing PPV move.

The irony of the situation made me realize that, after all these years, I was finally ready to become a WWF superstar.

I stole the Magsitral back to win the tournament for the newly created WAR tag team championships with my partner, Gedo. Our first title defense was against the New Japan team of Liger and a young boy named Takaiwa, who they had big plans for. I'd never heard of him and when reporters asked me to comment on our opponents, I told them so. "Liger is a legend and I've been looking forward to beating his ass for years," I said in true heel fashion. "But I've never even heard of this Takaiwa. He's too green to even be in the ring with me." I was just amusing myself, never expecting the quote to see the light of day.

But the reporters took my quote seriously and inadvertently created my first wrestling angle from it. My words were printed in all the magazines and started a minor controversy. Takaiwa got right to the point with his rebuttal. "I'm going to show him who I am."

Liger had worked in the States many times and I'm sure he knew I was just talking shit to create more interest in the match. But I don't think Takaiwa realized it.

By the time the match took place, I'd created my own angle by accident. The fans in Korakuen Hall had brought signs and anti–Lion Heart banners hung from the balcony. One of them featured a perfect drawing of me, colored green. Another said "Team No Respect, Know Takaiwa." Clever.

I met Takaiwa for the first time in the dressing room before the match and while he was cordial, I could tell that he wasn't my biggest fan. But he was a pro and when we got into the ring, the crowd was electric. We were in the main event in Korakuen in an interpromotional match for the titles and it was a big deal. Gedo and I played our heel characters to the max, much to the displeasure of the fans. We gave our opponents the finger, farted in their general direction, and played our title belts like guitars years before Hulk Hogan ever did. This over-the-top heel was the precursor to the Y2J character that I created years later.

When Takaiwa and I finally faced off, it was time for him to show me who he was. We locked up and when I told him to give me a big tackle, I sold it by bumping through the ropes onto the floor.

Febuary 1996. In Korakuen Hall I play my championship belt like a guitar—a year before Hulk Hogan started doing it. Liger and Takaiwa look on unimpressed, especially since I insulted them, creating a controversial angle as a result.

OOOOOOOOOOOHHHHHHHHHH!!!

Gedo joined me outside the ring and we gave each other a big hug to a chorus of boos. Smoky Mountain Wrestling had arrived in Japan and business was good. The basic principles of wrestling remain the same no matter where in the world you are. People like to see good guys facing bad guys with something at stake. In this case it wasn't just the titles at stake, but Takaiwa's personal pride as well.

He got a measure of revenge when he hit me with his Death Valley Driver before he was finally pinned by Gedo. It was a great finish, because even though he lost the match, he showed me who he was and was raised to another level in the fans' eyes in the process.

Mission accomplished.

A few months later I had what was at that point the defining match of my career, when I defended the WAR International Junior Heavyweight title against Dragón at the WAR 3rd Anniversary show in Ryogoku.

Dragón and I had worked together so many times that the fans were totally familiar with both of our repertoires. That meant we could play with their emotions by switching things up. This surprised the people and gave them something different from what they were used to seeing.

They would think, "Jericho's going to do the Lion-sault now," and when I jumped over Dragón to do it, he tripped me and went for a Magistral. Then I countered that with another reversal of my own.

Earlier in the day I'd gone to a Denny's (yes, they have Denny's in Japan) and came up with a number of ideas and concepts that I thought would work for the match. Unbeknownst to me Dragón had done the same thing and when we got together to discuss the match we were loaded with ideas.

The match was a culmination of the greatest hits of two performers who'd worked together dozens of times, like Kenny and Dolly. But we also came up with a bunch of new ideas including a top rope power slam and a reversal off of Dragón's spinning top rope Cancun Tornado Splash. The match was tremendous and became my calling card. When I needed to send a tape of my work to anyone, whether it was ECW, WWF, or WCW, I would just send that match. It was the perfect sample of who Chris Jericho was as a performer and what he could do in the ring, plus it took place in front of a sold-out raucous crowd in a prestigious Japanese arena.

I retained the title and beat one of Japan's biggest stars

at WAR's biggest show of the year. My credibility and name value were at an all-time high and when the match was over, we received a standing ovation from the 11,000 fans in attendance, one of whom was Mick Foley.

Mick was working in Japan for another company and had come to our show on a night off with Masa the superfan. I met him for the first time afterward and he seemed impressed.

"That was a great match. You guys stole the show."

Mick offered to help me out if I ever needed anything back in the States and said he'd put a word in for me with Paul E. Dangerously, the boss of Extreme Championship Wrestling—ECW—based out of Philadelphia. I'd been thinking about trying to get work in ECW for a while. The company had built part of its reputation on hard work and great matches and I thought that my hybrid Japanese/Mexican/Calgary style would fit in perfectly. Plus my career templates Chris Benoit and Eddy Guerrero were already working there. Most importantly, even though I had a great spot and a respected position within WAR, it was time for me to try to break into the big leagues again.

And this time I was ready.

So I mailed Mick a tape of the Ultimo Dragón match trusting that he would personally deliver it to Paul E. as he had promised.

He did and not too long afterward, I got a call.

CHAPTER 40

PRETTY BOYS WERE CRUCIFIED

Even though it hadn't taken long for Paul E. to call me after Mick gave him my tape, I'd been trying to get ahold of the guy for almost a year.

ECW had come into prominence as the premier independent American company and was famous for introducing the hardcore style of wrestling invented in Puerto Rico (and copied by FMW) into the U.S. It was also the first American company to shine the spotlight on wrestlers that were deemed "too small" by the big leagues. Before ECW, nobody ever gave guys like Benoit, Juventud Guerrera, Eddy Guerrero, Dean Malenko, or Rey Mysterio Jr. a chance, but Paul E. knew that their combination of technique and high-flying would help break the company to the masses. ECW was providing an outlet for guys with hybrid styles like mine and if I could make an impression there it would help finally break me in the States.

I first called Paul E. in November of 1994. He didn't call

me back so I continued to try every couple of weeks. Usually I only got as far as his answering machine until one time someone actually answered.

"Can I speak to Paul please? It's Chris Jericho."

"No, he's not here. This is his roommate Dave. I'll have him call you back."

Strangely, roommate Dave's voice sounded exactly like the distinctive voice of Paul E. and I'd heard him enough times on TV to know that I'd just spoken with him. I kept calling and a few weeks later he answered again, this time admitting his true identity.

"Hey, Chris, how are you doing?" he said nonchalantly. "I've got Jimmy Snuka on the other line. Let me call you right back." Denied again.

The runaround went on similar to the Ric Flair fiasco but the difference was Paul had never told me to call him. But my friends in ECW had.

Perry Saturn of the Eliminators kept telling me that Paul claimed to be interested in using me. "Paul is the worst at returning calls. But keep calling him, he'll eventually call you back." I figured if I bugged him long enough, he'd bring me in just to shut me up.

Finally after six months of unanswered phone calls, I was at home in Okotoks on a Saturday when Benoit called me at lunchtime. "Paul E. wants to you to come in to work against me."

My heart skipped a beat and I flipped out. "No way? Absolutely! When?"

"Tonight in Philly."

Philadelphia was a six-hour flight from Calgary. Even though it was already noon, I frantically called the airlines anyway but none of them had any flights that would arrive remotely on time. One of the ladies on the phone said, "I can't get you into Philly until tomorrow night. But I can get you into New York City tonight by eleven . . . is that okay?" Who was I . . . David Spade in *Tommy Boy*? If I could just convince Paul to move the show to the Big Apple, I'd be all set.

I was crestfallen when I had to tell Chris that I couldn't make it. I'd been waiting so long to work for ECW and was convinced that I'd missed my chance. However, if Paul had called me with such urgency once, he'd surely call me a second time, right?

Wrong.

I didn't hear another word from Paul or ECW until Mick Foley saw my match against Dragón in Japan. When he hand-delivered the tape and gave it the Cactus stamp of approval, Paul finally decided to give me a chance.

I returned to my apartment in Calgary one night at 2 A.M. in December of 1995 and found a message from Dave's roommate on my machine.

"Chris Jericho, Paul E. Dangerously. Please call me back as soon you can, night or day . . . I rarely sleep."

Since I'd been waiting for over a year to talk to the guy, I figured there was no better time than the present. I picked up the phone at 2:30 in the morning and dialed his number. He answered within seconds.

"Paul? This is Chris Jericho."

"Chris, I'm so glad you called. I have been trying to get ahold of you for a year."

With only one sentence, I knew he was full of shit. He knew damn well that *I'd* been practically stalking *him* for over a year. But he told his lie with such conviction and gusto that I immediately liked the guy. He was like a used car salesman trying to sell me a rusted '76 Volare when he went into his pitch.

"I saw your match with Ultimo Dragón and it was just unbelievable. Mick Foley, Perry Saturn, and Chris Benoit told me how good a person you are and I'd like to bring you in to make you a part of the ECW family. From what I've seen, there's no reason why you couldn't be the ECW heavyweight champion very soon."

It was the perfect time for me to start in ECW, as Paul had just suffered his first wave of defections: Benoit, Eddy, Malenko, Steve Austin, and the Public Enemy all had left for the big-money pastures of WCW and WWF. In showcasing the new breed of smaller, more exciting performers, ECW had unwittingly become a feeder system to the big leagues. But the exodus left a huge open spot for me to fill.

Paul prided himself in scouring the world for the best undiscovered talent and he had decided to bring in Rob Van Dam, Rey Mysterio Jr. and this sexy beast to shore up his roster. He made it clear that he wanted me to work whenever I was available. He was planning on making my first appearance into a big deal and vignettes began appearing on the ECW TV show trumpeting the arrival of the Last Survivor of Stu Hart's Dungeon, Lion Heart Chris Jericho.

Like the fans in Japan, Paul's audience was savvy to the wrestling business. They were hardcore tape traders or insider newsletter readers and familiar with all the wrestlers on the worldwide scene. A strong segment of the fans knew who I was because of the popularity of the second Super J Cup and my matches with Dragón. For the fans who hadn't heard of me, Paul's decision to promote me as the Last Survivor of the Dungeon gave me credibility and brought respect to my name.

Trumpeting my legacy provided me with the tougher edge I needed to get over with ECW fans. My long blond hair and pretty boy good looks were going to be automatic strikes against me. Paul's suggestion to me before my first match was to wet my hair, which would eliminate the glam rock element from my gimmick. In ECW, pretty boys were crucified, not welcomed.

My debut ECW show was going to be in Reading, Pennsylvania, but that was the only detail Paul had given me—we hadn't discussed money or any other arrangements. He was going to send me a plane ticket to Philly but mentioned nothing about hotel expenses. Some promoters paid for accommodations, some didn't. But I was a cheap bastard and I thought I'd see if I could arrange it.

So I called Paul's machine and said, "I was just wondering about my hotel expenses. We never discussed it but I assume you'll be taking care of that. If you don't call me back, I guess you're covering it." Since he was horrible at returning calls, my plan had just finagled (fun word) free rooms for my trip.

When I arrived in Philly I found that Paul had gotten the last laugh by booking me in a room with someone else. I knocked on the door a few times, but nobody answered. I kept knocking until I heard a flush and the door opened. The smell of weed and kaka wafted out, followed by my roomie, Rob Van Dam. I shook the hand of the man with whom I'd have a dozen great matches, and it was still wet from a post-dump washing.

The Whole Poop N Show.

My first match in ECW was against the Eliminators

with RVD as my partner. Because of all the press and hype ECW was getting worldwide, I was expecting a big-time atmosphere. I was surprised when I walked into the dark and dingy Slammer's Gym, which was no bigger than a community center. It felt like I was returning to the *Bloodsport* arena in Matamoros.

The first thing I noticed was the vibe of the fans. I wasn't in Kansas anymore—these critters were rabid. They were very knowledgeable and could tell instantly if someone wasn't up to snuff at their craft. You hear a lot about how certain writers or rock bands have a cult following—well, the ECW fans were a cult. They believed they were part of an uprising and had an elitist Us vs. Them mentality . . . with WCW and WWF being Them.

If the fans saw something they liked during the match, they would chant "ECDub, ECDub!" It was unusual for a crowd to chant the name of the company rather than the name of a wrestler, but the whole situation was unusual.

My match went well and I broke the Jericho Curse midway through when the crowd started chanting "Five-star match!" They took their wrestling seriously and knew the difference between a good and a bad match. They were like a Japanese crowd, if the Japanese crowd was on crack.

When I came through the curtain after the match, Paul E. was waiting for me with a smile on his face. He gave me a big hug and told me, "That was great! You hit the ropes harder than anybody since Steve Austin."

That was definitely the most unique compliment I'd ever received.

It was then that I saw Paul E.'s greatest strength: He was an exceptional motivator. He made his crew feel like a million bucks even though he was only paying them a couple hundred. Paul waited for every single wrestler to come through the curtain so he could congratulate them personally for their contribution to the show.

His encouragement meant more to his crew than money. I'm sure there were guys in the WWF who would've given a week's pay to get that kind of acknowledgment from Vince McMahon. Paul's currency was compliments and he spent it freely.

He was a master of accentuating the strengths and hiding the weaknesses of his roster. This was apparent when acts like Public Enemy and the Sandman went to the big leagues and were exposed as average performers when they weren't protected in the same way. Paul hid Sandman's weaknesses in the ring by turning him into a beer-drinking, hard-hitting son of a bitch (sound familiar?), and Public Enemy went from a stock tag team to a pair of hot-stepping table-breaking wiggers, who became the most popular act in the company.

With his limited financial resources, Paul had to use whoever was available to the greatest of their abilities. The fans truly loved or hated every performer on the roster and if they didn't, that wrestler wouldn't last long.

There was a family-type atmosphere in the locker room and I didn't sense the jealousy that usually existed toward a new performer in the fold. I felt welcome right off the bat. In that same locker room there was also a platoon of beautiful, scantily clad women roaming around like wildlife. Paul had stocked his company full of gorgeous girls on the theory that sex sells.

I was sold.

There were always women involved in the wrestling business, but these knockouts were in a different league:

Beulah, Francine, Woman, Miss Patricia, Lady Alexandria, Missy Hyatt; all of them drop-dead gorgeous.

I was blown away in particular by a tiny Asian girl named Kimona Wanaleia, who had one of the best bodies I'd ever seen. I couldn't take my eyes off her to the point where I couldn't concentrate on my work. It's hard enough to put together a match as it is, never mind being in the middle of a Cinemax flick to boob . . . er boot.

It wasn't just the girls who were distracting—the entire roster was a plethora of freaks and misfits. There were half a dozen guys walking around wearing tie-dye shirts and black-framed nerd glasses called the Dudleys. Their gimmick was that Mr. Dudley was a jobber (sorry Bubba) who'd spawned a whole brood of half-brothers with ricockulous names like Snot (my old SMF roommate Anthony), Spike, Bubba, Devon, Chubby, Big Dick, Sign Guy, and the Indian, Dances with Dudley.

There was an obese guy with a blue Mohawk, wearing a half shirt and short-shorts, named the Blue Meanie. While I appreciated the reference to the Beatles' *Yellow Submarine*, I thought it was the worst name for a wrestler ever. There was a fifty-year-old man with Captain Caveman hair and a Roman gladiator outfit named Salvatore Bellomo. Another guy called J. T. Smith had the gimmick of falling off the ropes and making mistakes in the ring, inciting the fans to chant, "You fucked up!"

The chant became J.T.'s legacy and you still hear it whenever a wrestler makes a mistake. I should know, as I've been the recipient of the dreaded chorus many times.

But the crowd loved a good chant and if they didn't like what they were seeing, they would start up with "End this match!" If one of the girls did something dastardly, a rousing refrain of "She's a crack whore" would sound throughout the building. If one of the heels did something evil, they would be greeted with "You suck dick!"

Fun for the whole family.

CHAPTER 41

CAN YOU DIG IT?

My victory over the Jericho Curse in ECW was short-lived when the bastard used Mapquest and found me during my second ECW match in Queens, New York. It was hard to believe that the New York City fans could be more brutal than the Pennsylvania brethren, but they were.

Paul booked me against RVD and wanted to use the match as our official TV debut. Rob and I had similar styles, similar size, and similar worldwide experience. He'd spent some time overseas and made a name for himself in Japan just as I had. But the match sucked worse than a toothless vampire. We were a step off on everything and there was no sign of the chemistry we'd had the night before. The fans turned on us, chanting "This match sucks," "Please go home," "End this match." Even the dreaded "You fucked up" chant reared its ugly head when I screwed up a simple arm drag.

At the time neither of us realized how bad the match actually was. Paul claimed he couldn't air it on TV because the tape in the camera was defective. It only took me five years to figure out that the tape was fine. It was the match that was defective.

A lot of the same fans from the Reading show were also in Queens and some of them had their own gimmicks. One guy brought his own signs and was one of the first fans to do so. Another wore the same straw hat and Hawaiian shirt at every show. Another dude with long black hair, beard, and black aviator shades looked exactly like Jim Martin the guitar player from Faith No More. All these guys sat in the exact same seat at every show.

The fans were a part of the ECW experience and they were proud to be a part of the revolution. The whole scene reminded me when I found the first Metallica record in Winnipeg in 1984 before they had any mainstream success. I got jealous when they started becoming more popular.

They were *my* band and nobody else could have them, dammit!

The hardcore ECW fans felt the same way. Whenever a wrestler left to go to bigger and more lucrative pastures, they were often greeted with chants of "You sold out," as if they were personally turning their backs on each one of the people in attendance.

I sure wasn't working in ECW for the money—I wasn't expecting to make a whole lot of cash. But I knew that being a regular there would increase my visibility and value overnight. I hadn't discussed a specific money guarantee with Paul and I was curious to see what he would give me for the weekend.

When I received my check, it looked like a doctor's

prescription—practically illegible. I had to study it for a few minutes to figure out that Paul had ended up giving me 150 bucks for the Reading show and 250 bucks for the Queens show. He also tacked on a $25 bonus.

Even though Paul couldn't pay a king's ransom, that $25 bonus might as well have been $5,000. It was a motivational tool that boosted my morale and made me proud to be a part of the company. Paul was notorious for bouncing checks, but I can honestly say that I never had a single problem cashing a check from Paul E. I also had a stack of pictures of him fornicating with a walrus, but that's a different story.

I went back a few weeks later for my debut at the famed ECW Arena. The Arena had developed a life of its own and was becoming as legendary as Korakuen Hall. Yet it wasn't an arena at all, but a bingo hall that had been converted into one. But after wrestling in bowling alleys, a bingo hall was actually a step up.

It seemed like the whole place was under construction. The backstage area was dirty and full of trash, with a grungy bathroom and a shower that was so filthy, a Mexican toilet wash would have been better.

Paul wanted my first Arena appearance to be a big deal, so he booked me against the Human Suplex Machine, Taz. Taz was the biggest star in the company and was known for destroying everybody he wrestled. He was another perfect example of Paul's adeptness at accentuating strengths, as the fans really believed he was the biggest badass in the company . . . even though he was smaller in comparison to some of the other wrestlers.

In the dressing room before the match, I heard a few people mention the name Alfonso while talking to Taz.

Since we were working together that night, I decided to address him on a first-name basis.

"What do you want to do out there tonight, Alfonso?"

He stared at me sternly, "What?"

"Ummm, your name is Alfonso, right?"

I thought he was going to choke me out when he told me that Alfonso was his manager's name. It seemed that Mr. Taz wasn't too fond of Mr. Alfonso either. Instead of breaking the ice, Taz almost broke my face.

Because Paul had built Taz into such a destroyer, the fans were convinced that I was going to be his pupu platter for the evening. In reality, the match was designed to make me into an instant star. The story was for me to hold my own against Taz, until finally maneuvering behind him and giving him a German suplex. It would be a huge deal because Taz rarely left his feet during a match and he'd never been suplexed before.

By giving Taz a taste of his own suplex medicine, the fans would know that ECW was taking me seriously as a contender, which would make them take me seriously.

It wasn't hard to see that the company took itself quite seriously as well. Before the show started, Paul addressed the entire crew from the top of a staircase and delivered a motivational speech that would've put Knute Rockne to shame. It was like Cyrus addressing the gangs in *The Warriors*.

"You are some of the most talented people in the entire wrestling business and nobody wants you. WWF has cast you out. WCW won't return your calls. They won't hire you because they are afraid you will outshine and embarrass every single one of their so-called wrestlers. And they're right. They don't want you, they won't take you, but I am honored to have you as a part of this company. I thank you for putting your bodies on the line to entertain these fans and give them the show that they deserve; a show that no other organization on this planet can give them. I sincerely thank you."

He might as well have finished up with, "Can You Dig It?"

I looked around and saw that this ragtag bunch of misfits were ready to kill for Paul E. at that point—and I was one of them.

Paul was Jim Jones disguised as a wrestling promoter and he had just served us a Big Gulp full of Kool-Aid. I drank it down like a fine wine and was more fired up for that match than any other in my life. I was determined to make Reverend Paul E. proud of my performance.

I took it to Taz with my Japanese stiff offense and when the big moment arrived, I suplexed the War Machine right off his feet. The crowd erupted with astonishment and surprise. They knew it was no coincidence that both Taz and ECW had allowed me to do that. Then, at the apex of my domination, Taz got behind me and returned the favor by suplexing me literally right on the top of head. He followed up by putting me in his katahajime submission finish (a judo choke hold), guaranteeing his victory.

But my subtle push continued when I didn't tap out. The story was that the suplex was so vicious, it had knocked me out cold. But I'd shown incredible fighting spirit in taking Taz to the limit and the fans accepted me as a member of the family. Paul's plan had worked.

Taz continued to apply his submission until the locker room emptied to try to save me. He murdered a few job guys, until Brian Pillman, a huge star who'd been one of my Stampede heroes, ran into the ring. Pillman distracted Taz long enough for me to get rolled onto a stretcher.

As I was being carted down the aisle, a fan leaned over the rail and said, "Hey Jericho ya faggot, why doncha go work in New York!" I guess not everyone in the Arena was ready to bake me a hero cookie.

The comment reminded me of a story my dad told me from when he was playing with the Rangers in the old Chicago Stadium. The arena had a staircase leading from the dressing room up to the ice and as he was climbing the steps a fan yelled, "Hey Irvine ya faggot, why doncha go back to New York!"

Same asshole, different Irvine.

As the stretcher took me through the curtain (where I was greeted by an ecstatic Paul E.) I saw Pillman rebuke Taz's challenge and jump over the rail into the arms of Philadelphia Eagle lineman Harry Boatswain. It fit Pillman's character to play the unorthodox chickenshit coward because it seemed like he'd gone completely insane in real life . . . or had he?

He was working in ECW after leaving WCW, where Pillman had convinced everyone in WCW that he'd gone crazy, to the point of conning WCW boss Eric Bischoff into firing him and legally letting him out of his contract. But he still kept showing up in the crowd at WCW events, causing disturbances on live TV and leading the fans and everyone in the company to think he'd lost his marbles. But it wasn't just for the shows—he was playing crazy all the time.

He'd shown up in ECW to continue the elaborate work and perfect his loony act. He was also doing an excellent job of convincing everyone that he'd lost it. He'd shown up at the Arena that day with his pants falling down from not having a belt. He went around to everyone in the dressing room asking them if they had an extra belt (who doesn't?) and ended up settling on a piece of twine.

Then out in the ring, the Sandman hit a jobber with his trademark kendo stick, knocking the guy loopy. The guy was obviously going to be fine, but that didn't stop Pillman from running around the dressing room, jumping up and down and screaming like a crack-addicted monkey in his gravelly voice, "Call 911! Call 911! For the love of Christ somebody please call 911!"

He was completely overreacting as if the guy had been beheaded. But he wouldn't stop and was making everyone in the room very uncomfortable, when right in the middle of his tirade with nobody looking, he gave me a wink.

I thought, "That guy is a genius. He's working everybody."

I was a big fan of Pillman's work, but I'd only met him for the first time that evening and I was confused as to why he chose to let me in on his elaborate ruse. Why did he trust me not to blow the whistle?

I'm sure it was because of our Calgary connection. He'd started in Stampede and still had great respect for the territory and all it had taught him. He also was a fan of wrestling and kept close tabs on what was going on within the business worldwide. Maybe he'd heard something about me and my history or how I'd gotten into the business the same way he had. Being trained in the Dungeon was like being part of a fraternity, so in a way we were frat brothers.

It was the only time we crossed paths in ECW, but we

spent a lot of time together that weekend and he gave me some brilliant advice.

"If you really want to make it in wrestling, you have to do something that's never been done before."

I took Brian's advice to heart and followed it throughout the rest of my career. The success of all my future work was always based upon that rule.

Brian was doing the crazy gimmick to build interest for his return to the big leagues. He wanted to end up in the WWF, but had an idea he'd been pitching to WCW in case he returned there. Pillman wanted to form a younger version of the Four Horsemen to feud with Ric Flair's legendary team. His idea was to call the team the Horsemen of the Apocalypse or the Generation X Horsemen. While the original team held up four fingers to signify the Four Horsemen, this team would cross their forearms and give a double four finger sign in the form of an X. Pillman's idea was to have Benoit and Eddy in the group and asked me if I'd be interested in being the fourth member.

Was I interested? Gee, let me check my calendar . . .

To get the chance to work with those guys would have been the biggest opportunity of my career. But Pillman ended up signing with the WWF and the idea never materialized. However, I never forgot his advice and it influenced my career greatly. Thanks Brian.

Pillman wasn't the only influential person that I crossed paths with in ECW, as my first weekend in the company was Mick Foley's last. He was going to the WWF and his second to last match in ECW was against me, the guy who he'd been instrumental in getting into the company in the first place. Our first ever match was a good one and I'd like to add that I won that hard-fought contest.

I would also like to add that Mick Foley has been a three-time world champion and a *New York Times* best-selling author, but the one thing he hasn't done is beat Lion Heart Chris Jericho in a wrestling match.

Not that I'm keeping track or anything.

CHAPTER 42

THE GOLDEN TICKET

While my match with Mick was one of my ECW high-light moments, my absolute hands-down favorite moment didn't even involve me. When I first started in the company, Kiss was in the middle of their huge reunion tour. The Blue Meanie was in a tag team with his partner, Stevie Richards, and their gimmick was to parody other wrestlers. One night in the Arena they came to the ring with two other guys dressed as Kiss and began lip-synching and strutting around to "Rock and Roll All Nite."

The crowd went bonkers for the Kiss tribute and everyone was having a great time watching these idiots make fools of themselves.

Just as the revelry reached its peak, "Enter Sandman" by Metallica cut Kiss off like road rage and the Sandman made his way to the ring drinking a can of beer. He took his kendo stick and caned the shit out of the Starchild and the Catman, spit beer into the face of the Space Ace, and kicked the Demon right in his Deuce.

It was hilarious and it made the Sandman my favorite wrestler . . . for one night only.

After the Arena shows, Paul E. put us up at a run-down Travellodge in the middle of a Philly crack neighborhood and all the fans knew exactly where we stayed. There were hundreds of fans in the bar and the lobby of the hotel after the show partying all night long. They weren't the annoying type of fans, but respectful and knowledgeable so it was cool to get to know them a little. Hanging with the fans also helped pass the time while we were waiting until 5 A.M. for Paul E. to tape the promos for the TV show.

He applied the same last-minute fly-by-the-seat-of-his-pants routine for most aspects of the promotion. I'd see him scribbling matches on a napkin for a show that was already in progress. All of the wrestlers would be dressed and on call to go on whenever he called our names.

Once as the first match of the show was already taking place, he said, "Chris, you're on in the third match against Mikey Whipwreck."

"Paul, Mikey's wrestling in the ring right now."

"How 'bout Too Cold Scorpio? Is he out there? If not, you guys are on third," Paul replied without blinking an eye.

I used my ongoing WAR tours to develop a foolproof way to impress the girls. I simply called them from Japan and just like Frank Costanza stopping short, it was my best move. It worked every time.

"How are you doing? I'm just hanging out in Tokyo and I thought of you." You could practically hear the helpless female melting on the other end of the line.

I used my best move on the lovely Kimona and it dazzled her so much, I started dating her. She became my ECW girlfriend, which was a better bonus than the twenty-five bucks Paul was giving me.

She made me a proud boyfriend indeed at the Arena one night when she saved the show after the ring broke.

Somehow during one of the matches, the ring just fell apart. There was a long delay while the crew tried to figure out how to repair it and the sold-out crowd was getting restless. Paul could sense a mutiny in the air so he told Kimona (who shockingly was a stripper) to go onto the balcony above the ring and perform a striptease. It took some convincing, but Paul poured a keg full of Kool-Aid over her and she finally agreed.

The lovely Kimona proceeded to calm the unruly mob with one of the sexiest erotic dances I've ever seen. I was watching her performance with Terry Gordy, who was one of the best big-man wrestlers of all time until a drug overdose left him with permanent brain damage. He stood next to me watching Kimona's display of artistic expression with a huge wad of tobacco in his mouth and said, "I ain't never seen nothing like this at no wrestling match."

Neither had I, but Paul made sure to give everyone the opportunity to see it by peddling the tape on the ECW TV show for the next five years.

A friend of mine in Los Angeles called me the next day to ask me about Kimona's famous dance. During the conversation, he mentioned an upcoming wrestling show that piqued my interest. Antonio Inoki, the boss of New Japan, was promoting the World Peace Festival, which featured wrestlers from Japan, Mexico, and the United States. WCW had a working relationship with New Japan and was planning to send some wrestlers from the company, including Benoit. I had a gut feeling that it would be in my best interest to be on that show, so I made a few calls to some of the local L.A. promoters I'd worked for and weaseled my way onto the card.

I was hoping to use the show as a tryout for New Japan, but it ended up leading me into an entirely different direction.

I met up with Chris at a party held the night before the festival and he insisted on introducing me to Eric Bischoff. Chris and I had worn suits to the party and even though we stood out like sore thumbs among the other guys, I was dressed for success when I met Eric.

Benoit had passed my Dragón match tape around the WCW higher-ups and Eric had seen it. Two sentences into our conversation, he cut me off and said, "Benoit has been recommending you like crazy and that's enough for me. Do you want to come work for me in WCW?"

And that was it.

After years of toiling away in foreign countries, high school gyms, bowling alleys, and bingo halls, I'd finally been given the golden ticket to work in the United States.

"Here's my number, call my secretary. We'll arrange a meeting and make a deal."

I couldn't believe how quickly it had transpired. Granted, Bischoff was signing anybody with potential to prevent them from going to the WWF. He was in the middle of a nasty wrestling war and he wanted to lock up as much talent as he could.

I'm not saying that Eric didn't know who I was, but I don't think he'd seen any of my work besides the Dragon match. I know damn well that he didn't see my work at the Peace Festival, because he left before the show started. I thought that it was strange that he didn't stick around to check out his new prospect, but in hindsight it was a typical WCW move.

A few days later I called Paul E. to tell him about Eric's offer and, to my surprise, he already knew. At that point, Paul had a huge influence on the business and had spies everywhere who told him everything. I think he still appreciated my honesty in telling him myself.

"Bischoff made me an offer to go to WCW, but I don't know if I really want to go."

"Well don't go then," he said matter-of-factly.

I didn't have to explain the reasons why I couldn't say no and he knew I was gone. But to my surprise, he explained that before I left he wanted me to win the ECW television championship.

It took a lot of trust for Paul to want that, as I had no contract with him. I could've won the belt and thrown it in the garbage can on live WCW TV. But he trusted me and I took that very seriously. We agreed it was best for business to keep the WCW deal a secret until my last night with ECW. We couldn't have done that now with the influence of the Internet, but back in those medieval times secrets could still be kept secret.

The plan was for me to win the title at the ECW Arena from Pitbull #2. The day I was supposed to leave Paul called and left a FedEx tracking number on my answering machine, explaining that my plane ticket had been FedExed to the airport and I had to pick it up.

Why would a FedEx be at the airport? Why wouldn't they just deliver it to my house?

I drove to the FedEx outlet at the airport, but when I gave them the number, they told me that it was a digit short, nine numbers instead of ten.

The night before the match I was still waiting for my plane ticket. Even though Paul was notorious for leaving flight arrangements to the last minute, this was getting ricockulous.

I was stir-crazy in my apartment waiting, so I left for a beer. When I came back a few hours later there was still no word from Paul. I called him every hour to no avail, until I finally said, "I've been calling you all night with no response. I don't care about your stupid belt and I'm not coming to your stupid show. Later."

I hung up and literally thirty seconds later, Paul called me back.

He was as friendly as can be and said cheerily, "Hey, what are you doing? I've been hanging out with a bunch of strippers and I just got home. I called you a few hours ago and left a message on your tape. There's a ticket waiting for you at the airport."

I had an answering machine with no messages on it and a caller ID with no calls on it, which proved two things:

1. I was a loser with no friends.
2. Paul E. was telling another bald-faced lie.

Jim Cornette once said that Paul E. would rather climb a tree and lie than stay on the ground and tell the truth. I was starting to agree, although this was probably Paul's revenge for me deciding to jump to WCW. I wanted to tell him him to go to hell, but he was one of those guys who was impossible to stay mad at. Besides, I was still excited that I was about to win my first American championship.

The match for the title was one of the best of my career and ended with me reversing Pitbull #2's top rope power

June 1996. The new ECW Television Champion. Paul E. put the title on me, even though he knew I had already signed with WCW.

bomb into a Frankensteiner for the victory. The move came out of nowhere and the crowd exploded out of their chairs when I won. It was a gas to watch the tape back and see their various euphoric reactions to my victory. On the eve of my exit, I had become a big part of the family.

After my victory, I jumped into the crowd and celebrated with the fans, even trading my belt for Hat Guy's Panama lid. I was the ECW TV champion at twenty-five years old and it was a great moment in Jeric-History.

I continued the celebration by hosting a victory party in my room until the wee hours at the Travellodge and woke up late for my flight. When I called the airline to get on the next one, they told me, "You should be able to fly standby on the next flight. Don't you worry and we're very sorry about your brother-in-law."

"My brother-in-law?"

"Yes, Mr. Irvine. We were so sorry to hear about the passing of your brother-in-law." I had neither a brother-in-law nor a sister.

Something was rotten in the state of Pennsylvania but I rolled with it, "Oh, yeah, yeah. I keep forgetting. I still can't believe it."

What I really couldn't believe was Paul E. had flown me in on a bereavement fare and hadn't told me.

The next weekend, I confronted him.

"Hey, the next time you're going to fly me on a bereavement fare, can you at least tell me so I don't blow my own cover and get arrested for fraud?"

Once again, Paul didn't bat an eye as he pulled a doctor's note pad out of his bag and said, "Did they hassle you? If they do, just give them this."

Then he took a pen and wrote in his illegible chicken scratch:

To Whom It May Concern,

Thank you so much for your compassion during this horrible time. You have been so understanding and the Irvine family thanks you.

Sincerely,

Dr. Horowitz

Now he was adding medical fraud to his list of felonies.

I lost the title one month later in a four-way elimination match against Pitbull #2, Too Cold Scorpio, and Shane Douglas. Paul surprised the fans again by having the champion (yours rockingly) be the first guy eliminated.

It was another memorable night highlighted by my first ECW brawl through the crowd. The fans were famous for bringing their own weapons for the wrestlers to hit each other with and there was quite a selection. Nintendo consoles, cheese graters, muffin pans, pencil sharpeners, and even a fishing net. What kind of evil violence could I dish out with a fishing net? Was I expected to capture my opponent like a huge butterfly and put him into a giant jelly jar with holes cut into its massive lid?

My next weekend in ECW was my last and Paul had one last laugh when he booked bereavement fares for me and a Calgary wrestler named Johnny Smith. This time another brother-in-law had choked on a grape or something.

Just a tip, kids: Don't ever think of marrying one of my sisters.

Johnny and I drove to the airport trying to figure out how we could have the same brother-in-law if we weren't related. We surmised that we would have to be married to sisters whose brother had died.

After my last match in ECW against Too Cold Scorpio, the crowd in the Arena started chanting "Please don't go." I'd been spared the "You sold out," chants because I think people were genuinely saddened at my departure. I know I was.

I had a tear in my eye as I grabbed the mike and cut an emotional promo praising the Arena, ECW, and all its fans. It was a genuinely bittersweet moment. If I could've stayed there forever and made good money in the process, I would've seriously considered it.

When I walked back through the curtain, Paul was standing there looking like he'd just lost his best friend. He gave me a hug like it was the end of an era . . . which it was.

I called Paul for advice many times afterward and he was always there for me—even though it took him forever to call me back.

A lot of people associate me with ECW and consider me an ECW guy. In reality, I only wrestled twenty-two matches for the company over the course of six months. But my connection to ECW isn't solely based on the amount of time I spent there, but rather on the attitude that I exuded while I was with the company.

I was tailor-made for the fighting spirit that the company was built on and I had the true respect for the wrestling business that everybody in ECW shared. There was nobody in the company that had been drafted from another sport or was in the business to make a quick buck or to become famous. We were all there because we loved wrestling and believed in the company and in ourselves. That's why it's difficult to explain or to understand what ECW was all about unless you were actually there.

I'm proud to say I fought in ECW and serving my tour of duty there helped take me to the big time.

Unfortunately making it to the big leagues of WCW almost killed my love for the wrestling business, in the same way that working in the minor leagues of ECW had intensified it.

CHAPTER 43

DOOMED FROM THE START

After the Peace Festival, it didn't take long to set up a meeting with Bischoff in Atlanta. There would be no Flair-style runaround this time.

WCW had recently taken the ratings lead over the WWF, so if things went well with Eric I would be working for the biggest wrestling company in the United States.

A few days after I'd received a plane ticket to Atlanta in the mail, I got a call from WCW booker Kevin Sullivan. He sounded almost annoyed, like he'd been forced to call me.

"Eric wants to fly you in for a tryout."

Sullivan spoke in a thick Boston accent and came off like a total dick. He arrogantly told me that he wanted to book me for a tryout so he could take a look at what I could do. I didn't have the heart to tell him I was already flying to Atlanta in a few days to negotiate a long-term contract with the boss.

Tryout? I don't need no stinking tryout.

In retrospect, Sullivan's call was an early warning about how the communication between the people in charge of WCW worked. The left hand didn't know what the right hand was doing or what it was hiring.

WCW was owned by Ted Turner and its offices were housed in the CNN Center along with TBS's and TNT's offices. WCW didn't arrange a ride from the airport, so I took the MARTA (subway) to my meeting with the multimillion-dollar corporation.

Eric wasn't ready when I arrived, so I was told to wait with Paul Orndorff. Paul was working behind the scenes in WCW after being one of Hulk Hogan's main WWF rivals in the 1980s as Mr. Wonderful.

He was friendly to me but I must've gotten him on a good day, because the rest of the office referred to him as Oscar the Grouch. He was full of advice and his first suggestion seemed of utmost importance to him: I had to get a flashy robe to wear to the ring for my matches. Apparently Paul was quite morose about the lack of flashy robes currently being worn in the business.

At least it was better than a loincloth.

When Eric finally arrived he was brash and arrogant; a tougher John Davidson, wearing jeans, cowboy boots, and a leather jacket. His outfit seemed far too casual an ensemble for the head of a multimillion-dollar company.

When we went to eat at a sports bar in the concourse of the towers, I started second-guessing my abilities. I was here to sign a contract and I'd never done any negotiating before—at least not at this level—so I wasn't very confident about the process.

WCW was spending a lot of money to get the upper

hand in its nasty ratings war with the WWF. Both companies aired live shows head-to-head on Monday nights and were pulling out all the stops to get the advantage. Bischoff had taken the lead by masterminding one of the greatest wrestling angles of all time (which he had lifted from Japan): the nWo invasion.

He'd convinced two of the WWF's top stars, Diesel and Razor Ramon, to jump to WCW and threaten to take over the company. They became the first members of the nWo and were causing chaos (on screen and off) to a huge response from the fans and were on the verge of bringing in their new secret third member. During our lunch I asked him like a mark, "So, who's the third member going to be?"

He looked at me with a smirk and said, "If I told you, I'd have to kill you."

DOH! I was trying to get a job in the company and here I was asking questions like a twelve-year-old fan. I should've asked Eric for his autograph while I was at it. There went fifty grand in Jericho salary down the toilet.

I wanted to grab the words and shove them back down my throat, but I still couldn't get off the topic.

"I'm sure that WWF owns the names Razor Ramon and Diesel. So what are you going to call them?"

"I'm not sure yet," Eric said. "But if worse comes to worst, I'll call them by their real names Kevin Nash and Scott Hall. We're not going to get too fancy with it."

I couldn't stop my verbal diarrhea and told him that Big Titan (who, ironically, would become the WWF's Fake Razor Ramon) and I had come up with names that would still allow them to use similar gimmicks.

"Instead of Diesel and Razor Ramon, you should call

them Octane and Philoshave Phil," I said with a grin. Eric didn't respond and I wilted like a sixty-year-old man's boner.

Awkward silence.

After I ate my lunch of crow, we went back up to Eric's office and he got right to the point.

"I'm not going to waste any time with bullshit, I want you to come work for WCW. I think you have the potential to be our version of Shawn Michaels. You have the look and the charisma and you could be a big asset for us. I want to bring you in and start you off hot."

I was honored by his compliments but I was confused by Eric's next statement.

"I'd love to see a Chris Jericho–Brad Armstrong feud. I mean, I really see this Brad Armstrong–Chris Jericho thing."

Talk about a mixed message.

Eric had just compared me to Shawn Michaels, one of the WWF's biggest stars. Then in almost the same sentence, he talked about starting me off in a feud against Brad Armstrong, who was universally regarded as a great worker but had been portrayed by WCW as a much smaller star than Shawn Michaels.

A feud with Brad didn't seem to be a fast ticket to stardom, but I respected Eric's vision and agreed. Then he asked me how much money I wanted per year. This was the moment of truth. I'd done a little math and figured out how much I was making in Japan and how much I thought I was worth to WCW. I summoned up my courage, took a deep breath, and went for it.

"Well, Eric, I thought about it and since I'm making

good money in Japan, I can't see myself coming in for any less than $100,000."

There . . . it was out.

It was a ludicrously high number and I expected him to laugh my inflated-self-worth ass right out of his office. Instead Eric nodded and said, "I see you in the category of Dean Malenko, Eddy Guerrero, and Chris Benoit and I don't want you to make any less than they do. I'll give you $135,000, which is what they're making."

My eyes bugged out of my head like Jim Carrey in *The Mask*.

A hundred thirty-five thousand dollars to do something I loved? Was he high?

But Eric wasn't finished.

"I'm also going to want you to move to Atlanta and that's not going to be cheap. So I'll give you another $30,000 a year to help you cover the cost of the move. And I want you to sign the deal for three years."

I was blown away by his offer despite the fact that he was negotiating against himself and telling me how much my fellow employees were making, and I was ready to sign for ten years. Keep in mind that the most I'd ever made in a year up to that point was about $50,000 and you'll understand why I was in shock. I'd just been exposed to the magical generosity of ATM Eric.

I accepted his offer, left his office, and called my dad to tell him what had happened. He was as awestruck as I was, but he told me a story about his first contract negotiation with the New York Rangers almost twenty-five years earlier.

In 1970, he'd had a really good season with the Rangers,

so he went to renegotiate his contract with the team's general manager, Emile Francis.

"You know, Emile, I had a good season and I think I showed my value to the team. I'd like to ask you for a raise to $27,000 a year." He'd been making $25,000.

Emile offered him $30,000 instead.

My dad walked out of Emile's office with a smile. A few minutes later, he began feeling like he'd made a mistake because Francis had given him more than what he asked for. A good negotiator asks for more than he thinks he can get and settles for less. If my dad had asked for $35,000, maybe he would've gotten it.

I'd fallen into the same trap. Had I asked for $200,000, maybe I would've gotten it but I didn't know any better. I had Constanza-d myself and negotiated for less money.

But I was still ecstatic with Eric's offer, even though I found out that with all the taxes and road expenses taken out, $165,000 wasn't the small fortune I originally thought it was.

Bischoff mentioned that he wanted me to start with WCW as soon as I could finish up my previous commitments with ECW and WAR. My life was about to get busier than ever.

So while I still had a few free days, I drove from Calgary to Winnipeg to visit my mom.

It was the end of the summer and her health had improved enough that she was able to spend a lot of time outside. She navigated the neighborhood in her motorized wheelchair and we were able to take a walk to our favorite restaurant, D-Jay's, for dinner. I was proud to accompany her.

She was adjusting to her injury and dealing with it. The next year, she even flew three hours to Calgary to attend my cousin Chad's wedding. She had used her iron will to rise to the challenge that God had given her.

One beautiful Indian summer evening she asked me if I could give her a ride in my Mustang convertible with the top down. It was unusual for her to want to leave the safety of her house, but I was too busy hanging out with my friends (or something equally stupid) and told her I'd take her for a ride the next day.

Then I got a call from WCW a few hours later telling me that I was needed for a TV taping the next day in Dalton, Georgia. I never did get the chance to give her a ride in the convertible and I kick myself for it every day. I've often wondered what she would've looked like with the top down and the wind whipping through her hair. I imagine she would've had a big smile on her face, but now I'll never know for sure.

I'd put her off when she was able and the chance had passed me by forever. It's the other major regret of my life.

Regrets are a terrible burden and even though I only have a few, they're a few too many.

The next day I flew to Atlanta and drove to Dalton with instructions to be at the arena at 1 P.M. I was on Japan time and arrived at the building at 12:45. When I got there, the place was deserted; no TV truck, no ring crew, and only two other wrestlers . . . Scott Hall and Kevin Nash.

They were sitting side by side in the corner like wall-flowers, so I went over and introduced myself. We exchanged pleasantries and Hall knew my name because he'd met my dad in an airport once. My dad was always my biggest fan and had put me over huge to Hall.

The three of us sat around laughing at how stupid we felt for being the only ones at work on time. But we were all new to WCW and since I had the Japanese mind-set and they had the similar WWF mind-set, we had been taught to get to work on time with no exceptions. It seemed the rules were a tad bit looser in WCW-land.

Hall and Nash hadn't yet adopted the bad attitudes they would later become infamous for and on that day we were at the same level. But it was the last day that would be the case.

Everyone else finally showed up and I was booked to wrestle my first match against Jerry Lynn. The office had recently given him a gimmick change and were portraying him as a masked superhero. They'd outfitted him with a cool purple and yellow costume and the clever yet cryptic moniker of Mr. J.L. I still haven't solved the mystery of what the initials of Jerry Lynn's masked identity stood for.

But I had other problems to solve. Mr. J.L. and I were given seven minutes for our match, including ring entrances, which worked out to roughly five minutes of action. In Japan, I was used to working twenty-minute matches on a nightly basis . . . but I wasn't in Kanagawa anymore.

When Terry Taylor, the assistant booker, told me that the company had decided I was going to be a babyface, I didn't think it was the best decision. The good-looking, blond-haired, muscular young babyface would have been a no-brainer a few years earlier, but in 1996 the world was changing.

Society as a whole was starting to accept the bad guy as the new good guy and the good guy as the new bad guy. WCW was behind the curve in that respect and I was doomed from the start when I was booked as a nameless faceless babyface. I'd just come off a very successful heel run in Japan and in ECW everyone was a heel anyway, so

turning into an instant babyface was a tough transition.
I was in the heel mode of wanting to make my opponent
look good, so I gave Mr. J.L. most of the match and stole
a quick win from him at the end. I did my best to have a
good match but an old friend still came a-calling.

Knock knock.
Who's there?
It's the Jericho Curse bitch!

The match went over like a dump in church. It was a
horrible, red reels debut and everyone knew it. Except me.

The chastising began the moment I walked through the
curtain where Paul Orndorff was waiting for me. "Dammit boy, you need a fancy ring robe with gems and sequins sewn on it!"

Then I saw Terry Taylor, who was famous for being
blunt, maybe too much so. "Wow did that ever suck. Was
that your first match ever? It was terrible. What were you
trying to accomplish?"

"Since I was winning the match, I wanted to make J.L.
look good in the process," I said defensively.

"That match wasn't for him. It was for you to show
what you can do and from the looks of things, you can't do
much. I don't even know if we can even show it on TV."

Ouch!

Terry was furious and I'd fumbled the ball badly. In
my defense, the booking committee knew it was my first
match in the company and that I'd been working Japanese-
style, but they still sent me out to sink or swim on my own
with no tips or advice.

It was typical of a larger problem that existed in

WCW—nobody was on the same page. Terry Taylor was one booker, Kevin Sullivan was another, and others like Hulk Hogan (who ended up being the mystery third member of the nWo), Hall, and Nash did whatever they wanted to do no matter what the bookers said. Bischoff was supposed to be in charge of it all, but he was a marionette that did whatever Hogan and his lackeys puppeteered him to do. It was hard to tell who the boss really was.

The disorganization continued when Terry decided that he wanted me to go to Orlando the next day for the TV tapings the company did at Universal Studios. I'd flown from Winnipeg to Dalton for one day, so I only had one change of clothes and one pair of tights. Since the Orlando tapings lasted for two weeks, I was unprepared for such a long stay.

Terry decided it was best for me to fly back to Winnipeg, grab my stuff, and come back to Florida. But the comedy of errors continued when I told him that I didn't live in Winnipeg and my stuff was actually in Calgary.

So I flew from Atlanta to Winnipeg, arriving at twelve noon, kissed my mom goodbye, drove fourteen hours back to Calgary, arriving at 3 A.M., turned down the only official booty call I've ever been offered, grabbed my stuff, and got back on a plane to Orlando at 7 A.M. All because they decided they needed me in Orlando with one day's notice, even though I'd been with the company for a month and they could have booked me weeks in advance.

YaskY.

CHAPTER
44

BASKETBALL
HIGHLIGHTS #12

The tapings in Orlando were for the syndicated *World Wide Wrestling* program that ran in smaller markets around the world. The show was at the bottom of the totem pole for the company and was devoid of all the top stars.

But WCW boasted a huge roster so there were still over 100 contracted wrestlers hanging around the backstage area of the Universal Studios lot. It looked like a casting call for *One Flew Over the Cookoo's Nest 2—Electric Boogaloo.*

There were a lot of familiar faces in the mass of misfits, including Tonga/Haku (who had now become Meng), Eddy Guerrero, Horace Boulder, and Chris Benoit. When I saw Benoit I could tell he wasn't happy. He pulled me into a corner and said, "What the fuck happened in Dalton? Terry told me that you stunk the joint out. The word is already going around that you aren't any good."

I didn't think my performance was *that* bad and I was surprised to hear such a harsh opinion had developed after only one match. I thought I'd be given the chance to acclimate to the new style, but WCW employed far too many wrestlers to spoon-feed a nonheadliner like me.

The browbeating continued: "You have to dress nicer too. You're wearing shorts and a tank top; you look like a slob. This is the big leagues, act like it." He was wearing dress pants and a nice shirt. Chris adhered to the dress code ten years before it was officially instituted.

His words freaked me out and my confidence was shot. I don't know if I felt worse about possibly getting fired or letting Benoit down.

My first *World Wide* match was going to be against the Gambler, a journeyman wrestler that I'd never seen before (or since). His gimmick was he was a Kenny Rogers impersonator.

Even though that gimmick would rule, his actual gimmick was of a Maverick-style riverboat gambler. It was a horrible feeling knowing that my future was in the hands of a man who did card tricks on his way to the ring. I didn't know if he was good or if he sucked, but my self-esteem was at such a low that I was going to leave the match up to him. I was gambling on the Gambler.

Having confidence is a huge part of being successful. When you have it, you can do no wrong. When you don't, all you can do is wrong. At that point all of my previous accomplishments didn't mean a damn thing.

This was my last chance.

The Gambler led the match and I followed him. He was a meat-and-potatoes wrestler so it was nothing fancy, but it was exactly what I needed. It was the type of basic match that I would've had in wrestling camp. No bells or whistles, just a good story and solid execution.

Lo and behold, we had a good little match and within five minutes I regained my confidence and once again became Chris Jericho—World Beater.

As ricockulous as it sounds, the KISS rule always works. I'm not saying to go put on Demon makeup and spit blood, I'm saying Keep It Simple Stupid. We kept the match simple and I was no longer stupid.

Since we filmed four shows a day in Universal, there was a possibility of wrestling four times a day. But the matches were a piece of goozleberry pie. The audience was always loud and excited because the matches were one of the park's attractions. People would go on the Back to the Future ride, get cotton candy, go to the wrestling matches, take a ride on the Diggler, whatever.

The tourists would file in while a guy dressed in a dog costume explained, "When that big sign over there lights up, put your thumbs in the air and cheer! When that sign tells you to boo, put your thumbs down and boo."

If you watched the show, you would see a bunch of people who had no idea what they were reacting to, putting their thumbs up and cheering, only to turn on a dime and instantly start booing when the next guy came out. They were the exact opposite of ECW fans and I was now a part of Turner Broadcasting Corporate Wrestling.

But I was also still a part of the wrestling fraternity and some things never change. Riddle me this: What happens when you take 120 cooped-up wrestlers and unleash them into the adult playground known as Downtown Disney?

The answer: complete chaos and debauchery on a nightly basis. It seemed the entire roster ended up at the disco 8 Trax, drinking, partying, and dancing until three in the morning. After that, the party would continue in one of the dozen nearby hotels that housed us. Many a time we'd go straight from the party back to Universal Studios for the tapings, hoping and praying that we wouldn't be booked on the 9 A.M. show.

Here's a secret. If you were a fan of the *World Wide* show, you watched many matches performed by severely hungover or still slightly loaded wrestlers.

I'm talking from experience.

One night I had a dream that I threw up in the sink. When I woke up I found out it was no dream. That day I was booked on the 9 A.M., 11:30 A.M., 2 P.M., and 4:30 P.M. tapings. Six bucks and my right nut says that one of the bookers saw me doing the hustle to "Disco Duck" in a drunken stupor at three in the morning and thought it would be funny to have me wrestle four times the next day. It wasn't.

But it was a great gig and the *World Wide* shows helped me to get into the groove of having fast-paced, exciting matches against guys like Benoit, Eddy, and Dean Malenko.

I was a little concerned with my entrance music though. After meticulously choosing such heavy songs as "Over the Mountain" by Ozzy, "Electric Head Pt. 2" by White Zombie, and "Silent Jealousy" by X, my new music was a synthesizer-drenched, castrated rip-off of "Only the Young" by Journey.

I've always put major thought into my intro music, as it sets the tone for my attitude and character in the ring. This song failed miserably in both cases. It might've been okay if used for a montage in a 1980s teen comedy but it was awful for a rocker wrestler with big energy. Even worse, I was watching basketball highlights on TBS one night and heard my ring music playing in the background. My oh-so-important intro song was actually a generic track from the TBS music library.

"Jericho needs ring music? Okay, give him Basketball Highlights #12."

In a way the intro song choice was perfect, because it was just as boring as my character was. I was a generic good guy with no discernible charisma, who won some and lost some. It was a dangerous place to be.

I'd been sheltered by the canned *World Wide* crowds but when I wrestled on my first Monday *Nitro* in front of actual paying fans, I didn't fare as well.

Nitro was Bischoff's answer to the WWF's *Monday Night Raw* and his idea to air it head-to-head against *Raw* in the same time slot sparked one of the biggest boom periods in wrestling history. It was an exciting time for fans and wrestlers alike and was one of the reasons why Eric had hired me in the first place. He wanted to scarf up as much available talent as possible and worry about how to use them afterward.

It hit me just how much talent he'd signed when I went into the arena in Palmetto, Florida, for my first *Nitro*. Unlike the *World Wide* tapings, all the big stars were there.

I walked into one dressing room and saw Ric Flair, Sting, and Lex Luger playing cards. I went into another dressing room and saw Randy Savage talking to Scott Steiner. I turned the corner and saw Hulk Hogan walking out of his private dressing room with Jimmy Hart.

I took a moment for myself and completely marked out. I'd followed Flair in my mom's car, waited in the Polo

Park Inn for Hogan's autograph, jumped out of my chair when Savage won the WWF title.

Now I was working in the same company!

I took a deep breath of professional and exhaled the mark. The heroes from my childhood were now my peers and I was going to act accordingly.

At Chris's suggestion, I'd gone out and bought some nice clothes, or at least I thought I had. I couldn't find proper dress pants, so I purchased a pair of ill-fitting tan jeans and a wrinkled, black button-up shirt. I looked like a five-year-old kid who'd dressed himself for Sunday school and the shorts and tank top were probably a better look.

I made a point of introducing myself to as many people in the locker room as possible, as I'd been taught in wrestling school. Most of the guys were cordial, but had no idea who I was. I approached Lex Luger and figured that talking to him about the gym he owned in Atlanta where I worked out would be a great icebreaker.

"Hey Lex, I'm Chris Jericho and I just wanted to say that I think you've got a kick-ass gym. How long have you had it?"

He looked at me with an annoyed face and said, "Who are you again?"

It didn't take long to find out that his pompous attitude was shared by most of the big names in the locker room.

My first *Nitro* match was against Alex Wright, a young high-flyer from Germany. We were given eight minutes for the match (including entrances), and since it was my live prime-time national TV debut, my mind was racing with all of the cool spots and moves I wanted to do.

I gave Alex all of my awesome ideas and he nodded.

"Out of those ten things you want to do, pick your best

three because that's all we're gonna have time for." He was now Dick Murdoch and I was the Japanese young boy. He wasn't being a jerk, just a realist.

By the way the match was booked it wouldn't have mattered what I did, I was still screwed.

Kevin Sullivan gave me the absolute worst finish that a debuting 1996 babyface could not have asked for. He wanted us to have a back-and-forth match, culminating with Alex jumping off the top rope at me on the floor. I would move out of the way and he would land on the barricade, leaving himself incapacitated. But instead of standing over my injured opponent screaming in victory, I was supposed to roll out of the ring and *help him up*.

The guy who once wrestled with a broken arm and beat a man with a punch to the face was going to make sure his opponent was okay.

The match would end with the both of us getting counted out because I refused to accept such a cheap win.

Bobby Heenan was on commentary and said, "What a stupid move Jericho just made. You've got to take the wins any way you can in the big leagues. Why didn't he want the victory?" He wasn't wrong.

Bischoff was also announcing, but he defended my decision.

"Chris Jericho is a stand-up human being. He plays by the rules and he wouldn't dream of taking a victory that way. He's a good kid."

Sickening I know. Each one of his words buried me deeper.

Even Heenan realized how shamelessly Eric was putting me over.

"Did you co-sign a loan for this kid?"

The squeaky-clean babyface might've worked a decade earlier, but it was now the wrestling version of rat poison: sure to induce vomiting.

To make matters worse, I did an interview with Mean Gene Okerlund directly after the match to explain my actions.

"I didn't want to win the match that way, Mean Gene. Hulk Hogan and the nWo would take a win like that, but not me."

Instead of focusing on myself, I had to talk about how the nWo were a bunch of meanies. Another total self-burial. In eight minutes, I'd portrayed myself as a goody-two-shoes who would rather talk about Hulk Hogan than himself. Who in their right mind would get behind a loser like that?

Not the WCW office, that's fer damn sure.

Despite the fact that Eric seemed to be high on me (Terry Taylor flat-out told me, "The boss digs you"), the rest of the booking team seemed to be digging me into a hole. My suspicions were confirmed when I had my first ever PPV match against Chris Benoit at Fall Brawl '96.

I knew Chris and I could tear the house down like we had at the J Cup, but my bubble burst like a pimple when Sullivan told us that the match should be structured 80 percent for Benoit and 20 percent for me.

It made no sense to book any important match that way, never mind one featuring the debut of a guy "the boss digs." Maybe Sullivan didn't like the fact that he'd looked stupid by calling me for a tryout after I'd already been hired by the boss. Maybe it was because he was about to start an angle with Chris and wanted him to look strong. Either way, he killed my morale dead.

Chris and I ignored Sullivan's order and had a good back-and-forth match anyway. Afterward, Sullivan said, "It was a good match, but you got in way too much offense."

Was I supposed to be the next Shawn Michaels or the next Barry Horowitz?

Things continued to get worse on my first loop of house shows. I was booked against Jerry Lynn and with none of the time constraints imposed at the TV taping, we were having good matches. They must have been too good because I was approached by Scott Hall.

"Listen, you guys are going way too long and doing too much stuff during your matches. Nobody is paying a dime to see you, so you shouldn't be out there for twenty minutes. Do a short match and hit the showers," he said arrogantly and sauntered away.

I was furious. Was he Scott Mascaras? He didn't like the fact that we were working hard and he had to follow us. Except his name value was a million times bigger than mine so he didn't have to do much to get a reaction. But in my case, hard work was all I had because nobody knew who in the hell I was. The nWo could've cared less about match quality but that's all I did care about and I wanted to slap him in the face for dissing me.

Benoit was as mad as I was. "It's not his place to say that. He's just pissed because he's lazy and wants us all to be lazy too. Don't listen to him." Benoit already wanted to kick Hall's ass, after he had drunkenly pissed on Chris's cowboy boots one night.

Hall's comments were indicative of the nWo's overall attitude as they were being paid millions and had turned into massive prima donnas. One night in Tupelo, Mississippi, there was a problem with the arena sound system and the intro music wouldn't play. Hall and Nash started complaining loudly that it was JoJo (their special term for something bush-league) and refused to go to the ring.

"In New York, there was always music. Isn't this supposed to be the big time? This is JoJo. If there's no music we're not going to the ring."

They were wrestling against Sting and Randy Savage and after a few minutes of nonstop, Warload-type bitching, Savage said, "Listen, I don't give a shit if there's music or not, I'm going to the ring."

Sting agreed and they walked to the ring without another word. Savage was one of the biggest stars in WWF history and he didn't think the lack of music was JoJo. Hall and Nash reluctantly followed, bitching and complaining all the way to the ring.

After the show Eddy, Chris, Dean, and I were driving out of town, having a few post-match beers in the car. Eddy had to take a leakus and when we pulled over, we were right next to the house Elvis Presley had grown up in. We knew because there was a big placard in the front yard advertising the fact. Eddy decided to piss in the bushes lining Elvis's house as a tribute. We all started laughing when Eddy, in the midst of his stream of consciousness, looked up and said, "Fuck Elvis! Who did he ever beat?"

I guess the King didn't play in El Paso.

CHAPTER 45

INDIAN CASTE SYSTEM

After floating around with no direction for the first few months of my tenure, Sullivan told me that I was finally going to be put into a story line.

"That's tremendous," I said with excitement. "Who's it going to be with? Eddy Guererro? Ric Flair? Randy Savage?"

"Nick Patrick," he replied.

Nick Patrick was a referee.

I'd worked all over the world to make it to the big time and my first angle was going to be against a referee. How low can you go?

It got worse when Sullivan told me that I was going to be managed in the feud by Teddy Long. Personally, Teddy was a great guy and a great performer but the problem was at the time Teddy's protégés lost most of their matches. As soon as Sullivan aligned him with me, I knew I was screwed. I was battling a referee in a one-arm-tied-behind-my-back match with Typhoid Teddy as my mentor.

Shawn Michaels never had it so good.

Things fell apart during the big match, when the rope tying my arm behind my back came loose and I had to pretend it was still securely fastened. It didn't matter anyway as the announcers hardly commented on the bout—they were too busy plugging the nWo.

The social aspects of WCW were equally as disheartening. The locker room was infested with politics and cliques (great title for a rap song), and the office gave special treatment to the powerful ones. Hogan and Savage had their own dressing rooms and didn't really talk to anybody else. Hall and Nash were in their own little unit and acted above everyone. Other guys like Scott Steiner, DDP, Paul Wight, and Booker T later became my friends, but within the WCW environment they seemed uptight and defensive. Booker even balked at working with Dean, Eddy, and me, complaining, "I ain't no cruiserweight," as if he would get leprosy from touching us.

There wasn't a lot of cross-pollination among the cliques. It was almost like regressing to high school, where you had to be careful about who you talked to and where you sat in the lunch room. Once I sat down in catering at Hogan's table and he looked at me like I'd just whipped him in the face with my Jack Johnson. Maybe I should've; it would've given him no choice but to talk to me.

The booking of the matches worked the same way. The guys who made a certain amount of money worked almost exclusively with each other. There was a level that you were placed at and it was rare to ever move to another level. It was like an Indian caste system. Whatever level you came in at was the level that you were destined to stay at.

I came in at $165,000 and that's where I would stay.

I hardly ever worked with someone who made, let's say, $750,000, because they were worth more than me and worked with the guys in their tax bracket. On the odd occasion that I did work with one of the big-money guys, it was usually in a quick squash. In WCW, a $750,000 salary had to be justified with a $750,000 push.

There was also a cavalcade of guys who were getting paid huge amounts of money and never worked at all. Horace Boulder, Hogan's nephew, was on the payroll for almost two years before he ever started working steadily. Randy Savage's brother, Lanny Poffo, was on the payroll for the whole three years I was with the company and I only saw him work ONE match. I'll bet you a free copy of this fine publication that he was making in the same ballpark as I was and I was wrestling twenty-two matches a month.

Sure I was making a decent wage, but ATM Eric was paying a lot of guys way more money to do less work. But it didn't matter to him, and he was fond of saying, "I don't care, it's not my money. It's Ted Turner's."

Because it wasn't his money, he seemed to have a real lackadaisical attitude and wore sweat pants, a leather jacket, and a baseball cap turned backward at most of the shows. He was running a multimillion-dollar company and looked like a change vendor at an arcade.

As smart as Eric was, he conceded so much power to Hogan, Hall, and Nash that they pretty much ran the show. The booking team would hammer out a *Nitro* episode and an hour before the show the nWo would rewrite it. Some nights we still didn't know the lineup ten minutes before the show aired live to millions of people.

Their attitude toward their work was piss-poor as well. I overheard Scott Hall asking Bret Hart one night in

Huntsville, Alabama, "Why do you care so much about this match? It's just a house show."

That attitude was shared by head booker Sullivan, who asked me once, "Why do you care so much about your match? Nobody else does. Just go in the ring and get it over with. This company is the *Titanic* heading toward the iceberg anyways." It was great to hear such positive words from the man who was technically in charge of my on screen career.

Ric Flair overheard Sullivan's words and though he had jobbed me out three years earlier, he was one of the few vets in the WCW locker room who gave a shit about the young guys.

"Don't ever stop caring about your work," he said with dead seriousness. "Around here a good match is all you have. It's the only thing that makes you rise above the bullshit."

Flair was right, because as a plain, dry piece of baby-face toast, a good match WAS all I had. The nWo were supposed to be the bad guys, the evil empire tearing the company apart, yet they booked themselves to be the most entertaining, coolest act on the show. They had crowd-pleasing catchphrases, cool merchandise, a great sense of humor, and nobody in the company ever stood up to them. The fans started to treat them as the babyfaces, which emasculated other babyfaces (like me) who had no angles, no balls, and no chance to show any personality. The era of the Cool Heel had arrived.

As WCW continued its domination over the WWF, Eric became increasingly drunk with power. To capitalize on the company's growing popularity, TBS had started another two-hour weekly show called *Thursday Thunder*.

Bischoff was looking to give the show a boost and decided at the last minute to re-form the Four Horsemen, who had broken up a few months earlier.

Flair had received permission weeks earlier to miss the show so he could attend his son's wrestling tournament, and when Eric found out, he fired him on the spot. Then he called a meeting with every WCW employee in the Target Center in Minneapolis.

"I'm going to starve that piece of shit Flair and his family. I'm going to make sure that they end up living on the street."

Eric also guaranteed that the WWF would be out of business within six months. With his ludicrous claims and gestapo tactics, Eric had become the Hitler of wrestling and was acting like he'd lost his fuckin' mind.

He constantly trumpeted to anybody who would listen that Hogan and the nWo were the sole reason why WCW had pulled ahead of WWF in the ratings war. He never stopped to think that another reason may have been the hard work of the leprosy-afflicted cruiserweights.

Nobody in the mainstream audience had ever seen the style of matches that we were delivering on a consistent basis (sometimes for twenty minutes or more) on live TV. We were carrying the load and giving the fans tremendous performances while Hogan and the boys were stinking out the joint with theirs. In their arrogance, they'll tell you that the people paid to see only them, and in my arrogance, I'll tell you that the people walked away from the shows happier because of our hard work.

The overall bad attitude and lack of attention toward 80 percent of the roster was leading to mutiny. I saw it firsthand at a *World Wide* taping before a match I had with Mike Rotunda.

Alex Wright and a jobber named Hardbody Harrison were standing face-to-face. Hardbody had one of those Mr. T. bendable pump-up bars and was brandishing it like a weapon.

"I wanna be the heel," he said in his Ebonics accent.

"No, I vant to be ze heel," Alex said in his German accent.

They were arguing over who got to be the bad guy, like a couple of eight-year-old kids who both wanted to be Darth Vader. The argument escalated to a pushing match and was broken up by referee Peewee Anderson.

"Stup it! Who's sposed ta bae the hee-ell?" Peewee said in his hick Georgia accent.

The scene had turned into a bad Dana Carvey routine, as the German, Ebonics, and bumpkin accents all blended into one. The comedy show continued when Alex wrenched the Mr. T. bar out of Hardbody's hand and conked him over the head with it. Hardbody pitied the fool and jumped on Alex. The two of them rolled around on the floor engaged in the worst fight ever. Meanwhile, my ring music was playing and I had to tear myself away from the catfight to go have my stupid match. It was far less entertaining than the match that was already taking place backstage.

It wasn't surprising that Hardbody had attacked Alex; he was in his own world anyway. He was constantly submitting weird angles and stories to the office, trying to get himself a push.

First he came up with the idea of painting his face and becoming Sting's black nemesis, Stang. Then he came up with another beauty that had Diamond Dallas Page (DDP) bringing a special magic diamond crystal to the ring. Hardbody would attack him, steal the crystal, and drop it into a tank of piranhas. This chicanery would force DDP to jump into the piranha tank to retrieve the magic crystal, live on PPV. I would've paid to see that one.

Maybe I should've hired Hardbody to write an angle for me too, as I was grasping at straws to get noticed.

I tried to jazz up my ring entrance by throwing my back up against the guardrail, goading the fans to pat me on the back and get their faces on TV. I was sick of seeing babyfaces (like Lex Luger) slapping the fans' hands and looking like they would rather be dipping their balls in hot pitch. Unfortunately for me, most of the fans who lined the barricades were guys, so when I vigorously threw myself at the rail it looked like I was trying to get groped by a bunch of dudes. Mission accomplished.

I also had another mission to accomplish by moving out of Canada. After avoiding it for a year it was time to leave Calgary as the flights were too long, the taxes were too steep, and Bischoff had been pressuring me to follow through on his original request.

I didn't have to worry about getting a work visa in the U.S., because I was born in New York when my dad was playing with the Rangers.

But I did have to worry about finding a place to live and because of my hectic schedule I had no time to look for a place in Atlanta. I was able to convince Eric to let me move to Orlando (like he cared) and I found an apartment during the two-week *World Wide* tapings.

So I packed up my Mustang, rented a U-Haul trailer,

and made the drive down to Florida with my friend Ajax. I noticed right away that my new hometown was filled with tourists and old people. Since I didn't know any vacationing seniors, I started looking for a church that could help me fill the rare downtime.

I hadn't attended church regularly since I'd been laughed out of St. Chad's in Winnipeg over seven years earlier. Plus after my mom's accident I had some issues with God and though I continued to talk to him every day, I hadn't felt the desire to return to church. But the time had come to get some fellowship but I had no idea where to go. So I let God decide.

I opened the Yellow Pages to the church section, closed my eyes, and pointed. God's fingers did the walking and landed on an ad for the Tabernacle Baptist Church. I went to check it out and when I did, I was blown away. It was like the church scene in *The Blues Brothers* with people jumping up and down and dancing, all singing up-tempo hymns while accompanied by a ten-piece band. The pastor, Steve Ware, told jokes and showed clips from popular movies to back up his sermon.

I'd never been to a church like it and I was surprised at how much *fun* it was. I was grateful that God had led me to Tabernacle via the Yellow Pages Ouija Board™. He must have known that my soul needed cleansing—and some detoxification.

On the road, I went out every night to maintain my sanity. Since most of the crew was on the same boat as I was, it was easy to form drinking alliances with various groups, each gang possessing different qualities and unique names:

1. The Chubba Bubbas

Hugh Morrus

Johnny Grunge

Rochester Roadblock

Rocco Rock

Chris Jericho

Special Quality—All the members accused the others of being fat, flabby, and chubby. A proper greeting was "Hello Fatso," followed by "Hello Chuboots." Girls of plus sizes and rotund shapes were appreciated, as was a one-legged woman. She was nicknamed Eileen. Think about it.

2. The Drunken Four Horsemen

Steve McMichael

Raven

Curt Hennig

Chris Jericho

Special Quality—Being the last people in the bar, NO MATTER WHAT. Must be able to gargle Jack Daniel's for over thirty seconds. Must party with anyone, no matter the age or sexual orientation, a rule that encouraged Raven to go on a midnight motorcycle ride with a seventy-two-year-old woman.

3. The Useless Pop Culture Trivia Triumvrate

Konnan

Raven

Chris Jericho

Special Quality—Being able to waste hours of time discussing such important matters as what Isaac from

The Love Boat's real name was (Ted Lange) and who was Meeno Peluce's half-sister (Soleil Moon Frye).

There were others, but you get the idea.

I spent most of my time with the core members of my Indian caste system, Benoit, Guerrero, and Malenko. I'd known Eddy and Chris for years, but I hit it off with Dean the best. I'd never met him before WCW, but everybody who'd ever worked with him told me how good he was. What they hadn't told me was how funny he was.

When the camera was on, Dean was a stone-faced no-nonsense performer who kicked ass and got the job done. But backstage, he was funnier than Will Ferrell. If he had projected his natural personality onto the screen, he could have had his own sitcom on the WB fo' sho.

He produced a steady stream of one-liners, no matter what the scenario.

When the overweight Brian Knobs walked around the dressing room in a thong, Dean mused, "That's not a G-string, that's the whole alphabet."

When we went to a strip club and watched an overly skinny stripper dance, Dean quipped, "I don't know whether to tip her a dollar or a food stamp."

Dean and I began to travel together. We had to pay all of our own expenses, so doubling up helped to save money and kill time during the long rides.

At first, Dean and I traveled together with Benoit and Eddy, but after a while four guys in the same car and in the same room got to be too much no matter how much money we were saving.

Plus Benoit and Eddy liked to get up at seven in the morning, have breakfast, and work out. Dean and I liked to sleep in until noon, have lunch, and work out. Why get up early when you didn't have to?

Eddy and Chris were very strict with their diets. They were the first guys I knew who checked the labels on food to find out the nutritional information. I ate whatever I wanted within reason (and looked like it) and Dean was the same way. One day I decided to mimic Chris and see what the hell the big deal with the labels was. I studied intently and looked up to see Dean across the aisle doing the same thing. Our eyes met and we burst out laughing at how stupid the situation was. We bought the donuts and left.

Then we had the bright idea to stay up all night after every *Nitro* until our flight left the next morning. We started our plan by going to the seediest clubs we could find in whatever town we were in. But that "thrill" soon wore off, so we thought it would be funny instead to keep everyone else awake. Because so many of the wrestlers had their rooms paid for by the company (not us), everyone was based out of the same hotel. As a result, it wasn't hard to con the hotel security guard into giving us the keys to the other guys' rooms.

Dean and I would open our victim's door and run into their darkened room wearing lucha masks and screaming our heads off. One night, we broke into the room of a bunch of Mexican minis, midget wrestlers from south of the border. We found all five of them sleeping on the same king-size bed in a K position.

It was kompletely hilarious.

My three amigos and I had all wrestled for the bigger companies in Mexico, Europe, and Japan, earning us the nickname the New Japan Four. The name didn't quite fit for me, because even though I'd worked in Japan dozens of times, it had never been for New Japan. I knew that WCW had a working agreement with New Japan and that was one of the reasons I'd been so excited to sign with them in the first place, but I still hadn't had my chance to go.

Just as I reached the end of my rope, New Japan called and saved my career.

CHAPTER 46

CHRIS BIGALOW, ORIENTAL GIGOLO

I had just finished vacuuming my apartment when I received a call from Brad Rheinghans (who I used to watch in the AWA), the American liaison for New Japan.

"New Japan needs you to send them your measurements. They want to bring you in to be Jushin Liger's new rival and you're going to have a costume like his."

Brad told me that I was going to debut as the evil Super Liger in front of 65,000 people at the Tokyo Dome. Liger was one of THE faces of New Japan Pro Wrestling and being introduced in this manner was akin to debuting at WrestleMania as Don Cena, John's evil twin.

So I bought a tape measure and gave my measurements. The company made me a replica of Liger's famous bodysuit, but I didn't get a chance to see it (never mind try it on) until I arrived in Tokyo the night before the show.

It was basically a skintight white wet suit, made of

material thicker than spandex. When I tried it on, it was like wearing a body cast.

When I put on the trademark Liger horned mask, it was like putting on the Gimp's gear. It had only a little hole for a mouth and the eyes were covered by a red mesh that totally restricted my sight. With my new Super Liger costume on, I couldn't see, I couldn't move, I couldn't breathe, and I felt like I'd been dipped in candle wax.

I would've been okay at an S&M convention but how in the hell was I going to wrestle?

Drastic changes were going to be necessary so I went into MacGyver mode and began altering my costume. I took a pair of scissors and cut the chin out of the mask, allowing me to breathe. Then I tried to figure out a way to open up the eyeholes without messing up the red mesh, but it was futile. So I put the mask on and wore it to bed to try and get comfortable with it.

The next day I was taken to the gigantic Tokyo Dome, aka the Big Egg, an intimidating structure that put major perspective on the fact that it was my:

First time wearing a mask.
First time wrestling with New Japan.
First time wrestling in a full bodysuit.
First time in the Tokyo Dome.

When I went to meet with my opponent, Kanemoto, I got the vibe that he didn't want any part of the match and wasn't happy about having to put me over. It was a recipe for disaster but I was ready for the challenge and I knew I would persevere. This was my big chance and nothing was going to stop—

Hold on, someone's at the door.

"Hello?"

"Yes hello, it's me . . . the JERICHO CURSE!"

The Super Liger match was a bigger bomb than a Pauly Shore comeback.

I walked to the ring on the football-field-sized walkway and couldn't see a damn thing the whole time. I had to stare intently at my feet with every step as it was the only way I could keep on the path. Every time I looked up, the red lights that dominated the lighting rig made me feel like I was in the middle of a strobe light rave party. And me without my glowsticks.

I had no peripheral vision, which made even hitting the ropes a challenge. I felt like Wilf from the Hart Brothers Camp.

With the crowd going mild for the match, I tried to get something going. I knocked Kanemoto out of the ring and got ready to do my trademark crowd-pleasing move of jumping straight to the top rope and drop-kicking my opponent off the apron.

But when I went for my big leap, my legs felt like they were painted with concrete. I didn't even come close to getting my footing and slipped right off the ropes onto my ass inside the ring.

The Dome crowds were notorious for being quiet and it was hard to hear any noise anyway as it dispersed in such an expansive building. But I sure as hell heard the sound of thousands of people laughing at me when I fell. Giggling crowds are the kiss of death in Japan; the Asian equivalent of "You fucked up!"

I ended up winning the match but Super Liger's fate had been sealed, especially when one of the New Japan employees took my costume "for safekeeping," the moment I took it off in the locker room.

There was a big party after the show that I had to attend while wearing the Super Liger Party Mask. I might as well have been wearing the Masque of the Red Death. I'd been painted with the scarlet letter and nobody at the party would even look at me, except for my friend Black Cat.

After waiting to work for New Japan for a half dozen years, I'd finally gotten my chance and delivered a barn burner of match . . . people were burning their barns in protest.

Failure be thy name.

In order to live up to the huge Liger legacy, I needed to put on an A+ performance, but I'd responded with an F-(for Fugettaboutit) abortion instead. Super Liger was

January 1997. At the Dome show afterparty, the only person who would talk to the disgraced Super Liger was my friend Black Cat. Everyone else shied away like I had scabies.

hung, drawn, and quartered, never to be seen again. Luckily, I was already contracted to return the following month as Chris Jericho.

When I returned to the States I heard Mark Madden on the WCW Hotline say, "Chris Jericho stinks in his first appearance as Super Liger." If word of my failure had reached America before I did, Super Liger really must've stunk worse than my nuts do. As a matter of fact, I didn't even wrestle in the Dome. I was attacked and stuffed into a closet and my assailant actually wrestled as Super Liger. Years passed before Kevin Federline would enter a wrestling ring again.

So I went back to New Japan the next month as plain old no-frills Chris Jericho. If my plane ticket and visa hadn't already been processed, I probably wouldn't have been brought back under any name. In my first match back I wrestled Takashi Iizuka, who had the reputation of making his opponents look good. I used to have the same reputation, but now New Japan felt I needed all the help I could get.

My confidence was shot once again after the Dome disaster (coming soon to a theater near you) but I still had a decent match with Iizuka. The next night I was in a tag match against the masked Samurai and Jushin Liger himself. While a lot of guys in wrestling can hide their true feelings and be nice to your face even if they don't like you, Liger isn't one of them.

He knew I could wrestle from my matches with WAR and that's why he'd come up with the Super Liger idea in the first place. But my performance at the Dome was miserable and he was furious with me. I'd almost tarnished his legacy and I'm sure he took some flak for suggesting the Super Liger character in the first place.

We discussed our match while an 800-pound Super Liger sat in the corner. I was told in no uncertain terms that Liger was beating me with his finish in the middle of the ring, clean as a sheet. I'm sure that the consensus was to get whatever they could out of me by having me lose to everybody on the roster.

Now I had something to prove and we had an exciting hard-hitting match that the crowd really enjoyed. Liger beat me but it didn't make any difference because I'd brought Sexy back.

Afterward Liger shook my hand and was clearly pleased. Even more importantly, I ran into the head booker, Riki Choshu, in the backstage hall.

"You Chris Jericho? You same guy as Super Liger?"

"Yes sir," I said nervously.

"Hmmm," he pondered while nodding his head. "Chris Jericho very good. Super Liger very bad."

"I think maybe Super Liger dead," I replied.

"I think maybe good idea," Choshu said and shook my hand.

And that's how I regained my Japanese mojo, baby.

Now that I was back on track, I threw myself into the Japanese style like never before. I'd always been enamored with the whole feel of the Japanese wrestling companies and New Japan was the biggest of them all. We worked in bigger arenas in front of bigger crowds. That also meant that there were a higher class of female fans who had no problem donating to the cause by using their parents' money to buy me expensive gifts and meals.

Chris Bigalow, Oriental Gigolo.

Being in the big leagues meant that the attitudes and the work rate were more serious as well. Every day I trained with the entire New Japan roster in the arena before the show. We would run laps and work out with the weights that were set up in every venue. I did a Japanese style workout where you took a deck of cards and threw them to the floor one at a time. Then you would do the number of squats (black suits) or push-ups (red suits) listed on each card, with the ace high, in quick succession. Sound easy? Try it, junior.

We did a lot of stretching in the ring, which confirmed my suspicion that Stu's training regimen we'd followed in Calgary was indeed derived from Japanese techniques. We did one style of back bridges that involved being stretched around a spare tire like a Gumby for minutes at a time and another style where we only used our necks for support. It was thirsty work and everybody did the stretching as a team. The camaraderie was cemented by the tradition of everyone wearing uniform track suits with their last names written on the back like hockey jerseys.

It was traditions like these along with the air of dignity surrounding the sport that made Japan my favorite country to work in. Benoit felt the same way and we were stoked when we found out that we'd been booked on the next tour together.

We were near the end of the fifteen-hour flight from Atlanta to Narita so I started filling out my customs form. I grabbed my passport to check the work visa number and almost threw up when I realized I'd brought the wrong one. Having both an American and a Canadian passport was one of the benefits to being a dual citizen; it was also one of the detriments especially when you are as scatterbrained as your fearless scribe. My visa stamp had gone into my American passport and I had brought my Canadian one instead. I was freaked out that the customs officials would simply send me back to the States. When we landed, I was placed into a holding room with the other dregs of society who had tried to sneak into Japan without the proper documentation and had been detained.

After spending an hour with Borat's extended family, a customs official rescued me. Since New Japan had such a high profile in the country, the company was able to smooth things out for me. But before I was allowed to go, I had to sign a form that literally said:

I, Chris Irvine, promise to never enter Japan again without the proper visa forms.

I'm surprised I didn't have to write it 100 times on the blackboard too.

Then they searched my bags for drugs and porno, fast-forwarding through my VHS copy of *Planes, Trains, & Automobiles* looking for boobies and confiscating my *Road House* video when they found some.

Kelly Lynch! Kelly Lynch! YEAHHH Kelly Lynch!

Benoit was one of my best friends, but you wouldn't have known it on the first night of the tour. When we were booked in a tag team match against each other, he attacked me before the bell and pounded me like a meat tenderizer.

Similar to when he'd slapped me at the J Cup, the attack was like having a bucket of ice water poured over my head. We took out our WCW frustrations by beating the living shit out of each other. During the melee I went for a spin kick and instead of connecting full force, I brushed the side of his face instead. He still took a bump and nobody knew the difference—nobody except him.

After the match I went looking for him but he'd pulled his usual Houdini act and I couldn't find him anywhere. I finally found him in the corner of a boiler room and asked what was wrong.

"I bumped off that spin kick. You didn't connect and I never should've bumped."

"Nobody noticed. The match was killer."

"No, it was a rookie mistake and I never should've done it."

He was a perfectionist and decided that he needed to purge himself by doing 500 hack squats right then and there. I'd thrown the errant kick, so I thought it was only fair to join in on his Opus Dei routine and cleanse myself too.

I hadn't done a single hack squat since wrestling school, never mind 500. After doing 300 my legs felt like they were going to detach themselves and beat me over the head for being so stupid, so I stopped. I don't think Chris noticed and he continued squatting with machine-like precision until he reached 500.

My legs were not pleased with their boss and they completely mutinied on me when I woke up the next morning. When I tried to get out of bed I collapsed on the floor while my legs stood beside me snickering. I crawled to the shower and sprayed hot water on my screaming limbs, hoping to reach a truce. They laughed in my face and knotted themselves tighter than Mick Foley. To make matters worse, when I showed up at the arena I found out that I was supposed to wrestle Liger in a championship match for the NJPW junior heavyweight title.

It was my first shot at the title and I was walking like the Tim Conway old man (dated reference). So I secluded myself in the corner and stretched my legs for an hour. I was able to pull off a decent match but I paid dearly the next day when I spent the whole afternoon in bed negotiating with the terrorists that had taken my pins hostage.

My legs went back to work the next night when I was put into a match with the legendary Great Muta. He was one the biggest stars in Japanese wrestling and a seasoned vet who knew all the shortcuts necessary to having a long career in the business.

Muta had Red Light Fever, which meant whenever the red light of the camera was on, he was an animal (just like me in Germany). He did all of his crowd-pleasing moves and had great matches every time. But whenever we worked in the smaller towns where there were no TV cameras, he worked at half speed and did just enough to get by. He probably extended his career ten years by pacing himself that way. When I asked him about it, Muta pointed to his head and said, "Wrestling is all up here. It isn't about moves and high spots, it's all about psychology and thinking."

He was right.

As the tour marched on, I started going stir-crazy. Being on the New Japan tour for three weeks, living and working in a foreign country, could mess with your head. The best way to alleviate the stress was to have a few cocktails. There were always fans who wanted to hang out with wrestlers and be a part of the revelry no matter the cost. So I developed the hazing process of drawing Kiss makeup on their faces with a permanent marker. If the diehard fan wanted to hang out, he would have to boast a star over one eye or cat whiskers under their nose. Then they would be allowed to stay and rock.

When four fans showed up and wanted to experience the initiation, I drew full Paul Stanley, Ace Frehley, Gene Simmons, and Peter Criss makeup with a silver permanent marker on their faces and taught them to do a move that mimicked each member. I had the Paul guy pucker his lips, the Gene guy stick out his tongue, the Ace guy acting spaced-out drunk, and the Peter guy scratching the air with an imaginary claw. Whenever I'd point to them they'd do the move on cue as if I was James Brown and they were the band. I still have fans come up to me with silver markers in their hands whenever I'm in Japan.

One of the top drawing tours of New Japan's year was the Top of the Super Junior Tournament, a round-robin that took place over a three-week period. It was an honor to be booked on the tour along with Doc Dean and Robbie Brookside, who I hadn't seen since Hamburg.

The party started the exact moment we saw each other again. We went out to Roppongi to celebrate and quickly met five dancers from England, who were promptly rechristened the Rice Girls.

Darby Rice had a little gut. Pizza Rice had mild acne. Cougar Rice was older but still hot. Punky Rice had multicolored hair and a nose ring and Shnozz Rice had . . . I'm sure you can guess. But besides Punky and Cougar (who Robbie and Doc claimed quickly), the others weren't my type and I didn't want them hanging around and ruining the vibe for any other interested parties.

But the Liverpool Lads insisted that the Rice Girls

come back to the Keio Plaza and continue the party. I went to my room alone as soon as we arrived, but a few minutes later I got a call from Doc. "Shnozz was being a real cock block, but she likes you so I sent her up to your room. Please keep her away for a while or else she's going to ruin everything."

It pissed me off, but I had to follow the code and take one for the team. A few minutes later there was a knock on my door and I opened it slowly as if I was in the midst of a dead sleep. Shnozz Rice was standing there, so I hung my coat on her nose and said, "Hey, I was just sleeping."

I lay down and pretended to go back to sleep. I felt her slide in bed next to me but I didn't move. I lay there wide awake for the next four hours hoping that she would get the hint and leave, but she didn't. Maybe I should have just nailed her and gotten some sleep instead.

A few weeks later the Jeri-Charm struck again and after spending some time doing the Haka with a model from New Zealand, I woke up late for the bus. I was scared of being tardy (I don't feel tardy), so I made the executive decision to be nice and let the delicious Kiwi stay in my room. I didn't really trust her and I padlocked my suitcase to the hanger pole in my closet so she couldn't steal it. When I came back twelve hours later she was gone, along with all of the alcohol in the minibar ($300), my extra room key ($50), and a pair of jeans ($100). My suitcase was still there, but its weight had pulled the hanger pole down and trashed my closet ($300).

That left me with a $750 tab.

Who says that the best things in life are free . . . and what was she planning to do with my jeans?

The Top of the Super Juniors tour was a blast and

Robbie, Doc, Chavo Guerrero Jr. (Eddy's nephew), nWo Sting (Jeff Farmer), and I had a nightly post-match ritual of playing a card game called Beale Street (which was renamed Destroyer) and drinking all the beer out of the hotel lobby vending machine, while singing the hits of the 1980s. Chavo had the superpower of being able to name any one-hit wonder's *other* hit. If I said "I Ran" by Flock of Seagulls, he would instantly fire back with "Space Age Love Song." He would've made the Flock and their swank hairstyles proud.

The tournament was carefully booked and I won four matches in a row, including a big win over eventual tournament winner, the masked el Samurai. Samurai wore a mask because he was an ugly mother. He also had the worst smoker's breath and would damn near kill you when he applied a chin lock and breathed in your face. Tear gas would've been more merciful.

But Samurai was a good worker and I'd been given the win over him because New Japan was setting me up to be a challenger for the junior title. Black Cat told me that NJPW wanted to bring me back for the next tour as long as Eric gave his permission. I didn't think that would be an issue and I was happier in Japan than in WCW anyway. The New Japan office liked me and I was about to become a challenger for the most prestigious junior title in the world. I was on a roll and nobody was going to stop me.

Nobody except Eric Bischoff that is.

Even though I practically begged him to let me return he didn't want to hear it and denied New Japan's request.

"Absence makes the heart grow fonder. They'll just want you more the next time. Besides Terry Taylor has some big plans for you."

I got up off my knees and wiped the tears from my face. Big plans? Me? Was it the feud with Roddy Piper that Bischoff had promised me months earlier? Or maybe an angle with Booker T. for the TV title?

"You're going to be the new cruiserweight champion."

Instead of happy happy joy joy, my heart sank.

Cruiserweight was a dirty word in WCW, a derogatory term. The belt meant about as much as a belt from JC Penney. If I'd been given a choice, I just would've gone back to Japan but, alas, there was no choice.

THIS IS SHOW
BUSINESS, BABY

The plan was for me to win the championship from
nWo member Syxx (1-2-3 Kid). Syxx losing his title
should've been a big deal, because it was the first time a
chink had been taken out of the nWo's armor. But instead
of happening on *Nitro* with millions of people watching, the title change was going to happen at a house show
(nontelevised) in Los Angeles in front of 7,000 people.
What made the idea worse was that I was going to win
immediately after Syxx wrestled a twenty-minute match
against Rey Mysterio Jr.

He was going to beat Rey and then I would run down
and goad him into giving me a shot. Too fatigued from
the previous bout, Syxx would be at a disadvantage and
I'd become the new champ. It was a great way for a heel to
win a title, but a horrible way for a babyface to win and the
fans responded by booing me right out of the building.

Shortly afterward, I pleaded with Kevin Sullivan to put

me in a few matches with big names to give me some credibility. He responded by booking me with Scott Hall in a five-minute squash loss on *Nitro*.

But Hall decided to rebel and let me win instead.

He kicked my ass for most of the match until I beat him with a small package, a basic move that I had to teach him in the dressing room beforehand. He had ten years of experience on me, but I had to teach him a freakin' small package. I might as well have tied his boots for him too.

After I got the pin the fans exploded in elation, but nanoseconds later he beat the snot out of me and left me lying in a pool of my own lost credibility.

After Eric signed almost every available performer in North America, he started bringing guys over from Japan. I was booked to face Gedo, my fellow Fuyuki-Gun-ner, at Halloween Havoc '97 in Las Vegas. I flew my dad in (Curt Hennig kept calling him Mr. Jericho and Flair thought he was NHL Hall of Famer Ted Lindsay) to hang out for a few days.

We were having a drink at the MGM Grand the night before the show and Terry Taylor approached me to say that they wanted Gedo to go over. It made no sense, as I was under contract as a regular employee and Gedo was only going to be in WCW for a week.

"Well at least you'll be on the show. The boss can take a look at you and see what you can do."

See what I can do? I'd been in the company for a whole year!

If Eric didn't know what I could do by now, losing to a foreign exchange student certainly wasn't going to help. When Eric showed up at the bar, I couldn't contain myself any longer. I'd never complained about doing a job before, but when I told him the plan he was just as surprised as me.

"Why are you supposed to lose, who are we promoting here? I'm going to change that immediately."

Maybe I shouldn't have said anything about the finish, because the next day Gedo almost killed me.

In the middle of a decent match in front of an apathetic crowd who had no idea who either of us were, I prepared to give Gedo my standing Frankensteiner off the top rope. It was the move I'd been using ever since Drew McDonald had suggested it in Hamburg years earlier.

For some reason when I jumped up to wrap my legs around his neck (no filthy remarks please), he gave me a double arm push to the chest. I didn't get the leverage I needed as a result and when I swung my head backward, I didn't clear the mat. I landed straight on top of my head with my legs flipping directly over my neck. A second later Gedo, who had still taken the proper bump, landed right on my head with his full weight.

The whole crowd in the MGM Garden Arena went silent and I lay there for a few seconds too scared to move, fearing I'd suffered the same fate as my mother. I was so terrified of what had just happened, I jumped straight up to my feet trying to prove to everyone (including myself) that I was okay.

It's interesting that when you're in a match and you really get hurt, it's hard to sell it. There is such fear of not knowing how badly you're hurt that it's hard to pretend you are and you just want to hop up on your feet as if nothing is wrong. It's the same principle as when you trip and bust your ass in front of a bunch of people.

The Lord was with me that night and I was fine—even

October 1997. Backstage with my dad at the MGM Grand Garden Arena the night that Gedo almost killed me.

though everyone who saw the botched move knew that tragedy had been narrowly avoided. I've never watched that match and I never will.

The office's original decision to put Gedo over in our match erased the last shred of optimism I still had that I might have a future in WCW. I started thinking about working someplace else because I believed I deserved better than what the company was giving me.

*   *   *

WCW was a great place for veteran stars to make easy money and be lazy doing it. However, it was an awful place for a young guy to try and make a name for himself. I knew that the WWF mission statement was to create new stars and that's where I needed to be more than ever.

I had an ace in my pocket to help me in my escape from the proverbial Alcatraz.

Even though I'd been working in WCW for over a year I had never signed my contract. I wasn't holding out for more money or having a legal disagreement, I simply had never put the pen to the paper and returned the contract to WCW's lawyers. Nobody seemed to realize it and I decided to see how long I could go without signing. It was astonishing that no one in the office had ever followed up with me about it, but this was the same company that once sent me a FedEx with nothing inside, so it wasn't too hard to believe.

As a free agent, I made a call to my friend Don Callis. I'd come up through the business with Don in Winnipeg and we'd worked together many times on the Tony Condello tours. He was working in the WWF as the Jackal and had the ear of head booker, Vince Russo. I asked Don to ask Russo if he would ever be interested in hiring me.

"Russo said whenever you want to come to the WWF, just say the word," Don reported a few days later. Those were the words I'd waited to hear since I pulled out of my mom's driveway eight years earlier at nineteen years old. I could show up in the WWF the next week and toss the WCW cruiserweight belt into the garbage if I wanted to. I was legally clear to do so and there was nothing stopping me.

Except myself.

As much as WCW had ignored me, I still couldn't justify walking away and screwing them over. I had never given up on anything in my life and if I quit WCW, I'd be admitting to everyone that I'd failed.

Plus Eric had given me a chance when the WWF never did and had even given me a raise (in good faith) a few months earlier. As much of an asshole as some of the bookers and wrestlers had been, Eric had always been fair with me and I didn't take that lightly. I signed with him for three years and if I backed out on that deal I would've felt like a real shithouse.

My desire to go to the WWF only got stronger when I went backstage at the Canadian Stampede PPV in Calgary. I wanted to see how the other half lived and I liked it. Hairstylists and makeup ladies touched up the performers while seamstresses worked on costumes. The wrestlers congregated together going over their matches with their agents, old-time wrestlers assigned to assist the young guys with their finishes. It was a far cry from Sullivan delivering a finish by holding his thumb up or down, leaving you to sink or swim unassisted.

I walked around the building until I ran into Vince McMahon himself. He stood broad-shouldered and imposing like Goliath in an immaculate suit, not a hair out of place. His do was so perfect I wondered if it was a toupee. He was the most intimidating individual I'd ever met. This was the man who had engineered the entire wrestling boom and I was standing before him.

"How do you like my town?" I asked, continuing the tradition of saying stupid things upon first meetings.

He looked at me sternly and said, "I like it just fine,"

and turned away. The man I'd dreamed of working for my whole life had just jobbed me out.

But I'd had enough of a taste to know without a doubt that the WWF was where I wanted to be. I placed one more call to Russo and he reiterated to call him as soon as I was legally able.

Only two more years to go.

In true Jericho fashion, I decided I was going to give it my all for those two years, so I devised a plan to get noticed and to get better. The first step was to do an interview with 1wrestling.com, challenging WCW to give me a chance and guaranteeing success if they did. I'd noticed that whenever Hall and Nash complained about something (which was often) they usually got their way and I followed their lead. The squeaky wheel most definitely gets the oil in this biz.

Second, I picked the brains of the handful of vets who seemed to give a shit about the younger guys: Arn Anderson, Ric Flair, Jimmy Hart, and Terry Taylor. Arn helped me with my matches and my selling. Flair came through with little details like how to kick out of a pin attempt with authority so that every fan in the building could see it. Jimmy complimented me on my vast array of ring costumes and pointed out that the majority of the crew wore the same gear in dark colors.

"This is show business, baby. You have to have some color and be flamboyant to stand out, darling." Jimmy was an old hipster and could get away with calling me darling.

He also had another interesting point.

"You can always tell who is over with the fans by the signs in the crowd. We can influence them to cheer and boo for who we want, but we can't walk into their houses and draw signs for them." He was right and whenever I tried out a new catchphrase if it appeared on a sign over the next few shows (like Ayatollah of Rock N Rolla), I knew I had a winner. If not, it meant the phrase wasn't going to stick (like Wocka Wocka Wocka).

Terry read my interview on the Web site and told me that I'd done the right thing. "Eric knows about it and you should go ask him for your release. I think you'll be surprised with his answer."

I didn't need a release since I wasn't under contract but I still met with Eric the next week and he cut to the chase.

"I read your little interview and I think you're right in a lot of ways. You're spinning your wheels and you're doing nothing. The problem is I can't do anything more with you right now because you don't have the familiarity with the fans that the top guys with years of TV exposure have."

You mean being on Winnipeg television didn't count?

It was a bullshit theory. The Rock didn't start off as WWF champion, but he still had feuds and angles from the moment he walked through the door, after never being on national television before.

"I think you have talent and I don't want to lose you, so just be patient."

Patience wasn't one of my strong suits but I had gotten my point across and I didn't have the guts to walk out of WCW anyway.

Next I started hanging around before every *Nitro* in the Box. The Box was a portable studio where all of the promos for the syndicated shows were filmed. Every week the company would make a list of wrestlers to come into the Box and do promos for the matches that would take place in the various towns the next week.

"Listen up, Menomonee Falls, WCW is coming to town Monday, August 30, and I'm going to kick Clint Bobski's ass," or what-have-you.

I hadn't done a promo in WCW yet, but that was where the money definitely was. You had to be able to sell yourself. You had to have the ability to connect with the crowd. Scott Hall was great at it and that's what made him a superstar . . . even though he didn't know how to do a small package. I'd learned two major lessons regarding promos from Bob Brown and Jim Cornette, but I was going to have to rock the mike at a higher level if I wanted to take my career to a higher ground.

So one afternoon, after a useless debate with Disco Inferno about whether or not Martin Short was funny (he is), I asked around if anyone would mind me hanging out in the Box. I sat in the corner and watched some of the greatest talkers in the history of wrestling sell themselves.

Flair, Anderson, Piper, Raven, Savage, Sting, Glacier—they all issued threats, boasted about themselves, insulted the fans, told jokes, and did whatever was necessary to entice the fans to buy a ticket. The promos were conducted by Gene Okerlund, the master of his craft. I learned just as much from watching him because he always knew how to get the point across, no matter what the skill level of his interviewee.

Like an Oscar-winning actor, the best talkers became their characters completely and lost all inhibitions. That's when it started clicking for me and it was the third major lesson I learned about delivering promos.

One afternoon Lex Luger refused to do promos because he had to go tanning. Since I was hanging around, I was asked if I wanted to give it a try. I jumped at the chance and my first official WCW promo was for Peoria, Illinois.

Would Jericho play in Peoria?

Not very well unfortunately—the promo wasn't very good. I was as wooden as a stake and didn't have much to say, but it was a start. From then on, whenever someone didn't show up or flat-out refused to do interviews, I filled in.

Pretty soon I was able to cut a decent forty-five-second promo. Shortly after that I was added to the weekly promo list and believe me I never turned down a chance to do one because I had to go tanning or eat a PB&J. I treated the Box as promo boot camp and it's where I finally developed into a good talker.

Doing interviews added an extra feeling of anticipation about going to work. I literally sat by the phone every week hoping to get the call to go to *Nitro*. When it finally came, I'd hang up the phone and do the *Nitro* Dance. If you want to see the *Nitro* Dance just ask me and I'll be happy to show it to you.

CHAPTER 48

CONSPIRACY VICTIM

I took Eric's advice about waiting things out but my patience was wearing thin, until I ran into Terry at a *Nitro* taping in Macon, Georgia.

"What's up?" I asked.

"Just your career. We're going to turn you heel."

It was music to my ears because I'd been lobbying to turn heel for months. I'd even asked to become a member of Raven's flock of misfits, but Eric had shot down the idea.

But he had finally decided that it was time for me to become eeeeeeevil and he was right. I'd achieved my greatest success as a heel and I knew I wouldn't be so handcuffed if I could act like the asshole that I was. It's much easier to make people hate you than it is to make them like you.

The plan was for me to go on a losing streak (I was already on one anyway), and after each loss I would snap and have a temper tantrum that would make a five-year-old proud. Terry was specific in his direction.

"Don't play it for laughs. Play it seriously like you just lost control."

So I pitched fits, smashed chairs against the ring post, and ripped the suit jacket right off of ring announcer David Penzer's back. Then I calmed myself down and, filled with remorse, apologized to him and the fans.

I brought Penzer a new jacket (only to tear it to pieces again later) and begged the crowd for their forgiveness. They gave it to me at first until they caught on to what I was doing and started booing me. Those boos were like hearing trumpets from heaven because they meant that I was actually getting over. The fans were forming an opinion about me and for the first time were interested in what I was doing.

Terry suggested that I start using a submission move as my finish instead of the Lionsault. He felt a submission would give me credibility and add a serious side to what was essentially an amusing character.

Terry's idea was to use a Fujiwara arm bar. In Japan I'd used a version of the Boston Crab where I would lean all my weight onto my opponent's neck, and I thought it would work better. I even had the perfect name, the Liontamer. Terry dug it and Lion Heart Chris Jericho's WCW career officially kicked into overdrive.

I decided that as a heel I wanted to be the polar opposite of the nWo. I had no interest in being the cool heel that defied authority and was intimidated by nothing and nobody. I wanted to be a coward and a blowhard. The type of person you wanted to punch in the face but didn't quite dare, so you hoped that he'd step in dogshit and track it all over his new carpet instead.

I modified my look by growing long sideburns and

tying a Gene Simmons/poodle topknot in my hair. I had
a white leather vest airbrushed with a big picture of myself on the back. I wore elbow-length gloves and walked
to the ring with an arrogant, almost effeminate glide. I
barged into the TV truck and changed my music from
the wimpy Basketball Highlights #12 to the slightly less
wimpy Basketball Highlights #17. It went from a lame
Journey rip-off to a lame Pearl Jam rip-off, but at least it
was a step up.

I gave myself nicknames such as the Paragon of Virtue, Your Role Model, The Ayatollah of Rock N Rolla
(shamelessly ripped off from *The Road Warrior*), and the
Epicenter of Excitement.

I would apologize about a dastardly deed and claim
that I would Never *Eeeeeeeever* Do It Agayn, pronouncing
"again" in a Canadian accent, pissing people off even more.
I spewed out whatever came into my head, the more prepos-
terous the better.

Signs started to appear in crowds proclaiming "Jericho
Is a Crybaby" or "Jericho Sucks," proving Jimmy Hart's
theory correct.

I'd mispronounce the names of the other performers
as if I held them in such low regard I wasn't quite sure
what their names were: Don Malenko, Roy Mysterio Jr.,
Jojo Dillon, Chris Benoyt, Tony Skiavone, Tooker B. The
more juvenile the better.

Before every match I'd cut an inane promo, starting
with "Onta Gleeban Glouten Globen" or "I Want You to
Want Me!" Then I'd leap into the air with an Eddie Van
Halen split-legged jump and my tongue sticking out.

I got serious during another promo and took off my
shades, only to reveal a second pair underneath. I would

rarely admit to losing and when I did I'd claim that my opponent was a one-hit wonder like Dexys Midnight Runners.

I was totally obnoxious and did whatever I could to make the fans think I was a jerk and an idiot.

People began to seriously hate me but even though I was becoming one of the most entertaining parts of the show, I was still relegated to my caste. At least I was having fun, which was the whole point of wrestling in the first place.

When Eric decided that he didn't want the Mexican luchadores to wear masks anymore, even though they were a part of their culture and tradition, it was decided that I'd beat Juventud Guerrera for his mask.

I insulted Juvie incessantly for weeks talking about how ugly he was without his mask, how he resembled Quasimodo, how the people would beg me to allow him to keep his mask on, etc. Juvie wasn't very strong with his English—his butchering of the English language was legendary. Combined with a voice that sounded like Fez, it was impossible for him to verbally defend himself.

After claiming for weeks that I was going to take his mask, I did by making him submit to the Liontamer in the center of the ring. No cheating, no controversy, no nothing. It was a shit deal for Juvie but when I appealed to the office to allow me to cheat to beat him, my suggestion was met with apathy. So I sat back and enjoyed being on the other side of the fence for once.

I wanted to remain the hated heel, but the bookers were making it more difficult than algebra. I'd already beaten Chavo Jr. a dozen times when we were booked together again in Fargo and given the usual finish: I would win with the Liontamer in the center of the ring.

It was an uninspired finish that we'd already done many times so I wanted to spice it up a bit. Chavo was doing a crazy gimmick where he'd made friends with a hobby horse named Pepe. I was supposed to beat Chavo clean and snap Pepe in half afterward. Keep in mind I was the bad guy.

Before the match, Chavo and I drove to a Toys R Us and bought a giant pogo stick and stuck its head on the end of an aluminum bat. We went back to the arena and stashed the bat underneath the ring.

I beat Chavo, and when I did, I snapped Pepe in two. While the crowd booed the hell out of me, Chavito went under the ring and pulled out José, Pepe's big brother. When I turned around, Chavito nailed me in the stomach and José exacted his revenge. The crowd loved it and the whole thing aired on live TV.

We didn't get anybody's permission to do the José angle, but nobody in the office said jack shit to us about it afterward. If I would have tried the same thing in Vince McMahon's company he would have fired me on the spot.

It was becoming a joke to see if anyone in the office was paying attention to my matches, so I started rubbing the front of my hair as hard as I could until it stood straight up like a member of Poison in 1986. I walked to the ring with a cheese-eating grin plastered across my face, looking like I was caught in a wind tunnel. I demanded only brown M&M's in catering. Strangely, some people in the crowd were starting to love it. Despite my efforts, I was becoming the dreaded cool heel.

But I was still being booed by 90 percent of the crowd when I orchestrated my WCW masterpiece: an angle with Dean Malenko. Dean wanted to take some much needed time off, so after defeating him on a PPV in Birmingham, Alabama, he did an interview saying he was going home.

In the course of three months, I built a hot feud with a guy who wasn't even on the show.

I made fun of him for taking his ball and going home. I buried his father, Boris, who had been a wrestler and was now actually buried as well. I called him Stinko Malenko and claimed he was now working the grill at Harry's Burgers in Tampa, all the while mocking his serious demeanor and wrestling style.

Dean was known as the Man of 1,000 Holds so I stole the Floyd Creachman angle I'd seen as a teenager and began calling myself the Man of 1,004 Holds. I knew four more.

On a *Nitro* in Chicago I pulled out a stack of connected computer paper and began reading off each one of my holds.

"Number 1—Arm Bar. Number 2—Body Slam. Number 3—Arm Drag. Number 4—Mexican Arm Bar." We went to commercial break while I was still listing them off. When I knew we were off the air, I started insulting the crowd and whipping them into a frenzy. When we came back from the break, I was now at Number 366— Russian Arm Bar, with the crowd booing the shit out of me.

I was finally interrupted by Prince Iaukea (currently residing in the "Where Are They Now?" file) and my pages were flung up into the air. I chased them around like a toddler chasing bubbles, screaming, "My holds, my holds!"

The comedy never ends . . .

I kept the feud alive by getting a negative of Dean's promo picture and blowing it up at Kinko's. Then I carried around a giant framed picture of him as a tribute. The ring crew wouldn't let me leave the portrait-sized picture on the truck, so I had to transport it (and the easel I rested it on) to and from work every week myself.

My incessant needling was paying off. The people were begging Dean to come back to shut me up. But I couldn't be stopped. I interviewed the portrait and when it didn't reply to any of my questions I commented, "This picture has more charisma than the actual Dean Malenko."

The whole angle culminated with a battle royal at a PPV in Worcester, Massachusetts, where I was immediately going to wrestle the winner for my cruiserweight title. I grabbed a mike and insulted the contestants as they made their way to the ring like I was hosting the Ugly Miss America Pageant.

"Here comes Silver King . . . with another 20,000 frequent flyer points, he'll be upgraded to Gold King. This is Billy Kidman . . . in a few more years he'll be twenty-one and will change his name to Billy Manman. Here is Juan Epstein's little brother el Dandy . . . and he's pissed!"

I was the Henny Youngman (dated reference #2) of wrestling.

Since there were only a few cruiserweights with any credibility, the majority of the combatants were jobbers that had little name value such as Lizmark, Lenny Lane, Ciclope, and el Grillo. El Grillo meant cricket in Spanish and was a character created by Dean and me as an inside joke on Eddy. He was infamous in the locker room for slapping his burrito on his inner thigh, making a sound resembling a cricket. Or so he claimed.

At the end of the battle royal, Juvie and Ciclope were the final two in the ring. Ciclope was low on the totem pole and it was surprising he'd lasted that long. Everyone assumed Juvie was going to be the victor.

But Juvie jumped out of the ring on his own, which left Ciclope as the winner. I ran into the ring to attack him from behind, but before I could, Ciclope pulled off his mask and revealed Dean Malenko.

The crowd went completely insane. It was one of the top three loudest reactions I've ever experienced during the course of my wrestling career and I've been in the ring with Steve Austin and The Rock at their peaks. When Dean took that mask off, it was one the most electric moments of my life. It was the biggest reaction on the PPV, nWo or no nWo.

Dean turned around and stared at me. Everyone in the crowd remembered my digs at his name, his gimmick, and his family. With each passing second, the anticipation built until he finally hit me and the shit was on.

He totally dominated me and three minutes later he was the new champ. I don't think I'm out of line saying it was the apex of both our careers in WCW.

A few weeks later *Nitro* was in Washington, D.C., and Terry wanted me at the arena early to film a vignette. I had no idea what they had in mind for me to do, but in classic WCW fashion neither did they. Nobody on the crew was quite sure either, so I took charge and mapped out a plan.

In what ended up being my WCW comedic masterpiece, we spent the day filming me trying to get reprisal for the horrible conspiracy committed against me by the evil Dean Malenko.

I scoured the Library of Congress looking for the official WCW rulebook. Then I stood on the streets of D.C. in a suit and tie holding a sign that said CONSPIRACY VICTIM with an arrow pointing down at my head. I tried to get into the White House but was sternly turned down for real by Secret Service agents who were *not* interested in being on TV. It culminated with my pleading my case to an actual conspiracy theorist who lived on the White House lawn.

"Dean Malenko was illegally registered in the battle royal and entered under false pretenses. Under those conditions, there is no way his victory should stand up in court." She listened intently and advised me that I had a chance due to the legal precedent set in the 1967 *Vandalay v. Mandelbaum* case or something along those lines.

The video was edited down to three minutes and made me look like the most pathetic crybaby on the planet. It also made me look like an entertaining mofo. Go to You-Tube and check it out . . . you won't regret it.

I continued to complain at every opportunity about the atrocities committed against me for the next few months. I read a letter on *Nitro* from Ted Turner himself that started off sympathetic to my cause but ended up with him admonishing me for my complaining and rescinding his invitation to go fishing with him in Canada.

While we said that the letter was from Ted, in actuality I wrote it. Eric originally insisted on writing it for me, but after giving me the runaround for four hours, I wrote the letter thirty minutes before showtime and read it unapproved.

Terry came up with the idea of bringing my dad onto a *Nitro* in Buffalo to further put me in my place. The Baby-Faced Assassin walked out in the middle of one of my ti-rades and browbeat me on live TV in front of millions of fans. He had never done a live promo before, but wrote it himself backstage and delivered it better than 80 percent of the wrestlers. He pointed to the retired hockey jerseys hanging in the rafters of the HSBC Arena and said I was an embarrassment to my family and an embarrassment to the legacies of Tim Horton and Gilbert Perreault. The crowd loved seeing the pompous jerk get yelled at by his daddy.

Terry wanted my dad to turn heel and help me to win my matches by hitting opponents with his hockey stick. Neither one of us was very excited about the idea espe-cially when my dad got stiffed on his payoff from the first show.

Even though I was making decent cash I still had to pay for all my expenses on the road. Wrestling is the only sport or form of entertainment where the performers are respon-sible for most of their own arrangements. The company provided our plane tickets, but once we flew into the town we were on our own. We were responsible for reserving and paying for our own cars and hotels. There were times when every hotel within a thirty-mile radius was sold out and we had no place to stay at all. I once spent the night with Eddy and Brian Hildebrand (the SMW ref who'd since been hired as a WCW ref) in our rental car in the parking lot of the Greenville–Spartanburg Airport on Eddy's birth-day. I put my alarm clock on the dash and we brushed our teeth with a bottle of water.

Feliz Cumpleanos, Eduardo.

I also wasn't making any money off of merchandise royalties because WCW was horrible at producing it for anybody except for the biggest names. Even though the crowd's reactions were much bigger for me than for someone like Ric Steiner, he had a T-shirt and I didn't. While the nWo was making hundreds of thousands off of merch, I once received a royalty check in the mail for 0 dollars and 0 cents. Stamps cost 37 cents . . . what was the sense in even mailing it?

So I organized a meeting with the merch guy and came up with an idea for my first T-shirt.

I'd already started calling *Nitro*, Monday Night Jericho, so my idea for a shirt was a takeoff of the *Nitro* logo, with Jericho replacing *Nitro*. But I needed something for the back of the shirt and I was stumped. Then I decided that I needed a name for my nonexistent fans, the same way that Hulk Hogan named his fans Hulkamaniacs.

I got a dictionary and a thesaurus and pieced together words that began with the letters CO onto my name. Jeri-Coalition, Jeri-Co-Conspirators. But nothing was really rolling off the tongue until I saw the word alcohol. It took me two seconds to compute Jerichohol into Jerichoholics and biggity bam, my trademark catchphrase was born.

Eric allowed the shirt to be produced and I wrote and directed a commercial that featured the silhouette of a raving Jerichoholic who needed treatment and a T-shirt to prove his loyalty. Suddenly the boom mike fell into frame, knocking the screen over and revealing that the Jerichoholic in question was really me. The commercial was top comedy and helped me sell some shirts too. I know this because my next royalty check was for 0 dollars and 37 cents.

* * *

If the company would've promoted me half as much as they promoted the Nitro Girls, I would've made millions. The Nitro Girls were WCW's version of the Dallas Cowboy cheerleaders. They would come to the ring in skimpy costumes and dance before commercial breaks and during the show. *Nitro* was three hours at that point and I guess they needed something to fill the segments.

The girls were made up of ex-NFL cheerleaders, strippers, and dance majors and they were gorgeous. They were also like lambs being led to the slaughter when they were set loose amongst the crew. They didn't have a clue how charming and lascivious wrestlers could be, but they found out pretty fast. I dated two of the seven myself. That's a 28.57 percent success rate.

Eric heard rumors and asked me, "I heard you dated that Nitro Girl with the nice rack."

That pretty much described all of them, and I didn't know what to say. I was afraid I'd get her (or even worse myself) in trouble.

Awkward silence.

"If you tell me you banged her I'll give you a raise," he offered, still awaiting my answer.

Uncomfortable awkward silence.

I came back with the same line he gave me when I'd asked him who the third member of the nWo was in the CNN Center a year and a half earlier.

"Eric, if I told you, I'd have to kill you."

He flashed his award-winning John Davidson smile and walked away muttering, "If you did, you're my hero."

I wasn't his hero, and I still didn't get a push.

CHAPTER
49

CRUISERWEIGHT PURGATORY

Eddy Guerrero and I were in the same boat in WCW. We both had good heat and could produce a good match with almost anyone in the company but we still couldn't break into the next level. We also traveled together a lot even though we were usually at odds. When it was my turn to rent the car it was always too small. When it was his turn to rent the hotel room it was always run-down. He needed the TV on to sleep, I needed it off. We drank a lot to stay sane and would end up arguing or rolling around on the floor of a Denny's somewhere over a leftover scrap of steak.

But for the most part we got along really well. We both liked Rush and watching movies in our hotel room on days off. *Romy and Michelle's High School Reunion* was our favorite. Got a problem with that? Stop laughing then.

In the political quagmire of WCW, we could trust each other and be ourselves with one another. Once we were driving through the wooded hills of Pennsylvania and when I glanced over to the passenger seat, Eddy was looking back at me with a goofy smile on his face and a plastic water bottle cap stuck in his eye like a monocle. It's one of my favorite memories of him, because that was the real Eddy before the weight of the world dragged him down.

We thought it would be a great idea for us to form a tag team and one week we found out we'd been booked as one. It wasn't supposed to be more than a one-shot deal, but we instantly clicked. We were almost a modern-day Gringos Locos (Eddy and Art's team in Mexico) because what I didn't have, Eddy did and vice versa.

We had extensive debates over our team name but we could never agree. I liked Bro, he liked Manzier.

I thought North and South of the Border was perfect as I was from Canada and he was from Mexico. He liked Eh and Wey, a combination of Canadian and Mexican slang words. But we really should've been called the Greatest Tag Team That Barely Ever Was.

We worked together every week for a month and stole the show every time. We were both kick-ass heels and complete cowards at the same time. After meticulously picking apart our adversaries, as soon as the tables were turned, we'd run into each other's arms and hug to a chorus of boos.

Our chemistry was so far off the charts that Ray Charles could've seen that we were championship material and a moneymaking act. But WCW was run by a team of Helen Kellers and we were broken up, never to be paired together again.

Eddy and I had made the cardinal mistake of getting over, which was a punishable offense for most of the roster in WCW. It seemed that some people didn't like the fact that we were making heads turn, so they simply chopped off our heads instead.

Our clique at that point included Eddy, Dean, Chris, Brian Hildebrand, Chavito, and me. We had some great times, the best of which went down at a biker rally in Sturgis, South Dakota.

Eric was an avid motorcycle rider and every year he booked the Road Wild PPV from the world-famous rally. The atmosphere was rotten because the bikers didn't give a shit about watching wrestling and most of them didn't even get off their bikes during the outdoor show. But it was Eric's yearly vacation and he and his buddies rode their bikes through the Black Hills to get to Sturgis.

The main event of the PPV that year involved the fierce Jay Leno. Eric was on a stunt casting kick and surprisingly Leno was better in his match than Dennis Rodman was in his. Rodman (who made around $3 million for the match) showed up an hour before his tag match and fell asleep on the apron while waiting for a tag. But since he's had sex with Carmen Electra and I haven't, he's the better man.

The night before Road Wild we went to see a Lynyrd Skynyrd concert. Skynyrd were big WCW fans and invited us to watch the show from the photo pit (free beer included) in front of 20,000 loaded bikers.

It was one of the best times in my life, seeing Skynyrd throw down "That Smell" and "Free Bird," with my closest friends jamming out beside me. Brian had just beaten cancer and as a huge fan of 1970s music, he was having a blast. Eddy had stopped drinking and was playing air guitar on a water bottle, while Dean, Chavito, and I picked up the slack and were hammered. Dean peed on the ground of the pit and Chavo's leg got caught in the crossfire. Hilarious for us, wet for Chavo.

I wish I could've bottled that night to carry around in my pocket forever. Being in the wrestling business is like fighting in a war: Some of your unit make it and some of them don't. It brings a tear to my eye to know that I'll never enjoy a night like that with those guys ever again.

There were still other guys in the company that I could've done without; Scott Hall seemed like a nice guy deep down inside, but the combination of power and substance had turned him into a real asshole.

For some reason he set his sights on me. He made me feel like I did when I was in the seventh grade receiving a daily beating from the school bully, Chuck Fontaine. I'd like to meet Chuck in a dark alley now . . . so I could run away screaming.

It was no secret that Hall enjoyed being a dick and he said on more than one occasion, "They pay me to wrestle, not to make friends" and "It doesn't say anywhere in my contract that I have to be nice to anyone. This is the wrestling business not the friendship business." He sure practiced what he preached.

One night after Hall's constant badgering, I got sick of it and finally stood up for myself. "You got something to say, Jericho? Don't sing it, bring it," he taunted. "I'll put an end to your little Terry Taylor push."

That pissed me off huge, because I'd worked my ass off for my little Terry Taylor push and I'd be damned if he was going to mock me about it. But I was intimidated by him and the nWo's influence within the company, so I held my tongue, much to the chagrin of my old pal Scott Norton.

Norton had taught me the fail-safe arm wrestling trick years earlier and we'd become friends while touring Japan. He let me escape with minimal injuries after he drunkenly dared me to rub Yaku Yaku (Japanese Icy Hot) in his eyes . . . and I did. He was blind for fifteen minutes, although I'm sure the multiple shots of straight tequila had something to do with it.

Norton looked me in the eye, man to man, and said, "You better shut his mouth right now. Because if you don't stand up to him I will and you'll look like a pussy."

Norton weighed about 350 pounds and looked like he could Hulk-smash his way through a wall, so hearing his words gave me all the backup I needed. I walked up to Hall and got right into his face.

"Leave me the fuck alone. Next time you mess with me, I'm coming at you. Understand?"

Hall looked at me in disbelief and said, "I don't have a problem with you. Come on, man, everything's cool." In classic bully fashion, as soon I stood up to him he left me alone. He was really friendly to me after that. Where was Norton when Chuck Fontaine was on my case?

The nWo had expanded to ridiculous proportions from its origins as a three-piece. How many of you remember Virgil, Ted DiBiase, and Mike Rotunda as nWo members? How about Horace Hogan (Boulder), Buff Bagwell, and Bryan Adams?

Most of the group was made up of ex-WWF superstars and it was obvious that Eric was enamored with Vince's old employees and wanted them in his top heel group. But his idea backfired when all of the new additions caused the nWo to lose its edge.

That's why I turned down Eric's offer to join. After all of my bitching about not getting a fair shake it was crazy to say NO to the nWo, but bear with me, constant reader.

I was booked to win the WCW Television Title in Rapid City, South Dakota, which was a big deal for me on many levels. Winning the TV title would give me my ticket to ride out of cruiserweight purgatory and into big boy land.

But the decision for me to get the big win over champion Steve Ray was made a scant twenty minutes before *Nitro* went live to air.

Eric told me that the Giant was going to assist me with my victory and I would then join the nWo.

But the dilution of the nWo meant that the majority of the members never had anything to do. When they came to the ring for their weekly endless opening promo, there wasn't enough room for all of them in the ring. They stood around laughing amongst themselves, knowing that they were rarely on camera because there were too many of them to be in one shot.

At that point, I was doing just fine on my own. I got interview time and segments that revolved around me. I was over despite the nWo's dominance and I would only get less over and lost in the shuffle if I joined them. So I thought about it and respectfully told Eric my thoughts on his invitation.

"I think it would be cool, but I've got a good thing going and I don't want to give that up by joining the nWo. I don't want to ride on your coattails and I don't want you guys to ride on mine."

It was a brash statement, but Eric didn't seem to care and he said, "If you don't want to be in the nWo, that's fine. But I still want the Giant to help you win the TV title so let's keep the same finish. We'll figure out why he helped you later."

They never did. Hope that answers your question.

CHAPTER 50

DWARFBERG

My next program started as a joke and ended up sealing my fate in the company.

Bill Goldberg was an ex-NFL player who'd stumbled into WCW. But with unmatched charisma and presence, he quickly became one the biggest stars of the 1990s. WCW booked him perfectly when he entered on a tear and went on a huge winning streak. The Streak became more famous than the Ray Stevens song (dated reference number three) and the fans followed it with bated breath.

However, Goldberg would have to have been wrestling a Mexico City ten-match-a-week schedule to even come close to the number of matches they were claiming he'd won. One week he'd be 42-0 and seven days later he'd be 58-0. Did stepping on bugs count?

Despite that, he was totally believable as a destroyer and his gimmick of tearing his opponents apart and spitting them out in less than three minutes had the fans eating him up with a spoon. When he beat Hulk Hogan in front of 50,000 fans at the Georgia Dome to become the new WCW champion, he became the biggest star in the business.

That's why I was surprised when I arrived at the Fall Brawl '98 PPV show and Terry told me I was going to be wrestling Goldberg. I was the TV champion and I thought it was strange that they would feed me to Goldberg in a three-minute throwaway match.

But Terry explained that I wasn't going to be facing the real Goldberg, but a midget version of him instead. I asked him why and he said, "No reason. I just thought you'd have some fun with it."

So I challenged Goldberg to a title vs. title match in my typical over-the-top Paragon of Virtue (that should've been another T-shirt) fashion and out came a dwarf. He looked like a Goldberg who'd spent the night in a trash compactor, right down to the famous tribal tattoo. I beat Dwarfberg in three minutes to a chorus of boos and that was the end of it.

Except it was only the beginning.

The next day I showed up in Greenville, South Carolina, and saw Goldberg in the backstage area. He came up to me with fire in his eyes and a defiant grin and said, "Well, Jericho, I hope it was worth it."

Confused, I asked him what he meant.

"People have been calling me all day and laughing at me. Well I don't do the comedy bullshit that you do and I just want you to know you're gonna pay the price for it."

I was surprised at his reaction because I thought we were on good terms. We both loved hockey and once went to a Boston Bruins game together. I thought he would've gotten a kick out of Dwarfberg. But as popular and successful as Bill was he was still very green about the business. As a result the backstage vultures were clouding his brain with manipulation, drooling at the thought of being the one to end his winning streak.

"I just work here, Bill. I wish I had the power to book the matches, but I don't."

He grunted and as he walked away he repeated, "I hope it was worth it, Jericho."

It really wasn't, because the segment wasn't very memorable. But someone must've liked it, because the next night at Thunder I was told to go to the ring and challenge Goldberg to a fight even though he wasn't at the show.

I didn't care that he was pissed about the previous night's show and I was happy to have an angle. So I went to the ring and bragged to the crowd about my won-loss record of Jericho 1, Goldberg 0. I challenged him to a match and had the ref count to 10. When he didn't show, I won the match by count-out and now it was Jericho 2, Goldberg 0.

Then I cut a scathing promo about how I'd been the one to finally tarnish his name. He was no longer Goldberg because I was renaming him Greenberg, a name that matched his experience in the business.

"Who's your daddy, Greenberg? Who's your daddy?"

The next week I went to a T-shirt shop and had a shirt made that said, "Jericho—2, Goldberg—0" and wore it to the ring. I knew the feud was getting over because there were signs scattered throughout the arena keeping score and saying "Goldberg Fears Jericho" and "Jericho's Next."

The angle that Terry Taylor booked to give me something to do on a Sunday afternoon had turned into one of the hottest angles in the company and, like my last hot angle, my opponent wasn't directly involved with it. But I was involved 200 percent and had a ton of ideas to further the story.

One of my bits (directly ripped off from *Spinal Tap*) had me getting lost on my way to the ring for a match against Wrath. I was planning to continue my mocking of Goldberg by coming to the ring led by a security team, one of his trademarks. (Supremely Cool Author's Note: If Goldberg was so tough, why did he need a full security team to take him to the ring? Things that make you go hmmmm.)

I debated using the local wrestlers in the building as my security force, but I thought it would be funnier if I came to the ring led by a crew of misfits instead. I had the perfect guy in mind to start off with.

I'd always see one of the company truck drivers hanging around and he had, shall we say, a very unique look. His hairline receded to his neck and he sported a massive gut. He frequently flashed a friendly smile that accentuated his missing front teeth and a pair of fanglike incisors that protruded out of each side of his mouth. He had a face only a mother could love and Mother Jericho wanted him for a bodyguard.

I approached him and asked him if he wanted to be on TV.

"Sure," he said with a punji stick grin. "Whaddya want me ta do?"

I patted him on the chest (cutting my hand on his teeth in the process) and handed him a cut-off wifebeater that caused his gut to hang over the belt of his dress pants. Then I took a marker and wrote on the front:

JERICHO
PERSONAL
SECURITY

The JPS was born.

My new bodyguard needed a name and I'd just seen the 1970s horror movie *Blood Sucking Freaks*. The flick featured a maniacal Oates (as in Hall and . . .) looking dwarf named Ralphus. The rest is Jeric-History.

Ralphus knocked on my dressing room door and we began our walk to the ring. But we weren't quite sure where it was. I opened one door and found a broom closet. Another led me into catering. I shouted "Hello Cleveland!" in tribute. Then I tried a third door and unwittingly walked outside into the parking lot as the door slammed shut behind me.

We'd rehearsed the bit earlier in the day and when the door shut behind me it had locked instantly. This time when the door shut I scrambled to pull it open and the damn thing opened easily. We were live, so I slammed my shoulder against the door and shut it again as if by mistake. The comedy continued when a curious security guard heard the noise and opened the door again to see what was going on.

Meanwhile Wrath was in the ring watching the entire spectacle on the 'Tron, and decided to come get me himself. He charged through the door and I ran from him as fast as I could until I reached my given mark. The mark guaranteed that I was out of the camera's sightline, and I stopped as Wrath ran past me as a joke. But the joke was on me because the mark was wrong and Wrath running past me while we both burst out laughing was caught on live TV.

What had started as a homage to *Spinal Tap* had turned into the real thing.

I ran into Goldberg in the airport the next day and he demanded that I stop doing the angle because he didn't do comedy.

I tried to explain to him that he wasn't doing the comedy, I was. Besides, the fans were digging it and at every show the Jericho–Goldberg signs multiplied while the reactions got stronger. But he still didn't understand that the more I mocked him, the more people wanted to see him destroy me.

Besides, I was having a blast with my comedy. My security force was increasing faster than the nWo: I'd sworn the Jerichoholic Ninja and Viva Las Jericho (I don't know what the hell it means either) into active duty.

The next week Greenberg finally got involved when he hit the ring and pulverized the new members of my valiant security force. But Ralphus and I escaped, making the score Jericho—3, Goldberg—0. To keep up with the tally, I put a piece of tape over the 2 on my sweet custom-made shirt and wrote a 3 in its place. People were really getting sick of my bullshit and the fans were itching to see him tear me apart.

The next week when I showed up for *Nitro* in Phoenix, Eric told me I was going to be wrestling Goldberg that night. I asked Eric what the story of the match was going to be.

"Story? The same story Goldberg always tells. He beats you up and pins you with the Jackhammer in three minutes."

I thought I'd entered the Twilight Zone, because he was talking to me like the previous six weeks of angles hadn't happened.

"What about our angle? The fans are really into it."

"There never was an angle. If there was, it ends tonight."

That was enough for me. Before my match with Dwarfberg, if I'd been booked to be the next victim of Goldberg's streak I would've done it, no questions asked. But the bookers got me into this and I'd made the angle work. I didn't expect to beat Goldberg and I didn't want to. But the Goldberg–Jericho angle was giving both of us an extra dimension and there was no way I was going to allow them to piss away all of my hard work.

"I've done some really strong work with this, Eric, even if it was just a throwaway. I don't want to waste it on a three-minute squash. I really think people will pay money to see him kill me. Let me have the best squash match of all time with him on PPV. He can give me ten Jackhammers if you want. I'm not saying I don't want him to beat me, I'm just saying that we've got something special here."

I don't know if Eric understood my point or if he just didn't want to put up with my bullshit, but he canceled the match.

I'd avoided one monster even though I'd created another one.

Ralphus became my full-time sidekick and was absolutely hilarious in his ineptitude. He understood nothing about wrestling and I don't think he even understood what he was doing on TV. When he escorted me to the ring I'd tell him to get mad and threaten the people who accosted me along the way, but instead he would wag his finger at them like a granny telling a five-year-old not to touch her flowers.

He tried to look menacing but with his half shirt and summer teeth he just looked comical. But the ladies loved him and he was enjoying his newfound fame. I showed up at the arena one day to see Ralphus dirty-dancing for his female fans behind the arena. The girls weighed in at about three bills apiece, but Ralphus didn't care . . . however, I was scarred for life.

I'd become Dr. Chrisenstein and I tried to reel in his ballooning ego by always referring to him by his real name of John Riker. I wanted him to understand that he wasn't really Ralphus. But he was too far gone and, quite frankly, who could blame him? He'd gone from a truck driver hauling lighting rigs to a nationally famous TV star in the space of a month all because of the space between his teeth.

"John, get these girls out of the backstage area," I said to him sternly.

"But they like me."

"I don't care. You can't bring girls backstage."

"But they want to hang out with me—look, they gave me flowers."

"Wow, those are nice. Can I see them?" He handed me the tulips and I beat them over his bald head.

When the Ralphus Rats started sitting in the front row, I was sickened to know that he had more groupies than I did. Even worse, he would spend all his time talking to the girls and not paying any attention to the match. The monster was loose.

His head got bigger than the gap between his teeth and

he started putting baby oil on his arms and stomach before he went to the ring. He began talking about hiring a
lawyer to negotiate his new contract. New contract? The
moron didn't have an old contract! I had to go to bat to get
him paid 500 bucks an appearance as it was.

Then he started showing up at house shows, "in case
he was needed." The first night, he was cheered so huge
that it killed my heel heat and I had to tell him to stop
coming. Sadly, Ralphus was over more than most of the
babyfaces.

Meanwhile Goldberg, who was the biggest babyface in
the company, had a lot of pull and decided our program
would end for good in Uniondale, New York. I found out
from Sullivan that I was losing to Goldberg and there
would be no debate whatsoever. Of course I had zero intention of following his orders.

I tracked down Eric and before I could say a word he
told me, "You're going to lose to Goldberg and that's it."

I didn't give a shit at that point because no matter what
anybody else thought, the angle was a moneymaker and I
was determined to live or die with it. If WCW didn't take
it as far as it could go, I might as well quit anyway. If they
didn't see this feud as a draw, then nothing I would ever
do in the future would be either.

"I'm not losing tonight."

"Go in my office right now," Eric said angrily.

He must've suspected that I was going to question
the match because Goldberg was already in Eric's office
along with a pissed-off Hulk Hogan. Some serious shit
was about to go down.

"This has gone on too long. We've accommodated

you long enough. Tonight you're losing to Bill," Eric explained.

The three of them waited for my response.

"I want to lose to Bill. I just want to do it right. People want to see him kick my ass and I believe they'll pay to see it."

Then I pled my case to Hogan using language I knew he'd understand.

"I thought this business was about making money. You've done it better than anyone, Hulk. This match will make money."

Hogan didn't disagree, but said, "It's never bad to lose to the champion."

"I'm sick of doing this comedy shit," Goldberg jumped in. "You could never last with me in the ring. I'm the guy who stands in fire for my ring entrance. I'm the guy who beat Hulk Hogan for the title."

"You're the guy who would go down right now if I kicked you in the nuts," I jackhammered back.

"Okay, okay, let's not get carried away," Judge Bischoff interjected. This was becoming *The People's Court* in tights.

"Well, what do you want to do?" Eric demanded. "What's your idea?"

"First of all, let us work this match at the next PPV (which was thirteen days away). Bill can squash the living hell out of me then."

"Okay, what are we going to do tonight then?"

Before arriving at the Nassau Coliseum that day, I'd come up with a plan.

"I'll go to the ring and call out Goldberg. Mean Gene can tell me that everyone knows he's not in the building, including me. I'll proceed to rip Bill a new asshole with insults. While I'm doing this, we'll show Bill arriving at the arena on the 'Tron. I'll be too wrapped up in my promo to notice him walking through the halls and into his dressing room, where he'll see me on the monitor. I'll finish my insults and leave the ring but when I'm walking down the aisle soaking up the adulation of the fans as if it's for me, Bill walks out of the entrance and stands behind me. When I turn around, he spears the hell out of me halfway down the aisle. Then we wrestle at World War 3 and he destroys me in the most entertaining squash match of all time."

Nobody said a thing and as the logic of my idea sank in both Bischoff and Hogan looked intrigued. But when Eric said he liked the idea, Hogan didn't agree.

"I don't know why you're making such a big deal out of this, but if you think you can make it work, then try it and he can beat you at the PPV. But if it doesn't work, Bill beats you next week and that's the end of it."

Everyone seemed happy until Goldberg said, "That's all fine and dandy, but I'm supposed to have the next PPV off."

Did anyone in this company give even a tiny squirt of a shit about the product?

With my plan approved, I went to the ring and buried Bill until Okerlund cut me off.

"Surely you don't think you can beat Goldberg."

"I do think I can beat Goldberg . . . and don't call me Shirley."

Airplane represent yo.

The crowd exploded when Goldberg showed up on the 'Tron. I left the ring waving and smiling like an idiot, only to turn around into the face of a pissed-off mountain of a man who'd had enough of the past two months of Jericho bullshit.

He fired up and speared the beBuddha out of me. On my twenty-eighth birthday no less.

I must've flown ten feet down the aisle and, to be honest, I deserved it. Goldberg had never dealt with someone so persistent and stubborn in the wrestling business before and I'm sure he was sick of looking at me. He took out his aggressions and completely annihilated me—and it was *awesome*.

Later in the night Hogan came looking for me in an area he usually dared not tread. The common locker room. It was the first time I'd seen him with the rest of us plebeians, but to his credit he came to give me props.

"Listen, brother, I just want to tell you that I was wrong and you were right. That was a great idea and it was great TV. I admire you for standing your ground." I was pleasantly surprised; he didn't have to say that. I'd spoken to him more in that one night than I had the prior two years combined and now he was apologizing to me. After that, we got along quite well. Told you I was friends with the Hulkster!

That week I came up with a plan for our squash match where I would wrestle in untied amateur shoes. When Goldberg speared me, I was going to kick them off and give people the illusion that he'd speared me clean out of my sneakers. Time for me to step off!

Of course when I showed up for TV the next week, the whole angle had been dropped and I started a one-week feud with Bobby Duncam Jr. I decided that day that my WCW career was officially over.

CHAPTER 51

NO TICKEE, NO LAUNDRY

I wanted out and I had less than a year left on my now signed contract. But there was a new problem because five months earlier I had verbally agreed to a new deal with Eric that was going to give me a substantial raise. Even though we verbally agreed to the deal and shook hands on it almost a half year earlier, I'd heard nothing about it since.

I knew that the deal was still on the table, but the lack of follow-up rubbed me the wrong way. If Hulk Hogan or Sting had agreed to a new deal, it would've been signed, sealed, and delivered before the day was done. It was initially a minor concern, but when the whole Goldberg situation went down I started second-guessing my decision.

The fact that I couldn't even get a PPV squash with Goldberg showed me that WCW didn't see me as a moneymaker or a big-league player. My attitude about the company at that point became the same as when you call a girl ten times and she never calls you back. You start off hoping she'll call, then you get bummed out, then desperate, and then you realize it's time to give up and move on.

Had he called me back anytime before the Goldberg angle was kiboshed, I would've signed. But the moment I found out that the angle had been shit-canned, I wasn't interested in being a part of WCW no mo'. Of course the day I found the angle had been dropped like a baby was the day Eric showed up with a contract for me to sign. He took it out of his little knapsack and told me to sign it on the spot. I hemmed and hawed and told him I needed a lawyer to look it over first. Jimmy Smits always said to do that on *L.A. Law* and if you can't trust Jim Smits, who can you trust?

Once I made up my mind not to sign the deal, I called Vince Russo. I told him that I wanted out and he suggested a meeting with Vince McMahon himself. So he made the arrangements for me to fly to Connecticut for a top secret meeting at Vince's house.

In the weeks leading up to the meeting, I avoided Bischoff like he had leprosy . . . or was a cruiserweight. If he was walking down the hall, I'd duck, dip, dive, and dodge into a nearby dressing room. He wasn't stupid and I'm sure he must've suspected that something was amiss. Finally he caught up with me in the United Center in Chicago and the first words out of his mouth were, "Have you signed that contract yet?"

"Well, my lawyer still hasn't—"

He interrupted me saying, "Get it back from your lawyer and get it signed for next week."

He was on to me and the jig was up.

The next day, I went to the airport and picked up my ticket to La Guardia. I was surprised that it wasn't first-class, but that was wishful thinking on my part. When I landed, McMahon's limo driver was waiting for me with "Robinson" written on a placard, the secret code name that Russo had given me to ward off any curious fans.

Why couldn't I have been Mr. Pink?

We drove through the dense woods of Connecticut, finally arriving at Vince's mansion. I'd chosen my clothes carefully, knowing Vince's propensity for big guys. I wore a tight black shirt that showed off my arms and a pair of hiking boots to make me taller. Before I rang the doorbell, I did a few isometrics to make the veins in my arms pop out.

My heart was pounding when the door was opened by Vince's son. "Hey Chris, I'm Shane McMahon, come on in," he said with a big grin.

(Marking Out Author's Note: The following memories of Vince's house may be correct or they may not. I was so nervous that I don't really remember for sure what I saw, so cut me some slack, junior!)

Shane led me through the kitchen into a sunken living room. I saw a big oil painting of Vince on the wall and there was a long oak table in the center. Seated at it was the inner circle of the WWF. Jim Ross, Vince Russo, Ed Ferrara, and Bruce Pritchard were all gathered around and sitting at the head of the table like Don Corleone was Vincent Kennedy McMahon himself.

They all stopped talking and turned their heads when I walked in. A big smile spread across Vince's face as he stood up and said, "Chris, how are you doing, pal? Thank you so much for coming!"

Once again there wasn't a hair out of place and the clothes were immaculate even inside the comfort of his own home. I noticed how much presence Vince had in comparison to Eric. It was like comparing a king to a court jester.

I was expecting a secret meeting between Vince, Russo, and myself, but instead I was sitting in the middle of a WWF booking meeting. In retrospect, I can see that Vince was giving me the huge sell to come work for him, because a wrestler from another company would never be allowed in such a sacred inner sanctum meeting now.

Vince and his boys took a break from the meeting and after ordering in lunch from a deli, Vince took me aside for a talk. When he asked me how things were going in WCW, partially out of nervousness and partially out of frustration, I just started talking and talking and talking.

"Well at first I enjoyed it but now I know that it's time to go it's a good place for the older guys but for a young guy like me it's a dead end I've been doing everything on my own and I've been getting over good without any help from the office I feel I have a similar talent as The Rock only he's in the WWF getting a push and I'm stuck in WCW."

I went on and on, just pouring my heart out to this total stranger who was technically my occupational enemy. But to Vince's credit he listened intently, nodded when he should've, and gave me a chance to vent, even though I sounded at best like a raving lunatic and, at worst, a total mark who was comparing himself to The Rock.

But I'd been watching Vince for so long that I felt like I knew him and I just had to spill my guts and get it all out. I was hoping that he was going to say, "Well we're going to hire you and make you a big star!" But he kept his cards close to his chest and merely insinuated that we may work together someday. After all I was still under contract to the enemy.

After our little chat, the meeting resumed and when I was asked my opinions on the show, I gave them. They made me feel like I was already a part of the company. It was a total smoke-and-mirror show designed to impress me. It did.

After the meeting was done, Vince's housekeeper brought in a big plate of brownies and they were spectacular. The whole experience was surreal.

I'd been scraping and clawing my way around the world with the sole intention of someday working for the WWF. Now before I'd even had one match with the company, I was sitting at a table at Vince's house eating brownies and participating in a booking meeting.

It was like walking out of the black and white Kansas of the WCW world into the color Oz of the WWF world. Here's Vince McMahon wearing a suit in his own house in comparison to Bischoff slumming around in sweats and biker gear in front of his employees at a flagship *Nitro* event. Here's a team of professionals planning the show weeks in advance compared to a bunch of guys scrambling to get their shit together twenty minutes before the show. Vince was a larger-than-life presence, not some wannabe following the cool kids around, like Eric appeared to be doing at times.

After Vince and I finished our brownie, there was a moment where each of us silently debated whether or not to have another one. When we both looked at the plate at the same time our eyes met and we knew exactly what the other was thinking. It was a bonding moment that I'll never forget because it showed that Vince was human, just like me.

"Well, let's have another brownie," he said with a hearty laugh. "Nothing wrong with two gentlemen having a second brownie, right?"

So we did and shortly after I left his house. If I'd had Dr. Emmett Brown's DeLorean, I would've driven to 88.8 jigowatts (I know, I know) and gone ten months into the future. In my head, I was already having an occupational affair and mentally cheating on my bitchy WCW wife with the much hotter WWF girlfriend.

As far as I know, Eric never found out about my secret meeting (unless he's reading this book . . . sorry Eric) and he was on a mission to have me sign that contract. I couldn't hold him off anymore and finally told him I wasn't going to sign.

Truth be told, I felt bad about my decision because my word had always been my bond and I was going back on it. But I justified my actions by telling myself that since he'd taken five months to get back to me about the contract, he was in breach of our verbal agreement. I know I'm grasping at straws here, but if you're going to say I went back on my word at least add an asterisk.

Bischoff was furious. "You can't do that! What's wrong with you? We had a deal. You went back on your word."

To an extent he was right, although I could've brought up all of the promises he'd made to me that never transpired, but what was the point? I was OUT.

Eric wasn't going to let it go, calling me an asshole and a fucking liar. Then he said, "Well if you won't sign, it's like losing your ticket at a Chinese dry cleaner. No tickee, no laundry."

I wasn't sure exactly what that meant, until Jimmy Hart told me I was losing the TV title to Konnan on *Nitro* that night in Chattanooga.

He was making his point by taking away the title (and my laundry I guess) and I planned to make my point by having a great match with Konnan, a guy who wasn't exactly Chris Benoit in the ring. My mission was to go above and beyond to put on an awesome spectacle and I'm not lying now when I say that we did.

Since Bischoff was laying down the law and resorting to brass tactics, I needed to do the same and I turned to Kevin Nash of all people for help. I'd heard that Nash and Hall had used an agent to broker their deal into WCW. Having an agent in every other form of entertainment is commonplace, but in wrestling they are regarded as vermin.

Wrestling began as a carnival attraction a hundred years ago and as far as it has come as a viable entertainment entity, it's still quite primitive in its treatment of its employees and that will probably never change. But I thought if I had representation, I could avoid further personal conflicts with Eric and formulate a game plan to help me escape WCW.

Nash put me in touch with his agent, Barry Bloom. We met in New Orleans in yet another secret meeting and it was the smartest move I could've made. Barry orchestrated a foolproof plan for my escape and played Eric like a temperamental fiddle. At first Eric refused to deal with him due to previous bad blood, so Barry had me hire a lawyer in Atlanta named John Taylor. John had fought against WCW in the past and Bischoff was reluctant to deal with him too. I had hit the Bischoff hornet's nest with a stick and he was furious. So I was prepared for him to make the reminder of my time in the company a living hell. Surprisingly he didn't.

Maybe he forgot or maybe he just didn't care, but nothing happened. I worked an angle with Perry Saturn that culminated in a Loser Wears a Dress Match. What better way for Eric to embarrass me, right? Wrong. Perry wanted to do a Marilyn Manson gimmick and lost willingly.

I wrestled a battle royal during *MTV Spring Break* in Cancun. I won and went out drinking for fourteen hours straight with the host, a relative unknown named Kid Rock (who I referred to as Rock Kid) in celebration. Only in WCW could you get a bigger push (and a hell of a party) when you were leaving the company.

I didn't escape completely unscathed, as I got a call soon afterward that I'd failed the WCW testing policy. The banned substance found in my system was androstenedione (Mark McGwire's supplement of choice), which I bought at a GNC in the mall. The fix was in.

As penance, I had to attend a steroid counseling session with the company quack in Atlanta with two other wrestlers, Lenny Lane and Bobby Blaze. Lenny was about my size and Bobby was built like you (I keed) and none of us were typical poster boys for rampant steroid abuse . . . although I was a sexy beast and worked out hard. But it was strange that the three of us had been targeted while so many others in WCW were practically neon signs for it.

What was even more peculiar was the class itself. We sat in a room for two hours watching public service films that looked like they were made in the 1970s.

"Hello, I'm Lionel Hutz. You may have seen me in such films as *Weight Supremacists* and *The Golden Curls*.

That was before muscle-enhancing narcotics caused my testes to spontaneously combust." I took heed and threw all of my GNC products away.

After receiving another tongue-lashing from Eric about how much of an asshole I was for going back on my word (bor-ring), I was in my apartment in Clearwater, Florida, watching Wayne Gretzky's last NHL game. Tears were streaming down my face as I watched one my childhood heroes play his final shift. It inspired me to leave a tribute to the Great One on my answering machine.

"Hey this is Chris, leave a message because I don't want to talk to anyone. Unless of course this is Wayne Gretzky, the greatest of all time, in which case I'll pick up."

I continued watching the retirement ceremony, and my phone rang. After my stupid message played, I heard a deep voice.

"Chris, this is not Wayne Gretzky, this is Vince McMahon."

I was agog (still a great word) that:

a) Vince was actually calling me at *my* house; and
b) He'd had to endure such a goofy message.

I picked up the phone in a scramble and bumbled out a hello.

"Wayne Gretzky, huh?"

"Well, he just retired today."

"I know, I know. He's a god for you Canadians, isn't he?" Then he burst out in the patented VKM overexaggerated belly laugh.

After a few pleasantries were exchanged, Vince got right to the point.

"Are you going to come work for me? We really want you here."

That was all he needed to say. I had the head of WCW calling me a fucking liar and a piece of shit while the head of the WWF was calling me at my home asking me to come work for him. Vinegar and honey, right? It was an awesome selling technique by Vince and it worked, not that I needed much prodding at that point anyway.

After repeated attempts by Eric to have other WCW employees, from DDP, to Nash, to Eric's business partner, Jason Hervey, from *The Wonder Years* (Fred Savage wasn't available for comment) asking me to stay, he finally changed his tune and started being really nice.

He put together a new offer that with incentives could've ended up in the high six figures. But it was too little too late because on top of everything else, Eric had hurt my feelings. I felt damaged as a performer and as a person and it would've been difficult for me to go back to WCW smiling like nothing had happened.

I'd decided that $1 million (pinky finger on bottom lip) was the magic number that would make me think about staying. But they never offered it to me so I didn't have to consider it.

When I confided to my friends that I was thinking of leaving, they told me to get out and never look back. My dad told me, "Sometimes the devil you don't know is better than the one that you do." While I'm still not sure exactly what that means, I appreciated the advice.

Even Brian Hildebrand, who was honored just to be working in the wrestling business, thought it would in my best interests to take my chances elsewhere. Brian's cancer had returned and he was forced to take a leave of absence from WCW (which tore him apart), with the caveat that his job would be waiting for him no matter how long it took for him to get better.

Eric wasn't my favorite person at that point, but his treatment of Brian during his hard times was first-class. He even orchestrated a Brian Hildebrand Tribute show in Brian's home city of Knoxville (in the same building I'd wrestled with a broken arm four years earlier). Brian was quite touched by WCW's efforts and when asked what match he wanted to see on the show, he requested Benoit and Malenko vs. Eh and Wey, North and South of the Border, the Greatest Tag Team That Barely Ever Was . . . Guerrero and Jericho.

The four of us had wrestled the match before but always with limited TV time. This time there were none of those shackles and in an unprecedented move, Arn Anderson, who was running the show, put our match on last. It was the first and only time I was ever in the main event of a WCW show and the four of us responded by having one of the best matches of our careers.

Brian was too weak to work on the show, but he was sitting ringside the whole night. I grabbed the mike before the match and cut a vicious promo accusing him of faking his cancer to elicit sympathy from the stupid rednecks. Brian looked at me in defiance as the crowd booed the hell out of me, and I know he loved it.

The finish was the best ending to a movie ever. The ref got knocked out just as Dean put me in his Cloverleaf submission and Benoit put Eddy into his Crossface submission. Just as we tapped out, Brian slid into the ring and signaled for the bell with his trademark double-handed bang-bang motion to a massive pop. Everyone in the building gave him a standing ovation and the smile on his face was big enough for Oprah to bathe in. It will be etched in my mind forever (the smile, not the image of Oprah bathing).

I still have a picture of the five of us taken backstage after the show hanging in my office today.

Afterward, the five of us went back to Brian's house in Morristown to relax, reflect, and enjoy the rest of the evening. As a token of his esteem, Eddy gave Brian his Black Tiger mask (the character he played in Japan) and Brian did a dance of joy. When I gave Brian the gift of my Super Liger party mask he did a dance of indifference and went back to looking at his Black Tiger mask.

Poor Super Liger still got no love.

Brian had a vial of prescription marijuana to help him deal with the painful chemo treatments. I wasn't much of a weed smoker, but I got so high I became Cheech if he had smoked Chong. If you can't smoke weed, drink pure moonshine, and eat hash brownies with your dying cancer-stricken friend, then who *can* you smoke weed, drink pure moonshine, and eat hash brownies with?

SHE WAS MY DENSITY

Even though my career was a little shaky, things were looking up personally. After years of meeting Mrs. Right Now, I finally met Mrs. Right. I was eating in a Japanese restaurant that all the boys went to whenever we had a show in Tampa. Scanning the crowd, I saw Disco Inferno talking with a breathtakingly beautiful blonde. I was staring at her when she glanced over and busted me red-handed. When our eyes locked, I was completely enchanted.

But the fact that she was talking to Disco was a warning sign for me, because whenever you saw one of the boys talking to a good-looking girl, chances were that something had already happened between them, or was about to. But she was way out of Disco's league, which made me think, "How typical. The hottest girls are always attracted to the biggest dweebs."

When Disco finished his conversation, I asked him, "Who is that girl you're talking to?"

"Oh, that's my friend, Jessica."

When I heard the magic word "friend," the race was on and I insisted that he introduce us. He did and we didn't stop talking until the restaurant closed hours later.

Disco had been showing Jessica a copy of the new *WCW Magazine* that featured him on the cover (sign #147 that the company was going down the toilet) and also featured an article that asked me such hard-hitting questions like what was my a) favorite number, b) animal, c) Backstreet Boy (A.J. like a muthaaafuckaaaa), etc.

I said that ferrets were my favorite animal and she was intrigued because she had two of them at home. She told me that her favorite number was 7 and when we looked at the survey, my favorite number was also listed as 7. When I asked her for her phone number and entered it into my PalmPilot, it was the 77th entry.

It didn't take long to realize that she was my density . . . I mean my destiny.

I became so intrigued by her that suddenly there was nobody else in the entire restaurant. I went into total fence-building mode (when one of the boys gets so into a girl he gives nobody else a chance to talk to her) and ignored everybody else in the room.

I didn't notice when Eddy stole my swank fanny pack off the back of my chair and put it in the freezer for safe-keeping. I didn't notice when the food came or when the plates were taken away. I just noticed this awesome girl with the pretty smile and the prettier personality. But our amazing connection was almost torn apart when Raven broke down my fence and stomped into my yard.

The two of us had developed a system during our time in the Drunken Four Horsemen where if we saw a girl we liked, he became the bad cop and I was the good cop.

This way the girl had two flavors to choose from like a cheap-ass Baskin-Robbins.

But I didn't want to play that way with Jessica and tried to shoo the annoying Raven away. But he kept interjecting himself into the conversation and after a few lascivious remarks, flew in for the kill.

"Well, I'm going to go over to the Dollhouse," Raven said. "Do you want to come with me?"

The Dollhouse was an infamous strip club in Tampa, and it was now the enemy along with Raven, who was intent on stealing her away.

She looked undecided and the moment of truth had arrived. Was she going to go to the Dollhouse with Raven, who she'd never met before, or stay at the restaurant with me where she belonged? Jessica turned and asked me, "Are you going to go?"

I played it cool even though if she'd wanted to go to the Dollhouse you know damn well I would've followed her.

"I don't think so. I'm just gonna stay here."

She dazzled me with her smile and said to Raven, "No thanks. I'm just going to stay here."

Angels burst out of heaven singing, bells chimed, babies gurgled with laughter, and birds snuggled in the trees. All was now well in the world.

We left separately and by the time I got home that night, she'd already left a message on my machine. There was no two-day buffer zone for her. I called her the next day and was disappointed to find out that she was going to her dad's cabin in northern Minnesota (she'd grown up only five hours away from Winnipeg) for three weeks.

We spoke on the phone every day while she was gone and the daily conversations helped us build a strong foundation for our relationship. We got to know each other well before anything physical happened. It was the exact opposite of the way most relationships begin and showed us that we had something special.

By the time she came back from Minnesota, she was already my girlfriend even though I'd kind of forgotten what she looked like. When I saw her again, she was more beautiful than I remembered and we've been together ever since. (Great Caesar's Ghost, that line is going to get me some brownie points when she reads it.)

Right after I met Jessica, I sprained my ankle in Las Vegas during a match against Booker T and was told by the doctor that I couldn't wrestle for six weeks. I only had sixteen weeks left on my contract, so the injury was a blessing in disguise.

When Eric realized that I wasn't going to re-sign my contract, he suspended me from appearing on TV. That darned suspension really taught me a lesson, especially since I still received every penny of my weekly check in the interim.

It's good work if you can get it.

Now when you think of the new millenn
you associate it with something spectacular,
an event so big it signifies a new era in
history... and in this case a new era in <u>WWF</u> history.

🔔 And a new era is ~~sadly~~ desparately
needed in this once profitable prod company. What
used to be a cutting edge, captivating,
trend setting promotion, has now become (a

✓ ~~shell~~ of it's former self, ~~stagnating~~, ~~dull~~
uninteresting, boring, ~~spectacle~~ a loser in an winnable rating war that in ~~and~~ of a ~~boring~~
and that's why I'm here.
dis-need reserves (chapter-string arena)

✓ This Jericho has come to save the WWF!

CHAPTER 53

TIME TO ROCK

During my suspension, Barry was negotiating with Jim Ross, who in addition to being the best announcer in the business (and a hell of a Foreword writer) was also the head of WWF Talent Relations and Vince's right-hand man.

JR was a huge football fan and made an effort to recruit all of his new signings the same way a football team would. He made a point of flying down to Tampa to have yet another secret meeting with me. Was I in wrestling or the CIA? He and his associate Gerry Brisco gave me a big pep talk touting the virtues of working in the WWF compared to WCW and discussed plans the company had for me.

The WWF's contract offer was a three-year deal at $450,000 a year, with an intricate system of bonuses based on attendance and pay-per-view buys. If you worked hard in the WWF and succeeded, you were rewarded and made more money. During all the years I worked in the WWF I never made less than double my guarantee, sometimes triple.

In the meantime, WCW had upped their offer to where with bonuses it almost reached the magical seven-figure mark, but it was too late. Even though the WWF was offering half the money I would've agreed to a bag of used hockey pucks to work for Vince. Or a bag of brownies.

It wasn't about the cash and it never had been. It was about finally achieving my elusive dream and enjoying my career again. All of the bullshit I'd experienced in WCW had drained my love for wrestling and I wanted it back.

Since I was suspended from TV and had been taken off the road, I got to spend four straight months with Jessica. We knew we had something special when we saw each other every day and still wanted more.

Eric however had had enough of me and felt that it was best for Chris Jericho to just disappear from WCW. My name was never mentioned and I was never seen on *Nitro* again. It was probably the right decision, as no matter what form of burial he might've thought of, I just would've taken it and got more over in the long run anyway. WCW had taught me the valuable lesson of taking any scrap of TV time given to you and using it to make an impression.

That lesson would benefit me for years to come.

I also used the time off to work on another one of my dreams.

One of the greatest feelings in the world is hooking up with other musicians and playing music. It's the ultimate form of both individuality and teamwork and a total creative rush. I'd never stopped playing, but since I'd moved away from Lenny in Calgary, I hadn't found anybody to jam with. I missed being in a band and now that I had the time to rock, I picked up the phone and called a guitar player in Atlanta named Rich Ward.

Rich was the backbone of the pioneer rap-metal band Stuck Mojo, and had been touring the world for years like I had. I'd seen Mojo in concert a few years earlier and I was impressed by their energy, their music, and their allegiance to wrestling.

They had wrestling dolls lined up on the amps, wore championship belts while playing, and threw out wrestling-influenced catchphrases like "To be the band, you got to beat the band" and "That's the bottom line 'cause Mojo said so."

Mojo had filmed a video starring DDP for their song "Rising" and our paths crossed when Rich came backstage at a WCW show in San Antonio during a Mojo night off. Rich and I were kindred spirits right from the start. We had the same sense of humor and liked a lot of the same bands, including Stryper. I was amazed because even though Stryper had been a huge influence on the early part of my career, it was rare to find somebody else who would admit digging them.

When I mentioned that I'd been playing bass and singing in bands for years, he threw out a curious offer. "I have a cover band called Fozzy Osbourne. Whoever is in town comes down and we jam on our favorite cover tunes. You should come sing with us sometime, it's a blast."

I loved the idea, but I never had enough spare time to make it happen. However, I kept in touch with Rich and when I hurt my ankle, he was the first guy I called. We booked a few shows, put together a loose set list, and I flew to Atlanta to rock.

Our first gig was at a club called the Hangar in Marietta,

Georgia. About 300 Jerichoholics and members of the Stuck
Mojo Dojo showed up. I was freaking out, because ever since
I'd seen my first concert (the Police/Synchronicity Tour '83)
I'd always dreamed of playing a full gig of my own. Now we
weren't exactly Van Halen in 1978 as far as quality, but we
were good enough for Rich and me to feel a spark. There was
something special about the chemistry of his guitar riffs and
my vocals right off the bat. We played again the next night in
Spartanburg, South Carolina, in front of about twelve people
and that was supposed to be the end of it.

But a funny thing happened on the way to the Casbah.
Both Stuck Mojo and Chris Jericho were popular within
our respective realms and due to the strange supergroup
lineup of the band, a buzz started to build. Mojo's manager started fielding offers from record companies who
were interested in signing us sight unseen and sound
unheard.

(Interactive Portion of the Book: Download "Dream
Weaver" by Gary Wright and press play now.)

We were in the middle of a bidding war after playing only two gigs and my dream of being a rock star was
starting to come true.

ONLY THE GOOD
DIE YOUNG

My dream of becoming a WWF superstar was about to come true and I began scouting my new company. To familiarize myself with the story lines and performers I studied every WWF television show, more specifically *Monday Night Raw* and the monthly PPVs.

On May 23, 1999, I was watching the *Over the Edge* PPV from Kansas City. I had just made Jess and myself dinner and as I sat down to eat, I saw Owen Hart on the TV doing an interview about his upcoming match. Now there were many reasons why I wanted to sign with the WWF, some of them major, some of them minor. One of them was that being in the WWF would give me the opportunity to finally work with Owen Hart.

Ever since I first saw him in Stampede thirteen years earlier, he was one of the reasons I'd decided to become a wrestler in the first place. Even though we'd worked for many of the same companies worldwide, except for that one plane ride from Calgary to Los Angeles, we'd never crossed paths. He'd become a big star in the WWF and was currently playing the masked Blue Blazer, a super-hero who was decidedly un-super due to his squeaky-clean, goody-two-shoes antics. When I sat down on the couch to watch his always entertaining match, I noticed that the camera was panning the crowd. After a few minutes of the increasingly long and awkward crowd shots, I said to Jess, "Something is wrong here."

At that moment the cameras switched over to Jim Ross and his sidekick, Jerry Lawler, sitting at the announcer desk, their faces pale and ashen.

JR said something like, "Owen Hart has suffered a serious accident. He's had a serious fall."

My stomach plummeted and I thought, "He fell? What is he talking about? What do you mean he fell?"

I knew it wasn't a gimmick because both announcers were crying real tears and soon after, so was I. Owen had fallen fifty feet from the rafters into the ring when an apparatus that was supposed to lower him snapped. He died pretty much on impact.

I was overwhelmed with feelings of desperation and helplessness much the same way I was when Magic told me that Art had died. I ran out of my apartment and called Benoit to tell him. There was no answer and I left a message ending with the same question I'd asked Magic: "What are we going to do?"

I hardly knew Owen, but his journey through the business mirrored mine and I considered myself to be a surrogate member of the Hart family. He was an inspiration . . . almost a hero . . . to me and I couldn't comprehend what had happened. I've often had this fantasy that on the day of the accident I have a premonition that something bad is going to happen to Owen, so I call the Kemper Arena and manage to warn him just in time, saving his life.

But I didn't have any such premonition.

The next Monday I went to my first funeral for a friend (I've been to too many of them since) and all of the respect and sympathy shown toward Owen and his family was overwhelming. The entire WWF roster was there and the streets of Calgary were lined with thousands of people sharing in the massive grief. The Hart family was the royalty of Calgary and Owen was the crown prince. He was one of those guys that nobody ever said a bad word about and you could tell how much he was loved from the number of people paying tribute to him.

He was planning on getting out of wrestling in a few short years to spend more time with his wife and two young children. They were scheduled to move into their new dream house the very next week. It's an overwhelmingly dismal story and it still hurts to think about it.

Only the good die young, all the evil seem to live forever.

At the funeral home, Owen rested in an open casket. I leaned over and hugged him as the tears flowed down my face and I asked him the question I had been thinking all day: "What happened, man? We were supposed to be tag team champions someday."

I kissed his cheek and said goodbye to the nicest guy I hardly ever met.

There was a first-class list of wrestlers paying tribute to Owen that day. I have a picture of Stu Hart, Bret

Hart, Hulk Hogan, Chris Benoit, Terry Funk, Dory Funk Jr., Shane Douglas, Davey Boy Smith, and me standing together at Stu's house after the funeral, all of us world champions at one point.

While the reason for the summit was terrible, the experience itself was actually a good one and it provided a small bit of closure. It was also a riot listening to Stu tell all of his stories while some of the greatest wrestlers of all time gathered in awe, hanging on to his every word. At eighty-four years old, he was still feisty. He even coerced a reluctant B. Brian Blair into allowing him to apply a shoot hold.

"This one can turn a man's eyes completely bloodshot," Stu said frankly as he applied pressure and then thankfully let go on his own. If he hadn't, I'm not sure that any of us could've made him let go, nor did we want to get close enough to try.

I saw Keith Hart for the first time since he tried to snap my teeth in half almost nine years earlier. I went and shook his hand, then we both stood there awkwardly. A fly landed on his face and when I went to shoo it away, he went into a fighting stance like he expected me to attack him.

Maybe he thought I wanted revenge . . . or a refund.

As I was leaving Stu's house, I saw the Hulkster. He was the only guy from WCW to show up at the funeral (besides Benoit) and I thought it was a very classy gesture on his part. I talked to him for a few minutes until he came flat-out and asked me, "Are you going to go work for Vince?"

I was still keeping my plans of defection on the down

low, but on that day I didn't care too much about keeping secrets.

"Yeah, I think I'm going to give the WWF a shot."

He looked me in the eye and said, "Can you take me with you?"

With Chris and Nancy Benoit and Stu Hart at Owen's funeral in May 1999. I debated for weeks whether or not to include this picture and I changed my mind a dozen times. In the end, I felt that to pull this picture would suggest that Chris and Nancy never existed. But they did exist and they loved each other and I loved them. So it stayed.

CHAPTER
55

THE CLOCK HITS ZERO TONIGHT

I didn't take Hogan with me, but I was officially WWF-bound. My signing was announced on the WWE Web site a full month before my contract with WCW was up. I thought for sure that Eric would run me through the wringer on TV as a result. But he must've considered me damaged goods because he still didn't do a thing.

On the day my deal expired, I sent Eric a fax thanking him for the opportunity he'd given me. Even with all the animosity and bad feelings between us, he still gave me a chance with the company and paid me a huge amount of money to wrestle on national TV. At the very least I owed him a thank-you for that.

Now that I was an official WWF superstar, I was on the phone with Russo constantly, discussing ideas and scenarios. He seemed to be as excited about me coming in as I was because my arrival into the WWF was going to be a huge deal and the company was already thinking of ideas for my debut. So was I.

I was dropping off some mail at the post office when I saw a clock on the wall counting backward. Underneath the clock it said, "Countdown to the New Millennium." It was six months before the year 2000 and the clock was keeping track of the time until New Year's Eve:

176 days, 17 hours, 8 minutes, 12 seconds, 11 seconds . . .

I thought, "That would be a cool way for someone to come into the—wait, that's a cool way for *me* to come into the WWF!" The WWF was famous for airing vignettes weeks before a new character's arrival to build anticipation and excitement. I'd just discovered my vignette. I called Russo and he promised to run my idea past Vince that day.

The Millennium Clock idea was . . . ahem . . . timely, because I'd been trying to think of a replacement for the Lion Heart name for a while. I'd been using it for years and I wanted to come into my new company with a new look, a new name, and a new nose. Well two out of three ain't bad.

So it was goodbye Lion Heart, hello Millennium Man. I would enter the WWF promising to be *the* performer to take the company into the year 2000 and beyond.

Russo called me back a day later and said that not only did Vince love the idea, but he was going to calibrate the clock to start a month before my debut. This way, it would hit zero right at the exact moment of my first WWF appearance on the August 9, 1999, edition of *Monday Night Raw*.

A month beforehand, I flew to the WWF offices in Stamford, Connecticut, to nail down the details of my

7/26/99

Eric,

I just wanted to express my appreciation to you for giving me the opportunity to work for WCW for the last three years. I really enjoyed it and I won't forget the favorable experiences that I had within the company.

I hope I have the pleasure of working with you again in the future.

All the best,

Chris Irvine n/k/a Chris Jericho

The fax I sent to Eric Bischoff after I signed with the WWF.

debut. I met with Jim Johnston, who wrote the music for all of the superstars. We spent an hour talking about who I was and what my character's attitude was, so he could get a feel for what my entrance music should sound like. Instead of recycled TBS basketball music, I was getting a custom-made fancy-pants song written just for me.

I met with Kevin Dunn, the producer of *Raw*, to talk about my entrance video and his plan of using a double blast of pyro to give my arrival extra impact. As I took promo shots and went over merchandise ideas, again I felt like I had stepped into Oz. Except Oz was now spelled WWF and Dorothy was bigger, sexier, and sporting a topknot. Come to think of it, I looked more like the Cowardly Lion.

I went in for a meeting with the Boss himself. His office had a view of the Stamford skyline and was decorated with WWF memorabilia. I sat down in a plush chair that was worth more than my apartment and he pulled a script out of his desk for the movie *Toxic Avenger IV*, which included a part written specifically for me.

"You've been here a day and you're already a movie star," he grumbled.

My star-making role as Toxie's new sidekick was never mentioned again, but it was a nice dangled carrot anyway.

Then Vince hit me with a bombshell. His idea was to have the Countdown to the New Millennium clock reach zero right smack-dab in the middle of a promo by The Rock. I was floored because interrupting The Rock took me to the highest level right off the bat. It was a great example of VKM's genius, as he'd taken my already good idea and increased it a thousandfold. We were a good team already.

Then Vince asked me what my finishing maneuver was and I explained it was a submission similar to the Boston Crab. He was reluctant to have me use a submission, feeling that I was more of an explosive pin fall type of guy. I would've used a sweaty sock as a finish if he'd wanted me to and I wasn't going to disagree. But I told him whether I was using a pin fall or a submission, I wanted to call my finish the Y2J Problem. Y2J was a take-off on the much ballyhooed Y2K problem that was apparently going to destroy us all at midnight on January 1, 2000. It didn't, although I personally was destroyed on that night.

He smelled what I was cooking straight away and said, "That's not going to be the name of your finish. That's going to be your name period."

"The Y2J Problem?

"No, just Y2J."

The rest is Jeric-History.

I was a nervous wreck the night the clock was supposed to first appear on *Raw*. I'd been in the business long enough to know never to count on anything until it happened. I still didn't quite believe that I could actually be going to the WWF.

Sure enough midway through the show, the screen went to a neon blue graphic that said "Countdown to the Millennium" while the numbers clicked backward. 28 days, 1 hour, 4 minutes, and 11 seconds . . . 10 seconds . . . 9 seconds, each click accompanied by an awesome whooshing sound effect.

It was definitely happening.

I spent that week writing my debut promo. In WCW I'd done a lot of my promos improv, but with this one I wanted to get everything just right beforehand. This was a different world and there would be no Onta Gleeben Glouten Globens allowed here. I had a few ideas about what I wanted to say and when I put pen to paper, the whole thing flowed out of me within ten minutes.

I was going to talk about how complacent the WWF

had become and how they were in need of a new savior to carry them into the next millennium. That savior was their role model. That savior was the Ayatollah of Rock N Rolla. That savior was Chris Jericho.

I flew into Detroit the night before my debut in Chicago to observe the WWF behemoth at work. They were filming the *Sunday Night Heat* show for MTV and I watched the whole production from the Gorilla Position (named after WWF legend Gorilla Monsoon), the brain center of the operation where Vince and his crew called the shots.

It was such a change from WCW where there was no Gorilla Position, no Giraffe Position, no nothing. Just an empty hallway and a curtain. But Vince was hands-on running everything, just like the Wizard manipulating everything from behind the black curtain.

The only thing that bothered me about joining the WWF was some of the provocative angles the company was doing, like when the World's Strongest Man Mark Henry received oral pleasure from a transvestite. I thought that stuff had no place in wrestling and I tried to get veto power in my contract if I was ever asked to participate in an angle I felt to be questionable.

Vince gave me his word that if I was ever asked to do something I felt awkward about, all I had to do was say no. I remembered his words when I watched the *Heat* show that night.

A character named Meat had his drink spiked with Viagra, which forced him to wrestle with a huge boner. This effect was subtly achieved by stuffing a dildo down Meat's Calvin Klein underwear-looking trunks.

The finish of the match saw his opponent the Big

Bossman take his nightstick and whack poor Meat in the cock.

I watched all of this in amazement thinking, "What have I gotten myself into?"

The next morning when I arrived at the Allstate Arena in Chicago, I suited up in my new Y2J costume of a pair of Harley-Davidson leather pants and a silver rave shirt that I bought from a hip-hop shop.

I was taking Jimmy Hart's darling advice of wearing color to the max. Besides, I had a lot to live up to if I was going to dub myself "the most charismatic showman to ever enter your living room via a television screen." I put my hair into the Gene Simmons topknot, combed the billy goat beard I'd grown for the occasion, looked in the mirror, and gave myself a Billy Idol sneer.

Y2J had arrived, muthatruckers.

My costume complete, I walked out of the dressing room as cocky as a male porn star, acting like I owned the place. I ran into Vince, who was getting a cup of coffee in catering. He looked me up and down, his eyes settling on my ricockulous hairstyle.

"It's cheap heat, Vince."

"Indeed." He nodded with a weird look on his face and strutted away.

I went over my promo with Russo and he didn't have any major concerns or changes. The Rock joined us, we rehearsed the whole thing once in catering, and that was it. Rocky and I were both trained professionals and we knew what to do. As the heel, I had some choice insults for him and as the babyface he had some tremendous comebacks for me. If everything went the way it was supposed to, it was going to be a classic moment.

I rehearsed my ring entrance in the empty arena and when I saw my new entrance video and heard my new music, I was in awe. The video was a montage of lights and cars speeding down the city street at night combined into a sleek and sexy package. Just like me.

My music was even better, with the opening tagline of "Break the Walls Down" setting the tone as a heavy, grooving guitar riff kicked in. The tune made me feel like walking up to the Pope and kicking him right in the rosaries.

In a moment that brought everything full circle, I ran into Jesse "The Body" Ventura backstage. Except he was now Jesse "The Governor" Ventura, the head of the state of Minnesota, and he was promoting his one-time-only return to the WWF for the upcoming *SummerSlam* PPV.

I went up to him and said, "Jesse, I don't know if you remember me, but I met you in Winnipeg at a hockey tournament you played in with my dad. I told you that I wanted to be a wrestler and you gave me some great advice that helped me get here today."

I don't know if I expected him to jump up and down, pat me on the back, and give me the keys to Brooklyn Park, but he really didn't give much of a reaction at all. He actually kind of jobbed me out saying, "Good for you kid. Another Jesse success story," before walking away with a cigar clenched between his teeth. My grandma was right!

The day changed to night and before I knew it it was show time. *Monday Night Raw* started with a hailstorm of bombs and fireworks, as the whole crew gathered around the backstage monitor to watch Jim Ross hard-selling that night's show.

"The clock hits zero tonight. What could this mean?" JR screamed with excitement.

A lot of the Chicago fans already knew what the clock signified. Some of them had brought Role Model signs and others were chanting "Je-ri-cho," but all of them were ripe with anticipation about what the clock was going to reveal.

Like a Viking warrior, I was ready for battle when I was called to Gorilla Position to get ready for my cue. The Rock's music began and the two of us hit knuckles as he stepped through the curtain to a thunderous reception.

I said a quick prayer thanking God for the opportunity and asking for his help in making it a success. Midway through The Rock's promo the Countdown Clock appeared and the crowd exploded. The Rock turned his steely stare toward the gigantic 'Tron displaying the graphic.

15...14...13...

This was it. After nine years of backbreaking physical and mental challenges, I was finally here.

12...11...10...

The crowd worked themselves into a frenzy as the numbers spiraled backward toward zero.

9...8...7...

Everything I had done to get here and all the accolades I'd amassed meant absolutely nothing at that moment.

Nobody cared that I had the best match of the Super J Cup in Japan or that I won the match of the year in Mexico. Either I could cut it in the big leagues or I couldn't. I'd have one chance to show what I could do with my promo and one chance only.

6...5...

But one chance was all I was going to need, because this sucker was getting knocked out of the park all the way out of Chicago and back to Winnipeg.

4...

My career and my twenty-eight years flashed before my eyes.

3...

My dad was going to be so proud.

2...

My mom was going to be so proud. She would get to watch me on her TV tonight and I loved her so much.

1...

The pyro went off with double force and I walked through the curtain straight into my dream come true.

REQUIEM

In a lot of ways, being in the wrestling business is similar to being in a war. The people you work with and work against become like army buddies. You count on each other, watch each other's backs, and trust each other with your lives. They become your surrogate family because you spend more time with them on the road than you do with your actual family. You share each other's highs and lows, dreams and realities, joys and pain.

You may not see your army buddies for days, weeks, months, or even years, but when you finally reunite it doesn't seem like a day has passed. There's a unique bond shared by all of us in this business that, like it or not, lasts a lifetime.

Unfortunately, some of those lifetimes are much shorter than others and a lot of the brothers talked about in this book will never read it.

There's no question that I owe a part of this book to every performer I've ever had the pleasure of watching, meeting, and working with throughout the years. I have a deep respect for each of them for having the courage to follow their dreams and seeing them come true.

But it's to those who left before the party was over that I truly dedicate these tales:

Jerry Blackwell, Andre the Giant, Davey Boy Smith, Floyd Creachman, Owen Hart, Stu Hart, Brian Pillman,

Mike Lozanski, Ed Whalen, Rhonda Singh, Bob Brown, Hammer Rick Applegate, Ken Timbs, the Great Goliath, Oro, Eddy Guerrero, Chris Benoit, el Texano, Art Barr, Dexter Barr, Daniel Benoit, Roberto Rangel, Indio Guajardo, Brian Hildebrand, Chris Candido, Dick Murdoch, Rad Radford Louie Spicoli, Sambo Asako, Rio Lord of the Jungle Rick Williams, Hiromichi Fuyuki, Bam Bam Bigelow, Johnny Grunge, Teddy Petty, Big Dick Dudley, Harry Boatswain, Terry Gordy, Pitbull #2 Anthony Durante, Road Warrior Hawk, the Gladiator Mike Awesome, PeeWee Anderson, John Kronus, Bad News Allen Coage, Curt Hennig, Black Cat Victor Mar, Bobby Duncum Jr., the Big Bossman Ray Traylor, and Woman Nancy Benoit.

God bless you guys and thank you.

CJ

ABOUT THE AUTHORS

CHRIS JERICHO lives in Tampa, Florida, with his wife, Jessica, and their three children. He still occasionally wears spandex in his living room while listening to Iron Maiden and doing the Macarena. You can visit his Web site at www.chrisjericho.com.

PETER THOMAS FORNATALE is a freelance writer, editor, and Jerichoholic. He lives in Brooklyn, New York, with his wife, Susan, and Black Lab, Mugs.

VISIT US ONLINE
@ WWW.HACHETTEBOOKGROUPUSA.COM.

AT THE HACHETTE BOOK GROUP USA WEB SITE YOU'LL FIND:

CHAPTER EXCERPTS FROM SELECTED NEW RELEASES

ORIGINAL AUTHOR AND EDITOR ARTICLES

AUDIO EXCERPTS

BESTSELLER NEWS

ELECTRONIC NEWSLETTERS

AUTHOR TOUR INFORMATION

CONTESTS, QUIZZES, AND POLLS

FUN, QUIRKY RECOMMENDATION CENTER

PLUS MUCH MORE!

Bookmark Hachette Book Group USA
@ www.HachetteBookGroupUSA.com.